UNEARTHING FRANCO'S LEGA

CONTEMPORARY EUROPEAN POLITICS AND SOCIETY

Anthony M. Messina, Series Editor

EDITED BY
CARLOS JEREZ-FARRÁN AND SAMUEL AMAGO

UNEARTHING
FRANCO'S LEGACY

Mass Graves and the Recovery
of Historical Memory in Spain

University of Notre Dame Press
Notre Dame, Indiana

Library of Congress Cataloging-in-Publication Data

Unearthing Franco's legacy : mass graves and the recovery of historical
memory in Spain / edited by Carlos Jerez-Farrán and Samuel Amago.
    p. cm. — (Contemporary European politics and society)
    Includes bibliographical references and indexes.
    ISBN-13: 978-0-268-03268-5 (paper : alk. paper)
    ISBN-10: 0-268-03268-8 (paper : alk. paper)
1. Franco, Francisco, 1892–1975—Influence.   2. Political violence—
Spain—History—20th century.   3. Murder—Spain—History—
20th century.   4. Mass burials—Spain—History—20th century.
5. Spain—Politics and government—1931–1939.   6. Spain—Politics and
government—1939–1975.   7. Spain—History—Civil War, 1936–1939.
8. Collective memory—Spain.   9. Spain—Social conditions—1975–
I. Jerez Farrán, Carlos, 1950–   II. Amago, Samuel, 1974–
    DP264.F7U54   2010
    946.082—dc22

                                                            2010001660

To those who fought and continue to fight for justice and the defense of democratic rights, arduously gained, perilously maintained.

Contents

Acknowledgments

We would like to express our gratitude to all those who made the publication of this book possible. Foremost, we wish to thank our contributors not only for the articles and commentaries that now comprise this volume but also for their generosity and patience through all stages of the editorial process. We thank them especially for taking time to share their thoughts and reflections on this important theme. Our thanks are also due to the Program for Cultural Cooperation Between Spain's Ministry of Culture and United States Universities for financial support offered to do the necessary research work to write the introduction, and to the Institute for Scholarship in the Liberal Arts and the College of Arts and Letters at the University of Notre Dame for the grant support that has made this book possible.

Thanks are also due to Juan Sanchez for editing support; to Doris Bergen for her encouragement, pointers, and intellectual generosity; to Char Prieto for the interesting and inspiring conversations held about this topic; to Scott Mainwairing for taking an interest in the conference that served as the starting point for this book and for referring us to the present publisher; and to the anonymous external readers for their ideas, concerns, and suggestions. We are grateful to Harry Karahalios, Bryan Scoular, and especially Roger Tinnell for their generous help with translations. Elizabeth Van Jacob and the reference staff of the Hesburgh Library deserve our gratitude for their invaluable bibliographic savoir faire. We are indebted to our colleagues and students at the University of Notre Dame with whom we have discussed many key issues that now form a crucial part of this book. In particular, Samuel Amago wishes to thank his students from the senior seminar of fall 2008 for their enthusiasm and fresh insights into the theme. He is also grateful to Amy Keenan-Amago for her acute critical eye and companionable interest in Spain's recent history and its cultural representations.

This volume was inspired by a symposium organized by Carlos Jerez-Farrán, held at the University of Notre Dame, October 28–29, 2005, entitled Franco's Mass Graves: An Interdisciplinary International Investigation, which was made possible by the generous support of the Henkels Lecture Series at the Institute for Scholarship in the Liberal Arts, the History Department, the Nanovic Institute for European Studies, the Office of Research of the Graduate School, and the Helen Kellogg Institute for International Studies at the University of Notre Dame. As organizer and main editor of the present book, Carlos Jerez-Farrán is also grateful to the Embassy of Spain in Washington, DC, and the Program for Cultural Cooperation Between Spain's Ministry of Culture and United States Universities for assistance in promoting and supporting the symposium.

Introduction

Carlos Jerez-Farrán and Samuel Amago

In a lecture he delivered in Buenos Aires in 1933, Federico García Lorca, Spain's most celebrated poet and playwright, observed that "a dead man in Spain is more alive when dead than anywhere else in the world: his profile hurts like a razor's edge."[1] Although the remark was made somewhat flippantly, it carries more irony today than Lorca could ever have imagined. More than thirty thousand people, including Lorca, fell victim to Francoist political executions. Seventy-two years later, their bodies, unlike Lorca's own, have been exhumed from the numerous mass graves into which they were dumped all over the country, and they have become both culturally and politically some of the most "alive" dead bodies in contemporary Spain. They have become living mementoes of the power of the dead to speak beyond language as they mutely but eloquently remind the nation of the crimes perpetrated against its own people during and after the Civil War. These mass burial sites and the bones they contain are part of the Franco legacy, especially of the years of the Civil War and the dictatorship that followed, when thousands of political detractors were massacred and secretly dispatched to the anonymous graves throughout the Spanish landscape.

Owing to the conspiracy of silence imposed by the Franco regime and perpetuated even after his death, the whereabouts of the tens of thousands of the General's victims were seldom discussed in private or in public, even though their resting places were known by neighboring residents. As is often the case with authoritarian governments, the silence that followed what happened during and after the Civil War was due mainly to the fear inflicted on the populace by the prevailing ideology. This collective pact of silence (known in Spain as the *pacto del silencio*) was also created in part by the genuine fear some Spaniards felt of seeing their country slip back into a painful past that was still all too vivid in their minds, especially at a time when the newly born democracy was in a process of consolidation. Consequently, during the transition years of the late 1970s and early 1980s, the experience of the Civil War was deliberately played down. As Paloma Aguilar has put it, "During this same transition period, both right and left agreed that the bitterest aspects of the past should not be aired in public debate. The memory of the Civil War was used, and then only implicitly, to facilitate the many social and political agreements and pacts made during this period. The transition to democracy was the almost obsessive desire to avoid a repetition of the war or the failings of the Second Republic" ("Agents" 103).

The Socialist Party (PSOE) that prevailed in the general elections of October 1982, just seven years after Franco's death, preferred not to deal with the subject in order to avoid provoking adverse reactions from the Right. From the other side of the political spectrum, members of the Partido Popular (PP), the right-of-center party that governed in Spain from 1996 to 2004 (all democrats but direct heirs of Francoist ideology and tactics and, in some cases, even former members of his government) were—and continue to be—reluctant to talk about this recent past, claiming that at best such discussion is an exercise in futility, a return to a historical past that contributes nothing of value and can only provoke social and political divisions that, they claim, have already been overcome.[2] According to this reasoning, "coming to terms with the past" for the Partido Popular would entail, in Theodor Adorno's terminology, "wishing to turn the page and, if possible, wiping it from memory" ("What Does" 115). Even twenty-five years after the consolidation of Spanish democracy, when the Spanish parliament has approved a new law recognizing officially the suffering of thousands of victims of Franco's regime, ordering the removal of statues erected in his honor, and condemning the forty years of rule that followed his victory, representatives of the PP continue to remind the nation of the same kinds of perils experienced in the past, using nearly identical rhetorical language when trying to avoid airing unpalatable truths.[3]

Regardless of the efforts made to silence the past, the way the Spanish Civil War continues to intrude on current politics was made all too evident in the aftermath of the March 2004 terrorist incident in Madrid, an attack that most commentators suggest cost the governing PP the presidential election. The two main opposing parties, moved by the political opportunity they saw in the incident, blamed each other for employing tactics reminiscent of the ones that provoked the Civil War some seventy years ago: the PP accused the winning PSOE of manipulating the terrorist assault for its own political advantage, while some members of the governing Socialist Party, on the other hand, accused José María Aznar and the soon to be defeated PP of preparing a coup d'état much like the one that had brought to power their ideological forefathers after a similar electoral defeat in February 1936. As Antonio Feros indicated in his analysis of the event, "the fact that a 70-year-old conflict should so quickly come to mind indicates how deeply ingrained the civil war is in the collective memory of the country and how it continues to have a profound influence on the ways Spaniards speak about national politics" (9). Accusations of this kind are an example of the political tensions that are still alive in Spain and of the ongoing difficulties involved in extracting the country's past from its present.[4]

Although Franco's regime and its contemporary heirs have spent decades trying to control collective memory by a variety of means—such as obliterating official records, sanitizing universities of suspected political dissidents, barring access to historical archives (thus enforcing a national amnesia about what happened during the Civil War and the years of dictatorship that followed), and withdrawing financial and logistical support for the exhumation of located graves—there has nevertheless been heard a public desire to confront Spain's recent past more persistently every year. As Geoff Pingree and Lisa Abend remark, "the so-called Pact of Silence, which effectively curbed open discussion of the past in order to secure the country's move towards democracy, has over the past few years given way to a chorus of demands to confront the past" (22).[5] This return of the repressed, to draw on Freudian terminology, can be seen as the inevitable result of the peculiar nature of the transition Spain experienced as it went from a repressive dictatorship on the one hand to the formal restoration of what is today a constitutional democracy, all without "the self-critical working through of the past" that a process of this kind requires (Suleiman 5). Instead of admitting that much of what happened during Franco's dictatorship needed to be recognized before moving on, the new democratic government, agreeing to abide by a mutually beneficial Amnesty Law of 1977, decided to turn the page on the past as if nothing had happened, recommending instead a kind of amnesia that would only delay matters further. And yet, as Suleiman has observed regarding the cultural manifestations of the traumas of the Second World War, "the deeper the political and ideological divisions that characterized the event and its aftermath, the more difficult it is to forget an offense by the opposing side, especially if the forgetting itself becomes a contested object of legislation" (224).[6]

As a result of a combination of factors—including a more permissive political climate, the stimulus to reflect on the past that resulted from the collapse of Communism in 1989 (Richards), and the discovery in 2000 of the burial site in Priaranza del Bierzo that initiated the current waves of exhumations—it is only over the course of the last ten years that Spaniards began to discuss openly the consequences of their turbulent past and recognize the long, silenced suffering shared by thousands of countrymen who saw members of families fall victim to the excesses of this war. As part of the long overdue effort to confront their past and come to grips with it wherever possible, an ever-increasing number of volunteers, led by teams of forensic experts, anthropologists, political activists, relatives of the disappeared, and sympathizers with their plight, set out to identify and exhume the numerous mass graves that are scattered throughout the country. As of July 14, 2008, according to Natalia Junquera and Luis Gómez, 171 burial sites had been excavated and a total of 4,054 bodies exhumed. This literal digging up of past violence has brought to light gruesome facts about the thousands of victims who disappeared mysteriously, the manner of their execution, and in some cases the reason for their death.

The ongoing resolution to come to grips with Spain's national past has generated much interest among historians and journalists, politicians and political scientists, writers and film producers, church representatives and ethicists, many of whom have approached the subject as witnesses of the Civil War and its legacy. The attention this episode of Spanish history is attracting has reached an audience far wider than the national one, as readers of the international press will have noticed in the last eight years or so.[7] As a consequence of this delayed reckoning, hardly a year has gone by without the inauguration of a new museum exhibit on this historic event, sometimes held concurrently with another exhibit and for extended periods of time, as was the case with Franco's Prisons and The International Brigades, held in the fall of 2002 in Barcelona. Prior to these exhibits, in September of that same year King Juan Carlos officially inaugurated an exhibit in Madrid on the Republican exodus to neighboring France. More recently, in 2005, the Círculo de Bellas Artes in Madrid held a photographic exhibit on the 33,000 orphaned children who were expatriated during the war and sheltered by families in different parts of the world.[8]

The large number of autobiographical accounts and memoirs that continue to be written by people who grew up in Republican families during Franco's dictatorship, together with an increasing output of works of fiction, history books, TV documentaries, newspaper articles, and public commemorations dealing directly with the Civil War, is unprecedented in Spain. This cultural production represents yet another facet of the current unabated surge of memory that attests to the central place this chapter in Spanish history continues to have in the present. As Pierre Nora remarks in his analysis of the reconstruction of the French past, "Memory has been promoted to the center of history," as if the current interest in exhuming a national past, physically, symbolically, and psychologically, were the way modern Spaniards have found to refill a "depleted fund of collective memory" and to arrive at truths deeper than those offered by an epoch devoid of history (qtd. in Sivan and Winter 2). This unabated interest indicates that the time has come for Spain to revise its past and publicly confront Franco's legacy just as the people of Germany, France, the Netherlands, and Italy have confronted and condemned the repressive regimes of the 1920s, '30s, and '40s and civilians' role in them. Even if Spain had to wait for more than seventy years to recover a "consciousness of historical continuity" that had atrophied, Spaniards are now living up to the claim that "enlightenment about what happened in the past must work, above all, against forgetfulness that too easily goes along with and justifies what is forgotten" (Adorno, "What Does" 117 and 125).

The present volume grows out of the need to address this ongoing debate from a variety of disciplinary perspectives and aims to offer a comprehensive account of how the Spanish Civil War continues to make itself felt in the present. Some of the essays included in this book are expanded versions of papers initially presented at a conference on Franco's mass graves held at the University of Notre Dame in the fall of 2005. The book, much like the conference that inspired it, gathers together a wide range of international experts from several disciplines—history, cultural studies, literary criticism, anthropology, and journalism—who discuss one common theme: how the Spanish Civil War and the years that followed are being remembered collectively by modern Spaniards, and what factors contributed to the ensuing silence, its distortions, and its denials. Each of this volume's four parts is preceded by an introduction and commentary by experts in each of these respective disciplines.

The preceding pages of this introduction will no doubt make clear that this collection of essays departs from a decidedly critical stance. Each chapter begins with the assumption of what the editors consider a series of historical facts: that in July 1936 a military rebellion led by General Francisco Franco and other members of Spain's military elite emerged to challenge the country's democratic institutions and elected government. And while some historians have suggested that the causes of the Civil War lay perhaps in the first military rebellion against Republican democracy led by General Sanjurjo in 1932, or in the Asturian general strikes that occurred in October 1934, we instead understand that it was, in fact, the illegal and undemocratic coup d'état led by General Franco that was the generative cause of the country's bloody fratricidal war. Further, we take for granted the fact that the Spanish Civil War ended with a thirty-six-year repressive dictatorship that systematically denied human rights to Spanish citizens and overtly and covertly sought to eradicate any ideological or political opposition. The mass graves that continue to be unearthed today are a testament to these historical facts.

This collection of essays concentrates principally on the cultural, political, and historical ramifications that the Francoist repression has had in the democratic present. While we do not deny that the Spanish Republic suffered from many problems before the start of the war or that those who fought against the Fascists between 1936 and 1939 committed many atrocities of their own, the reader will not find in this volume any sustained accounts or analysis of the killing undertaken by Republicans against Nationalist rebels or their sympathizers, principally because of the above stated reasons, but also because the regime had ample opportunity to memorialize its dead. As Helen Graham has pointed out, it was the military coup that allowed the culture of brutal violence to flourish, and "its original act of violence was that it killed off the possibility of other forms of peaceful political evolution" (18). Indeed, "if there had been no military rebellion then there would have been no extra-judicial killing—anticlerical or otherwise"—by Republican sympathizers (38). And it cannot be forgotten that Franco, after all, took full advantage of his nearly forty years in power to perpetuate his own version of Spanish history and to memorialize those who fought in his crusade against the Republic. Although we recognize that there remains work to be done on understanding why Spain's "political Left has not sufficiently tackled its responsibilities for extra judicial killings during the war" (Labanyi, "Politics" 123; see Loureiro), the essays included in this volume explore the history of Spain's defeated Republicans and their sympathizers, and analyze the unofficial histories that have been all but forgotten.

The primary focus of part I, "Franco's Mass Graves and the History of Forgetting," deals with the repercussions of Franco's dictatorship on the defeated. Soledad Fox, whose work on the Republic intersects in many ways with the issues raised here, provides an insightful introduction. Paul Preston then offers an analysis of the convoluted way in which extreme right-wing parties during the Second Republic and the authoritarian four-decade rule after Franco's victory campaigned to demonize and destroy "the entire Left of the political spectrum," which was seen to be conspiring against traditional Catholic and monarchic Spain. This was partly carried out, Preston argues, through the regurgitation of anti-Semitic sentiments dating back to the early Middle Ages in Spain, which reappear during the fifteenth and sixteenth centuries, and are deployed once again during the dictatorship of Primo de Rivera in the 1920s. This campaign of political vilification included the association of Bolsheviks, Socialists, Africans, and Freemasons, all of whom were characterized as an infernal mix engaged in the diabolical corruption of a supposedly healthy body politic. Just as the Nationalist general Mola was among the first to involve sacred principles as guides in what was after all a sociopolitical conflict (Casanova, *La iglesia* 79), these ultraconservative groups went to incalculable lengths to demonize the liberal agenda of the Republican government in order to win the support of those Spaniards who saw leftist ideology as hostile to their religious values, their political ideology, and their economic interests.

These concerted efforts—often used by persecutors whenever the security of individuals or the cohesion of a given community is threatened (Girard)—were based, according to Preston, "on a convoluted logic whereby Bolshevism was a Jewish convention and the Jews were indistinguishable from Muslims, and thus leftists were bent on subjecting Spain to domination by African elements." The irony is that this defamation and persecution was partly carried out by descendants of Jews themselves and by generals who, like Mola, were put in charge of the colonial army in Morocco to repress social unrest and aid the Nationalists' endeavor to oust the democratically elected government of the Republic (see Preston, *Coming*). The same can be said of Father Joan Tusquets, a Catalan priest who played a vital role in propagating the theory contained in the *Protocols of the Elders of Zion* of a worldwide Jewish conspiracy to destroy Christianity. As Preston remarks, "despite, or perhaps because of his own remote Jewish origins . . . his investigations into secret societies had developed into a fierce anti-Semitism and an even fiercer hatred of Freemasonry." As postmodern theory has demonstrated, the Other is often inextricably within, just as the excluded is required for the construction of the identity of the excluder. One is reminded of a similar case occurring a couple of decades before Tusquets's attacks, that of Otto Weininger, a Jew, a homosexual, and author of *Sex and Character* (1903), a widely disseminated book that became well-known for its misogynist attitudes and its virulent anti-Semitism. The main difference between Weininger and Tusquets is that the former committed suicide upon finding out about his own "criminal" sexual nature, that is, upon "recognizing his own otherness as a homosexual and a Jew, and masochistically accepting the 'correctness' of the Aryan antipathy to his 'subversive' ambiguity of race *and* gender" (Dijkstra 401–2). Father Tusquets did not kill himself. He lived on for more than fifty years after his invited visit to Dachau, if only to admit how shocked he was by what he had seen during that visit.

The deep moral and theological dilemmas raised by the Church's involvement—addressed implicitly in Preston's essay—are taken up more explicitly by another expert on the contemporary history of the Catholic Church in Spain, Hilari Raguer Suñer.[9] In his essay, "The Spanish Church and the Civil War: Between Persecution and Repression," Raguer analyzes the connections between the Vatican and the Catholic Church in order to show how the latter's intervention was more bellicose and supportive of the excesses committed by the Franco regime than the former. The Vatican is portrayed as having played a double game, combining on the one hand a covert collaboration with the Republicans during the war and, on the other, maintaining a cordial but tense relationship with the Fascist government in Burgos. It was only after the Nationalists won the war that the Holy See granted official recognition to Franco's victorious regime.[10] Raguer goes on to contrast the conduct of some members of the Church with the otherwise exemplary behavior of a handful of clergymen whose main aim was to uphold the Christian values in which they believed, denouncing publicly and at their own peril the killing of persecuted Republicans. Such was the case with clergymen Marcelino Olaechea and Father Huidobro. In order to show that not all Church representatives were supportive of the atrocities they were witnessing, Raguer draws on the example of Aita Patxi, a chaplain who offered himself as sacrificial victim to save a Republican prisoner's life. Sadly, Patxi later found that the prisoner had not been pardoned, as the military had told him (likely to get the priest out of the way), but been executed the following morning.

As was the case in post-Holocaust Germany, by the end of the Franco dictatorship one would have expected the Church to have shown a less passive attitude to what it had witnessed, to have made some public statement admitting its guilt, or, at least, to have condemned the atrocities committed by Franco. But nothing of the sort has come from its representatives so far, which tends to suggest that perhaps they colluded by their silence in those acts revealed by posterity. As Robert Ericksen and Susannah Heschel have remarked about the German churches after the Second World War, silences like these can be construed as a "strong indicator of the attitudes held during previous years" (11). Some of the inevitable questions that arise from these investigations are these: What humanitarian and religious convictions activated resistance in some priests and compliance in others? Why did so many high-ranking members of the Church fail so dismally to react when they were witnessing some of these atrocities? (Ericksen and Heschel, 4). Was their conduct justified on the basis of the persecution the Church suffered as a result of the anticlerical excesses before and during the war? Where does the moral authority of the Church in Spain rest when it participated in this kind of conduct?

In "The Faces of Terror: Violence during the Franco Dictatorship," Julián Casanova, a world expert on the Spanish Civil War and on the complex role the Catholic Church played in this event, analyzes the era of terror that dawned in Spain as soon as Franco proclaimed himself head of state, especially in the provinces that had remained faithful to the Republic during the war. He lists the measures of punishment legitimated by Franco's regime, the travesty of the judicial system that was created, the proliferation of regional tribunals, the executions by firing squad of those who were suspect of opposing the National Movement, and their subsequent anonymous internment. The violent political repression and human rights violations perpetrated by the regime were considered to be a just retribution against a group of people deemed barely human, partly because of the social stigma that came with being a "Red."

A portion of the essay deals also with the public humiliations and harsh conditions that imprisoned women had to endure, a topic also taken up by Fernández de Mata in the commentary he offers on the challenges to gender-based constructions that the sudden empowerment of women posed for men during the Republic (see his essay in part IV). This topic has received increased attention since the 2002 publication of Dulce Chacón's best-selling, prize-winning novel *The Sleeping Voice*. What is surprising to learn from Casanova's essay is that this treatment, which was meant to "exorcise the demons from the body," was performed under the official moral stamp of the Church and the Sección Femenina, a right-wing organization founded in 1933 and presided over by Pilar Primo de Rivera, sister of the president of the Falange, whose main objective was to educate Spanish women according to the Christian principles upheld by the movement. If the "intangible effects" of the repression the nation experienced were deployed primarily from above, they were also reproduced from below, as a result of the social, political, and material advances accrued from collaborating with the government.

This all confirms the fact that "the traumatic collective memory that most Spaniards have, even today, of the Civil War is explained not only by the events of the war of 1936 to 1939, but also by the experience of millions of Spaniards in the aftermath of the conflict itself" (Aguilar, "Agents" 84). The social and political "purge" Spain went through and the legal system of repression Franco established would not have been possible, Casanova claims, without the direct involvement of the Church. This was the main reason why it enjoyed the protection, privileges, and power Franco bestowed on it throughout his dictatorship.

Michael Richards's essay, "Grand Narratives, Collective Memory, and Social History: Public Uses of the Past in Postwar Spain," focuses more directly on the relations between history and memory. The essay draws subtle distinctions between historical knowledge and the mnemonics involved in recollecting the past, while posing compelling questions for historians. Richards asks, for example, "how to achieve the necessary critical distance from a period whose contested meanings are still part of contemporary political and social debates: How do historians operate from a vantage point *between* memory and history when recollections are still alive?" One of the salutary effects of the recent movement to recover historical memory in Spain, Richards claims, is that it "has mounted a sustained critique of the social and political 'amnesia' after Franco's death and has provoked some profound questioning of the democratic Transition as the founding myth of contemporary state legitimacy." The other positive value of this growing national reckoning with its past—which the essays by Ignacio Fernández de Mata and Francisco Ferrándiz in this volume ratify—is that "these memories and representations have focused largely on individuals, their experience of the war, and their suffering in the postwar period and have offered a corrective to a previous predominance of structures and ideologies in historical analysis." Besides demonstrating how history as an analytical discipline benefits from the social memory of a given group, Richards proposes a deconstructive approach to "our myriad images of the Spanish war" in order to "understand the process by which the narratives were produced and evolved (for example, the evolution of the 'crusade' construct into the 'fratricidal struggle' image). Dismantling them is the task of historians *and* broader movements for the recuperation of memory."

Part II of *Unearthing Franco's Legacy* is dedicated to the documentary films and *testimonios* (testimonies) that have played a crucial role in the recovery of historical memory in Spain.[11] This section is introduced by Anne Hardcastle, a specialist in contemporary Spanish cinema and cultural studies, who elegantly underlines the central issue uniting the three essays included in this section: their shared sensitivity to how ideologies and meanings are constructed in cultural texts that aim to uncover lost or repressed memories of the Spanish Civil War and the years of *franquista* repression. All three essays are reflexively concerned with understanding the trappings of historiographical representation and attempt to account for how memory texts—be they documentary films or *testimonios*—function in the cultural realm to make meaning out of the past.

The first essay in this section, "Investigative Journalism as a Weapon for Recovering Historical Memory," is by Montse Armengou Martín, a journalist who has worked since 1985 for Televisió de Catalunya, the regional public television station of Catalonia based in Barcelona. She has codirected, with Ricard Belis, three award-winning documentary films, *Los niños perdidos del franquismo* (*Franco's Forgotten Children,* 2002), *Las fosas del silencio* (*The Spanish Holocaust,* 2003), and *El convoy de los 927* (*927 on the Train to Hell,* 2004), which were all produced by the weekly program *30 Minuts.* Two of these titles—*Los niños perdidos del franquismo* and *Las fosas del silencio*—were subsequently published as books. The importance of Armengou's contribution to the process of recovering historical memory in Spain can hardly be overstated. In her essay included here, she describes her firsthand experience as an investigative documentary filmmaker: how she labored not only to discover and reconstruct lost accounts of Franco's repression but also to generate public visibility for repressed and forgotten collective memories. Armengou emphasizes that journalists are ethically obliged to give a voice to those who have been silenced. Along with newsreel footage, legal documents, historical analysis by historians, and video footage that constitute her documentaries, Armengou stresses the crucial importance that personal memories play in the construction of these televisual histories of the Spanish Civil War and Franco dictatorship. Echoing some of the points made by Jo Labanyi in her own essay, Armengou indicates that personal memories and *testimonios* play an important part in constructing a truly collective history, and therefore they must be included in any responsible historiographical account.

Gina Herrmann's essay, "Mass Graves on Spanish TV: A Tale of Two Documentaries," takes as its point of departure two documentary films that were broadcast less than a year apart but that present very different attitudes toward the historical memories they try to represent: Armengou and Belis's *Las fosas del silencio* and Alfonso Domingo and Itiziar Bernaola's *Las fosas del olvido* [*Mass Graves of Oblivion*, 2004]. Herrmann analyzes both documentaries in Derridian terms, linking televisuality to the political by investigating the methods by which these programs were made and what their authors have chosen to emphasize in the construction of their narratives. Through a combination of perceptive formal analysis and subtle theoretical framing, Herrmann highlights the fundamental differences between these two documentaries and takes Domingo and Bernaola to task for their ultimately specious representation of historical events. She convincingly exposes how their *Fosas del olvido* manipulates "archival images, words spoken in interviews, and editing techniques" to imply an even distribution of culpability among "*rojos y fachas.*" She points out that Armengou and Belis, on the other hand, take pains to imbricate their documentary within a concrete historical and political context that allows the thinking spectator to come to his or her own conclusions. While wartime abuses are nearly always committed by both sides, Herrmann—as do most of the contributors to this volume—rejects any implicit or explicit *equiparación* (equivalency) of the two sides that fought the Spanish Civil War. The main responsibility for the Civil War rests, after all, on the rebel generals who initiated their coup d'état in July 1936 against a democratically established Spanish Republic.

In "Testimonies of Repression: Methodological and Political Issues," Jo Labanyi explores how *testimonios* allow the speaker (and, by extension, the reader) "to think about the war in helpful ways." The essay argues that the responsible collection, organization, and publication of oral testimonies of the Civil War and postwar years can help to establish not so much a politics of truth but a politics of feeling. As such, Labanyi argues that the *testimonio* can function as both a legal document used to assign accountability and a crucial insight "into emotional attitudes toward the past in the present time of the speaker." Labanyi's discussion of the various *testimonios* that have come out in recent years explores how those memories, even when they are unreliable, allow the speaker to engage in a very real way with a personal experience of reality that has important ramifications for the collective whole. Labanyi writes, citing Elizabeth Jelin's work on postdictatorship Argentina, that "memory is not a slice of the past waiting . . . to be 'recovered'" but rather "a process that operates in the present and cannot help but give a version of the past colored by present emotions." Memory, she writes, is "affected by all sorts of interferences from subsequent experiences and knowledge," for it is an ongoing process of working through things that takes place in the present. This "working through" is an important part of the recovery of memories in a way that will be meaningful to us in the present. In the process of assessing these *testimonios*, Labanyi encourages us to go beyond the false dichotomy of "victim" and "perpetrator" by investigating instead the significant grey areas that continue to exist between these semantic categories. By including highly personal oral accounts within more traditional histories, and by including interviews in their entirety, historians may create a public awareness of "the complex structures of present-day feeling that they reveal." Labanyi concludes that it is important that editors, publishers, and scholars resist the temptation to remove the *testimonio* from its historical and personal contexts, for we must take into account the "specificity of memory as a mental process," not as unmediated access to historical truth.

Antonio Gómez López-Quiñones points out that "since the mid-1990s, the Civil War has enjoyed a period of cinematographic and novelistic popularity" (*La guerra persistente* 11). But in spite of this popularity, there have been few honest reckonings of the role that many Spanish novelists played during and after the Franco dictatorship. The inability or unwillingness of many men and women of letters to acknowledge reflexively their own roles during and after the Franco regime has only recently earned attention. When the Nobel laureate Günter Grass revealed in August 2006 that, as a young man, he had briefly served as a member of the SS, for example, there appeared in the Spanish press a number of essays and editorials expressing alternately disappointment, surprise, and condemnation. The novelist Javier Marías came to Grass's defense in the Sunday magazine of *El País* and proposed that perhaps it was time for Spaniards to begin to look at their own complicity—

overt or implicit—in the pall of silence that continues to cover the historical period that began with the Spanish Civil War and continued through Franco's dictatorship. He wrote, apropos of Spain's own sordid recent history, that "mientras proliferan los sesudos o frívolos artículos sobre cualquier intelectual extranjero repentinamente 'manchado,' en España sigue siendo casi imposible contar—sólo contar—las pringosidades fascistas o stalinistas de nuestros escritores" (while we have seen a proliferation of articles both frivolous and wise dealing with just about *any* foreign intellectual who has been suddenly "dirtied," in Spain it continues to be almost impossible to talk—and only talk—about the oleaginous Fascist or Stalinist dealings of our own writers). With his characteristic severity, Marías insists that it is indeed high time that Spain begins to look inward at its own complicity in the quiet continuation of Franco's repressive legacy during and after the war, reminding his readers that Spain's own Nobel laureate, Camilo José Cela, willingly offered his services as an informer for Franco's regime and moved voluntarily from Madrid to Galicia during the Civil War in order to join the rebel forces there. Cela later served proudly as an official censor during the dictatorship. Another popular and critically acclaimed novelist, Gonzalo Torrente Ballester, for his part, was an enthusiastic Falangist and Francoist ideologue.

In the article in *El País*, Marías, whose name is often mentioned as a possible candidate for a Nobel Prize for literature, faults both the political Right and the Left for not daring to explore the roles that certain Spanish authors and intellectuals played during and after the Spanish Civil War. His cantankerous condemnation of Spanish national culture bears citation in full, as it relates directly to the central problems addressed in this volume:

> En este país grotesco, ni la derecha ni la izquierda tienen el menor interés en que se sepa la verdad, y ambas están aún dedicadas a maquillarla a su favor, cuando no a tergiversarla con desfachatez. No cuente usted lo que escribieron o hicieron Cela, Laín Entralgo, Tovar, Maravall, Ridruejo, Sánchez Mazas, D'Ors, Giménez Caballero o Foxá, porque no fue nada malo, exclama la derecha, o empezó a serlo sólo cuando se apartaron del falangismo o de la dictadura, los que lo hicieron. No cuente usted lo que escribieron o hicieron Aranguren, Haro Tecglen

o Torrente Ballester, porque acabaron siendo muy "progres" y amigos nuestros, exclama la izquierda indignada, y menos aún Bergamín, que fue rojo de principio a fin. Por ambos lados la consigna es callar. Todo lo contrario que con Grass, Heidegger, Jünger o Cioran, no digamos con Drieu la Rochelle o Céline.

In this grotesque country, neither the Right nor the Left have the slightest interest in making the truth known, and both sides are still determined to touch it up—if not completely and shamefully distort it—to their own favor. Do not mention what Cela, Laín Entralgo, Tovar, Maravall, Ridruejo, Sánchez Mazas, D'Ors, Giménez Caballero, or Foxá wrote or did, because it was nothing bad, exclaims the Right . . . or at least it only began to be when they distanced themselves from *falangismo* or the dictatorship (those who actually did so). Do not mention what Aranguren, Haro Tecglen, or Torrente Ballester wrote or did, because they ended up being very progressive friends of ours, exclaims the indignant Left, and much less Bergamín, who was a Red from the beginning to the end. On both sides the agreement has been to keep quiet. This is all the exact opposite of Grass, Heidegger, Jünger, or Cioran, not to mention Drieu la Rochelle or Céline.

Marías explains this generalized reticence to discuss the past as a kind of political cynicism that springs from a self-interested double standard by which both the Left and the Right sought to promote their own perspectives. He continues,

No sé cuántos [años] habrán de pasar para que la verdad interese de veras (la redundancia es a propósito, hoy interesa de boquilla), pero está claro que setenta no han bastado, cuando aquí corren ríos de tinta sobre el pecado de Grass, que apenas si nos concierne, y se sigue amordazando con malos modos a quienes alguna vez mencionamos los de nuestros compatriotas intocables.

I don't know how many years will have to pass before the truth begins truly to interest us (the redundancy is purposeful, today the truth is of interest only in theory), but it's clear that seventy years have not been enough, since there have been rivers of ink spilled here on Grass's sins, which barely concern us, and we continue to muzzle rudely those of us who dare to mention one of our untouchable compatriots.

Apropos of this widespread silence about the pasts of public intellectuals, José-Carlos Mainer has remarked that Franco's legacy has been very difficult to exorcise, but that it continues to be a very familiar (and sticky) skeleton lurking in the nation's closet ("fue (es) un cadáver en el armario que acaba resultando familiar y que siempre es pegajoso"). Compared with other disastrous events that befell Europe during the twentieth century, the Spanish experience with Franco has been frustratingly difficult to acknowledge or metabolize: "el franquismo fue demasiado largo, contaminó toda nuestra experiencia de las cosas y, aunque culturalmente fuera inhóspito, se hizo costra de costumbre" (Franquismo lasted far too long; it contaminated our entire experience of things and although culturally it was not welcome, it became an ingrained, permanent reality).

Public declarations like Grass's have been all too uncommon in Spain, where no intellectual has made public his or her regret for having supported Franco's regime. *Intelectuales tránsfugas* (Turncoat Intellectuals) is the lead theme of a special edition of *Babelia, El País*'s Saturday literary supplement, dedicated to this subject. Inspired by the Grass confession, the issue is dedicated to the contrastive analysis of Spanish letters during and after the Franco dictatorship. A massive black-and-white photo on the front page of the issue tellingly features the poet Dionisio Ridruejo, who happily accompanies General Yagüe as he walks through Plaza de Cataluña after the Fascists took Barcelona in 1939.[12] The literary supplement dedicates five pages to the topic, whose overarching title is *"La responsabilidad de los intelectuales"* (The Responsibility of Intellectuals). An article by Miguel Ángel Villena, *"Entre el miedo y la impunidad"* (Between Fear and Impunity), compiles commentaries by contemporary Spanish novelists who comment on the noteworthy silence of the older generation of Spanish novelists who continued to publish and speak publicly after the consolidation of democracy in the early 1980s. (Villena's essay appears, significantly, below a photograph taken of Cela during the Nobel ceremony in Stockholm in 1989.)

Here, the novelist Suso de Toro affirms that there has not been one real case of auto-criticism or regret from a public intellectual associated with Franco or his regime: "si aceptamos que el golpe militar y el franquismo fueron un error histórico terrible, deberíamos esperar algún gesto como el de Grass. Pero ningún franquista se ha arrepentido, no. Ni siquiera Dionisio Ridruejo fue capaz de asumir la culpa, indudable en su caso" (if we accept that the military coup and Franco's regime were a terrible historical error, we really should expect some kind of gesture like Grass's. But no *franquista* has ever repented, no. Not even Dionisio Ridruejo was capable of assuming his guilt, which was doubtless in his case) (qtd. in Villena). Meanwhile, Rafael Chirbes asserts that in some cases the Spanish transition to democracy had the perverse result of turning collaborators into heroes: "No podemos olvidar que Cela fue nombrado senador y que Torrente Ballester fue elogiado una y otra vez" (We must not forget that Cela was named as a senator and that Torrente Ballester was praised time and again) (qtd. in Villena). For his part, Pedro Altares indicates that often during the Transition anti-*franquistas* and the political Left were forced to renounce necessary compromises because of a generalized fear: "miedo a hurgar en el pasado o a rescatar el odio" (qtd. in Villena). As several of the authors included in this volume have highlighted, in the words of Rafael Chirbes, "el gran acuerdo de la transición . . . pasó por no remover el pasado" (the great agreement of the Transition was to not disturb the past) (qtd. in Villena). Villena concludes his essay with the observation that, alongside the generalized fear that intellectuals suffered during the Transition, "la impunidad aparece como la sensación más citada al analizar el papel de la cultura bajo la dictadura" (impunity appears as the most mentioned feeling when one analyzes the role played by culture under the dictatorship).

In Germany, France, and Italy Fascist collaborators were publicly named, brought to justice, or censured, or they openly confessed or expressed regret, but this same auto-critical process did not and has not occurred in Spain. Enrique Gil Calvo laments that in Spain, "los fascistas españoles se permiten el lujo de ir con la cabeza bien alta y solo se ven obligados a dejar de presumir de las barbaridades que han cometido" (qtd in Villena; Spanish fascists are free to walk around with their heads held high; they only find themselves obliged to stop boasting about the barbarities they had committed). In many cases, the identity of perpetrators and collaborators remains secret, and the darker episodes of Franco's repression have never been discussed or recognized in public. As Gil Calvo claims, "Es la doble moral típico de este país" (qtd. in Villena; It's the typical double standard of this country). Calvo expresses his disappointment in the fact that the Transition brought with it the pact of silence and collective amnesia that is, in part, the subject of this book. The result of this generalized oblivion is that Spanish intellectuals who were involved with the regime were able to keep quiet about their past actions, and in exchange they tacitly agreed to become supporters of the new democracy established after the death of Franco. Villena asserts, "lo que parece indiscutible es que este país se pelea continuamente por los fantasmas de un pasado turbulento, complejo y, desgraciadamente, poco estudiado" (what seems absolutely indisputable is that in this country we are constantly fighting for the ghosts of a turbulent, complex, and, unfortunately, little studied past).

The essays included in this section of *Unearthing Franco's Legacy* attempt to address this historical lacuna and to explore these issues as they have manifested themselves in the cultural realm. The novelist Manuel Rivas has written extensively on the relationship between literature, history, silence, and memory from a decidedly Galician perspective. His remarks in a 2006 interview published in *El País semanal* are relevant to the main issues that Joan Ramon Resina and Samuel Amago explore in their essays in part III, as he points with some optimism to the redemptive qualities that words can have in the face of the willful oblivion that continues to permeate contemporary Spanish culture. Rivas explains that while silence has been pervasive, no silence can ever be total: "Esa pretensión de extirpar, de eliminar lo que representaba media España, no es posible. Las palabras viven y crecen también en la sombra. Hay formas de resistencia y de transmisión. La memoria tiene su propia estrategia" (qtd. in Pérez Oliva 14; This attempt to extirpate or eliminate what half of Spain stood for is not possible. Words also live and grow in the darkness. There are forms of resistance and transmission. Memory is its own strategy).

The power of words to memorialize the dead lies at the center of Joan Ramon Resina's essay, "The Weight of Memory and the Lightness of Oblivion: The Dead of the Spanish Civil War," in which he engages movingly with how death, memory, monuments, and ritual are and must be linked in the construction of ethical humanistic society. In his subtle argument, Resina analyzes the importance of all struggles against institutionalized forgetting, the power that images of the dead have in the cultural sphere, and the mnemonic role of monuments to the dead. A common theme shared by many essays included in *Unearthing Franco's Legacy* has to do with how amnesty and oblivion have important ramifications in the cultures of the present. Resina surveys the ways in which "the exhumation of corpses in the presence of immediate relatives showed the impossibility of establishing a clear distinction between history and memory," and he examines how "rituals of remembrance facilitate the disentangling of the living from the departed." In this way, public rituals honoring the deceased sustain society in a larger sense, and thus, the "Antigone Agenda" (as Hermann terms it in her essay in the previous section) is all about how "culture is disrupted by the refusal of ritual and the [negation of] the work of mourning."

In the classic text, the tyrant Creon's imposition of his will goes against one of the founding principles of culture, which is "the sublimation of violence into reassuring . . . images" of memory that will allow us to live nonviolently with those we may fear or do not understand. In the worst of cases, "under the aegis of horror," Resina writes, "sovereignty is synonymous with the tyrant's death-bringing power, while the images of carnage that he spitefully calls forth become the cornerstones of the new state." The carnage that has emerged as the cornerstone of the Francoist state is represented chillingly by the skeletons that appear in the mass graves that dot the Spanish landscape. Resina argues that these mass graves, which continue to be exhumed, with the help of the memory of the survivors, "establish new overriding memories, which reorganize the relevance of the past." But Resina's reading of recent Spanish history is complex, and he allows that at the same time, as we see in the *testimonios* and documentary films discussed in part II, "memory retains the ethical force of witnessing and . . . rises easily to the status of a political factor." The sheer volume of writing on the subject, along with the calcifying character of Spain's constitution in the political realm have made it increasingly difficult to hold the state accountable because the state is not a continuous entity. Resina insists throughout, however, that the refusal of post-Franco governments—conservative and liberal alike—to confer symbolic burial on the victims of Franco's regime represents, ultimately, "a fatal avoidance of responsibility."

Amago's essay, "Speaking for the Dead: History, Narrative, and the Ghostly in Javier Cercas's War Novels," attends to the rhetorical and ethi-

cal power that narrative has to memorialize the dead while also assuaging the fundamental human need to tell the stories that haunt us.
Amago argues that, much like the unearthing of mass graves that has
inspired this volume, Cercas's recent fiction is self-consciously obsessed
with digging up and giving meaning to the forgotten stories of the past.
He considers how Cercas's war novels, *Soldados de Salamina* and *La velocidad de la luz,* demonstrate the profound manifestations—physical
and psychic—that untold histories can have on their narrators, and he
analyzes the role of narrators in general—be they fictional or real—in
recuperating lost accounts of historical happenings. The essay concludes
by suggesting that reflexive narratives offer perhaps the truest method
of engaging with the complexities implicit in the writing of history, for
by drawing attention to the process by which memory becomes narrative and events become history, these kinds of stories draw attention to
the responsibility of novelists and historians to tell the tales that have
not been told, especially those that have been silenced.

Part IV, "Unearthing the Past: Anthropological Perspectives on
Franco's Mass Graves," is introduced by Tony Robben, a scholar whose
expertise is drawn from similar anthropological studies carried out in
Argentina. His essay attests once more to the universality of the Spanish
phenomenon that concerns us here, partly because of the global nature of the war and also because it deals with humankind's unlimited
potential to cause irreparable destruction. The essays that Robben comments on contain anthropological observations from two experts who
bring firsthand experience in the actual excavation of the burial sites
they study: Fernández de Mata in the province of Burgos and Ferrándiz
in Valdediós (Asturias). Their essays offer valuable personal accounts
of investigations into the repression that followed the war, the state of
fear created by the Nationalists during and after the war, and the inability
among Republicans to mourn their dead properly. They also serve as
examples of the shift that is taking place "from the history of collectivities and structures toward individuals and human agency" that Richards sees as symptomatic of the new focus that "recent manifestations
of collective memory" have taken in Spain.

In "The Rupture of the World and the Conflict of Memories" Ignacio Fernández de Mata sees memory in Spain as being "at the heart of
contemporary redefinitions of nationhood, civil society, citizenship, and

democracy." He addresses the plight of the defeated from four perspectives: the difficulties involved in remembering and transmitting the traumas experienced by their victims, the violence perpetrated by Franco's troops, the explanations of this genocide offered by different social groups, and, finally, the conflicts of memory created today by the exhumation of Franco's mass graves. Fernández de Mata's essay, which in several ways complements Casanova's and Ferrandiz's accounts of the culture of terror institutionalized by the dictatorship, explores the social, political, and economical opportunities that the lower middle classes saw in the coup, the allegiance they pledged to Francoist politics, and, adversely, the discrimination experienced by the vanquished. His essay speaks to key questions asked by commentators of similar atrocities elsewhere, such as how we might negotiate the past and the discomfort of guilt, especially when those responsible for this past "often feel remorse and live with guilty consciences, but few accept the responsibility of their participation in the events and ask for forgiveness."

The uncomfortable and embarrassing position with which some perpetrators have had to struggle is vividly portrayed in his examples of a former civil guard and a Falangist in Aranda de Duero, both of whom "reveal that they want to remove part of their guilt by cooperating with the relatives of the assassinated victims, while simultaneously denying that they in fact have any guilt to remove." The essay confirms the need expressed elsewhere by Mieke Bal "to legitimize traumatic memory in order to lessen the hold they continue to have over the subject who suffered the traumatic event in the past" (Introduction viii). Fernández de Mata deals also with the personal conflicts these exhumations have had on victimizers and victimized alike, and the unsettling effects this process may have on those who struggled "to construct an identity that distanced them from the Reds and was valued positively by Francoism." Among the latter, Fernández de Mata lists the example of the mayor of a town near Villamayor de los Montes, a member of the PP who opposed the exhumation of a recently located mass grave, even though it was known to contain the remains of his own Republican father. Another example of identities being destabilized, as Fernández de Mata avers, is the one constituted by descendants of Republican families who have accommodated to the conditions imposed by the victors' prevalent ideology and "blamed their murdered parents not only for their deaths but for the problems they caused for the surviving family members." Self-justifying attacks like these are not unique to the Spanish phenomenon, as they echo other counteraccusations made in post-Nazi Germany, which stated that "such things could not have occurred if the victim had not presented some kind of provocation" (Adorno, "What Does" 116). If the sudden surge of memory means one thing for the descendants of the perpetrators and something else for the victims, there are times when political orientation, age, and material prosperity stand in the way of making this distinction altogether convincing. As Stanley Cohen has remarked about similar "ideological shifts" during and after the Pinochet era in Chile, "well-informed, middle-class people, who must have known about the disappearances and tortures, simply denied what was happening. After the transition to democracy, they openly acknowledged that these abuses happened, but switched to justification: current stability and economic success have vindicated the junta; it was necessary to save the country from the chaos that Allende caused" (137).[13]

The fear imposed by the Nationalists as part of a political and military consolidation of power is addressed also in Francisco Ferrándiz's essay, "The Intimacy of Defeat: Exhumations in Contemporary Spain," in which he demonstrates how the "memory-work taking place around mass graves, whether they are exhumed or not, has been progressively making visible a formerly neglected cartography of terror and repression that encompasses many landscapes and localities throughout the country." Ferrándiz focuses on one particular incident that occurred in Valdediós in 1937: the execution by a firing squad of seventeen staff members of a psychiatric hospital whose bodies were dumped into one of the burial sites that has been exhumed in the northern province of Asturias. His essay draws on personal testimonies afforded by relatives of the victims interviewed by the author. Ferrándiz also addresses the difficulties involved in sharing personal traumatic experiences without their losing impact or, worse, being turned into clichés or commodified by the media to be sold in the form of popular narratives. Ferrándiz interviews some of the most vulnerable of the victims, like Emilia and Esther, the wife and daughter, respectively, of one of the murdered members of the hospital staff. All Emilia recalls is that "Asturias had fallen, some soldiers came, there was a Mass, there was a meal, and then 'there was death.' The closest Emilia gets to the killing is when recalling her husband told her, when his name was called, 'Do not worry. Nothing is going to happen to me just for taking care of mad people.'" These last words remembered vividly by the victim's surviving wife are significant for several reasons. They serve as an example of the indiscriminate killing that was carried out during the Civil War, but they also corroborate the fact that in cases like these "memory work is intertwined with grief work" (Sivan, "Private Pain" 178–79).

What is so compelling about Emilia's ellipsis is its emblematic power to convey on a personal scale the difficulties Spain is presently experiencing as it attempts to integrate its national past into a national narrative, partly because of the silence and invisibility imposed on what happened. This is what Ernst van Alphen, in his reflection on the Holocaust, calls "the inadequacy of the frames that are inflicted on the victims by the surrounding culture," and the impossibility of traumatic memories to become narratives (34). It is beyond human comprehension capacity to record what actually happened. As Doris Laub has observed about other atrocities bearing a disturbing resemblance to what happened in Spain, it was "the very circumstances of being inside the event that made unthinkable the very notion that a witness could exist" (qtd. in Cohen 131). Exhumations, Ferrándiz goes on to claim, can also be "understood and interpreted as a road map linking the political production of terror with the intimate experiences of the victims of repression."

Although the present volume focuses on contemporary Spain, the implications of the issues explored here transcend national boundaries, since the book deals with the way a nation's past is called up to bear on the present, and the repercussions it has at the social, cultural, and political levels. *Unearthing Franco's Legacy* also poses crucially important questions, such as how victims of crimes like the ones remembered might be induced to forget when, as Suleiman posits about similar experiences, some of the actions experienced by those directly affected by them are difficult to forget and forgive (217). Indeed, how should a nation deal with those responsible for the traumatic events of its past? Should bygones be bygones for the sake of preserving the peace and prosperity brought about by a fragile new democracy? Silence is always unacceptable, but so too is remembrance as a means of healing since, as Walter Benjamin warns, it can be used as a means to cover up crimes and thereby protect their perpetrators (Sivan and Winter 5). Are reconciliation and healing achievable when the nation is divided between those who would prefer to forget and get on with life and those others who want to see justice done? Can Spaniards come to terms with their past when the victimizers continue to have monuments in their honor maintained by the state, as is the case with Franco's colossal mausoleum, known as the Valley of the Fallen, and when the country "dares not turn into a punishable crime the exaltation of the dictatorship, as the case is with other European countries who suffered similar historical blemishes" (Prado 1)? Can bygones be bygones for Spaniards when the Vatican beatifies 480 victims of the atrocities committed by the militias loyal to the Republican government but continues to ignore the death and suffering of thousands of victims of Franco's brutality?

The universality of the issues discussed in this volume become more evident when we consider present political conflicts, unnecessary wars, and massacres that have resulted from similar abuses of power and military might. We only need to think of the Holocaust, *los desaparecidos* in Latin America, the Yugoslav Civil War, and the Rwandan genocide, together with other collective traumas too current to be named, to realize that the psychohistorical dynamics of ignored atrocities and systematic assaults on truth and memory are of universal concern. In all cases, denial is anathema because national amnesia—enforced or unconscious—about given genocides has the potential to provoke new ones. The central goal of this volume can be summarized with a quotation from the Uruguayan Luis Pérez de Aguirre's *Memoria de los detenidos desaparecidos*: "No se recuerda, no se juzga el pasado sólo para castigar o condenar, sino para aprender" (One remembers not to judge the past, to punish or condemn, but to learn) (qtd. in Casanova, "Otras memorias").

NOTES

1. "Un muerto en España está más vivo como muerto que en ningún sitio del mundo: hiere su perfil como el filo de una navaja barbera." The paper, titled "Teoría y juego del duende," was delivered in Buenos Aires on October 20, 1933. See García Lorca, 3: 312.

2. In the introduction to a special number of the *Journal of Spanish Cultural Studies* devoted to the politics of memory in contemporary Spain, Jo Labanyi points out that "apart from the condemnation of the Franco dictatorship by all parties in Congress on 20 November 2002," Spain's political Right has

been unwilling "to dissociate itself from or apologize for their predecessors' support for the extra-judicial murder of civilians" ("Politics" 124).

3. Such is the case with Máximo Rodríguez, speaker of the PP, when he rejected in 2006 the proposal to indemnify victims of Francoism in Galicia, stating that to support this new law would mean to fall into the same "sectarian and Manichean imposition of the Franco regime," adding that "to reopen wounds could provoke frictions and even social fissures considered to be overcome with the transition" (qtd. in Varela, 25). See Labanyi, "Politics," and Golob, along with Giles Tremlett's essay in this volume for more on the debate on the *Ley de la Recuperación de la Memoria Histórica*.

4. The frequent marches and manifestations organized by the PP in opposition to the PSOE's antiterrorist program and other policies have brought the iconography of the past into the present. The front page of *El País* on March 23, 2007, for example, featured a photograph of the latest march organized by the PP to protest the prosecutor's release of Arnaldo Otegi, leader of the outlawed Batasuna party. The photo features a group of hard-liners bearing preconstitutional Spanish flags and banners supporting the Falange—Spain's Fascist party and the only political organization allowed during Franco's regime—as they make their way through the streets of Madrid.

5. Paul Connerton observes, apropos of similar attempts to control collective memory, that "control of a society's memory largely conditions the hierarchy of power . . . and the organization of collective memory . . . , is not merely a technical matter but one directly bearing on legitimation, the question of the control and ownership of information being a crucial political issue" (1).

6. The link we make here and elsewhere to World War II is purposeful, as we regard the Spanish case, with Golob, as one part of what has become a globalized transitional justice culture.

7. The article by Elizabeth Kolbert, "Looking for Lorca," published in the *New Yorker* (December 22, 2003), brought the issue to a wide audience in the United States, as did a number of shorter articles published in a variety of newspapers: "Spaniards at Last Confront the Ghost of Franco" (*New York Times*, November 11, 2002) by Elaine Sciolino and Emma Daly; "Via a Grave Site, Spain Relives Harsh Divisions" (*Boston Globe*, August 22, 2004) by Charles Sennott; and "Even in Death, Franco Has the Power to Divide Spaniards" (*Los Angeles Times*, October 29, 2006) by Tracy Wilkinson. More recently, the investigation undertaken by Magistrate Baltasar Garzón of the whereabouts of approximately 137 war victims, the poet García Lorca among them, has moved center stage and received wide attention by the international press. Garzón's judicial indictment of Franco and thirty-four of his generals and ministers for crimes against humanity committed between 1936 and 1951 was the subject of a recent article in the *Economist* (October 25, 2008, 62–63). The indictment was later found unconstitutional.

8. In the United States, Francesc Torres presented his photographs of the excavations of mass graves at the King Juan Carlos I of Spain Center at New York University and at New York's International Center of Photography in the autumn of 2007. See Torres.

9. The dilemmas raised by the Church's involvement in the massacres and repression that took place during and after the Civil War, together with the support it gave to Franco's government, transcended Spain and "became a particularly acute problem of conscience" for leading Catholics like the French liberal theologian Jacques Maritain (Doering, 489).

10. It is telling that the first two official telegrams that Franco received after his victory in November 1939 came from Adolf Hitler and Pius XII (Preston, *Franco* 322).

11. Documentarians have been prolific during the last ten years, producing titles such as *Muerte en El Valle* (Christina Hardt, 1998), *La guerrilla de la memoria* (Javier Corcuera, 2001), *La memoria es vaga* (Katie Halper, 2004), *Los héroes nunca mueren* (Jan Arnold, 2004), *Presos del Silencio* (Mariano Aguado and Eduardo Montero, 2004), *La mala muerte* (Fidel Cordero and José Manuel Martín, 2004), *La columna de los ocho mil* (Ángel Hernández García, Antonio Navarro, Fernando Ramos, and Francisco Freire, 2005), *Santa Cruz, por ejemplo* (Günter Schwaiger and Hermann Peseckas, 2005), along with the two documentaries by Montse Armengou (discussed in essays in this volume by Gina Herrmann and Armengou herself). These and other titles have been broadcast on regional and national television stations and screened in art house cinemas throughout the country. Indeed, over the last few years documentary films have enjoyed an unprecedented popularity. In June 2005 a series of films carrying the title *Imágenes contra el olvido* was so successful that the Cine Doré in Madrid repeated the series in its entirety in October 2006. All of the films included in the series are now available for purchase in a boxed set sold at book and video stores throughout Spain.

12. The caption reads, "Frente a gestos como el de Günter Grass, pocos escritores españoles, de los que colaboraron con el franquismo, trataron abiertamente de su apoyo a la dictadura o renegaron de su pasado" (Considered alongside gestures like Günter Grass's, few of the Spanish writers who collaborated with Franco's regime dealt openly with their support of the dictatorship or renounced their past).

13. These kind of postdictatorship dynamics are no doubt behind the unfortunate impunity that perpetrators have enjoyed in Latin America and Spain. It is estimated that over 90 percent of the common crimes committed by the various Latin American dictatorships of the 1960s, '70s, and '80s (genocide, human rights abuses, crimes against humanity, etc.) were never addressed, nor were their perpetrators brought to justice. See Aznárez.

PART I

Franco's Mass Graves

and the History of Forgetting

Violence and Silence

The Repressed History of the Franco Regime

Soledad Fox

Atrás quedaba una nación en escombros, agotada y aterrorizada, en manos de una minoría cruel y tremendamente eficaz en el uso negativo del poder. Se sucedieron años de exterminio sistemático de toda oposición y de aparente triunfo de los negadores de la libertad política, de la dignidad humana y de la justicia social.

—José Rubia Barcia, *Prosas de razón y hiel*

When Manuel Fraga Iribarne was minister of tourism and propaganda in the 1960s, he coined the well-known and cheerful slogan "Spain is different!" to attract foreigners to the sun and beaches of a country still scarred by its Civil War and under the reign of Franco's authoritarian regime. The benevolent image promoted by the government was immensely successful in masking the sociopolitical reality of Spanish life, but in light of the evidence that has emerged in the last few decades, a much more accurate description of the country would have been "Spain is one big prison" or "Spain is a mass grave."

The following essays offer a detailed portrait of the nature and consequences of Nationalist ideology and violence before, during, and after the war. Though each is very different in its sources and approach, there are many common threads. Themes that stand out are the complex role of the church, the constant menace of imprisonment and death that pervaded and shaped all aspects of Spanish life during the war and the postwar period, and the ideological apparatus that served throughout to justify the use of violence against Republicans.

—— In the midst of the Spanish Civil War, Hannah Arendt noted that "even Franco, in a country where there are neither Jews nor a Jewish question, is battling the troops of the Spanish Republic while mouthing anti-Semitic slogans" ("The Jewish Question" 43). The full ramifications of this insight are brought to the fore in Paul Preston's chapter "The Theorists of Extermination: The Origins of Violence in the Spanish Civil War," which reveals just how surprisingly fruitful anti-Semitism proved as an ideological theme in a country where there was hardly a Jewish presence. Preston echoes Arendt when he writes: "Spanish 'anti-Semitism without Jews' was not about real Jews so much as an abstract construction of a perceived international threat."

This essay exposes the cultural and ideological foundations of the campaigns of violence that would terrorize Spain for decades. In order to have a proper understanding of what fuelled the Nationalists' repressive tactics and what made them widely acceptable in the eyes of so many Spaniards, Preston argues that one must look at the sociopolitical situation in Spain in the years leading up to the military coup of 1936. Particularly from 1917 onwards, the tensions between the "militant industrial and rural proletariat" on the one hand, and industrialists, landowners, and the middle class on the other, spiraled into violent and recurring confrontations. It was in this context that the image of a Jewish-driven revolutionary menace was fomented, using anti-Semitic rhetoric sometimes imported, sometimes indigenous to Spain's past, and the idea propagated that "an alliance of Jews, Freemasons, and working-class internationals was conspiring to destroy Christian Europe, with Spain as a principal target." After 1931, the Republic's measures to separate church and state and diminish the power of the former made it easy to sell the spurious notion that all Republicans were anti-Catholic, anti-Spanish, hence foreign and part of the Jewish-Bolshevik-Masonic conspiracy. Anti-Semitism was thus used to justify a program of violence against the Left. Moreover the religious and racial overtones, in the context of Spain, lent a particularly Catholic flavor to anti-Semitic prejudice, giving the Church a leading role in political life. Nobody could have guessed how fruitful and enduring this platform would be, as it would justify "any means necessary for what was presented as national survival." This ideology was spread widely via anti-Republican magazines, newspapers bulletins, and pamphlets. The rhetoric of these publications had a captive audience that included landowners, industrialists, and military officials. The military, an outdated and overpopulated institution, was especially threatened by Republican calls for army reform.

One of the leading figures in this propaganda war against the Republic was the Catalan priest Juan Tusquets Terrats (who was descended from a Jewish family). Tusquets's best-selling writings were instrumental in disseminating the *Protocols of the Elders of Zion*, the notorious manifesto that accused the Jews of conspiring to destroy Christianity. His message, which would resonate directly with General Franco (and later implicate Tusquets in the military plot against the Republic), was, in Preston's words, that "Spain and the Catholic Church could be saved only by the destruction of the Jews, Freemasons, and Socialists, in other words, of the entire Left of the political spectrum." Tusquets's work had sufficient success for him to be invited by the International Anti-Masonic Association to visit the newly built German concentration camp at Dachau. He influenced many leading Spanish Nationalists, including the planner of the 1936 military rising, General Mola, who also wrote about Spain's "decay" at the hands of "international organizations" (i.e., Jews), and characterized Nazi persecution of Jews as the necessary step that permitted Germany to "rise again."

Onésimo Redondo, founder of the anti-Republican newspaper *Libertad* and the Fascist party Juntas Castellanas de Actuación Hispánica, also believed and spread the ideas of the *Protocols*. His own writings on Spain's "enemies" called for "a few hundred young warriors in each province, disciplined idealists, to smash to smithereens the dirty phantom of the red menace" and urged Spaniards to "cultivate the spirit of violence, of military conflict." Preston points out that Redondo's anti-Semitism was derived more from fifteenth-century Castilian nationalism than from Nazi models, though Redondo did translate Hitler's *Mein Kampf* into Spanish. In Redondo's rhetoric, Moors, Jews, and the Left were all merged into one: "By asserting that Marxism was a Jewish in-

vention and implied the 're-africanisation' of Spain, Redondo was identifying Spain's archetypal 'others,' the Jew and the Moor with the Right's
new enemy: the Left. The war Spain needed to wage was a new 'reconquista' and ideologues such as Redondo offered a 'murderous justification of violence against the left.'" Anti-Semitism was no hindrance
to anti-Arab sentiment, which could also be useful to the right-wing program. General José Sanjurjo, the director general of the civil guard, had
compared the poor Spanish workers of Castilblanco to Rif tribesmen,
and the press would echo his views, adding their own qualifiers such
as "bloodthirsty savages and Marxist hordes."

As tensions in Spain grew more dramatic, the Right's use of propaganda became more widespread and ruthless. During the revolutionary
strikes of 1934 in Asturias, eventually crushed by General Franco, the
insurrectionary miners were portrayed in the right-wing press as "creatures of a foreign, Jewish-Bolshevik conspiracy." The much-criticized
fact that Franco had used Moorish troops in Asturias was given a positive spin by propagandists: the rebels, being half-foreign themselves,
deserved no better than to be put down by Moors.

Thus well in advance of the uprising, the enemy of the Right had
been established, in a bizarre sort of Russian doll set-up, as a Moorish
barbarian, inside a Jew, inside a Freemason, inside a Communist, inside
a Republican. This confusingly defined foe was characterized as treacherous, violent, anti-Christian, and murderous—attributes that accurately
sum up the behavior of the Right. The irony, of course, is that in their
rhetoric of hatred the Nationalists were in fact offering a revealing self-
portrait in a classic case of collective projection.

In this section's second essay, Hilari Raguer Suñer debunks the idea
that the Vatican was as aggressively anti-Republican as the Spanish episcopacy. Based on documents illustrating diplomatic relations between
the two Spains and the Holy See during the period of 1936–1939, "The
Spanish Church and the Civil War: Between Persecution and Repression" explains that the Holy See in fact was slow to grant official recognition to the rebels—despite the fact that these claimed to be "defending
the Church and fighting against those who were persecuting priests."
Franco's alliance with Mussolini and Hitler, along with news of the repression in the Francoist zones, made the Vatican wary of committing to
the rebels, and they remained in contact with the Republican leadership

through the second year of the war. "If in the end the Church dropped this contact and officially recognized Franco," Raguer asserts, "it was only because Franco won the war."

Within the Spanish episcopate itself, Raguer shows, positions on the war often lacked the coherence that has retrospectively been attributed to them. An example of this is the collective letter in support of the Nationalist uprising signed by the Spanish bishops on July 1, 1937—a missive of which not all bishops approved. Raguer also highlights the humanitarian values of a few exceptional clerical figures, such as the bishop of Pamplona, Marcelino Olaechea Loizaga. At a ceremony of Acción Católica, Olaechea publicly denounced the lynching of *rojos*, which was common practice in villages following the burial of nationalist soldiers.

Another dissenter within the clergy was Father Fernando Huidobro Polanco, who urged the Nationalist military authorities to impose some kind of limitation on imprudent use of the death penalty for Republican prisoners: "One doesn't necessarily deserve the death penalty for the mere fact of being affiliated with the CNT or the UGT; not even for taking arms in order to defend mistaken ideals that are sincerely considered the best for society." He had been horrified by killings he had witnessed, which he assumed to be at the hands of disobedient madmen. He did not realize that the killers were, on the contrary, "disciplined legionaries" mercilessly carrying out the instructions of General Mola, with the blessing of Franco, Varela, and all the commanding officers. Even for the relatively progressive Huidobro, however, some Loyalists (murderers of priests, women, and so forth) did deserve to die. Ironically, he himself died in Madrid, officially killed by a Russian shell, but Raguer suggests that a legionary murdered him. Had it been proven that Russians were responsible for his death, he would be on his way to sainthood, but when it came out that "the wrong side" may have killed him, his beatification process was stopped. Huidobro's controversial legacy, then, shows how wartime ideology lived on for decades.

Aita Patxi was also an exceptional cleric, as Raguer highlights in a biographical sketch of the greatly admired Basque priest. Venerated for his austerity and spirit of self-sacrifice, Patxi repeatedly offered his own life to the Nationalist authorities to save Communists or Republicans from execution. The majority of the clergy, however, seemed to be able to handle the violence that had become a part of their daily lives with great calm, efficiency, and even enthusiasm. The chaplains in the prisons and concentration camps emerge as an especially sinister group, who would often "insult the prisoners and . . . tell them that they weren't worthy of the benevolence that the Caudillo showed them." In the magazine for priests of the Company of Jesus, *Sal Terrae,* there were heated debates about the Church's role in the mass executions of prisoners. The dilemma did not, however, touch on the moral issue of the widespread use of the death penalty, but hinged on whether prisoners sentenced to death should be granted extreme unction and, if so, at what point. Father Regatillo, the advice columnist of the publication, eventually put his colleagues' minds to rest by stating that extreme unction should be administered, ideally, "after the first shot, and before the coup de grace."

The detailed portrait that emerges from Raguer's essay is an unsettling one of a church whose bishops and priests actively collaborated with, and justified, military and police violence. The generally unified stance that this clergy would come to adopt is all the more disturbing given the tremendous power they would wield not only during the war but in the ensuing decades, in a society where "one's employment, freedom, or even life depended on the endorsement of the priest." In terms of the "recovery of historic memory" the role of the Church in Spain is still far from being resolved. The Spanish episcopacy (unlike those of Germany, Argentina, Chile, and other countries in similar situations) "has repeatedly rejected the suggestion of publicly making an apology for the role the Spanish Church played during the Civil War and in the repression of the postwar period."

The horrors of the postwar era described in Julián Casanova's "The Faces of Terror: Violence during the Franco Dictatorship" make clear that ideologically justified violence, torture, and death continued long after the alleged peace of April 1, 1939. The war had not done enough, in the eyes of the victors, to eradicate and punish all traces of the Republic, and in order to guarantee its supremacy Franco's regime would use forceful and repressive means to ensure its longevity. The victors insisted on exacting what they saw as their just revenge on anyone who might disturb their imposed social order: "Secularism and the workers movement would be eradicated through a process of terror, and a reign of order, soon to be called *franquismo*, would establish its hegemony."

The most basic purging of Republicans and leftists was achieved by imprisonment and execution, and the numbers of the victims can be traced throughout Spain. For example, executions by military order in Albacete between 1939 and 1953 totaled 1,026. By 1950, 1,280 people had been officially executed in Jaén; in Madrid, 2,663 had been shot as early as 1945. In total, at least 50,000 men and women were executed between 1939 and 1949, and countless additional victims died in makeshift concentration camps (in which 270,000 prisoners were interned between 1939 and 1940).

There was, as Casanova points out, not even a semblance of justice for the victims at any point between their arrests and their execution: "Between 1939 and 1945, thousands of individuals were judged in Franco's courts, which carried out a travesty of justice on a daily basis." In the proceedings of these kangaroo courts, nothing was ever proven, as it was already taken for granted from the outset that the accused was "Red." Thus the so-called legal system of the new regime acted with complete disregard for the law and spontaneously exercised what Walter Benjamin calls "the highest form of violence," that over life and death ("Critique" 242). The 1939 Law of Political Responsibility posed as a law-preserving measure, but was in fact a "law" justifying partisan violence. All those found guilty or guilty by association of opposing the Nationalists actively or passively were deemed "beyond the law" and lost their rights and property. "By October 1941, 125,286 cases were brought against some 200,000 persons," and though the law was modified in 1942 and repealed in 1945, many open cases were not fully processed until 1966. Casanova also points out that the 1940 Law of Repression of Masonry and Communism survived, albeit under a new tribunal, until 1977.

One of the most sinister aspects of the repression highlighted by Casanova is the widespread collaboration with the regime throughout Spanish postwar society: "The military justice system found an abundant number of efficient collaborators who helped carry out detentions, torture sessions and assassinations." The combined forces of the army, the Guardia Civil, Falangist and Carlist militias, and informants of all kinds ensured that few escaped. Repression passed from uncharted chaos to punishments couched in more legalistic terms, but in practice the beatings, torture, and executions remained the same. The ideology of extermination that was forged before the war flourished in the postwar era, and the "Reds" were considered scum of which Spain had to be cleansed. Society in general was governed by fear and by the pressure to cooperate, making denunciations of friends, neighbors, and family quite common. Centers were set up where citizens could report people they knew, and "from the very first day, there were long lines of citizens, many of whom arrived in search of retribution." Spain became a self-censoring country of conformists, spies, and victims. According to the author, not even in Nazi Germany was there ever such a successful system of collaboration. All public offices were immediately purged, ensuring that no subversive elements remained and that loyal Francoists were employed.

The religious angle was crucial to the success of the repression for "the jail and such businesses were both blessed by the Church, which was complicit in the general repression of the postwar." The fallen on the Nationalist side were remembered and glorified as "martyrs," and this rhetoric alone provided ample justification for the Church's support of the revenge on the vanquished. The Spanish clergy seized the postwar period as an opportunity to reclaim the power they had lost, in their perception, at the hands of the Republic. Many priests became eager informants and collaborated actively in the blacklisting process. "In particular," Casanova writes, "they showed their approval for the legal extermination of the vanquished. . . . They were deeply involved in encouraging feelings of envy, vengeance, and hate that pervaded Spain's small rural communities."

The regime's menacing propaganda permeated every single aspect of daily life in Spain and targeted all citizens regardless of their age, gender, or class. One of the key subjects Casanova emphasizes is the role of education in the postwar period. The education system was crucial to the "re-Catholicizing" of Spain and to what was, in effect, the "de-educating" of the Spanish people. One need only look at the schoolbooks for children from the time (for example, Editorial Luis Vives's *Historia de España*) to see how Spanish history past and present was rewritten as propaganda. In schools and universities, secular and progressive teachers were purged, and the Church helped turn education into a purely authoritarian experience aimed at bringing students into submission and conformity.

In time, Franco was clever enough to brush away Spain's Axis stigma (and, in the Cold War, other countries were eager to accept this sanitized version), but within Spain little changed. The Catholic Alberto Martín Atajo, appointed by Franco to the Ministry of Foreign Affairs, helped to forge the new image of a non-Fascist Spain but did little to make the image conform to reality. He did nothing to end the persecution of "Reds." Nor did the Spanish Church want to hear anything about forgiveness or reconciliation. Like Raguer, Casanova points out that "the Catholic Church came out ahead in its exchange of favors with the murderous political regime and was delighted with the benefits it derived from the dictatorship."

After reading Casanova's portrait of the physical and social repression after the war, it comes as no surprise to be told that, in Spain, the Civil War and its consequences "have not yet been effectively absorbed and understood as a collective experience." In "Grand Narratives, Collective Memory, and Social History: Public Uses of the Past in Postwar Spain," Michael Richards outlines the problems that historians face today when writing about a period characterized by the historian of Vichy France, Julian Jackson, as still inhabiting "a twilight zone between history and memory." Richards places the aftermath of the Spanish war in the context of other revolutions and civil wars, in which "a gulf is placed between opposed concepts of 'the nation' and ideas of legitimacy, society, and citizenship." It is difficult, in such cases, to differentiate between war time and postwar time because of the absence of factors that contribute to such a distinction (formal cease-fire, peace treaty, intervention by international peacemakers).

For Richards, the epic or tragic grand narratives of the Civil War can be reduced to three "big stories": "religious crusade or holy war, class war analysis, and the fratricidal struggle ('war between brothers')." The representations of memories of the war that have emerged in the past few years operate as a challenge to these narratives, but are also inevitably shaped by them. In considering the different meanings of history and memory within the Spanish context, Richards suggests that we can compare "mythical constructs and . . . popular challenges" to current historical practice.

In the regime's version of good versus evil, the Republic had been nothing but a "proto-Stalinist monolith" in an anti-Communist narrative that is still alive and well today. While the Nationalists were "martyrs" in the postwar discourse (as Casanova points out), fallen Republicans were not even victims. "The 'homecoming' for Republicans with the death of Franco in 1975 would be silent and without public recognition, because of the tacit agreement to forget the past, which was the price of the peaceful Transition to democracy." Residual fears of the dictatorship have delayed until recently a popular movement to recover the past and the bodies of Republican victims from their mass graves.

Throughout the postwar time period, the Francoist rhetoric of the conflict as a "crusade" and the regular commemorations honoring the Nationalists in their fight against "foreigners" effectively constituted the official version of Spain's recent history for future generations. This ideology, and the way it permeated Spanish life, is clearly illustrated in Richards's quote from Julián Grau Santos (born in 1937): "gradually it was instilled in me and I always believed that Spain had won the war against foreign enemies of our historic greatness." Since the Republic was fully and officially blamed for the war for so long, the relationship between truth and reconciliation has been especially complicated.

Spaniards were collectively forced into a state of resignation during the postwar decades. Richards equates this state not with passivity but rather with "a wholesale political disillusionment" as well as "a conscious and active decision by millions of people (many of them migrants) to take on painful sacrifices in the interests of generations to come. This was social and cultural reproduction in the aftermath of and in the face of the worst defeat imaginable."

Though the regime's rhetoric evolved over the decades (from "crusade" to "war," for example), its official historians always resisted reexamining the official version. The vehemently pro-Franco "state bureaucrat-cum-historian" Ricardo de la Cierva, when asked in 1970 what the war meant three decades later, refused to consider the larger significance of the conflict for Spanish society. De la Cierva maintained that the Alzamiento Nacional had been a beginning for Spain and, as Richards quotes, "never a reference point for moving backwards."

Since the 1970s, many factors colluded to impede the development of discourses on the war that could seriously challenge the official version.

After Franco's death, the process of reconciliation, officially at least, was defined in terms of forgetting and silence. Taking De la Cierva's cue, the Transition to democracy presented itself as a forward-looking process and thus thwarted efforts to understand, let alone come to terms with, the past. There was a tacit public agreement that the past had to be sacrificed for the success of the present and future. "History was not confronted, let alone conquered—the official version appeared to be accepted for the sake of peace, but this was tantamount to ignoring history."

According to Richards, the recent movement to recover Spain's memory and history, with its focus on individual experience, is a "sign of a move from the history of collectivities and structures toward individuals and human agency." This change has brought about new challenges for historians, who are now addressing a much broader Spanish public. Richards sees the media explosion of works on the war and the dictatorship (books, memoirs, TV documentaries, internet forums) as a form of "history from below" or a popularized narrative of the civil war. The problem with this development, according to his perceptive insight, is that the Spanish audience lacks the historian's vantage point and is thus also prey to similarly appealing tales from the other side that are also having great success in the Spanish market: "The unquestioned moral clarity pushed to the forefront by both sides, in the context of a rather low level of general historical consciousness in society, can be unsettling and tends, in effect, to perpetuate the long story of competing versions from Left and Right."

Richards argues that memory and history—separate though overlapping forms of recovering the past—are crucial to one another. Memory needs history in order to have a context, and memory is a crucial part of social history. Memory in Spain needs history not because the former is biased, or more subjective, but because Spanish discourse is still so heavily polarized. Thinking in historical terms can allow "a multiplicity of memories to be heard rather than to be resubmerged within such catch-all concepts as 'the memory of the defeated' or 'Republican memory.'"

These issues bring to mind one of the countless recent confrontations in the Spanish media on the question of recovering the past. In his column in the right-wing mouthpiece Libertad Digital, the best-selling and self-styled "revisionist historian" Pío Moa responded to a comment by the Hispanist Ian Gibson on the excavation of the mass graves of Republican victims in Spain. Gibson was quoted as saying, "If I had a grandfather buried like a dog in a ditch, I would want to find him. Any Christian should be able to understand that human beings need to be able to bury their dead properly." Moa accused Gibson of sowing discord and added that "Gibson, like the majority of the Left and the Popular Front, are not Christians; what they are is anti-Christians, the ones who burned churches, monasteries, libraries, and schools simply because they were Christian institutions. Furthermore they assassinated thousands of clergy and lay people for the same 'reason.' "[1] Moa then offered the Irish author a bit of menacing wisdom, evocative of a gypsy curse or a line from a horror film: "Here is some advice, Mr. Gibson et al.: leave the dead alone, because in the end the dead will turn against you."

Moa and his followers continue to launch a stubborn and vitriolic resistance to the project that has come to be known as *la recuperación de la memoria histórica*. Though these attacks try to perpetuate Francoist dogma, and though their spirit aims to echo the intimidation tactics of the regime, they ring retrograde and hollow. As these essays show, there is no longer a repressive force capable of stopping or negating the proof—whether in the form of human remains or archival documents—of the nature and volume of the decades-long violence perpetrated against Spanish Republicans and those associated with them. As Michael Richards writes in his conclusion, there is no effective argument against the process of "unearthing memories" of the Civil War in Spain, a process that is "both necessary and inevitable."

NOTE

1. Pío Moa, "Un Consejo a Gibson," Libertad Digital, Sept. 8, 2007, http://www.libertaddigital.com/opinion/pio-moa/un-consejo-a-gibson-38772/.

The Theorists of Extermination

THE ORIGINS OF VIOLENCE IN THE SPANISH CIVIL WAR

Paul Preston

In the first third of the twentieth century, Spain's agrarian oligarchy, in an unequal partnership with the industrial and financial bourgeoisie, was menaced by a militant industrial and rural proletariat. In August 1917, the Left's feeble revolutionary threat was bloodily smothered by the army. Thereafter, until 1923, when the army intervened again, social ferment occasionally bordered on undeclared civil war. In the south, there were the rural uprisings of the "three Bolshevik years." In the north, the industrialists of Catalonia, the Basque Country, and Asturias, having tried to ride the immediate postwar recession with wage cuts and layoffs, faced violent strikes and, in Barcelona, a terrorist spiral of provocations and reprisals.

In the consequent atmosphere of uncertainty and anxiety, there was a ready middle-class audience for the notion disseminated by extreme right-wing Catholics that an alliance of Jews, Freemasons, and working-class internationals was conspiring to destroy Christian Europe, with Spain as a principal target. The idea that there was an evil Jewish conspiracy to destroy Christianity went back to the early Middle Ages in Catholic Spain. In the early nineteenth century, the Spanish extreme Right had come to believe that the Freemasons were the tool of the Jews and that their objective was to establish Jewish tyranny over the Christian world. The Carlist daily *El Siglo Futuro* had peddled such views since the last quarter of the nineteenth century, precisely at the moment that Spanish society was being destabilized by the kaleidoscopic processes of rapid economic growth, social dislocation, regionalist agitations, a bourgeois reform movement, and the emergence of trade unions and left-wing parties. Through Freemasonry, the Jews were alleged to control the economy, politics, the press, literature, and the entertainment world through which they propagated immorality and the brutalization of the masses. In 1912, the Liga Nacional Antimasónica y Antisemita had been founded by José Ignacio de Urbina with the support of twenty-two Spanish bishops. The bishop of Almería wrote that "everything is ready for the decisive battle that must be unleashed between the children of light and the children of darkness, between Catholicism and Judaism, between Christ and the Devil" (Álvarez Chillida 279; see also 201–3).

In Spain, as in other European countries, anti-Semitism reached a new intensity after 1917. It was taken as axiomatic that Socialism was a Jewish creation and that the Russian revolution had been financed by Jewish capital, an idea given a spurious credibility by the Jewish origins of prominent Bolsheviks such as Leon Trotsky, Julius Martov, and Fedor Dan. Spain's middle and upper classes were chilled and outraged by the various revolutionary upheavals experienced in Spain between 1917 and 1923. The fears of the Spanish elite were somewhat calmed in September 1923, when the army intervened again and a dictatorship was established by General Miguel Primo de Rivera. While Primo de Rivera remained in power, his ideologues worked hard to build the notion that in Spain, two bitterly hostile social, political, and indeed moral groupings were locked in a fight to the death. Specifically, in a pre-echo of the function that they would fulfill for Franco, they continually stressed the dangers faced from Jews, Freemasons, and leftists.

These ideas essentially added up to delegitimizing the entire spectrum of the Left, from middle-class liberal democrats, via regional nationalists, to anarchists and Communists. This was done by blurring distinctions between them and by denying their right to be considered Spanish. The denunciations of this "anti-Spain" were publicized through the right-wing press; the regime's single party, the Unión Patriótica; as well as through civic organizations and the education system. During the dictatorship, they served to generate satisfaction with the regime as a bulwark against the perceived Bolshevik threat. When the monarchy fell, they fed the paranoia that met the establishment of the Second

Republic. Starting from the premise that the world was divided into "national alliances and Soviet alliances," José María Pemán declared that "the time has come for Spanish society to choose between Jesús and Barrabás" and claimed that Spain was divided between an anti-Spain, made up of everything that was heterodox and foreign, and the real Spain, which was the historical Spain of religious and monarchical values (28–29, 105, 308–9).

In 1931, the year of the passing of political power to the Socialist Party and its urban middle-class allies, Republican lawyers and intellectuals sent shivers of horror through right-wing Spain. The Republican-Socialist coalition intended to use its suddenly acquired share of state power to implement a far-reaching program to create a modern Spain by destroying the reactionary influence of the Church, eradicating militarism, and improving the immediate conditions of the wretched day laborers with agrarian reform. This huge agenda inevitably raised the expectations of the urban and rural proletariats while provoking the fear and determined enmity of the Church, the armed forces, and the land-owning and industrial oligarchies. The transition from the hatreds of 1917–1923 to the widespread violence that engulfed Spain after 1936 was long and complex, but it began to speed up dramatically in the spring of 1931. Within hours of the Republic being declared, monarchist plotters had begun collecting money to create a journal that would propagate an armed rising against the Republic. Within a month, they had successfully collected substantial funds. Their efforts would see their first fruit in the military coup of August 10, 1932. And its failure would lead to a determination to ensure that the next attempt would be better financed and entirely successful.[1]

Many on the Right took the establishment of the Republic as proof that Spain was the second front in the war against world revolution. *El Siglo Futuro* announced in June 1931 that the new prime minister, Niceto Alcalá Zamora, his minister of the interior, Miguel Maura, and his minister of justice, Fernando de los Ríos Urruti, were Jews and that the Republic had been brought about as a result of a Jewish conspiracy. The Catholic press in general made frequent reference to the Jewish-Masonic-Bolshevik conspiracy. The more moderate Catholic daily, *El Debate*, referred to De los Ríos as "the rabbi" (*rabino*). The Editorial Católica, which owned a chain of newspapers including *El Debate*, would soon be publishing the deeply anti-Semitic and anti-Masonic magazines *Los Hijos del Pueblo* and *Gracia y Justicia,* which would reach a weekly circulation of 200,000 copies (see Tusquets, *Orígenes* 30–44, 137–42; Luis 153–62; Blinkhorn, *Carlism* 46, 179; Álvarez Chillida 181, 334–38).

Traditionally, Spain's social hatreds saw the civil guard and the army lining up in defense of the possessing classes. Between 1931 and 1936, however, two linked factors provided pervasive and far-reaching justifications for the use of violence against the Left. The first was the Republic's attempt to break the power of the Catholic Church. The Republic's anticlerical legislation would provide an apparent justification for the violent enmity of those who already had ample motive to see it destroyed. The religious issue would in turn produce another crucial factor in nourishing right-wing violence. This was the immensely successful propagation of theories that left-wingers and liberals were neither really Spanish nor really human and that, as a threat to the nation's existence, they should be exterminated. In books that sold by the tens of thousands, and in daily newspapers and weekly magazines, the idea was hammered home that the Second Republic was foreign and sinister and must be destroyed. This notion, which found fertile ground in right-wing fear, was based on the contention that the Republic was the product of a conspiracy masterminded by Jews and carried out by Freemasons through left-wing lackeys. The idea of this powerful international conspiracy— or *contubernio* (filthy cohabitation), one of Franco's favorite words— justified any means necessary for what was presented as national survival. The intellectuals and priests who developed such ideas were able to connect with both the hatred of the *latifundistas* (big landowners) toward *jornaleros* and the urban bourgeoisie's fear of the unemployed.

The Catholic intellectual—and later cardinal—Ángel Herrera Oria edited the newspaper *El Debate* and created the political party Acción Popular, which later developed into the largest mass party of the Right, the Confederación Epañola de Derechas Autónomas. Its manifesto drew on many of these ideas of the racial and national worthlessness of the left-wing masses and presented the Republic as the revolution carried out when "the contagious madness of the most inflamed extremists sparked a fire in the inflammable material of the heartless, the perverted, the rebellious, the insane" (Monge i Bernal 114–15). The implication was that the supporters of the Republic were subhuman and, like pestilent vermin, should be eliminated. "The sewers opened their sluice gates and the dregs of society inundated the streets and squares, convulsing and shuddering like epileptics" (Monge i Bernal, 122).

In the eyes of the Right, the Republic was the regime of the rabble, which was remotely controlled by a sinister conspiracy of Jews, Freemasons, and Communists. This idea was heard with ever greater insistence as right-wing hostility to the Republic was mobilized fully in the wake of the parliamentary debate over the proposed Republican constitution. The text separated church and state, introduced civil marriage and divorce. It curtailed state support for the clergy and ended the religious monopoly of education, not only secularizing the official education system but also preventing religious orders from engaging in education. This constituted, on paper at least, a tremendous financial blow. The Church was essentially paying the price of its identification with the rich and the powerful, and with the monarchy and the dictatorship. Catholics regarded the Church as the guardian of Spain's essence and identity. They were outraged that the Republic was effectively decreeing that it become a voluntary association supported by those willing to pay. The proposed reforms were denounced by the Catholic press as a godless, tyrannical, and atheistic attempt to destroy the family (*El Debate*, August 18, 19, 1931; see Lannon 181).

The legalization of divorce and the dissolution of religious orders contained in Article 26 of the constitution raised the ire of the Catholic establishment, which attributed the measures to evil Masonic machinations. As part of the campaign against the constitution, a group of Basque Traditionalists created the Asociación de Familiares y Amigos de Religiosos (Association of Relatives and Friends of Religious Personnel). The AFAR attracted considerable support in Salamanca and Valladolid. It published an anti-Republican bulletin, *Defensa*, and many anti-Republican pamphlets. It also produced the violently anti-Masonic and anti-Semitic weekly magazine *Los Hijos del Pueblo*. It was edited by Francisco de Luis, who would eventually run *El Debate* in succession to Ángel Herrera. De Luis was a fervent believer in the theory that the Spanish Republic was the plaything of an international Jewish-Masonic-Bolshevik conspiracy (see Tusquets, *Orígenes* 30–44, 137–42; Blinkhorn 46, 179; and Álvarez Chillida 181, 334–48). Another leading contributor to *Los Hijos del Pueblo* was the integrist Jesuit Father Enrique Herrera Oria, brother of Ángel. The paper's wide circulation was in large part a reflection of the popularity of its virulent satiric cartoons attacking the Second Republic as the tool of the Jewish-Bolshevik-Masonic conspiracy. The magazine regularly accused prominent Republican politicians of being Freemasons and thus at the service of the international conspiracy against Spain and Catholicism. It thereby contributed to the popularization on the Right of the notion that this foreign *contubernio* had to be destroyed (see Vincent 183–84; Heras 713–50).

Right-wing rhetoric about the Republic reflected the feelings and the fears of those most threatened by its reforms. In the case of the *latifundistas,* fury at the sheer effrontery of their laborers in voting for Republican candidates reflected a sense of social, cultural, and indeed near racist superiority over those who worked their estates. That the Republican-Socialist coalition should openly declare its intention to improve the daily lot of the wretched day laborers implied a sweeping challenge to the very structures of rural power. The hostility of the landowners toward the new regime was first manifested in a determination to block Republican reforms by any means, including unrestrained violence. Fed by the rhetoric of the Jewish-Masonic-Bolshevik conspiracy, the hatred of the *latifundistas* for their *braceros* would find its most complete expression in the early months of the Civil War. Then, they would collaborate enthusiastically with Franco's African columns as they spread a wave of terror through southwestern Spain. The landowners' loathing of the landless laborers and their families paralleled that of the colonial officers for the subject tribesmen that it was their job to repress.

The attitudes of the landowners were paralleled by those of army officers infuriated by the Republic's attempts to streamline the bloated officer corps. This was especially true of the brutal Africanistas, who had benefited most from an inflated number of battlefield promotions. One of the most prominent of them was General José Sanjurjo. As director general of the civil guard, he was at the nodal point of praetorian discontent with the new regime. It was hardly surprising that he should be one of the first Spanish soldiers to make the link between the subject tribes of Morocco and the Spanish Left. He made a seminal speech on the subject in the wake of the atrocity at the remote and impoverished village of Castilblanco in Badajoz on December 31, 1931, when villagers had murdered four civil guards in an outburst of collective rage

at long-term systematic oppression.[2] Speaking to journalists, Sanjurjo
blamed the entire incident on the Socialist deputy for Badajoz, Margarita Nelken, "a foreigner and a Jew, to all intents and purposes a spy." He
went on to compare the workers of Castilblanco to the Moorish tribesmen he had fought in Morocco. He commented, "In a corner of the province of Badajoz, Rif tribesmen have a headquarters," and declared—
mendaciously—that after the disaster in July 1921 at Annual in northern
Morocco (where the Spanish colonial army had been roundly defeated
by the rebel tribesmen commanded by Abd'el Krim), "even in Monte
Arruit, when the Melilla command collapsed, the corpses of Christians
were not mutilated with such savagery."[3]

Taking their cue from Sanjurjo, right-wing journalists compared the
rural population of Extremadura with Rif tribesmen, Berbers, savages,
bloodthirsty savages, and Marxist hordes. In general terms, the way in
which the right-wing press reported the events of Castilblanco reflected
the belligerently racist attitudes of the rural elite. The inhabitants of
Castilblanco, and by extension the rural proletariat as a whole, were presented as an inferior race, horrible examples of racial degeneration. It
was common for them to be described as subhuman and abnormal.
Colorfully exaggerated descriptions pandered to the ancestral fears of
the respectable classes: the allegation that a woman had danced on the
corpses recalled the witches' Sabbath (F. Valdés; "La tragedia" Jan. 7;
"La tragedia" Jan. 9; "Aún quedan"). The often explicit conclusion was
that the rural proletariat should be treated using the same methods that
had defeated the colonial enemy in Morocco ("La guerra"; "Los sucesos").
The civil guard was a central part of the complex of violence building
up within Spain and was invariably to be found on the side of the landowners. During the week following the incident at Castilblanco, the civil
guard would wreak a bloody revenge that saw eighteen people die.

The attitudes of the Africanista officers and civil guards were merely
the most violent dimension of right-wing hostility toward the Second
Republic and the Left in general. Their behavior received encouragement and justification in the murderous hostility to the Left voiced by a
number of journals and newspapers. In particular, several influential individuals spewed out a rhetoric urging the extermination of the Left as a
patriotic duty. They insinuated the racial inferiority of their left-wing and

liberal enemies through the clichés of the theory of the Jewish-Masonic-Bolshevik conspiracy.

The idea of an evil Jewish conspiracy to destroy the Christian world was given a modern spin in Spain by the dissemination from 1932 onwards of the most influential work of the genre, *The Protocols of the Elders of Zion*. Drawing on French, German, and Russian myths, this fantastical concoction purveyed the idea that a secret Jewish government, the Elders of Zion, was plotting the destruction of Christianity and Jewish world domination.[4] The first Spanish translation of *The Protocols* had been published in Leipzig in 1930. Another translation was made available in Barcelona in 1932 by a Jesuit publishing house, which then serialized it in one of its magazines. Awareness and approval of *The Protocols* was helped greatly by the enormous popularity of the work of the Catalan priest Juan Tusquets Terrats (1901–1998), author of the best seller *Orígenes de la revolución española*. Tusquets was born into a wealthy banking family in Barcelona on March 31, 1901. His father was a descendant of Jewish bankers, a committed Catalanist, and a friend of Francesc Cambó. Ordained in 1926, Tusquets was renowned for his piety and culture. As a teacher in the seminary of the Catalan capital, he was commissioned to write a book on Madame Blavatsky's theosophism. In the wake of its success, he developed an obsessive interest in secret societies.[5]

Despite, or perhaps because of, his own remote Jewish origins, by the time that the Second Republic was established, his investigations into secret societies had developed into a fierce anti-Semitism and an even fiercer hatred of Freemasonry. In a further rejection of his family background, he turned violently against Catalanism and gained great notoriety by falsely accusing the Catalan leader Francesc Macià of being a Freemason.[6] Working with another priest, Joaquim Guiu Bonastre, he built up a network of what he regarded as his "informants," that is to say, Freemasons who told him about lodge meetings. His ostentatious piety notwithstanding, Tusquets was not above spying or even burglary. One of the principal lodges in Barcelona was in the Carrer d'Avinyó next to a pharmacy. Since Tusquets's aunt lived behind the pharmacy, he and Father Guiu were able spy on the Freemasons from her flat. On one occasion, they broke into another lodge and set a fire in order, in the ensuing confusion, to steal a series of documents. These "researches" were the basis for the regular, and vehemently anti-Masonic, articles that he contributed to the Carlist newspaper *El Correo Catalán*. He later alleged that, in retaliation for his articles, the Freemasons twice tried to assassinate him. From his account, it seems that they did not try very hard. On the first occasion, he cheated death simply by getting into a taxi. On the second, he claimed, curiously, that he was saved by an escort provided by the anarcho-syndicalist newspaper *Solidaridad Obrera*. This benevolence on the part of the anarchists was all the more curious given their passionate anticlericalism.[7]

Tusquets used *The Protocols* as "documentary" evidence of his essential thesis that the Jews were bent on the destruction of Christian civilization. Their instruments would be Freemasons and Socialists, who would do their dirty work by means of revolution, economic catastrophes, unholy and pornographic propaganda, and unlimited liberalism. In Spain, he denounced the Second Republic as the child of Freemasonry and accused the president, the piously Catholic Niceto Alcalá Zamora, of being both a Jew and a Freemason.[8] The message was clear: Spain and the Catholic Church could be saved only by the destruction of Jews, Freemasons, and Socialists—in other words, of the entire Left of the political spectrum. Tusquets's book *Orígenes de la revolución española* not only sold massively but also provoked a noisy national polemic that served to give even greater currency to his ideas. His central notion that the Republic was a dictatorship in the hands of "Judaic freemasonry" (*la masonería judaica*) was further disseminated through his many articles in *El Correo Catalán* and a highly successful series of fourteen books (*Las Sectas*) attacking Freemasonry, Communism, and Judaism. The second volume of *Las Sectas* included a complete translation of the *Protocols* and a section entitled "*Su aplicación a España*," which asserted that the Jewish assault on Spain could be seen not only in the Republic's persecution of religion but equally in the movement for agrarian reform and the redistribution of the great estates (see Tusquets, *Los poderes* 35–46; Tusquets, *Orígenes* 35–36, 41, 99, 126–27; Canal 1201–7).

So great was the impact of his writings that in late 1933 Tusquets was invited by the International Anti-Masonic Association to visit the recently established concentration camp at Dachau. He commented that "they did it to show what we had to do in Spain." Dachau was established as a camp for various groups that the Nazis wished to quarantine: political prisoners (Freemasons, Communists, Socialists, and liberal, Catholic, and monarchist opponents of the regime) and those they defined as asocials or deviants (homosexuals, gypsies, vagrants). More than fifty years later, Tusquets would claim to have been shocked by what he saw. Nevertheless, at the time, the flow and the intensity of his anti-Semitic and anti-Masonic publications did not abate (see Subirà 25; Bonada).

Tusquets would come to have enormous influence within the Spanish Right in general and specifically over General Franco, who enthusiastically devoured his anti-Masonic and anti-Semitic diatribes. He produced a bulletin on Freemasonry that was distributed to senior military figures, and Franco's brother-in-law and right-hand man from 1937 to 1941, Ramón Serrano Suñer, would later praise his contribution to "the creation of the atmosphere which led to the National uprising" (see Riera 126–27; Serrano Suñer 7). But Tusquets did more than just develop the ideas that justified violence. He was on the periphery of the military plot against the Republic through his links with Catalan Carlists (see Raguer Suñer, *Salvador* 40; Nadal 265). From the early 1930s, with the help of Joaquim Guiu, Tusquets had assiduously compiled lists of Jews and Freemasons in part on the basis of information provided by a network of what he called "my faithful and intrepid informers." Their search for the enemy extended to societies of nudists, vegetarians, spiritualists, and enthusiasts of Esperanto. When Tusquets finally became a collaborator of Franco in Burgos during the Civil War, his files on alleged Freemasons would provide an important part of the organizational infrastructure of the repression.[9]

Endorsement of the *Protocols* also came from the founder of the ultra-right-wing monarchist theoretical journal *Acción Española*, the marqués de Quintanar (who was also Conde de Santibáñez del Río). At an event held in his honor by fellow members of Acción Española at the Ritz, he alleged that the disaster of the fall of the monarchy came about because "the great worldwide Jewish-Masonic conspiracy injected the autocratic Monarchies with the virus of democracy to defeat them, after turning them into liberal Monarchies" (quoted from the account of the event published in the May 1932 issue of *Acción Española*). Julián Cortés Cavanillas, also of the Acción Española group, cited the *Protocols* as proof that, through prominent Freemasons, the Jews controlled the anarchist, Socialist, and Communist hordes. Freemasonry was the "evil offspring of Israel" (*maléfico engendro de Israel*). That the new Republican-Socialist government contained Freemasons, Socialists, and men thought to be Jewish was proof positive to many on the extreme Right that the alliance of Marx and Rothschild had established a bridgehead in Spain (see Cortés Cavanillas 25, 33–34). Reviewing a French edition of *The Protocols of the Elders of Zion,* with total seriousness as if it were factual truth, the marqués de Eliseda managed to imply with a veiled reference to Margarita Nelken that Castilblanco was the result of Jewish involvement: "The Jews are true parasites who exploit those who are incapable of producing" (*Los judíos son verdaderos parásitos que explotan los que son incapaces de producir*).

General Franco was a subscriber to *Acción Española* and a firm believer in the Jewish-Masonic-Bolshevik *contubernio*. Significantly, among the many other senior military figures sharing such views was General Emilio Mola, the future "director" of the military coup of 1936. The tall, bespectacled Mola had the air of a monkish scholar, but his background was that of a no-nonsense veteran of the African wars. Born in Cuba in 1887, the son of a captain of the civil guard, and a harsh disciplinarian, he rose to military prominence serving with the Regulares Indígenas during the African wars. He had been promoted to brigadier general for his role in the defense of the fortification of Dar Akobba in September 1924. His memoirs of the campaign, wallowing in descriptions of crushed skulls and billowing intestines, suggest that he had been utterly brutalized by his African experiences (see Mola Vidal 197–98, 200). On February 13, 1930, in the wake of the fall of the dictatorship of General Primo de Rivera, he was appointed as director general of security. Mola was a surprising choice, given his lack of experience in police work. Until the collapse of the monarchy fourteen months later, he devoted himself to crushing labor and student subversion as he had crushed tribal rebellion in Morocco (see Blanco Escolá 61–64). To this end, he created a crack antiriot squad, physically well-trained and well-armed. He became immensely well-informed about the doings of the Republican opposition by dint of setting up a complex espionage system under the title Sección de Investigación Comunista. Its success derived from the use of undercover policemen who infiltrated left-wing groups and then acted as agents-provocateurs. This same network was still substantially in place in 1936, when Mola used it to help his conspiratorial activities in the preparation of the military uprising (see Blanco Escolá 79–81, 187–88).

Mola overestimated the menace of the minuscule Spanish Communist Party, which he viewed as the instrument of sinister Jewish Masonic machinations. This reflected the credence that he gave to the fevered reports of his agents, in particular those of Santiago Martín Báguenas and of the sleazy and obsessive Julián Mauricio Carlavilla del Barrio. Mola's views on Jews, Communists, and Freemasons were also colored by information received from the organization of the White Russian forces in exile, the Russkii Obshche-Voinskii Soiuz (Russian All-Military Union) based in Paris. Thereafter, even after he had lost his position, he remained in close contact with the ROVS leader Lieutenant General Evgenii Karlovitch Miller. Although less virulently anti-Semitic than some of his colleagues, General Miller was, like Alfred Rosenberg, a Baltic German. Their view of Communism reflected the fact that, because of the Bolshevik revolution, they had lost their families, property, livelihood, and homeland. They seized upon the idea that the Jews had masterminded the revolution and must be prevented from doing the same in Western Europe.[10]

When the Republic was established, convinced that he would be arrested for his work in defense of the establishment, Mola went into hiding for a week before giving himself up. Influenced by the paranoid reports received from Carlavilla and the dossiers supplied by the ROVS, he came to believe that the triumph of the democratic regime had been engineered by Jews and Freemasons. In late 1931, in the first volume of his memoirs of that time, he wrote that he had been awakened to the threat of Freemasonry by a pamphlet received from France: "When, in fulfilling my duties, I investigated the intervention of the Masonic lodges in the political life of Spain, I became aware of the enormous strength at their disposal, not through the lodges themselves but because of the powerful elements that manipulated them from abroad—the Jews" (347).[11]

By the time Mola came to write the second volume of his memoirs, *Tempestad, calma, intriga y crisis*, he was more explicit in his attacks on Freemasons and Jews. He himself implied that this was because, in addition to the reports of General Miller, he had read the work of Father Tusquets and *The Protocols of the Elders of Zion*: "Upheavals within Spain have always been influenced from abroad, more often than not because of the international politics of the day. However, in the present case, this has not influenced our affairs although that does not mean that there was no external cause. There was — the hatred of a race, transmitted through a cleverly manipulated organization. I refer specifically to the Jews and to Freemasonry" (Mola 574–75).

In December 1933, Mola wrote the conclusion to his bitterly polemical book *El pasado, Azaña y el porvenir,* in which he gave voice to the widespread military animosity toward the Republic in general and toward Manuel Azaña in particular. Mortified by what he perceived as the unpatriotic antimilitarism of the Left, he attributed this mainly to the fact that "decadent nations are the favorite victims of parasitical international organizations, used in their turn by the Great Powers, taking advantage of the situation in weak nations, which is where such organizations have the most success, just as unhealthy organisms are the most fertile breeding ground of the virulent spread of pathological germs. It is significant that all such organizations are manipulated if not actually directed by the Jews." He saw the Russian revolution as the work of the Jews and used this to justify Nazism: "The German Chancellor—a fanatical nationalist—is convinced that his people cannot rise again as long as the Jews and the parasitical organizations that they control or influence remain embedded in the nation. That is why he persecutes them without quarter" (Mola 1166–67).

Since 1927, both Mola and Franco had been avid readers of a journal of anti-Comintern affairs from Geneva, the *Bulletin de L'Entente Internationale contre la Troisième Internationale.* As director general of security, Mola passed information from his network of agents to the Entente in Geneva, where it was incorporated into the bulletin sent to Franco and others. The Entente had been founded by the Swiss rightist Théodore Aubert and one of the many White Russian émigrés in Switzerland, Georges Lodygensky. Its publications were given a vehemently anti-Semitic and anti-Bolshevik turn by Lodygensky and praised the achievements of Fascism and military dictatorships as bulwarks against Communism. An ultra-right-wing organization that had close contacts with Antikomintern, an organization run from Josef Goebbels's Ministry of

Information, the Entente skillfully targeted and linked up influential people convinced of the need to prepare for the struggle against Communism, and supplied subscribers with reports that purported to expose plans for forthcoming Communist offensives. The material from the Entente devoured by Franco, Mola, and other officers portrayed the Second Republic as a Trojan horse for Communists and Freemasons determined to unleash the godless hordes of Moscow against Spain and all its great traditions.[12]

The ultra-right-wing press in general regarded the *Protocols* as a serious sociological study. Since there were few Jews in Spain, there was hardly a "Jewish problem." In any case, Spanish "anti-Semitism without Jews" was not about real Jews so much as an abstract construction of a perceived international threat. Some of these beliefs were central to integrist Catholicism and harked back to Judas Iscariot's betrayal of Jesus Christ and to medieval myths and fears about Jewish ritual killings of children. However, they were given a burning contemporary relevance by fears of revolution. The notion that all those belonging to left-wing parties were the stooges of the Jews was supported by references to the numbers of left-wingers and Jews fleeing from Nazism who were given refuge by the Second Republic. As far as the Carlist press was concerned, the incoming Jews were the advance guard of world revolution and intended to poison Spanish society with pornography and prostitution (see Cohn 326; Vincent 217–19; Álvarez Chillida 302–3, 324–25; and Blinkhorn 179).

Conservative intellectuals argued that through such subversive devices the Jews had enslaved the Spanish working class. One alleged consequence of this subjugation was that the Spanish workers themselves came to possess "oriental" qualities. The Spanish radical Right began to see the working class as imbued with Jewish and Muslim treachery and barbarism. The most extreme proponent of this view was the late nineteenth-century Carlist ideologue Juan Vázquez de Mella. He argued that Jewish capital had financed the liberal revolutions and was now behind the Communist revolution and in union with the yellow peril and the Muslims in order to destroy Christian civilization and impose Jewish tyranny on the world. Even King Alfonso XIII believed that the rebellion of tribesmen in the Rif was "the beginning of a general uprising of the entire Muslim world instigated by Moscow and international

Jewry" (Álvarez Chillida 286–88). The Carlists took these ideas to extremes. Their ideologues argued that "the four horsemen of the Apocalypse, Judaism, Communism, Freemasonry and Death," already controlled Britain, France, and Australia and soon Spain would fall under their dominion. Another asserted "the inferiority—racial—of almost all the oriental peoples of today . . . Chinese, Indians, Arabs, Abyssinians and Soviets" (Blinkhorn 180–81).

The Carlists and General Mola were among a number of influential figures who through their writings and speeches fomented an atmosphere of social and racial hatred. Another was Onésimo Redondo, a fervent believer in the *Protocols*. Redondo had studied in Germany and was also close to the Jesuits. He was much influenced by Enrique Herrera Oria, brother of the founder of the Asociación Nacional Católica de Propagandistas and editor of *El Debate*, Ángel Herrera. Father Herrera had encouraged Onésimo in the belief that Communism, Freemasonry, and Judaism were conspiring to destroy religion and the Fatherland and recommended that he read the virulent anti-Jewish and anti-Masonic tract by Léon de Poncins, *Las fuerzas secretas de la Revolución. F∴ M∴— Judaismo*. It was thus that Onésimo became aware of the *Protocols*, of which he translated and published an abbreviated text in *Libertad* of Valladolid (see below), a version later reissued with notes explicitly linking its generalized accusations to the specific circumstances of the Second Republic (see Herrera Oria 12–13; *Protocolos*; and Redondo, "El autor" 201–4, 223–26).

Although hardly a national figure, his case merits attention because his hometown, Valladolid, where his ideas were disseminated, experienced greater political violence than other Castilian provincial capitals. As a young lawyer, Onésimo Redondo had been linked to Acción Nacional (later Acción Popular), the Catholic political group founded on April 26 by Ángel Herrera and principally supported by Castilian farmers. In early May 1931, he had created its provincial organization in Valladolid and headed its propaganda campaign for the parliamentary elections of June 28, 1931. On June 13, Onésimo brought out in Valladolid the first number of the fortnightly, and later weekly, anti-Republican newspaper *Libertad*. After the elections of June 28, 1931, had given a huge majority to the Republican-Socialist coalition, Onésimo rejected democracy, severed his ties with Acción Nacional, and in August 1931 founded a Fascist party, the Juntas Castellanas de Actuación Hispánica (the Castilian Hispanic Action Groups) (see Monge i Bernal 126–32; Jiménez Campo 129–30; Montero 98, 385; and Mínguez Goyanes 24–30).

On August 10, 1931, *Libertad* published a fiery proclamation by Onésimo Redondo. It revealed his passionate commitment to the traditional rural values of Old Castile, to social justice, and to violence. He wrote, "The historic moment, my young countrymen, obliges us to take up arms. May we know how to use them in defense of what is ours and not at the service of politicians. May the voice of racial good sense emerge from Castile and impose itself upon the great chaos of the moment: let it use its unifying force to establish justice and order in the new Spain." This advocacy of violence set the tone for the organization. For him "nationalism is a movement of struggle, it must include warlike, violent activities in the service of Spain against the traitors within" (see Martínez de Bedoya 19–22; Redondo, *Estado* 42–43). Certainly, Redondo and the JHAC injected a tone of brutal confrontation to a city previously notable for the tranquility of its labor relations (see Prado Moura 135). He called for "a few hundred young warriors in each province, disciplined idealists, to smash to smithereens this dirty phantom of the red menace." His recruits quickly armed themselves for street fights with the predominantly Socialist working class of Valladolid. He wrote of the need to "cultivate the spirit of violence, of military conflict" (Martínez de Bedoya 30). Over the next few years, Onésimo Redondo's enthusiasm for violence grew progressively more strident.

Redondo's anti-Semitism was derived more from fifteenth-century Castilian nationalism than from Nazi models, although he did translate Hitler's *Mein Kampf*. Anti-Semitism would recur frequently in his writings. In late 1931, for instance, he wrote of the coeducational schools introduced by the Second Republic as an example of "Jewish action against free nations: a crime against the health of the people for which the traitors responsible must pay with their heads" (Álvarez Puga 25). In November 1931, the Juntas Castellanas de Actuación Hispánica fused with Ramiro Ledesma Ramos's La Conquista del Estado to form the Juntas de Ofensiva Nacional Sindicalista. The new group adopted the red and black colors of the anarcho-syndicalist CNT and took as its badge the emblem of the Catholic kings, the yoke and arrows. It was antidemocratic and imperialist, demanding Gibraltar, Morocco, and Algeria for

Spain and aspiring to "the extermination, the dissolution of the Marxist parties" (see Ledesma Ramos 255–57; Sánchez Diana 125–26; Mínguez Goyanes 40; and Martínez de Bedoya 34–35).

In Valladolid, Onésimo was devoting ever more time to the conversion of his forty or fifty followers into warriors of what he now called *"milicias regulares anticomunistas."* Soon they would be involved in bloody clashes with left-wing students and workers in the university and in the streets of Valladolid. At considerable expense, pistols were being bought, and much time was spent on training. Already by the spring of 1932, Onésimo Redondo was writing about the inevitable civil war to come—"The war is getting nearer; the situation of violence is inevitable. There is no point in refusing to accept it. It is stupid to flee from making war when they are going to make war on us. The important thing is to make preparations so as to win, and, to win, it will be necessary to take the initiative and go onto the attack" (see Martínez de Bedoya 40–47, 51–57; Mínguez Goyanes 42, 170–73). An article he wrote in the Fascist monthly *JONS* in May 1933 reflected the growing virulence of his thought:

> Marxism, with its Mohammedan utopias, with the truth of its dictatorial iron and with the pitiless lust of its sadistic magnates, suddenly renews the eclipse of Culture and freedoms like a modern Saracen invasion. . . . This certain danger, of the Africanization in the name of Progress, is clearly visible in Spain. We can state categorically that our Marxists are the most African of all Europe. . . . Historically, we are a friction zone between that which is civilized and that which is African, between the Aryan and the Semitic. . . . For this reason, the generations that built the fatherland, those that freed us from being an eternal extension of the dark continent, raised their swords against attacks from the south and they never sheathed them. . . . Isn't there a risk of a new domination of the African element? . . . For this reason, the great Isabel ordered Spaniards always to watch Africa permanently, to defeat Africa and never be invaded by her again. Was the Peninsula entirely de-Africanized? Is there not a danger of a new kind of domination of the African factor, here where so many roots of the Moorish spirit remained in the character of a race in the vanguard of Europe? We ask this important question dispassionately and we will answer it

right away by underlining the evident danger of the new Africaniza-
tion: "Marxism." Throughout the world, there exists the Jewish or Sem-
ite conspiracy against Western civilization, but in Spain it can more
subtly and rapidly connect the Semitic element, the African element.
It can be seen flowering in all its primitive freshness in our southern
provinces, where Moorish blood lives on in the subsoil of the race.
There bloody and materialist propagandas feed off the southern fire
of "holy war." The follower of Spanish Marxism, especially the Andalu-
sian, soon takes the incendiary torch, breaks into manor houses and
farms, impelled by the bandit subconscious, encouraged by the Sem-
ites of Madrid; he wants bread without earning it, he wants to laze
around and be rich, to take his pleasures and to take his revenge . . .
and the definitive victory of Marxism will be the re-Africanization of
Spain, the victory of the combined Semitic elements—Jews and Moors,
aristocrats and plebeians who have survived ethnically and spiritually
in the Peninsula and in Europe. (Redondo, "El regreso" 154–59)

By asserting that Marxism was a Jewish invention that implied the
"re-Africanization" of Spain, Redondo was identifying Spain's archetypal "others," the Jew and the Moor, with the Right's new enemy: the
Left. Moreover, this sophistry was not limited to the Communists who
professed loyalty to the Soviet Union but extended to the Left in its
broadest sense. His conclusion, shared by many on the Right, was that a
new *Reconquista* was needed to prevent Spain from falling into the hands
of modern foes. Anti-Semitism could be found across most of the Spanish Right. In some cases, it was a vague sentiment born of traditional
Catholic attitudes toward the fate of Jesus Christ, but in others, such as
Onésimo Redondo, Emilio Mola, or Mauricio Carlavilla, it was a murderous justification of violence against the Left.

The identification of the working class with foreign enemies was
based on a convoluted logic whereby Bolshevism was a Jewish invention and the Jews were indistinguishable from Muslims, and thus leftists were bent on subjecting Spain to domination by African elements.
It had the advantage that it presented hostility to the Spanish working
class as a legitimate act of Spanish patriotism. According to another
member of the *Acción Española* group, the one-time liberal turned ultra-
rightist Ramiro de Maeztu, the Spanish nation had been forged in its

struggles against the Jews (arrogant usurers) and the Moors (savages without civilization) (see Maeztu 197–99; Villacañas Berlanga 350–78). In one of his articles, the monarchist leader José Calvo Sotelo neatly encapsulated the argument by referring to the Socialist leader Francisco Largo Caballero as "a Moroccan Lenin" (2: 225).[13]

Even José María Gil Robles, the leader of the mass Catholic party CEDA (Confederación Española de Derechas Autónomas)—albeit less explicitly than Sanjurjo after Castilblanco or Onésimo Redondo— managed to convey the view that violence against the Left was legitimate because the Left was racially inferior. His frequent use of the historically charged word "reconquest" linked enmity toward the Left in the 1930s to the central epic of Spanish nationalism, the reconquest of Spain from the Moors. During his campaign for the elections of November 1933, on October 15 in the Monumental Cinema of Madrid he declared: "We must reconquer Spain. . . . We must give Spain a true unity, a new spirit, a totalitarian polity. . . . For me there is only one tactic today: to form an anti-Marxist front and the wider the better. It is necessary now to defeat socialism inexorably." Gil Robles continued with language indistinguishable from that of the extreme conspiratorial Right: "We must found a new state, purge the fatherland of judaising freemasons. . . . We must proceed to a new state and this imposes duties and sacrifices. What does it matter if we have to shed blood! . . . We need full power and that is what we demand. . . . To realize this ideal we are not going to waste time with archaic forms. Democracy is not an end but a means to the conquest of the new state. When the time comes, either parliament submits or we will eliminate it." In the autumn of 1933, CEDA election posters declared that Spain must be saved from "Marxists, Freemasons, Separatists and Jews." The belligerent implication was unmistakable. The entire forces of the Left—anarchists, Socialists, Communists, liberal Republicans, regional nationalists—were anti-Spanish (see *CEDA* Oct. 31, 1933). Violence against them was therefore legitimate—and indeed an urgent patriotic necessity.

As violence became more common in both the towns and the countryside, Onésimo Redondo's rhetoric became more radical. He apparently found no comfort in the fact that the Right had regained power in the elections of November 1933. In January 1934, he wrote, "Get your weapons ready. Learn to love the metallic clunk of the pistol. Caress your dagger. Never be parted from your vengeful cudgel!" and "Wherever there is an anti-Marxist group with cudgel, fist and pistol or with higher instruments, there is a JONS" (Martínez de Bedoya 71–72, 82–84).

A major leap in the Spanish Right's association of the working-class Left with Jews and Muslims took place in October 1934. In protest against the entry of the CEDA into the government on October 6, the miners of Asturias mounted a revolutionary uprising. Initially, the proposal to put Franco formally in command of troops in Asturias was rejected by President Niceto Alcalá Zamora because of his reputation as a ferocious Africanista. Nevertheless, the minister of war, the radical Diego Hidalgo, gave Franco informal control of operations, naming him his "adviser," using him as an unofficial chief of the general staff, by dint of marginalizing his own staff and slavishly signing the orders drawn up by Franco (see Alcalá Zamora 296; Vidarte, *El bienio* 290–91). What delighted the Spanish Right was that Franco responded to the rebellious miners in Asturias as if he were dealing with the recalcitrant tribes of Morocco.

Franco's approach to the events of Asturias was colored by his conviction, fed by the material he received from the Entente Anticomuniste of Geneva, that the workers' uprising had been "carefully prepared by the agents of Moscow" and that the Socialists, "with the experience and technical instructions from the Communists, thought they were going to be able to install a dictatorship" (see Suárez Fernández 1: 268–69; Hills 207; and Franco Bahamonde 11–12). That belief justified for Franco and for many on the extreme Right the brutal use of troops against Spanish civilians as if they were a foreign enemy.

With a small command unit set up in the telegraph room of the Ministry of War, Franco controlled the movement of the troops, ships, and trains to be used in the operation of crushing the revolution (see Franco Salgado-Araujo 114–16; Arrarás, *Franco* 189). Uninhibited by the humanitarian considerations that made some of the more liberal senior officers hesitate to use the full weight of the armed forces against civilians, Franco regarded the problem before him with the same icy ruthlessness that had underpinned his successes in the colonial wars. Unmoved by the fact that the central symbol of rightist values was the reconquest of Spain from the Moors, Franco did not hesitate to ship Moorish mercenaries to fight in Asturias, the only part of Spain where the crescent had never flown. He saw no contradiction about using the Moors because he regarded left-wing workers with the same racialist contempt he possessed toward the tribesmen of the Rif. Visiting Oviedo after the rebellion had been crushed, he spoke to a journalist in terms that echoed the sentiments of Onésimo Redondo: "The war in Morocco, with the Regulares and the Legion, had a certain romantic air, an air of reconquest. But this war is a frontier war and its fronts are socialism, communism and whatever attacks civilization in order to replace it with barbarism" (Martin 129–30). Ironically, although the colonial units sent to the north by Franco consisted of the Spanish Foreign Legion and the Moroccan mercenaries of the Regulares Indígenas, in an outburst of xenophobia and anti-Semitism, the right-wing press portrayed the Asturian rebels as creatures of a foreign, Jewish-Bolshevik conspiracy (see Balfour 252–54).

Inevitably, within Spain and abroad, there were widespread criticisms of the use of Moorish troops in Asturias, the cradle of the Christian reconquest of Spain. José María Cid y Ruiz-Zorrilla, parliamentary deputy for the right-wing Agrarian Party for Zamora and minister of public works, responded with a declaration of double-edged racism: "For those who committed so many acts of savagery, Moors were the least they deserved, because they deserved Moors and a lot else" (*El Noroeste* [Gijón] Oct. 26, 1934, qtd. in Díaz Nosty 359). A book published by the Oviedo branch of Ángel Herrera's Asociación Católica Nacional de Propagandistas suggested in similar terms that the crimes committed against clerics by the revolutionaries deserved to be punished by exposure to Moorish atrocities. In his preface, José María Rodríguez Villamil, a chief state prosecutor and a member of the Oviedo branch of the ACNP, wrote, "May it never again be necessary that those against whom Pelayo rose up twelve centuries ago [the Moors] should have to return again to Spain and to Asturias to free us from the Moorishness [the working-class left] emerging at the foot of the mountains of Covadonga" (qtd. in Asociación Católica 14). In the majority of Catholic writing about the events of October 1934, there is an assumption that the revolution was an attack on Catholicism and that the suffering of religious personnel is analogous to the suffering of Christ at the hands of the Jews (see Sánchez, *Fact and Fiction* 151–52).

Along similar lines to the writings of Onésimo Redondo were those of Francisco de Luis, who had succeeded Ángel Herrera as editor of *El Debate*. De Luis was an energetic evangelist of the Jewish-Masonic-Bolshevik conspiracy theory. His magnum opus on the subject was published in 1935 with an ecclesiastical imprimatur. In it, enthusiastically quoting Tusquets, the *Protocols,* the Carlist press, and General Mola, he argued that the purpose of Freemasonry was to corrupt Christian civilization with "oriental" values. His premise was that "the Jews, progenitors of freemasonry, having no fatherland of their own, want all men to be without one." Thereby freed of patriotic and moral impulses, the masses could be recruited for the assault on Christian values. In his interpretation, Catholics faced a struggle to the death because "in every Jew there is a freemason: cunning, deceitful secrecy, hatred of Christ and his civilization, a thirst for extermination. Freemasons and Jews are the begetters and controllers of socialism and Bolshevism" (see Tusquets, *Orígenes* 30–44, 137–42; Luis 6, 99–102, 158–60, 191; Blinkhorn 46, 179; Álvarez Chillida 181, 334–38).

There was little difference between the pronouncements of Francisco de Luis and Onésimo Redondo and those of a friend and one-time subordinate of General Mola, the policeman Julián Mauricio Carlavilla del Barrio (see Conolly). He specialized in undercover work, infiltrating left-wing groups where he would then act as an agent provocateur. By his own account, he did so on his own initiative, without informing his superior officers. His efforts included involvement in, and later frustration of, assassination attempts against both Alfonso XIII and General Miguel Primo de Rivera during the opening of the great exhibition in Seville in May 1929.[14] When General Mola became director general of security in early 1930, Carlavilla informed him of his clandestine activities, which he described as "my role as catalyst within the highest circle of the revolutionaries" (Carlavilla, *Anti-España* 18).[15] At the orders of General Mola, Carlavilla set about writing a detailed report on the supposed activities of the Communist Party in Spain. A wild mixture of fantasy and paranoia, the report was sent by Mola to the Entente Internationale contre la Troisième Internationale at the end of 1930. It would not be unreasonable to surmise that its contents were fed into the bulletins that the Entente sent to its subscribers, including General Franco.

The report formed the basis of Carlavilla's first book *El comunismo en España* (see Carlavilla, *Anti-España* 439).

Between 1932 and 1936, Carlavilla wrote a series of best sellers, using the pseudonym Mauricio Karl.[16] The first, *El comunismo en España*, described the various Socialist, anarchist, and Communist elements of the working-class movement as the enemy of Spain that would have to be defeated. The second and third, *El enemigo* and *Asesinos de España*, argued that the enemies masterminding the left-wing assassinations in Spain were the Jews who controlled Freemasonry ("their first army"), the Socialist and Communist Internationals and world capitalism. Spanish greatness in the sixteenth and seventeenth centuries was the fruit of the expulsion of the Jews, and further greatness would require a repetition. Since there were hardly any Jews in Spain, that meant their lackeys, the Freemasons and the Left. The only hope of stopping the destruction of Christian civilization and the establishment of the empire of Israel lay in joining German Nazism and Italian Fascism in defeating the "sectarians of Masonic Jewry." He asserted that General Primo de Rivera, who died of natural causes, had been poisoned by a Jewish Freemason and that the Catalan financier Francesc Cambó was both Jewish and a Freemason.

One hundred thousand copies of the third of his books, *Asesinos de España*, were distributed free to army officers. It ended with a provocative challenge to them: describing Jews, left-wingers, and Freemasons as vultures hovering over the corpse of Spain, he wrote, "The Enemy howls with laughter while the nations that serve Zion play diplomatic dice for the cadaver's land. Thus might be the real end of Spain who was once feared by a hundred nations. And so it will be because her sons no longer know how to die. Nor how to kill."[17] Carlavilla was expelled from the police in 1935 as a result of what he would later describe as persecution for his anti-Masonic revelations. In May 1936, he fled to Portugal after taking part in the attempted assassination of Manuel Azaña during the celebrations of the anniversary of the Republic's founding. He was also believed to have been involved in attempts on the lives of Francisco Largo Caballero and Luis Jiménez Asúa. It was claimed that the assassination plans were masterminded by Mola's crony, Comisario Santiago Martín Báguenas. In Lisbon, Carlavilla linked up with the exiled General Sanjurjo and remained on the fringes of the military plot.

Shortly after the outbreak of war, he went to Burgos, where he was welcomed onto the staff of General Mola. Carlavilla worked for a time there in Mola's headquarters alongside Father Juan Tusquets (see *Claridad* May 4, 1936; Arrarás, *Historia* 2:503; Cabanellas 1:274; Ortiz Villalba 158–59; Barbero 39).

It was hardly surprising that the great majority of Africanista officers were in favor of a violent action against the Second Republic or that Emilio Mola should be given the job of coordinating the plot. The Africanistas had already found themselves in key positions from May 1935 as a result of the appointment of José María Gil Robles as minister of war. Franco was made chief of the general staff. Many loyal Republican officers were purged from their posts, because of their allegedly undesirable ideology. Others, of known hostility to the Republic, were reinstated and promoted. Gil Robles and Franco quietly established Mola in a small and secluded office in the Ministry of War to prepare detailed plans for the use of the colonial army in mainland Spain in the event of further left-wing unrest (see Martínez de Campos 32; Iribarren 44; Cierva, *Francisco* 2:162). Emilio Mola was then made general in command of Melilla and shortly afterwards head of military forces in the entire Moroccan protectorate. Medals and promotions were distributed to those who had excelled in the repression of the October uprising. Franco ensured that reliable reactionaries were posted to the command of many units in Morocco and the Spanish mainland. He commented later that these commanders would be key pawns in the uprising (see Gil Robles and Beltran de Heredia 234–43; López Fernández 40–43; Franco Bahamonde 15). The election results threatened but did not totally derail the Africanistas' schemes. The change of government saw the most suspect officers posted far from Madrid: Franco to the Canary Islands, Godet to the Balearic Islands, and Mola to Navarre. But they were quick to plan their response in terms of a conspiracy to overthrow the Republic.

Having already ensured the collaboration of the most influential officers in Morocco and sure of the police network, Mola held the most important strands of the future rebellion in his hands. It had been assumed by the Republican authorities that, in Navarre, Mola, whose books had given him something of a reputation as a military intellectual, would have few dealings with the deeply reactionary local Carlists. In fact, within three days of his arrival on March 14, he met the man who was to become his chief liaison with the local Carlists, B. Félix Maíz, a thirty-six-year-old Pamplona businessman. They hit it off immediately, discovering a shared enthusiasm for *The Protocols of the Elders of Zion.* Even before the elections of February, Maíz had been plotting with local military figures who took a chance on introducing him to Mola. To Maíz's delight, Mola, who was still receiving paranoiac anti-Communist reports from the ROVS in Paris, told him that "we confront an enemy that is not Spanish." Maíz, whose memoirs include lengthy extracts from the *Protocols,* believed that a war to the death was imminent between Christians and the stooges of the Jews, "the great beast—tightly-knit hordes emerging from the swamp of evil." The terms in which Maíz viewed the political situation were even more extreme than those of Mola: "there are moving around Spain complete teams of creatures injected with rabies who are seeking Christian flesh in which to sink their teeth" (see Maíz, *Alzamiento* 23–28, 52–56, 61–63, 67, 162).

With such a view of the enemy, it was but a short step to Mola's first secret instructions to his fellow conspirators, issued in April. He wrote, "It has to be born in mind that the action has to be violent in the extreme so as to subdue as soon as possible the enemy which is strong and well-organized. It goes without saying that all leaders of political parties, societies and trade unions not part of the movement will be imprisoned and exemplary punishment carried out on them in order to choke off any rebellion or strikes" (see Bertrán Güell 123). It was an instruction that would have pleased the theorists of extermination.

NOTES

1. See Vegas Latapie, *Pensamiento* 88–92; Vegas Latapie, *Escritos* 9–12; Vegas Latapie, "Maeztu." See also González Cuevas 144–45, 165–68, 171–75.
2. See Albar. For a description of Castilblanco, see Vidarte, *Cortes* 308–9, and Jiménez Asúa et al. For a biography of Margarita Nelken, see Preston, *Doves of War* 297–407.
3. See *ABC,* January 1, 2, 3, 5, 1932; *El Debate,* January 2, 1932; *La Nación,* January 4, 5, 1932; *El Sol,* January 3, 1932; *La Voz Extremeña,* January 5, 1932. See also Espinosa Maestre, *La columna de la muerte* 498.
4. On the genesis of the *Protocols,* see Cohn.
5. On Tusquets, see Mora 231–42; Ferrer Benimelli 191–97; and Canal.

6. On Tusquets' accusations against Macià, see Tusquets, *Orígenes* 150–51; Tusquets, *Masones* 104–5; Raguer, *Unió* 279–80; and Vidal i Barraquer 2: 386, 638, 3: 935.

7. On the burglary and the alleged assassination attempts, see Mora 234–35.

8. See Tusquets, *Orígenes* 101 and 137. Alcalá Zamora wrote in protest to Archbishop Vidal i Barraquer on March 26, 1932; see Vidal i Barraquer 2: 644–46.

9. See Tusquets, *Orígenes* 51–57, 95–96, 122–26, 170, 177, 207–15. On the compilation of lists, see also Archivo Histórico Nacional.

10. See Vigón 57–58, 63–64; Maíz, *Mola* 25–28, 43–44, 84–86, 238. Evgenii Miller had been a dictatorial governor-general and commander of the White military and political forces in the northern region of Russia (Archangel) during the Russian civil war, then representative of General Wrangel in Paris and chief of staff of the Russian army from 1922 to 1924. Thereafter, he was one of the key figures among the military émigrés between the wars. In 1930 he became president of their organization, the Russkii Obshche-Voinskii Soiuz after the abduction (in Paris) of its former head, General Kutepov, by the OGPU. Miller himself was then abducted by the NKVD, again in Paris, in 1937. He was shot in Moscow in May 1939 on the orders of Beria. On Miller, see Goldin and Long; Robinson 174–77, 208–10, 224–25, 236; Gorboff 135–36, 151–58; and Stepan 18–23. I am grateful to Dr. Jonathan Smele for his help on the White Russian connection.

11. From *Lo que yo supe: Memorias de mi paso por la Dirección General de Seguridad* in Mola, written in 1931 but not published until January 1933.

12. See Southworth, *Conspiracy* 128–91; Crozier 92; Hills 157; and Suárez Fernández 1: 197–98. On the many White Russian émigrés in Switzerland, see Cohn 243–55.

13. He claimed to be quoting an unnamed acquaintance.

14. He gave his own account of this in *Asesinos de España*; Carlavilla, *Asesinos* 60–68, 76–81.

15. See Carlavilla, *Anti-España* 434–38. In his memoirs, General Mola describes the work of an unnamed undercover policeman; see Mola 758. Carlavilla claims that this was a reference to his activities; see Carlavilla, *Anti-España* 436.

16. See Karl. On Carlavilla, see Southworth, *Conspiracy* 207, 212–13; Álvarez Chillida 320–21. According to Ricardo de la Cierva, his name was Mauricio Carlavilla de la Vega; see Cierva, *Bibliografía*. However, one of his later books, published when he no longer felt the need for a pseudonym, is signed "Mauricio Carlavilla del Barrio 'Mauricio Karl' "; see Carlavilla, *Sodomitas*. Mola acknowledged knowing Carlavilla well; see Mola 624.

17. On Hitler and Mussolini, see Karl 21–24, 85–89, 196–207. On the army, see Karl 320–21. On Cambó, see Karl 74–75; Rodríguez Puértolas 1: 309; García Venero 309.

The Spanish Church and the Civil War

BETWEEN PERSECUTION AND REPRESSION

Hilari Raguer Suñer

The great historian Pierre Vilar concluded his closing remarks at a colloquium about the French and Spanish civil wars by saying: "We should remember that history consists of what some would like to forget and of what others cannot forget. The historian's job is to figure out the reasons why some try not to remember and why others cannot help but remember" (Vilar). In 1986, the Spanish bishops declared, "Students of history and society have to help us to know the entire truth about the events leading up to the Civil War, its causes, its battles, and its consequences. This knowledge about historical reality is indispensable if we are going to truly recover from it" (Spanish Episcopate).

THE VATICAN AND THE SPANISH CIVIL WAR

When one speaks of the Church's involvement in the Spanish Civil War, it is crucial to distinguish between the position taken by the Vatican and that of the majority of the Spanish episcopacy.[1] Although they were on opposing sides, both the Francoists and the pro-Republicans have agreed both during and after the war that the Holy See had given its complete support to the military uprising. But in reality the Vatican was much more human and a lot less bellicose than the Spanish bishops proved to be. This is eloquently shown in the evolution of diplomatic relations between the two Spains and the Holy See between 1936 and 1939. The 1936 Pontifical Yearbook documents full diplomatic relations. The 1937 Yearbook (written six months after the beginning of the uprising) shows the double representation—active and passive—of the two Spains: of the "Government of Burgos" and of the "Government of Valencia." In the case of the Valencia government, Ambassador Zulueta is recognized by Rome, and the Nunciature of Madrid continues to be open. The Burgos government, on the other hand, is listed as having only a "provisional and unofficial Chargé" as the pope's envoy to Franco, Cardinal Gomá, and an "unofficial Chargé" of Franco as emissary to the Holy See, the Maquise of Magaz. In the 1938 Yearbook, one finds increased public relations with the "National Government of Salamanca" at the level of "Chargé d'Affaires"—Monsignor Antoniutti in Salamanca and Churruca in Rome. But in the section dedicated to the "Government of Valencia," one can still see that relations have not been formally broken; the chart represents both active and passive relations of the Holy See, and ellipses have now replaced names and positions. It is only in the 1939 Pontifical Yearbook (drawn up at the end of 1938) that Franco's government effectively takes the place of the Republic. There is no mention of the Republic, and in the "National Government" section of the Yearbook (the only recognized one) the only representatives listed—as in 1936, when the Republic was the only recognized government—are the papal envoy Cicognani and Ambassador Yanguas.

   Why did the Holy See take so long to recognize the rebels, who claimed that they were defending the Church and fighting against those who were persecuting priests? There are two reasons. First, Hitler and Mussolini's support of Franco worried the Church; they feared that the new regime would be of Nazis and Fascists, with whom the Vatican already had increasing problems despite its respective concordats with the Germans and the Italians. Second, the Vatican had received accounts of repression in the Francoist zone. In particular, the Vatican had heard of the execution of Basque priests and of the expulsion of Bishop Múgica. During the second year of the war, the Vatican, which had a tense relationship with Franco, maintained indirect and covert contact with the Republic. If in the end the Church dropped this contact and officially recognized Franco, it was only because Franco won the war.

A terrible religious persecution was immediately unleashed in all the cities where the military insurrection failed. During the first months of the war, until public order was gradually reestablished, it was enough that someone was identified as a priest, a religious or secular member of a religious organization, or one who conserved religious relics for him to be assassinated without due process or any legal formality or the possibility of any defense. I will not expand here on the religious persecution since it is only too well known.[2] Suffice it to say that the extremists handed the useful title of "crusade" to the rebels on a plate.

THE COLLECTIVE EPISTLE

The position of the Spanish episcopate was made clear above all in its collective epistle on July 1, 1937 (exactly a year into the war). The letter was composed by Cardinal Gomá at Franco's request. Many who have not actually read the epistle have wrongly praised it or criticized it for declaring the Civil War a "crusade." In fact, the epistle expressly says that the war was not a crusade: "While war is one of humanity's most tremendous scourges, it is at times a heroic solution, the only way to put matters in the hands of justice and to return them to the reign of peace. Because of this, the Church, as the daughter of Peace, blesses the emblems of the war, has founded military orders and has organized crusades against the enemies of the faith. This is not our affair. The Church did not want this war and it did not ask for it."[3]

Gomá and Pla i Deniel, as well as other bishops, had noted the religious nature of the war in their previous epistles, speeches, and sermons and had called it a "crusade." But Gomá decided not to use that particular expression in the collective letter, most likely because he believed that it would displease the Vatican. Instead, he described it as an "armed plebiscite."

There is a section of the Spanish bishops' epistle that has been often overlooked. While the epistle as a whole was composed in support of the uprising, one particular passage of the document explains that the Church could not unconditionally support a regime that was still *in fieri*:

With respect to the future, we cannot predict what the last day of the struggle will bring. We emphasize, however, that the war has not been undertaken to establish an autocratic State over a humiliated nation, but that it wants to bring back the national spirit with the Christian liberty and vigor of earlier centuries. We trust in the prudence of the men of government, who will not want to accept foreign models for the configuration of the future Spanish State. Rather, the future leaders will wish to take into account the demands of the domestic life of the nation and the trajectory marked by the past.

What is most relevant here is the absolution that the collective epistle imparts on the Francoist repression:

All wars have their excesses; the national movement will no doubt also have them; no one can calmly defend himself against the wild attacks of a cold-blooded enemy. Condemning in the name of justice and of Christian charity all the excesses that might be committed—whether by mistake or by subordinates who have methodically exaggerated foreign information—we pronounce that the judgment we rectify does not correspond to the truth. We assert that there is an insurmountable distance between the principles of justice of its administration and the form that it is applied in either side.

The bishop of Vitoria, Mateo Múgica, did not share the same opinion. In a June 1937 letter to the Holy See, he explains the motives for his refusing to sign the collective epistle: "According to the Spanish episcopacy, justice is well administered in Franco's Spain. But this is not true. I have an extensive list of fervent Christians and exemplary bishops who have been assassinated with impunity, without any legal recourse, and without any juridical formality" (qtd. in Iturralde 348–49).

BISHOP MARCELINO OLAECHEA

We should note a rare and almost singular exception within the Spanish episcopacy: the bishop of Pamplona, Marcelino Olaechea Loizaga, who spoke out against the unjust treatment of prisoners. The bishop demonstrated exceptional bravery when, on November 15, 1936, he publicly condemned the frequent practice of certain executions that, in truth, would be better called lynchings. Often, when a young man died at the front and was brought back to his village to be buried, the funeral service would end with a swift execution—without any judicial procedure whatsoever—of some local Communists. Olaechea publicly denounced the practice at a ceremony of the Acción Católica. At the service, which consisted of awarding insignias to some townswomen, he said, "*Mercy! Mercy!* By the sacred law of clemency! *No more blood, no more blood!* . . . No more blood than that which the Lord wishes to spill when He intercedes in the battleground to save our glorious and agonizing Fatherland; this is the blood of redemption that mixes, by God's compassion, with that of Jesus Christ, to seal with the seal of life the new Spain, vigorous and kicking, which is at this moment undergoing the pains of birth" (Ballester 28). Later, the prelate puts all of his oratorical talent at the service of a humanitarian message. He describes in crude fashion the custom that was being repeated at funeral after funeral:

> Catholics! When the dead body of a hero arrives in the village for defending God and Country at the battle front, and they carry him on shoulders—the young ones, his brave comrades who, crying, mourn him—and a flock of crying relatives and friends arrive to accompany the coffin, you feel the raging blood in your veins and the raging passion in your chest and you cry out for vengeance. . . . There should be, you say, a man or a woman who should pay by dying for the tears you have shed (your heart is overflowing with grief). But then a woman that arrives at the coffin, extends over him her arms and speaks with all her strength: "No, no; get back! The blood of my son is the blood of redemption; I hear his voice, just like Christ's voice on the Cross; come closer and listen what it says: Mercy! Nobody touch my son! Nobody should suffer! Everyone should be forgiven! If you could see the blessed soul of my martyr, which God has accepted into His kingdom, he wouldn't recognize you. If you gave yourself over to vengeance and I could curse you, I and my son would curse you."

Everyone in the village knew each other, and everyone knew who voted for whom. We can imagine the anguish of those who were known

[handwritten note in top margin: Connection to Movie baptising all kids]

leftists when the funeral of a Nationalist volunteer was announced. In such an environment, the mere fact that, before the conflict exploded, an individual did not regularly attend Mass could later prove fatal. Olaechea, besides movingly condemning those lynchings, also confronted the issue of the nonbelievers who go to Mass out of fear, and declares the only acceptable attitude for those who consider themselves true Christians:

> I see an enormous mountain of heroism rising in each village, and an unfathomable soul of anguish and fear. Of fears. Souls that come to the Church in a mad rush, fearfully looking for baptism and matrimony, confession and the Eucharist. They come with sincerity; but they didn't come before. They have broken the chains that imprisoned them and they run to the burning consolation of the [Christian] faith. But in their soul they bring with them a fear that pierces them like a dagger. And we have to win them over with the sincerity of our faith, with the sincerity of our affection, with social justice and charity.

Olaechea made sure that this document was published not only in the ecclesiastical bulletin but also in the local press. He ordered that the parish priests read it at the solemn Mass of the first holiday and that they comment on it "in the spirit in which it was dictated."

"Saving human lives and obtaining pardons," writes Vicente Ballester, "was Don Marcelino's principal undertaking during the years of the fighting. Those of us who lived with him knew that the doors of the Episcopal Palace should always be open—whether it be day or night, late night or daybreak—in order to answer the telephone calls, to receive the families of those who were condemned to death. As far as I know, through his efforts he was able to obtain twenty-eight pardons for death penalties" (28–29).

THE ACCUSATIONS OF FATHER HUIDOBRO

In 1936, Father Fernando Huidobro Polanco, S.J., studied philosophy in Germany and was a favorite student of Heidegger.[4] He wholeheartedly felt the spirit of the crusade, and he tried to join the rebel army as a chaplain in Navarra, but they already had too many priests there. He went to Talavera de la Reina and joined as a chaplain of the legion in the Castejón column, in which he marched as far as the gates of Madrid. In that march he witnessed the slaughters of the "Column of Death" (Espinosa). As he had been such a proponent of the rebels' cause, his protests against the soldiers' actions acquired an incontrovertible value. He wrote two documents, one for the military authorities and another for the legal military authorities, each with the title *On the Application of the Death Penalty in Actual Circumstances: Norms of Conscience*. In these he proposed to "shape the consciences of the Commanders and Officials of the Army, who, given the circumstances, enjoy extraordinary powers of justice. Though they are obliged to exercise these powers, we hope to help avert any excesses that might stain the honor of our armed forces." The document is an irrefutable witness of what was happening: the military was carrying out exactly the kind of actions of which the priest was expressing disapproval.

In the first document, intended for the military authorities, he writes, "All mass condemnation, regardless of guilt or innocence in all these prisoners, is murder, not justice. . . . The killing of those who throw away their arms or those who surrender is always a criminal act. . . . The excesses that those subordinates have been able to carry out are in clear contradiction with the decisions of the High Command, which has declared several times that we should love the punishment of the leaders, and reserve for the seduced masses a later judgment, where there will be a place for pardons."

In the second document, intended for the legal military authorities, he writes,

The assassination of women, priests and other harmless persons; the perpetrators of these revolting crimes demonstrate a subhuman grade of perversion of nature, and at times reveal a revolting sadism. Those who have committed crimes that the [Penal] Code sanctions with grave penalties could deserve the death penalty. And if they aren't mentally unsound or idiots, one can presume that they deserve this punishment. The same can be said of those who have guided or led a movement based on an ideology such as Communism, which carries within itself the seeds of horror. I refer to those who have excited the masses by way of newspapers, pamphlets, or books. . . . On the other hand, we have to act with extreme caution when dealing with the misled masses. . . . One shouldn't necessarily deserve the death penalty for the mere fact of being affiliated with the CNT or the UGT; not even for taking arms in order to defend mistaken ideals, but ones that they sincerely considered the best for society.

Father Huidobro sent his rules to many military authorities and numerous military chaplains. It is known that they were read by Castejón and even Varela. Father Huidobro wrote to Varela on November 14, at a moment when the general was swiftly pressing forward toward Madrid. In the letter, the priest addresses the general as the future conqueror of Spain and begs him not to let his glorious name be tarnished by some of his subordinates who have bragged of the many assassinations that they would soon commit. On December 3, Varela responded to Huidobro from Juncos, congratulating him for his opinions and also assuring him that they were of the same mind. Writing on the top margin, Father Huidobro dared to send his rules to Franco himself through his assistant, Lieutenant Carlos Díaz Varela. Huidobro added an article denouncing concrete cases of excesses that had been committed. Díaz Varela surmised that the General was too busy to attend to such minor details, so he sent Huidobro's documents to General Yagüe, who commanded the Fourth Legion Unit, which Huidobro served as chaplain. Huidobro, however, insisted that Franco should see his rules, and Díaz Varela replied that he had sent the manuscripts to the General, who upon reading them was "infuriated" and "regretted not being warned by these acts." On November 25, Díaz Varela wrote to Father Huidobro from Salamanca: "I was able to inform the person you wished about your formal complaints. He found them well-grounded and he denounced—as they deserve to be—the excesses that you have denounced. . . . Those extra limitations brought about by some mad people are deplorable, and they only serve to discredit the cause and offend God."

Father Huidobro's error stemmed from the conviction that the killings he had witnessed were executed by some "crazy people," against the instructions of the good and Christian generals, when in fact the men were disciplined legionaries who were mercilessly carrying out the premeditated instructions of the "director" of the national movement,

General Mola, and were approved of by Franco, Varela, Yagüe, Castejón, and all the commanders of the columns.

Despite the established story that Father Huidobro died at the front in Madrid, killed by a Russian shell, several persons have convincingly claimed (though I have still not been able to obtain a document that proves it) that the bullet that ended his life came from someone in the legion who felt threatened by Huidobro's reports.

The question of who killed Huidobro is an important one in the eyes of the Church. In fact, the uncertainty has halted his progress to sainthood. When his beatification was begun, it was generally accepted that he had died from a Russian shell. But when this story was cast into doubt by claims that he was killed by someone from the same legion, the process was brought to an end. If he was killed by the Russians, Huidobro is a saint. If, on the other hand, he was killed by the "Nationalists" because he was denouncing the indiscriminate killings, he could never be canonized (as in the case of Bishop Oscar Romero).

THE BOMBING OF CIVILIAN VILLAGES

Resentful of the persecution of its clergy, the Spanish episcopate took no pity upon the victims of the terrible bombings by the German and Italian air forces, who tried out new weapons and methods that would eventually be used in the Second World War (see Langdon-Davies; Barrio).

The Basque priest Alberto Onaindia, who was in Guernica the day of the famous bombing immortalized by Picasso, wrote a moving letter to Cardinal Gomá in which he described what he had just seen. In the letter, he pleads to his superior for a humanitarian intervention:

> Sr. Cardinal, interpreting the sentiment of the most Christian people in the world, in the name of my brethren, and in the name of the religion that we represent, I implore you to use your authority so that the war is carried out through legal channels, if this war is going to be called legal. As a rule, we don't deal with murderers. Forgive me, Sr. Cardinal, but I wish that your highness called things by their name.

I cannot begin to describe the atrocities: the persecution and killing of children and women, the burning alive of hundreds of persons, the spreading of grief with rubble and ashes.

Will the people responsible for all this ruin burn Bilbao as well? The person in charge of Radio Sevilla has promised to destroy the city.

Gomá's heartless response was the following: "I deeply regret what happened in Vizcaya. . . . But I permit myself to answer your anguished letter with a simple advice: Bilbao must surrender; right now there is no other solution" (357).

A year later, there was no Picasso to denounce the bombings of Barcelona in March 1938, although they were a lot more devastating than those in Guernica. The Holy See, in a letter published in the *Roman Observer*, publicly condemned them as unnecessary slaughters that lacked any military justification (see Villarroya i Font; Raguer Suñer, "La Santa"). But the Spanish Church kept silent. Those bombings were meant precisely to terrorize the population. Mussolini recognized this in a telegram in which he orders his men to *"terrorizzare le retrovie"* (terrorize the vanquished left behind). Furthermore, the bombings were tactical exercises; the war was being prepared. Two years after the bombings of Barcelona, London would experience them in an even worse degree. On June 18, 1940, Churchill, in one of his most dramatic speeches, said to the House of Commons, "I do not underrate the severity of the ordeal which lies before us, but I believe our countrymen will show themselves capable of standing up to it like the brave men of Barcelona."[5]

PRISON CHAPLAINS

The testimonies of the hard-heartedness of the chaplains in prisons and concentration camps are countless. The chaplains would insult the prisoners and tell them that they were not worthy of the benevolence that the Caudillo showed them. When the Christian politician Carrasco i Formiguera was arrested along with his wife and six of his eight children, he was taken to the provincial jail of Burgos, while his wife, their month-old baby, and the wet nurse were sent to the women's jail of the same city. The rest of the children were sent to San Sebastián; the older girls were put in a women's jail, and the three younger children, Raimon (thirteen years old), Josep (eleven), and Neus (nine), were sent to an orphanage that had been converted into a jail. The nuns who ran the penitentiary-orphanage were cruel to the children. The young girl spent her days washing enormous heaps of the nuns' clothes. The first Sunday the three children waited for communion as they always did when they went to Mass with their parents, but the nuns did not allow them to receive the Eucharist because they were Communists and because they had to confess first. They duly confessed, and the priest made them pray as penitence an "Our Father" for the conversion of their father.

There was no concern for the lives of the convicted, but the chaplains were anxious that the sacraments be observed. According to Calleja, the prison chaplain of Yagüe said that he regretted the death sentences he had to pass, but he always made sure that the victims could confess before their execution (see Calleja 179–80).

In the previously cited Episcopal letter of July 1, 1937, the Spanish bishops stated that they were consoled in having been able to say that "in their deaths, which were sanctioned by law, the great majority of our Communists have been reconciled with the God of their parents. In Mallorca only 2% of the unrepentant have died; in the South no more than 20% died without confession; and in the North the number of impenitent does not reach perhaps even 10%. This proves the deception to which our village has fallen victim" (Gomá, "Carta"). Bishop Miralles of Mallorca felt very satisfied in being able to say, "Only 10% of our dear sons have refused the holy sacraments before they were executed by our virtuous officers" (qtd. in Thomas 186; see also Bernanos 74).

 The pastoral care of the prisoners on death row is one of the darkest examples of the Spanish Church's attitude regarding the repression during the war and its immediate aftermath. On previous occasions I have cited a book that was published in 1942 by the chaplain of the Modelo Jail of Barcelona in which one finds the following passage:

> In this world, only the condemned man knows the fixed hour in which he will have to appear before that judge whose judgment—supreme, decisive, and final—is the only one that can interest him for the whole

of eternity. "When will I die? Oh, if only I would know!" say the inner voices of millions upon millions of consciences. Well, the only man who has the incomparable good fortune of being able to answer this question is the condemned man. "I will die at 5 o'clock this morning." Can one give a greater gift to a soul who has walked through life on a path that has not been that of God?

I was shocked by the cynical heartlessness of this prison chaplain until I learned that these words, as well as the entire work, were not authored by him. As Vincent Comes Iglesia has demonstrated, they were written by a prisoner who had been condemned to death: Luis Lucía Lucía (see Iglesia).

The January 1938 issue of the magazine for priests of the Company of Jesus, *Sal Terrae*, published guidelines for the administration of extreme unction, which were deemed appropriate for reprinting in the Official Bulletin of the Archbishop of Toledo on March 15. Their author was Father Eduardo Fernández Regatillo, S.J., one of the most famous of the moralist-canonists of his time. In his advice column he responded to the following question: "Can extreme unction be given, and should it be given to those convicted of the death penalty?" His response was the following: "This is an extremely timely question, because there are hundreds of convicted persons by the maximum penalty of the military tribunals; they are commonly executed in front of the firing squad; and the accused of the most numerous and severe crimes are sent to the garrotes and the gallows." In spite of the high number of executions, the question that Father Regatillo raised was not the morality behind the many executions that were being carried out. He limited his concern, rather, to whether the sacrament of extreme unction was lawful, or at least valid. After speaking with various religious authorities, the learned theologian concluded that, for his part, extreme unction was a sacrament meant for the ill at death's doorstep.[6] The convicted who were about to be executed were not necessarily ill, but they were certainly about to die. The situation was dubious, but taking into account that when dealing with the sacraments one should be generous, Father Regatillo would conclude that it was better to administer the sacraments, even though it should be done "*sub conditione.*" He ended his discourse with a detail from ceremonial rubrics: the most opportune moment for extreme unction for the accused would be "after the first shot, but before the coup de grace."

A notable exception to this attitude is that of Brother Gumersindo de Estella (see de Estella). In his moving memoir, he refers to a large number of people executed after a kangaroo court. The majority of them had not seen the assigned officer for their defense until the day of the war tribunal. Some spoke of the proofs they had of their innocence, but they were not given the opportunity to bring them forth. Many were victims of despicable private revenge plots. The prison chaplains constantly insulted the prisoners, and the priests preached condemnatory sermons to their literally captive audience. Brother Gumersindo could not save them, but he treated them with respect and compassion, which was in itself a great relief.

AITA PATXI

Aita Patxi[7] is the Maximilian Kolbe of the Basque clergy. Like that blessed Polish priest, who, in a Nazi concentration camp in 1941, offered to take the place of an imprisoned father who was to be executed in retaliation for an escape, Aita Patxi is a hero of the cloth. His civilian name was Victoriano Gondra y Muruaga, but when he entered the Congregación de la Pasión, or Padres Pasionistas, they gave him the name that in the Basque language means Father Francisco of the Passion.

During the Civil War Aita Patxi was a chaplain of a battalion of *gudaris,* the soldiers of the Nationalist Basque army. He was imprisoned at the end of the Vizcaya expedition, in June 1937. His performance as priest during the war was heroic. He was thin, timid, peaceful, and feeble and always seemed to lack energy, even though he would rise during moments of danger in order to aid the wounded or to give last rites to a dying soldier. When he carried his heavy suitcase, which contained a portable altar and everything necessary to celebrate Mass, he would still rigorously observe the procedures for the ceremony of the Eucharist: not only did he fast before Mass, but he would not even drink a drop of water. This is why everyone in the battalion—believers and nonbelievers alike—venerated him. In the Euskadi army there were

both Asturian regiments, in which the majority of the soldiers were Socialists and Communists, and regiments of the Basque National Party,
which were comprised mostly of pious practicing Catholics who had
healthy habits. Ramón de Galarza, in his *Diary of a Gudari Condemned
to Death* (*Diario de un gudari condenado a muerte*), tells of the surprise of
the chaplains of Francoist prisons when they saw how pious and honest
these "separatist-Red-commies" were.

Like many other Basques, Aita Patxi was not a man of war, but he
believed the Basques had the right to defend themselves against those
who would take away their national and democratic rights. He maintained this opinion even though Cardinal Gomá, in a pastoral letter that
the bishops of Pamplona and Vitoria had signed, told them it was *non
licit,* or not permissible. On the other hand, Aita Patxi did not simply
tolerate the fighting; when the troops were demoralized by the bombings and attempted to run away, he tried to control them by ingenuously
telling them, "Don't run away—it's a sin!" He never concealed his contempt for the military coup. Once he was captured by a *requeté* priest,
who ordered him at gunpoint to turn in his arms; Aita Patxi showed
him his breviary, which was the only weapon he was carrying. After-
ward, when he was a prisoner, he was asked during various investigations whether he had turned himself in or if he had been captured. Even
though he would have been released had he admitted that he had turned
himself in, he always replied in his terse Basque-Castilian: "Captured—
I never turned myself in." After the Euskadi defeat, Aita Patxi and the
rest of the battalion were taken to the San Pedro de Cardeña concentration camp. He kept his ragged religious habit as a treasure, and though
he was not allowed to celebrate Mass, he led his suffering fellow prisoners in many rosaries and other prayers.

On August 10, 1938, he was allowed to go to Toledo in order to see
Cardinal Gomá, who was the military's general vicar. Gomá was surely
expecting that Aita Patxi would ask him to intercede for his freedom.
But what Aita Patxi requested instead was permission to celebrate Mass,
the right to hear confessions, as well as the authorization to practice the
sacraments for the imprisoned. The cardinal verbally authorized Aita
Patxi's request, but when he asked Ramón Iglesias (the future bishop of
Seu d'Urgell) to formalize the agreement in writing, he was told that
the cardinal's word was enough. Aita Patxi understood the words that

Gomá had given him as the Word of God, and he believed Gomá's reason for leaving him in the prison: "It is God's will that you are here, in the ranks of the workers."

It happened one day that an Asturian prisoner—who, it seems, was a Communist—attempted to escape but was caught and summarily condemned to death. Even though the poor young man was not a believer, Aita Patxi wanted to be with him the night before his execution. During the night, however, while the condemned was talking about his family, Aita Patxi wondered whether he could do something a bit more practical than merely being with the prisoner until the moment of his death. Aita Patxi went to the commanding officer of the camp and asked him, as a favor, if he might take the condemned's place in front of the firing squad. According to the testimonials of the *gudari* prisoners, the commanding officer was a brusque man, but under his tough skin he had a good heart. He was astounded by Aita Patxi's proposal and told him that he would need to consult with his superiors since he did not dare execute a priest. He postponed the execution for the time being.

But whether by his own initiative or because of orders received from Burgos, the officer devised a plan to make sure that the priest was not bluffing and that he was in fact ready to take the condemned man's place. At ten o'clock in the evening he sent a squad of four soldiers dressed in helmets and armed with rifles with the bayonet attached to the sleeping barracks to escort Aita Patxi to the commander's office. Aita Patxi had only told one of his fellow companions of his formal request. He peacefully said good-bye to them with "*¡zerurarte!*" ("see you in Heaven!"). When he arrived at the commander's office, he was told that the government had accepted his petition of substitution. Aita Patxi thanked him, prayed for a few minutes, and then said, "I am ready." Aita Patxi was taken to the firing wall, and the firing squad assembled in front of him.

We have two coinciding testimonies for this dramatic moment. One of the two testimonies comes from the commanding officer himself, who recounted the incident later in the Miranda de Ebro concentration camp, to which he had been transferred. According to the two witnesses, while Aita Patxi was cheerfully praying for the life that he had been able to save, everyone else in attendance was crying. The commanding officer suddenly stopped the dramatic scene short by shouting, "Go away, Father!" He informed the priest then that the government had pardoned

[margin annotation: offered to die instead of man]

Killed him anyway

the life of the Asturian prisoner because of his intervention. Aita Patxi went to sleep a happy man that night, but the following day he was devastated when he learned that earlier that morning they had executed the man whose life he had tried to save with his own.

The same situation occurred again some time after that. The prisoners from the north had been sent to the work camps, where they had to dig trenches and mines at the war front of Madrid. There had been a formal order that if any of the prisoners crossed the line to the Republican side, some of their comrades would be executed. Despite the formal order, some of the men crossed over, and as a result five of the prisoners of the same battalion were arbitrarily chosen and sentenced to death. When the workers were selected and lined up, Aita Patxi joined the line unnoticed, without saying anything to the condemned group. The lieutenant in charge of the operation ordered the priest to move away, but Aita Patxi replied, "If you want to kill these poor men without trial, you might as well kill me too." There was general amazement, hesitation, and various discussions. In the end no one was killed.

It is thus clear that the most evangelical of all of the priests who exercised their ministry with the prisoners was not an official prison chaplain, but rather the prisoner that Cardinal Gomá did not want to free or recognize as part of the licensed clergy.

OPPOSITION TO THE NEGOTIATED PEACE

At the beginning of 1938, when the war had become bloodier than ever due to the bombings and the battle in Ebro, some Spaniards living in exile—those who did not identify with either of the warring sides and who were part of what was called "the third Spain"—undertook an international campaign for foreign intervention so that the war would come to an end (Preston, *Las tres Españas*). They belonged to the Paris Committee for Peace, which was organized by Jacques Maritain, Alfredo Mendizábal, and Joan Baptista Roca Caball. At the same time, Cardinal Vidal i Barraquer wrote from his exile to Franco, Negrín, and also the principal European leaders with the same intention. The Vatican, either out of humanitarian principles or because it did not want it said that the Church was not promoting peace, encouraged Cardinal Vidal i Barraquer in an indirect and discreet manner. The pacifists (as Vidal i Barraquer expressly stated in his letters to the secretary of state) feared that if Franco achieved a total victory without any foreign intercession, there might be massive reprisals (which is what in fact happened). Franco was infuriated by this campaign because he wanted an unequivocal victory that would guarantee him absolute power. It is precisely for this reason that he was artificially prolonging the war, which, with the help of Italy and Germany, could have—and should have—ended a lot earlier. Consequently, just as he had done a year earlier with the collective epistle, Franco obtained the public support of the bishops, who collectively generated a written campaign condemning the peace efforts. The Francoist propaganda machine collected all of the declarations of the bishops and disseminated them widely.

The pinnacle of the Episcopal campaign against peace was the intervention of Cardinal Gomá during the International Congress of the Eucharist in Budapest, which was celebrated at the end of May 1938. Admiral Miklos Horthy, who had mounted a Fascist dictatorship characterized by ferocious anti-Communism and anti-Semitism (which would lead him to eventually become an ally of Hitler during the Second World War and declare war against the Soviet Union in 1941), was in power. One easily understands the cordiality with which he greeted the Spanish mission. Cardinal Gomá stayed in the Royal Palace. But the International Congress was not merely comprised of pilgrims or devotees of the Eucharist: this was a political mission presided over by Cardinal Gomá, who was representing the Spanish government, according to Bayle, and was accompanied by Mariano Puigdollers, the director general of ecclesiastical matters, among other public figures.[8] The attendance of General Moscardó, the "hero of Alcázar," had also been scheduled, but "his military operations had not allowed the celebrated General to make the anticipated trip."[9] Beyond the Eucharist, Gomá talked about the holy war that would liberate Spain from the grip of Communism and affirmed that the only possibility for peace was contingent on Franco's complete victory.

The men who had worked for peace were called traitors to Spain and apostates of the Church, although time has proved them to have been right. While Cardinal Vidal i Barraquer conveyed a desire for the insurgents to win the war in his reports to the Holy See and stated that any peace plan should be "based on Franco's leadership," he thought that without an international intervention Franco would have a free hand for indiscriminate payback. This was what in fact happened. If that campaign for international intervention had succeeded, the postwar repression would not have been so brutal. Also, the consequent reconciliation would not have been so difficult.

THE ENDORSEMENTS

The collaboration of not a few parish priests in the repression represents a serious concern. One might have hoped that the bishops would have made sure that the priests under their purview considered the tremendous responsibility they had to their parishioners. But the opposite proved to be true. In cases in which one's employment—especially the case with teachers—one's freedom, or even one's life depended on the endorsement or a certificate of the priest, the archbishop of Santiago, referring to the "shock" felt by some people because of the certificates some generous priests had issued, ordered that "all priests should refrain from giving certificates of religious good conduct to those who were affiliated to Marxist societies or in concomitance with any such anti-Christian societies; nor should they issue certificates that are going to provoke adverse reactions from the military or civil authorities. Priests should expect the latter to request in writing or by word of mouth that they issue such certificates; then will they certify whatever needs to be certified, without any qualms, and without human consideration of any kind" (qtd. in Álvarez Bolado 240).

Some bishops appropriated for themselves these letters from the archbishop of Santiago. The archbishop of Lugo went even further: he dictated that the certificates "should always refer to a determined time period," since there were people who complied during the monarchy but not during the Republic, "or that in the last few years they haven't received the sacraments and have not contributed to the maintenance of the cult and the clergy; only for the last few months have they acted like fervent Catholics" (qtd. in Álvarez Bolado 298).

On the other hand, the bishop of Seu d'Urgell, Justino Guitart, refused to collaborate in this repression. The examining magistrate of political responsibilities of the provinces sent Guitart a large list of left-wing persons from the region and demanded that he report everything he knew of their political actions and their possessions. The Reverend Jesús Castells, who was then the archivist of the archdiocese and secretary to Father Guitart, told me in an interview that the bishop, who was a lawyer, personally looked into the case and replied that there was nothing in that file that reflected the information requested. The examining magistrate arrogantly replied that he had not asked him what he had found out in the archives, but rather that he investigate, with the help of people faithful to the regime, the activities and possessions of the Republicans in the list that he had sent him. As a result, the bishop dictated the following reply: "My position as Secretary Chancellor of the Chamber and Government of his Eminence Bishop of this Archdiocese prevents me from making official and unofficial inquiries about the political and social actions of the aforementioned persons or their material wealth" (Raguer Suñer, "El bisbe").

MAKING AN APOLOGY

Unlike the humble action of the bishops of Germany, Argentina, Chile, and other countries that have experienced similar histories to Spain's, the Spanish episcopacy has repeatedly rejected the idea of publicly issuing an apology for the role the Spanish Church played during the Civil War and in the repression of the postwar period. Thirty-two years after the end of the Civil War, when Cardinal Enrique Vicente y Tarancón chaired the Spanish Episcopal Conference, in the assembly of bishops and priests, celebrated in Madrid in September 1971, the following proposal was put to the vote: " 'If we say that we have not sinned, we make a liar out of God and His Word is no longer with us' (1 John 1:10). Hence we need humbly to recognize this and ask for forgiveness because we did not know during that time how to be true ministers of reconciliation in the heart of our community that was divided by a war between brothers."

This document obtained 137 votes in favor, 3 null and voids, 78 against, 19 *iuxta modum,* and 10 blank votes. Since the vote did not reach the two-thirds majority that was needed according to the regulations of the assembly, the members debated for possible revisions to the proposal and finally voted again, adding a word: "we did not *always* know." But perhaps because some of the original proponents of asking forgiveness changed their mind or, more probably, because others were displeased with the new, attenuated version with "always," it obtained fewer votes, though they carried a majority with 123 for, 0 null and voids, 113 against, and 10 abstentions (see *Asamblea* 161). Although it was not formally approved, that vote was a great moment of sincerity and self-criticism for the Spanish Church, a moment that has not been repeated. Years later, for example, on the occasion of the beatifications of martyrs of the Civil War, the clergy has spoken of forgiving but not of asking forgiveness.

In a letter to Cardinal Vidal i Barraquer, the Republican Catholic minister, Manuel de Irujo, recalled how he had tried to facilitate the reconciliation of the Church with the Republic by denouncing religious persecution to the government of the Republic, by saving priests and other threatened individuals, and by appealing for the reestablishment of public worship. He also attended to the imprisoned bishop of Teruel and even offered to send him to the Vatican on the condition that he stay in Rome until the end of the war. He said, quite hurt, that he had failed. But his failure, he said, was not the fault of the government but was due to the lack of cooperation from the ecclesiastical authorities. Feeling like a failure in his noble effort to be faithful both to the Republic and to the Church, he ended his letter with the following words: "Bear in mind that there have been martyrs in both zones, that the blood of the martyrs, in religion as well as in politics, is always fertile, and that the Church, perhaps for what it was, will figure as a martyr in the Republican zone while lining up in the firing squad in the Francoist zone."[10]

NOTES

1. For a detailed analysis of this issue, see Raguer Suñer, *La pólvora*, and the revised and expanded English translation, *Gunpowder and Incense*.

2. Despite its limitations, the classic study to consult is still Antonio Montero Moreno's *Historia de la persecución religiosa en España, 1936–1939*. When it appeared, I wrote an extensive review of it in *Revue d Histoire Ecclésiastique*; see Raguer Suñer, Review.

3. The Spanish Church did not participate in the conspiracy to overthrow the Republican government, but it did contribute to the retrenchment that led up to the conflict. Furthermore, some prelates had been informed of what was in the works. They desired (as did most rightists) that a military coup d'état would put an end to the Popular Front, but those who revolted were not "part of them."

4. See Peiró; Valdés; Sanz de Diego. Included in Sanz de Diego are twelve complete documents written by Huidobro about this theme along with an excellent introduction.

5. To avoid any offense to Franco at such a delicate moment of the war, this sentence was omitted from Hansard (the record of the proceedings of the House of Commons) and, indeed, seems to have been reported only by the *Daily Telegraph*, a copy of which is preserved in the library of the Abbey of Montserrat.

6. The liturgical reform in the wake of the Council of Vatican II has reestablished, in a return to the most genuine tradition, the classical conception of this sacrament as an "unction to the sick" and not—as it had become in practice—unction of moribund or agonizing persons, who, in fact, were sometimes already deceased.

7. I have based this section of the chapter on the biography of Aita Patxi written by Father José Ignacio Lopategui, a *pasionista* priest. In this work, the author has collected statements by many witnesses, believers and nonbelievers, Basques and non-Basques. I am currently preparing a new biography in which I will make explicit some things that Lopategui could not say given the political situation of the time.

8. Unless otherwise indicated, the information that follows is taken from Constantino Bayle's introduction to the compilation of the wartime writings of Cardinal Gomá, *Por Dios y por España*, which is included in the report published in *La Paix Civile*, May–June 1938.

9. The great myth about Moscardó, creation of the Francoist propagandists, was shattered by H. R. Southworth in *El mito de la Cruzada de Franco*. Following in the footsteps of Southworth, I have tried to demonstrate, based above all on the statement of General Moscardó in the General Cause about the execution in Barcelona of one of his sons, that the "hero of the Alcázar" was not a participant in the uprising. In fact, he did not know its date, and on July 19 he had had to leave Barcelona with some lieutenants, among whom was his son José. All of them had been invited to the Olympic Games in Berlin, and he did not declare a state of war in Toledo until July 21. The true artificer of the resistance in the Alcázar was the lieutenant colonel of the civil guard, Pedro Romero Basar, whose role had to be downplayed in order to forge the myth of Moscardó. As a matter of fact, Franco made the most out of this myth to pave his way to become the head of the Nationalist state. See Raguer Suñer, "L'altre."

10. "Tenga presente que en las dos zonas se han hecho mártires; que la sangre de los mártires, en religión como en política, es siempre fecunda; que la Iglesia, sea por lo que fuere, figurará como mártir en la zona republicana y formando en el piquete de ejecución en la zona franquista." The quotation is found in Irujo's unpublished letter to Vidal i Barraquer, dated July 4, 1938. In the May 26 bulletin *Euzkadi*, Irujo had published, under the pseudonym "Xavier de Iranzu," an article titled, "The Republic in the Church," in which he wrote, "Whether we Catholics wish it or not, History will remember that the Church figured in the formations of those executed by the rebels, where hundreds of thousands of persons have fallen, assassinated to the calls of "Long live Christ!", which constituted the greatest violation one could commit against a doctrine that was born out of love, understanding, charity, and tolerance. . . . We all know the Church of martyrs. We cannot imagine a Church of executioners." In his reference to persons "fallen" and "assassinated," Irujo seems to include the victims both at the front and behind the lines.

The Faces of Terror

VIOLENCE DURING THE FRANCO DICTATORSHIP

Julián Casanova

The war ended April 1, 1939.[1] With it ended not only the class struggle and political contests but also the secular Republic and revolutionary atheism: these demons were exorcised from the body politic by Franco, who claimed divine protection for his victorious army. Spain would begin a new era, which would be marked by its purity, free from the "corruption" of political pluralism, liberalism, and foreign philosophies, not to mention the "Reds," all of whom would be disarmed and captured. The new order, founded on the ruins of Republicanism, would completely eliminate all signs of the society that came before it. Secularism and the workers' movement would be eradicated through a process of terror, and a reign of order, soon to be called *franquismo*, would establish its hegemony.

In the last days of the war the complete destruction of the vanquished was deemed an absolute priority. Especially in the last provinces conquered by Franco's army, killings were rampant, and Franco's soldiers enjoyed the free hand of impunity that had been granted to them by their leader from the very first days of the war in July 1936. Later, after the formal end of the fighting, a new period of mass executions, incarcerations, and torture began. In Cataluña and the province of Valencia, the regions where many of the Republicans and leftists were able to escape to neighboring France, the executed numbered nearly four thousand and five thousand, respectively. In Albacete 1,026 men and women were executed by military orders between April 1939 and 1953. In the city of Jaén the authorities registered 1,280 executions from the end of the war to 1950. There were 935 executions (or assassinations) in eighty-two of the municipalities of the western province of Badajoz by 1945. In the Cemetery of the East, known in Spanish as Cementerio del Este, in Madrid, there were 2,663 victims registered by that same year.

The hand of vengeance was heavy in the zones occupied by Franco's troops from the beginning of the war, as well as in the territories conquered in the course of the conflict. Nearly a thousand men and women were executed in the postwar period in the western, Republican part of Aragón. In Málaga there were 710 executions, and 1,100 in Granada. But this is only the number of people who appear in the registers; many more were taken for a *paseo* in which they were summarily executed. Such unrecorded "walks" with no return, which began in Granada and Aragón in the summer of 1936 and in Málaga in February 1937, put an end to thousands of people's lives.

Upon the rout of the Republican army in the summer of 1939, hundreds of prisoners were sent to impromptu concentration camps throughout Spain. In the last months of 1939 and in 1940, officials of the regime recorded the internment of more than 270,000 prisoners, a number that lowered continually over the next two years as a result of the many executions, as well as illnesses and malnutrition caused by the poor conditions of the camps.

The complete or partial information that is available about thirty-three provinces indicates that there were more than 35,000 executions that can be accounted for in the postwar period. It is true that among the provinces appear the majority of those that remained Republican throughout almost the entire war, but reliable statistics about Vizcaya, Badajoz, Toledo, Santander, and Madrid are still needed. One should add to official numbers the hundreds of cases of violent deaths by summary execution, which reached their apogee in the summer of 1939. Also, according to official sources, 4,663 prisoners died of hunger and disease. The conclusion one reaches according to our current knowledge of the postwar period is clear: at least 50,000 men and women were executed in the decade following the war. And in addition to this number it is essential that one considers the deaths caused by the dismal conditions of the regime's many camps and prisons.[2]

THE MONOPOLY OF VIOLENCE

The primary characteristic of the terror that was implemented at the conclusion of the war is that it was organized from the top down. In the wake of the explosions of violence that rocked the recently conquered cities and the disorder in the form of *paseos* and arbitrary actions by autonomous powers (such as the squadrons of the *falangistas*) arose a more mundane—but no less terrible—form of repression overseen by military courts. Once the state legitimated a number of extraordinary measures of punishment by making them the law of the land, the councils of war imposed a new kind of terror characterized by its coldness, by the bureaucratic and droning passing of death sentences. Between 1939 and 1945, thousands of individuals were judged in Franco's courts, which carried out a travesty of justice on a daily basis. In the proceedings of these kangaroo courts, nothing was ever proven, as it was already known from the outset that the accused was a "Red," which meant, in the words of the erudite Gonzalo de Aguilera, that he or she was to be considered an "animal" (Richards, *Un tiempo* 49–50). As Francisco Moreno writes, "Everything was outlandish [*esperpéntico*] in the judicial proceedings [which consisted of] a mere rubber stamp for physical elimination. No proofs were ever put forth, nor was there an effort to give a clear account of the facts of the case. Moreover, the lawyer for the defense was a member of the tribunal, whose role was precisely to do absolutely nothing" (321).

As the Capuchin priest Gumersindo de Estella writes in his memoirs, such judicial farces played out in the absence of real defense lawyers began during the war. By way of signals and pantomime, the condemned prisoners of the Torrero jail related their travails in the tribunal to a man of the cloth, who helped them spiritually in their last days. Despite the end of the war, nothing changed: the same ritual of death was repeated, and prisoners could expect nothing but desperation when they appeared, defenseless, before Franco's cynical judges (see de Estella).

Many family members moved heaven and earth to save their loved ones, but the deceitful authorities only fed them lies and false promises. Gumersindo de Estella writes, for example, of a mother who told him on February 12, 1940, how she had been well received in Madrid and that she was confident that her son was going to be pardoned. "Poor woman!"

the priest writes in his diary: the mother did not know that Franco had already signed the death warrant for her son, Juan García Jariod, a twenty-two-year-old actuary, and that the document had been sent to Zaragoza to be carried out. He was shot the next day, February 13, along with eight other prisoners. Three days later his pardon arrived (216–17).

That mother, like many people at that time, did not know how swiftly and dispassionately the Caudillo signed death sentences. It is probably fortunate that these mothers and other family members did not know that Franco and his officials constantly made jokes at the expense of their loved ones. As illustrious victors like Ramón Serrano Suñer or Pedro Sáinz Rodríguez would tell later in the carefree manner afforded by the passing of time, Franco's officials would inform the General about who would be executed, just so he would be "in the know." That is, once the sentences were passed by the councils of war, the auditor of the headquarters, Lieutenant Colonel Lorenzo Martínez Fuset, would present Franco with the list of condemned prisoners for the *enterado* (debriefing). Often at the side of the Caudillo when he received these documents was the chaplain José María Bulart, who was known to joke at the expense of the condemned. "What?" he would comment wryly, "*Enterrado?*" (a play on words meaning "They are buried?"). Unsurprisingly, whenever the good father Bulart received petitions for clemency, he invariably threw them in the wastebasket.[3]

The first assault of the vengeful violence on which *franquismo* was founded came on February 9, 1939. The Law of Political Responsibility, which was passed that day, set up the framework to punish those who, since October 1, 1934, had "contributed to or abetted the subversion of the order to which Spain had fallen victim" and those who, since July 18, 1936, "had opposed or who might oppose the National Movement with physical acts or with damaging passivity." According to the law, "individuals, considered as both juridical subjects and as physical beings" would be punished especially if they had belonged to or joined certain groups. Among these were all those "political and social groups" that had formed part of the Popular Front, the "allies of the Front and separatist organizations," and all "who had opposed the triumph of the National Movement." If found guilty by association, the individuals, who had to take responsibility for their politics, would be deemed "beyond the Law" and would suffer the "absolute loss of their rights as citizens

of Spain and the complete loss of their property," which would be appropriated by the state.

According to Rafael Díaz-Llanos y Lecuona, after "the war was won
by arms—a hundred times victorious—and the heroic dedication of
the soldiers of Spain," this "historic" law "would consolidate the peace
by force of justice, separating (provisionally or definitively) the dangerous and noxious elements from society." As the lawyer, judge of war
crimes, and university professor adds, the law would also work to rein-
tegrate the citizens who are "worthy of that name so that they work towards the glory of the fatherland in their homes, their shops, their offices, and in the countryside" (5).[4]

Once the wheels of this despotic law of repression and confiscation
were set in motion, the damage ran deeper for the vanquished, as the
legal road was laid open for arbitrary and extrajudicial persecution. By
October 1941, 125,286 cases were brought against some 200,000 persons who would suffer the "force of justice," a misnomer for what was
really a state-sponsored program of sacking and pillaging. The law, partially modified in 1942, was repealed on April 13, 1945, but dozens of
cases in process were not closed until November 10, 1966.

In October 1941, the regional tribunal of Granada had opened more
cases than any other, with 20,174, while Zaragoza had closed more cases
than any other, with 2,854. After Granada, the most active regional tribunals and courts were those of the territories that had remained in Republican hands until the end of the war, namely Valencia, Madrid, Barcelona, and Albacete. But the law also affected thousands of persons in
territories that had been occupied by the insurgent Nationalist army
since July 1936. In Valladolid, for example, more than 5,000 cases had
been processed by October 1941. Similarly, by that same date 3,057 cases
had been opened in Pamplona and 2,866 in La Coruña. Even in the two
least-populated territories, Ceuta and Melilla, the tribunals were working at full speed, having processed 1,848 and 1,516 cases, respectively.

The severe sanctions made possible by the law were, according to article 8, of three types, each carried out by legions of the regime's officials:
"restrictions on activity," which included the prohibition against employment as professionals; "limitations on the liberty of residency," which
could include being "relegated to Spain's African territories," imprisonment, or exile; and "economic penalties," which could mean the partial

or total loss of possessions or payment of fines (Carrillo 20). Those who had been denounced by their neighbors and later condemned by the court soon found themselves sunk in complete and utter misery.[5]

As the law states, the judge should "request reports on the political and social history of the accused." These reports would "include detailed descriptions of activities both before and after July 18, 1936, from the mayor's office, the local leader of the Spanish Traditional Falange and JONS, the parish priest, and the commander of the civil guard of the town in which he or she currently lives or last lived." By listing the bodies to be consulted—the church, the army, and the regime's politicians— the law implicitly laid out the circle of omnipresent powers of the post-war period. Indeed, these bodies of the regime, which often overlapped (the mayor, for instance, was typically also the local leader of the Move-ment), used their unlimited powers to coerce and intimidate thousands of citizens of Spain who, even in the long years of peace, had little con-trol over the destiny of their possessions or their lives.

The repressive legal system erected after the war, characterized by its numerous special judicial bodies, remained essentially the same throughout the entire period of the dictatorship. When a law was re-pealed, the new laws would reiterate the repressive character of the ones they replaced. This is what happened, for example, with the Law of State Security of March 29, 1941: it was repealed six years later, only to be replaced by the law against banditry and terrorism of April 13, 1947, which upheld the death penalty for a wide range of crimes. Another ele-mental instrument of persecution, the Law of Repression of Masonry and Communism of March 1, 1940, enjoyed an even greater continuity. (This is not surprising, given how obsessed Franco and his officials were with the idea that all of Spain's ills were caused by Communists and Freemasons). The special tribunal that established the law was dis-mantled on March 8, 1964, but the majority of its anti-Communist and anti-Mason activities were taken over in 1963 by the Tribunal of Public Order, which survived Franco's death. It was finally abolished by law on January 4, 1977.[6]

The military justice system found abundant and efficient collabo-rators who helped carry out detentions, torture sessions, and assas-sinations. The right arm of the justices was, of course, the police and the *guardia civil*, who responded, in theory at least, to the Ministry of

Government but who, militarized in the wake of the war, carried out
their repressive activities throughout all the towns and cities of Spain
in unchecked fashion. When the police or the civil guard needed extra
help, they found plenty in the first years after the war from the militias
and "information and investigation" services of the Falange, which kept
an eye on the "Reds" and denounced them. The *falangistas* often "helped
out" in the jails by beating prisoners.

The beatings and torture also evolved, like the terror in general, from
a "vengeful" phase to a "legal" and "judicial" phase. For some time after
the victory of April 1, 1939, spitefulness and cruelty abounded. Hundreds of prisoners known for their leftist past or who, like the poet Miguel Hernández, were known for their ideas, were beaten and tortured.
Some of these prisoners committed suicide. Others, less fortunate, were
beaten to death, though the records never showed this. Instead, the official version was that the "law of flight" had been applied: those who
had attempted to escape had been executed by the armed forces.

The legalization of torture arrived with the *Fuero de los españoles*
(Declaration of the Spaniards), a political text that declared the rights of
citizens under *franquismo*. It was approved on July 17, 1945, the ninth
anniversary of the military uprising. According to article 18 of this document, "No Spaniard can be detained except in the form and in the cases
prescribed by the Laws. In the period of seventy-two hours, all prisoners will be either freed or turned over to the judicial Authority." But in
practice, as Marc Carrillo notes, "the idea of a limited period of detention by the government was a pure fallacy . . . that was sustained throughout the dictatorship" (27). Indeed, the prisoners would be held for days,
and sometimes weeks, during which time they were humiliated and
tortured. The Political-Social Brigade carried out the "diligences" in famous places such as the police station of Via Laietana in Barcelona or
Security Headquarters at the Puerta del Sol in Madrid, both of which
would remain forever marked in the anti-Francoist memory. There were
instances when detentions were not even registered. This was the case
in numerous of these interminable "diligences": there were no records
of the arrest, no doctors, and no legal defense whatsoever.

When the *Fuero de los españoles* was passed, thousands of prisoners
had already been condemned to the maximum penalty and executed
by firing squads. Spain itself had become a jail, although the exact num-

ber of prisoners will never be known because we do not have docu-*overcrowding*
ments from the many work camps in Spain or the militarized colonies
and camps. In Modelo Prison in Valencia, there were 15,000 prisoners
during some months of 1939 and 1940, though the prison was built in
1907 for only 528 persons. In Modelo Prison in Barcelona there were
10,000 prisoners. As no more would fit, they had to use the adjoining
correctional facility as well as other buildings, including the vaults of a
factory of Pueblo Nuevo in the city's suburbs. Given the state of affairs,
it is not at all surprising that the general director of prisons, Máximo
Cuervo Radigales, would complain in a private note to Franco a year after
the end of the war about how difficult it was to process all of the prisoners: "Because of the lack of a sufficiently experienced Judicial Body to
handle the volume of present prisoners, we have had to use many inex-
perienced lawyers that lack both professional capabilities and the requi-
site military specialization" (Vinyes, "Territoris" 53).[7]

In 1943 there were still more than 100,000 prisoners. That year
15,947 persons were paying their penalties in the 121 work camps scattered throughout Spain. Their labor consisted mainly of reconstruction
jobs, building highways, or work in the swamplands. The number of
prisoners was lowered by executions and deaths from illnesses, as well
as the necessary pardons because of the "administrative collapse," but in
1946 the prisons were still three or four times over the limit for which
they were built. According to *Le Livre Blanc sur le système pénitentiaire es-
pagnol,* a solid investigation carried out by a delegation from the Comis-
sion Internationale contre le Régime Concentrationnaire, in 1952 there
were prisoners of war in Spain who had still not been sentenced. In this
context, it might be noted that in this justice system dominated by military tribunals that offered no guarantees and demanded no proof of
guilt, the average time between detention and trial was two to three
years. Of the prisoners with the longest sentences—between twelve
and thirty years—87 percent were politicians.[8]

The harsh repression during the postwar era was not inevitable. Instead, the incarceration of so many men and women and the constant
torture, executions, and deaths from hunger and illnesses were the punishments deemed necessary by the regime for the vanquished "Reds."
Given the logic by which "Red" invariably signified "scum" that had to
be cleansed from the body politic, legal subtleties were meaningless.

As Michael Richards has observed, the negative epithet "Red" would come, after the war, to refer "not only to political affiliation with the left, as it had before, but also to a general 'filthiness,' the fact of being different, of being a pariah" (*Un tiempo* 87).

Many of those "Reds" were, in the words of the José Antonio Pérez del Pulgar, "hardened criminals that were beyond redemption in this world." They should not be allowed to return to society, but should "pay for their guilt somewhere apart from the decent people of Spain." Some, the Jesuit conceded, were "adaptable to the social life founded on patriotism," but only after hard manual labor. This and other similar assertions he writes in *La solución que España da al problema de sus presos*, a pamphlet published in 1939 that endorsed the virtues of the Central Organization of Social Redemption through Work (Patronato Central de Redención de Penas por el Trabajo), an institution created by order of Franco's Ministry of Justice on October 7, 1938.

Pérez del Pulgar, together with his supporters Martín Torrent and Máximo Cuervo, attributed the creation of that regime of redemption through hard work to a new "extremely Christian" conception of the penitentiary system advocated by the Caudillo. The penitentiary, based on the "laws of the Indies, which were inspired by [Spain's] great theologians," proscribed for itself the job of "lovingly looking over and educating prisoners in the ways of the Church." Everything about the prison system was dressed in the mantle of religion, and its creators waved the flag of Christianity continually, as when they declared that "the prisoners not only had the right to work and that their work be rewarded, but also the right to redeem their sins through their labor."

Under such lofty trappings of Christianity there existed, nevertheless, a baser reality. The overcrowded prisons emptied out little by little without the need to declare an amnesty, that forgiveness that would have allowed the winners of the war to shake hands with thousands and thousands of defeated and to recognize that the conduct of many "Reds" did not merit criminalization. The system set up to carry out prisoners' convictions turned out to be also an excellent source of cheap labor to many businesses and even the state. In Asturias, for example, they built new prisons around the mercury and coal mines so as to exploit prisoners more effectively. Similarly, in the mercury mines of Almadén and the coal pits of León and the Basque Country, numerous prisoners were forced to work under such strenuous conditions that many of them would not survive the mercilessly long days of labor. The jail and such businesses were both blessed by the Church, which was complicit in the general repression of the postwar period. In fact, in the first years of *franquismo,* they could not be distinguished from each other. Political prisoners were given work, and the "free" workers were disciplined with political and religious propaganda.[9]

The Central Organization of Social Redemption through Work was led by a clergyman named by the cardinal. As was the custom in the administration set up by the victors (in the mayors' offices, the FET, the JONS, etc.) the local branches were run by a parishioner and staffed by secretaries who were known to be "charitable and devoted women."

Among Spanish women, there were also, of course, victors and vanquished. In 1940 there were at least 20,000 female political prisoners. In the first part of that year, the women's prison of Las Ventas in Madrid, which had been constructed to hold up to 100 women, had a steady population of about 2,000. According to Ricard Vinyes, Sister Felipa García, a nun from the Daughters of Charity of Saint Vincent de Paul, acted as head of the disciplinary board and administrator of the jail. The same group of sisters oversaw the cooking and cleaning of various jails. Sister Felipa bragged about the discipline that prevailed in Las Ventas in particular. In order to achieve such a state they had to prohibit all packages, as well as all communication with the outside world. Also, the prisoners were punished with harsh jobs they had to perform "until they showed a proper amount of contrition and their will to reform."

Sister Felipa formed a perfect team with the prison's chaplain, Eliseo Cots Carbonell. Both were very satisfied with the "religious progress made by the prisoners." They ruled over the jail together, directed the choir, oversaw flag-blessing ceremonies, and organized a number of activities for the religious holidays for the women in their care. On one of those festive days, for example, the prisoners enjoyed a speech given by the inspector of Catalan prisons and director of the Modelo Prison in Barcelona, Isidro Castillón López, who spoke to them about the beauty of the Spanish landscape, of Don Pelayo and the Catholic kings, and the defeat of the Marxist hordes by the immortal Caudillo.

More important than history to the women in the jails was the condition of the prisons, where cases of typhus and tuberculosis were widespread. The prison's doctor, Enrique Fosar Bayarri, often complained at the meetings of the discipline board about the lack of medicines and sanitary materials. In 1939 there were forty-four children under the age of four who were jailed with their mothers. Many of them died of meningitis or of hunger, and some were even assassinated, if we are to believe the horrifying tales found in books by Tomasa Cuevas and Juana Doña.

The children formed part of the life of the women's prisons. Many of the children who survived the jails were later separated from their mothers and put in assistance centers and religious schools under the auspices of the Central Organization of Social Redemption through Work. In 1942 9,050 children were placed by the organization. As Ricard Vinyes has noted, there were many more girls than boys in the austere and rigid religious centers. Punishments and misery were deemed part of an ideal education for the daughters of "Reds" in order to turn them into good Catholic girls.

The majority of the "common" prisoners practiced prostitution, an activity that had taken off "vertiginously" in the postwar period. As the public prosecutor of the Supreme Court, Blas Pérez González, puts it in a report he presented to the government in September 1941, the "exacerbated economic hardships" were, according to the prosecutor, the principle cause of this rise in prostitution, as well as the increase in the number of sexual assaults and rapes. Martín Torrent, who opened and censored prisoners' letters to "be aware of the general spiritual state of the house," transcribes the letter of a woman who confesses to her husband in prison that it is simply impossible to live on a mere fifteen pesetas a week. "What can I do?" she writes. "Can I let you and the kids die of hunger? Or is it that you don't think that I love you all and that I would let our kids die of hunger and not receive even a basic education?" (102).

These women, writes Torrent, should realize they ought to suffer the trying circumstances occasioned by the victory of good over evil "rather than sell their honor as women, wives, and mothers." The families of the "Reds," he adds, should know how to bear the disgrace of the defeated, which included, for men and women alike, the threat of confiscation. "Red" women, the military, clergy, and other *franquistas* believed, were meant to suffer, to sacrifice themselves, and to cleanse themselves of their own sins or for not having been effective in steering their husbands down the path of righteousness.

Elvira

The regime deemed it necessary to keep watch over these women, reeducate them, and purify them—with castor oil, if necessary—to exorcise the demons from their body. As they were seen as carriers of guilt, their heads were shaved in order that others could even more easily point out the guilty "*pelona*" (bald woman). The Women's Section (Sección Feminina) and the Church, who made sure this was a daily image during the 1940s, not only supported the women being thrown into physical and moral misery but also provided their own brand of propaganda: they continually contrasted these bad women with model females such as the Virgin Mary, Isabel the Catholic, and Saint Teresa of Jesus. "Red" women were an offense to a society that was morally opposed to adultery, divorce, and abortion, all of which were heavily penalized under Franco.[10]

The victors of the war determined the fate of the vanquished for decades by means of a variety of mechanisms and manifestations of terror. First, the regime used physical violence in vengeful and arbitrary fashion and carried out numerous summary executions. This was a continuation of the "fiery terror" that Franco's soldiers had used throughout the war and that continued, albeit on a much lesser scale, through 1943. After the end of the war, the violence was controlled by the military authorities. Terror thus became institutionalized and upheld by the repressive legislation of the new state. This state of terror, a continuation of the state of the war, transformed Spanish society through the destruction of entire families and by inundating daily life in Spain with the constant threat of punishment and through numerous instances of carrying out that threat. What remains to be seen are what Conxita Mir has called the "intangible effects" of the repression: fear in general and the dread of being watched by the state in particular, as well as constant humiliation and marginalization. Though the *franquista* state would show different amenable faces to the world in its lifetime, it was, from the beginning to its last days, repressive. As many different studies have shown, not only did the regime define itself principally as repressive, but it manifested its brutality in countless ways.[11]

DENUNCIATIONS: THE VIOLENCE FROM BELOW

This machinery of terror organized from above would not have worked without a great number of Spaniards willing to grease its wheels. The loyalist elements of society (the Church, the military, the Falange, and diehard rightists) zealously supported the effort to purge society of threatening elements. The regime also found a number of willing collaborators in the form of informants among those who wished to take advantage of the opportunity to get rid of men and women who had been—or could be—labeled as "undesirable," as "animals," or as troublemakers. The purging was, after all, both a political and a social phenomenon, and people looked after their best interests given the chance. Furthermore, there was the social pressure to cooperate in this process: when someone was denounced by his or her neighbor, people kept quiet for fear of being accused in turn for defending the person in question. And there was a strong consensus that the punishments being given were politically necessary.[12]

After Franco conquered Valencia on March 30, 1939, the Column of Order and Police of the Occupation (Columna de Orden y Policía de Ocupación), led by Colonel Antonio Aymat, started the "cleaning," a crackdown that, according to Vincent Gabarda, took the lives of 4,174 "Reds," as well as 1,165 prisoners who died in the jails and concentration camps. On the first day of the postwar period, Aymat and the other officers in charge set up centers at which citizens could denounce their neighbors. And from that first day, there were long lines of citizens, many of whom arrived in search of retribution. Others wanted to avoid at all costs accusations of leftist sympathies. A warning published by the military government implied that silence would be punished: "Every person who knows of a crime committed during the years of Red domination is obligated to denounce the crime . . . so that the justice, the animating spirit of our Caudillo, may be observed."

The citizens of Franco's Spain were told that they should keep a constant lookout, and to be "relentless" in carrying out the necessary work of good Spaniards of uncovering and denouncing "any person who might have committed any crime." To not share knowledge about a possible crime was considered a crime: that of concealment.

In every corner of Spain it was a time of hatred, denouncements, and silence. In Málaga, for instance, as Matilde Eiroa has shown, in the first months of 1939 many men and women were detailed "for not having informed the authorities about the arrival to the city of Marxist individuals who participated in activities against the uprising." It was not enough to have taken thousands of "Reds" on their final *paseo* after Franco's troops occupied Málaga in February 1937; the regime also worked to break any ties of friendship and solidarity in order to impede the spread of any "germ" of resistance.

To collaborate by informing on one's neighbors also implied the commencement of a wide array of summary legal procedures put into place by the victors. Denouncements acted as a kind of social glue among the victors, and for that reason the regime insisted so strongly on active participation and penalized passivity so harshly. To denounce "crimes" of the "delinquents" was something done by "good patriots" who were forging the "New Spain." The act of informing on one's neighbors thus became the foundation for justice under Franco.

The authorities encouraged denouncements in the workplace as well. Barcelona's city hall, for example, obliged all government functionaries to act as policemen. As the order states, "You must tell the proper authorities who the leftists are in your department and everything you know about their activities" (Molinero and Pere Ysàs 97). One had to follow such orders not only to show one's loyalty to the National Movement but also to keep one's job.[13]

In an environment in which paybacks became the way to assure a paycheck, thousands of men and women were denounced as leftists, thereby leaving many positions open for those who, having shown their loyalty through treachery, would advance through the ranks of the provincial and local governments. A law passed on February 10, 1939, institutionalized the purging of public offices, a process that the military rebels had begun (without laws) since the summer of 1936. After the law was passed, each ministry designated "instructors" (*instructores*) to investigate the conduct of the functionaries, and those who were found to be "clean" were called in as witnesses against their fellow citizens.

The law, and the purging process in general, had a double objective: first, to deprive those who opposed the regime of their jobs and their means of economic survival as an exemplary punishment, and second, to guarantee jobs for all those who had served the Nationalist cause during the Civil War and who had proven their allegiance to the Movement. One of the reasons the dictatorship of Franco was able to survive was precisely because of the "unbreakable union" of those who had benefited from the Caudillo's victory.

An elevated percentage of "vacancies"—in some places, up to 80 percent of positions—were reserved for ex-soldiers, ex-prisoners of war, relatives of the "martyrs" of the crusade, and all those who proved their complete commitment to the principles of the victors. "Throw the neutral people in jail!" writes Luis de Galinsoga, Franco's hagiographer and director of the *Vanguardia Española*. As he continues in this same vein, "It is a crime in our day and age for a Spaniard to be neutral regarding Spain and life in Spain. One must be for or against the biological unity that we call Spain when it is judged by History" (qtd. in Abella 20).

Spain was united both politically and religiously. It had been cleansed, in the words of Galinsoga, of the "delinquents like Companys."[14] The next task at hand was for the citizens to readapt themselves to the new way of life in the postwar era. In the Republican areas of Cataluña, Valencia, Aragón, Castilla-La Marcha, Murcia, and Andalucía, factory owners saw to the cleansing of their workforce of Marxist elements (especially those who had joined unions), and landowners gave the boot to peasants who had taken part in the leftist revolution. Many men and women lost their jobs; others, especially in the countryside, were forced to move to other cities or towns. Persecuted and denounced by informants, militant unionists, who stood out for their support of the Republic, suffered more than anyone. Even the least involved, many of whom were illiterate, were effectively silenced by the Regime.[15]

One year alter the war ended, the dictatorship put into place the legal system for denouncements, an instrument used by the state to better stimulate people to inform on others. Not even in Nazi Germany, where the Gestapo encouraged and promoted the collaboration of citizens with the authorities, was the participation of the civilian population fashioned in such a far-reaching manner. Some National Socialists tried to put a similar system into place, but they were not successful.

The Ministry of Justice created the "General Investigation of Criminal Activities and Other Aspects of Life in the Red Zone from July 18,

1936, Until Its Liberation" by decree on April 26, 1940. Its declared goal was to "investigate everything concerning crimes and everything about them: their causes and effects, the ways in which they were carried out, the degree of culpability of the authors of the crime, the identification of the victims and appraisal of the damage, both material and moral, caused by the criminals, whether it be against persons, goods, religion, culture, artworks, or to the national patrimony."

The "General Investigation" achieved various objectives. It gave citizens a chance to vent their feelings about the "Red terror" and solidified the collective memory about the widespread horror of that time. It compensated the families of victims of the violence and with such rewards confirmed the social divide between the victors and the victims, who were concurrently penalized and marginalized. Above all, it became the instrument for the denouncement and persecution of citizens who were not involved in any crimes. As the scholars who have studied the "General Investigation" have shown, especially regarding Cataluña, Aragón, and Levante, the officials in charge of investigations often used false evidence to condemn people to long years of prison or to execution. Various studies have shown that the members of the public, whom Franco manipulated through propaganda about the "Glorious Crusade," generally supported the *franquista* regime's policies and practices and were, by proxy, the Caudillo's willing executioners.[16]

The war and the victory also induced the appearance of voluntary hangmen. One incident that illustrates this phenomenon is told by Gumersindo de Estrella, the chaplain of the jail in Torrero (Zaragoza). On June 13, 1938, the clergyman says, everyone was waiting for the hangman to arrive to execute Esteban García Solanas. Because the executioner was very late, a member of the Brotherhood of the Blood of Christ, the organization in charge of burying the dead, said, "resolutely," that "as the hangman has not come, I am ready to carry out justice." All who heard him, writes the Capuchine priest, "interpreted his words and bearing as a sign of his profound allegiance to the Movement and to the Church."

To survive in such an environment, one had to be more insensitive than the next person, as each denouncement distanced one further from being suspected of disloyalty. Many had to transform themselves into a new person and swallow their past by erasing any trace of dissidence and covering up any record of ever having expressed a desire for liberty. In the harsh austerity of the forties and fifties, writes Frances Lannon, "religious conformity was essential for those who wished to have a job, to ascend in the workplace, or to attain any other ascension, and to be secure in general." Spain had become an economic, political, and cultural autarchy. The vanquished were persecuted and hungry, while the victors were hungry for vengeance. Both sides were marked by the war, but the losing side had taken the worst, with so much death and misery everywhere and Catholic morality constantly shoved down their throats.

Many relatives of the victims of the "Red terror" were the most active participants in the postwar repression. Conxita Mir has shown that in rural Lérida, for instance, there were very close "consanguineous ties" among the informants. (Most of these were men, but women did not stay on the sidelines by any means). To denounce someone became for many the first act of political allegiance to the dictatorship. People were "surveilled and silenced to the point that the entire society had turned into a legion of spies for the government. The collaboration of the population in their submission to power was absolutely crucial in the smooth transformation of a politics of the masses that had existed before the war in Spain to a dictatorship" (Lannon 259).

Since the majority of the political and union leaders (especially those in Aragón and Cataluña) had been able to leave the country, many of those who suffered the regime's harsh punishments had nothing to do with the actions that were ascribed to them. But no one was there to defend those who stayed. To blame someone was easy, but to stand up for the accused was to put one's neck out.

All of the denunciations by the security forces, the clergy, the *falangistas,* and ordinary people, as well as the endorsements and statements of good conduct necessary to stay alive, in themselves represent an eloquent testimony to the degree of involvement of the general population in the establishment of this system of terror. This fact implies, in turn, that the dictatorship did not survive solely by violence and terror, nor did it prosper only by repression. Without the participation of the Spanish public, the terror would have been limited to violence and coercion. Once the bloodiest years were over, what surfaced was a system of self-surveillance in which zero tolerance was permitted for disloyalty to the regime, and any resistance was stamped out with the help of the citizens themselves. As time passed, the dictatorship changed its methods. Without the threat from the outside, Franco could offer a gentler, "sweeter" face. When he appeared in public, it was not as an enforcer of the law, but as a leader who inaugurated public projects and rewarded the hard work of Spaniards.

But while the dictatorship may have developed a seemingly gentler side, Franco never made an attempt to erase its bloody origins. In fact, his government would commemorate the Civil War time and again as a foundational moment. The dictatorship recemented its bonds with the extensive coalition of the victors while never missing an opportunity to further marginalize and humiliate the vanquished. Such repression was not "inevitable," but the victors deemed it necessary and considered sentences of death or prison as a fitting fate for the "Reds." There was always the opportunity to pardon prisoners on death row, to free the majority of incarcerated men and women (and children), and to provide hygienic conditions and food in the prisons. But no punishment was deemed harsh enough for the "animals," who deserved everything they got.

The repression was, in the words of Enrique Moradiellos, "a profitable political and social strategy: without such 'purifying' and 'purging' of enemies, such a comprehensible consolidation, which contributed to the longevity of the dictatorship, would not have been possible." In fact, one could say that the dictatorship, which weathered so many decades and so many international contexts, was forged through a "pact of blood"; through the terror, which consisted greatly of paybacks, unity was achieved. The vanquished were paralyzed by fear and incapable of formulating any response to the regime (Moradiellos 237).

The few voices inside Spain that encouraged reconciliation and pardons were silenced. During the first decade of the dictatorship, there was no possibility of suturing the wounds in Spanish society or stopping the vengeful punishment and violence. This was something that everyone—from Franco to the last parish priest of the Catholic Church—agreed upon. Indeed, when the war was transformed into a Crusade, religion stimulated greater violence. Even after the war, the Church did not mitigate the violence but rather approved of it, and the Church itself enjoyed a long period of prosperity. Not only did the dictatorship protect the Church, but lavished it with privileges, defended its doctrines, and crushed its enemies. The Church, its hierarchy, the clergy, and hundreds of thousands of believers participated in the front lines in asserting the righteousness of Christian doctrine and legitimizing the repression of the vanquished. Indeed, many laypeople helped, especially in controlling and monopolizing the education of the country's youth and in helping the unfortunate "Reds" and atheists to see the error of their ways. One had to be strict but caring, they believed, with those who had defied the social order and had abandoned the Catholic faith.

RELIGIOUS FUNDAMENTALISM

In no other authoritarian regime in the twentieth century did the Church assume such political responsibility and play such a central role in policing the country's citizens as Spain. Neither the Protestant Church in Nazi Germany nor the Catholic Church in Fascist Italy were as intimately involved with the government. After the civil wars in Finland and Greece, the Lutheran and Orthodox churches signed pacts of friendship with the victorious Right, which defended patriotism, traditional moral values, and patriarchal authority in the family, but in neither of these countries did the religious authorities call for bloodshed, in contrast to the Catholic Church in Spain, which was vehement in its calls for retribution. It is true that no other Church had been persecuted with such cruelty and violence as the Spanish Church. But once the war was over, far from turning the other cheek, the Church used the memory of its martyrs to justify paybacks against the vanquished.

I would like to concentrate on three basic ideas in the following pages. The first is that the Catholic Church was not only implicated but fully involved in the legal system of repression organized by Franco and his cronies after the Civil War. The second is that the Catholic Church sanctioned and glorified that violence not only because the blood of thousands of martyrs called out for vengeance, but also—and above all—because it helped solidify the position of power in which it found itself. In one instant, with the military coup d'état of July 1936, decades of secularism were made to disappear by a regime that would give the Church in Spain a hegemony and monopoly beyond its wildest dreams. Throughout the pages that follow, it is important to remember that the symbiosis of religion, fatherland, and Caudillo was crucial for the dictator's survival in the wake of the defeat of the Fascist dictatorships in the Second World War.

The Law of Political Responsibility of February 9, 1939, gave the Church the opportunity to become an extralegal body of investigation, with each parish in charge of policing its parishioners. It was not enough that the Church, which enjoyed abundant privileges after the war, recover its role as the guardian of morality and good conduct. As Conxita Mir writes, "Thanks to the Law of Political Responsibility, the parishioners became an integral part of Franco's legal machinery. In fact, they were placed at the same level as the local government officials and local leaders of the Falange. The parishioners would use their expert knowledge of the littlest details of daily life of their neighbors to carry out justice" (*Vivir* 191).

It was nothing new in the postwar period that priests would fill out reports about delinquents, denounce them, or persecute them to their grave. As recent studies have shown, they had done this during the war zones occupied by the rebel military. The novelty lay in that the fog of war had lifted and that their policing role had been clearly engraved in law. Upon the approval of the law, which allowed the clergy to take the initiative in repressive actions, men of the cloth unambiguously announced the part they would play in Spain after the war: they would not be an instrument for reconciliation, but rather messengers of hate and vengeance. They would be the voluntary agents of the exterminating angel.

The proof of the priests' involvement is found in the reports submitted by the priests as subscribed by the instructing judges' pronouncements, as well as in the declarations made under the banner of the "General Investigation." It is true that not all the clergy actively participated in this police work; some refused to collaborate with the regime. But the few men who pointed out the negative consequences for the future of the country as a result of the unbridled persecution and who encouraged reconciliation were ridiculed by the majority. Gumersindo de Estella, one of the few priests who dared to lament both in private and in writing the assistance the Church was giving to the murderous regime, closes his diary with a sense of guilt, rage, and impotence. As he writes about his fellow clergymen after attending to a man to be executed on March 11, 1942, "The violence of the adversaries does not give us the right to hate, to disdain the vanquished, nor to abandon him" (314).[17]

Gumersindo de Estella knew that many of the prisoners who ended up before a firing squad had been denounced by priests. We know that this is the case, for example, from the records that we have from the rural zones of Aragón and Lérida, which had remained in Republican hands until the spring of 1938 and from where most of the prisoners executed in Zaragoza in the first years of the postwar era came. One has to suppose that the priests who went to those towns were angry and resentful about the anticlericalism that had formerly prevailed. But this does not seem to be the only reason that they persecuted the leftists and atheists. One other reason they sacrificed the supposed unfaithful was to render homage to their own martyrs, whose blood demanded vengeance. The political crimes carried out in peacetime were a direct response to the assassination of clergymen during the war. Such malevolence was rampant in the Catholic Spain of the postwar period.

The reports that have survived reveal a clergy that was bitter because of the violent anticlericalism and unacceptable level of secularization that Spanish society had reached during the Republican years. Not only had secularization pervaded public ceremony, but many Spaniards had stopped going to Mass, and the country was replete with rationalist teachers, militant workers, and secular Republicans. The clergy used Manichean language to condemn the Republic as "a time of the Red horde" and glorified "the Glorious Crusade." They considered people of order as good Christians and reserved negative and condemning epithets for subversives and anticlerical men and women. They also took advantage of the terror and fear to stuff the Church's coffers; the clergy would issue innocent reports about rich Republican professionals in exchange for donations to the Church.

It seems clear, therefore, that the Law of Political Responsibility made the priests, in collaboration with government officials, investigators of people's ideological and political pasts. Except in the few cases of priests who did not feel comfortable playing the role of official informant, the rest collaborated actively and voluntarily in the hunt for "Reds," thereby showing an unbreakable allegiance to Franco's dictatorship. In particular, they showed their approval for the legal extermination of the vanquished with their reports. In a more general sense, they were deeply involved in encouraging feelings of envy, vengeance, and hate that pervaded Spain's small rural communities.

In Spain, unlike in Germany or Italy or other societies that had suffered civil wars or dictatorship, the Church was able to impose its discourse of moral and political purity. Spain did not have Nazism or a Holocaust, but the victors treated the vanquished in a violent fashion. The rhetoric the regime and the Church used drew on the latter's racist history.

The Church turned a blind eye to the beatings, tortures, and deaths in the *franquista* jails and concentrated on "spiritual" control of the prisoners and on converting them. As Martín Torrent writes, the chaplains had not been given the right to free the prisoners condemned to death. In this matter Torrent followed the instructions of one of his idols, José Antonio Pérez del Pulgar, to the letter. In a cyclical he sent to the "interning chaplains named to work in the Central Organization of Social Redemption through Work," Pérez del Pulgar, the ideological creator of the labor camps, gave a piece of advice as to how to reconcile their dual role as apostles of Christ and agents of the "magnanimous" justice of Franco. "The chaplain should never speak in public or private about matters concerning the prisoners nor question the justice of the sentences," he writes, adding that they also should not "offer to intercede for the inmates or offer to obtain anything for them to ease their condition in the prison, even if such things might be permissible for other people" (qtd. in Raguer Suñer, *Divendres* 386).[18]

No intercession or any other type of intervention whatsoever was permitted. The chaplain's job was to peddle and impose Catholic morality—above all, obedience and submission—to the prisoners on death row and to those serving out long sentences. Their work consisted of political and ideological censorship, and they provided communion and confession in exchange for "little" favors they could concede, while castigating those who resisted the priests' project of proselytizing with the reports. The clergy was powerful both inside the jails and in society, and they exercised their power over the prisoners and their families. Indeed, the law gave the men in black the power to decide according to their own religious criteria in what way and for how long people should purge their sins.

The Catholic Church in Spain enjoyed its position of power for a long time. Among the other powers they had been conferred, thanks to the sacralization of the Civil War and its close ties with Franco's dictatorship, was control over the country's schools. The Church hierarchy had begun to make its mark on this crucial sector since the beginning of the war.

The ecclesiastical hierarchy, headed by Enrique Pla i Deniel, set out as one of its main tasks the labor of re-Catholicizing Spain. Even before the war ended, the clergy began an overhaul of the country's education system with the help of Franco, who placed Catholic intellectuals with Fascist ideas in charge of the Ministry of Education. Franco named Sáinz Rodríguez, a university professor from the extreme Alphonsist Right, to the post on January 30, 1938. Upon the conclusion of the war, Franco chose José Ibáñez Martín as part of his second government, which he formed on August 9, 1939. Ibáñez Martín, like José María Pemán, was part of the National Catholic Association of Propagandists (Asociación Católica Nacional de Propagandistas) and had been elected as a representative of CEDA, the Catholic political party, for Murcia in the November elections in 1933. He occupied the post for twelve years, which was sufficient time for him to finish off the job of purging the ministry begun by the Commission of Culture and Teaching (Comisión de Cultura y Enseñanza), which was headed by Pemán, who led the work of Catholicizing state-sponsored schools and allocating generous funding to the Church's schools. Ibáñez Martín's legacy also includes a litany of antimodernist pronouncements and fervent praises of the pedagogy of San José de Calasanz. Among the more ridiculous things he said during his terms were his statements about the formation of teachers and basic questions of education. On one occasion in 1943, for example, he asked, "How can a teacher ever hope to shape the soul of a student if he does not know how to pray? I have here the fundamental problem of Spanish education."

Ibáñez Martín kept Tiburcio Romualdo de Toledo and José Permatín, two radical Catholics from the times of Sáinz Rodríguez, as his right-hand men throughout his tenure. He also included some "old shirts" from the Falange: one instance more of the mix of Fascism and Catholicism that dominated Spanish society during the postwar period. Romualdo de Toledo, head of the National Service of Primary Education

(Servicio Nacional de Enseñanza Primaria) was a traditionalist who held as his model school "the monastery founded by Saint Benedict." Similarly, in 1937 José Permatín, head of the National Service of Mid- and Upper-Level Education (Enseñanza Superior y Media), defended a "careful and meticulous purging" of the teachers and professors. Such a process, he said, should not be vengeful, but scrupulous.

The clergy in charge of the education system sanctioned and sacked thousands of teachers who were the cream of the crop of the progressive and secular Left and divided up Spain's schools as booty among the families of falangists, loyalist soldiers, and Catholic families. In some provinces such as Lugo, for instance, "practically all the teachers were dismissed." This process took place at the university level as well, as Ibañez Martín, Catholic propagandists, and the Opus Dei made sure that professorships were offered only to the most faithful.[19]

The clergy did not stop at denouncing and persecuting professors and filling their posts with their own. They also acted as censors and converted the entire education process (from first grade to university) into an exercise of submission to authority and religion. According to Gregorio Cámara Villar, the goal of the system was to "form resigned and respectful subjects who bow their heads to order and the social hierarchy." The Church was the soul of the new state, which had come back to life after its death under anticlericalism. The Church insinuated itself into every corner of daily life: in schools, in the government and centers of power, and in social customs and practices (see Cámara Villar 67–68).

The clergy also made the working classes another central target of their project of re-Catholicization at gunpoint. As the working class had largely taken the side of the Republic, they were in especial need of being shown the light of truth. The clergy would exercise their new powers not only in the jails but also in the factories, where many of the "Reds" who had survived would continue to work after the war. This was the strategy of, for example, Balbino Santos Olivera, the bishop in Málaga who, after the Loyalist occupation of February 1937, became well known for his rants with Nationalist rhetoric about Franco's crusade.

According to Adela Alfonsi, "at the heart of the apostolic mission of the Catholic Action Group [Acción Católica] was the idea that poverty was inevitable and necessary, and emphasized the nobility of manual work." Resignation, discipline, and hard work were deemed "patriotic," in contrast with egoism, violence, and anarchy, traits that described the revolutionary scum. To be poor was natural; it was a sign that they were loved by God and must resign themselves to this fate, while the labor of the rich was to be benevolent and magnanimous. To show that he practiced what he preached when he spoke about the need to be charitable with one's good fortune, don Balbino invited sixteen poor youths to his table for Christmas in 1945. It was a portrait, with sumptuous food and fancy gifts, of Christian charity against the backdrop of the glum Spain of hunger and indigence.

In October 1947 Balbino Santos Olivera was replaced with Ángel Herrera Oria, who was less jingoistic than his predecessor but equally traditionalist and paternalistic. Herrera Oria, a lawyer by profession, had been a member of the National Catholic Association of Propagandists in 1909 and worked on *El Debate* in 1911, a newspaper that he directed until 1933, the year he occupied the presidency of the board of directors of the Catholic Association. He had also created the National Action (Acción Nacional), the right-wing political organization from which the influential Popular Action (Acción Popular) emerged. From lawyer, propagandist, and politician, he later became a priest, a bishop, and a cardinal, a post to which he was elevated in 1965 by Pope Paul VI.

Herrera, like Santos Olivera and the rest of the bishops in the Church during Franco's dictatorship, insisted that Spain's social problems were spiritual and moral in nature and had little time for arguments that they might be caused by an unequal distribution of riches and power. Charitable contributions, he asserted, were the solution for social injustice, and they had the extra advantage of offering something for the rich: eternal salvation. It was the same tune of resignation, subordination, and acceptance of the status quo that the Church had sung without success with the monarchy and that it ended up implementing by means of armed force (see Alfonsi).

With each year that passed, it became clearer and clearer that the imposition of Catholicism by force was not working and that the air of modernization and secularization that had circulated through Spanish society before the Civil War had not dissipated. Much of the population was still anticlerical and indifferent to religion. But the Church did not care about this social reality, as the costs of the re-Catholicizing (i.e., the jailing and humiliating of men and women, the violation of basic human rights, and the execution of thousands) cost them little. The Church was happy, as it had achieved what it always desired—a "divine totalitarianism"—a mix of Catholicism and Fascism, with which they occupied the public sphere.

Nothing disturbed the hegemony of the Church in the first twenty-five years of the postwar period, and the identification of the Spanish Catholic Church with Franco's dictatorship could not have been more intimate. All had begun with a military rebellion, which the Church blessed, and the relationship was consummated with a pact of blood and the symbiosis of religion, fatherland, and Caudillo, which came as a blessing during the crucial period after the Second World War. It was during this period in which the dictatorship was vulnerable to outside pressure that the Church could have changed by giving some sign of dissidence, forgiveness, or reconciliation. But the Church, enthralled as it was with the idea of a "divine totalitarianism" and overjoyed by its privileges, had no interest in an "unnecessary revisionism." Enrique Pla i Deniel, the ideologue of the crusade, could not have said it clearer than when he declared in 1945 that, "the hour of peace throughout the world should be the hour for consolidating the peace inside Spain" (Sánchez Recio 148). The prelate of the Spanish clergy asserted that "the past civil war and Crusade was an armed plebiscite that put an end to the persecution of the Church. Nobody wants another unnecessary revision, which might lead us to another civil war" (148).

A month before Pla i Deniel published that pastoral letter, Franco had augmented the presence of the clergy and prominent Catholics in his government. He kept Ibáñez Martín in the Ministry of Education and named José María Fernández Ladreda and Alberto Martín Artajo, two long-standing politicians and ex-representatives of the CEDA, to the ministries of Public Works and Foreign Affairs, respectively. In that time of "international ostracism," and in need of shedding the regime's Fascist skin, Franco tried to establish relations with other countries by the most direct way: by selling Spanish Catholicism, which would be accompanied by Spanish tradition and an anti-Communist stance.

Martín Artajo occupied his post for twelve years, in which time he helped to whitewash the image of *franquismo* for the world at large. He also did what most Spanish Catholics did at the time: he rejected any possibility of returning to a constitutional government, to the liberty of expression, and to the "dogmas of liberalism." He agreed with the consensus that the anarchists, Communists, Republicans, and other "Reds" were fine where they were—in jail, persecuted, or under surveillance. He wholeheartedly approved of stripping these men and women of their rights. It was one thing to disavow Fascism in order to reduce Spain's political isolation in the world. It was quite another to dismantle the authoritarian regime, to lose privileges, or to reconcile with the "Reds."

The old politicians of the CEDA and the relevant members of the ACNP thus contributed in decisive ways to institutionalize the new state of Spain ruled by the victors of the war. They "harmonized" the best of the Spanish tradition with modern ways of mobilizing the masses, such as the paraphernalia and symbolism they took from Fascism, as well as other methods derived from "divine totalitarianism," which was manifest in processions, schools, Catholic Action, the parishes, the pulpit, and even the jails. The Church adjusted itself to become a perfect fit with the dictatorship (Fascist or otherwise) and showed how in the daily striding toward Catholic regeneration their speeches, their elite leaders, and their organizations would last over the decades to come.

Catholicism and the Catholic clergy did not remain impervious to the socioeconomic changes that, since the beginning of the sixties, challenged the political apparatus of the Franco dictatorship. Spanish Catholicism had to adapt itself to that evolution by means of a series of internal and external transformations that various scholars have analyzed. According to José Casanova, the hierarchy of the Church looked with alarm on the "rapid secularization that accompanied the rapid industrial progress and urbanization" ("España" 144). And he writes, "Slowly, however, the more astute sectors of Spanish Catholicism began to speak of Spain not as a nation that was inherently Catholic and that had to be reconquered, but rather as a country of vocation (*país de misión*). Catholic faith could not be imposed from above; it had to be adopted slowly and voluntarily through individual conversions" ("España" 144).[20]

Before making this change, the Church, along with the victors, relished doing away with the unfaithful and all those opposed to the re-Catholicizing of Spain. During almost the entire dictatorship the Church never wanted to hear anything of forgiveness or reconciliation, contented as it was with the memory of the crusade. Even in September

1971, in the First National Assembly of Bishops and Priests, the clergy did not take on this matter in a formal fashion. At that meeting, some members of the assembly presented a resolution in which the Church asked forgiveness because it did not know at the time how to use its central position in Spanish society to be true ministers of reconciliation after a war among brothers. The proposition did not obtain the two-thirds of the vote necessary to be approved and included in the final report. It was submitted to a second vote, but again it was rejected with 122 in favor, 114 against, and 10 abstentions.

When the "indomitable Caudillo" died on November 20, 1975, the Spanish Catholic Church was no longer the monolithic entity that had supported the crusade and the bloody vengeance of the postwar era. But what remained of the legacy of the golden age of privileges was impressive, nevertheless, in terms of education, its propaganda apparatus, and the media. "No leader of any time in our history," said Carrero Blanco to Franco in December 1972, "has done more for the Catholic Church than Your Excellency, who provided this help in service of God and the Fatherland, to which you have dedicated your life in exemplary fashion" (Gómez Pérez 170–71). Carrero estimated that in the years Franco was in power the Church had received 300,000 pesetas from the state.[21]

The Catholic Church came out ahead in its exchange of favors with the murderous political regime and was delighted with the benefits it derived from the dictatorship, which was erected over the ashes of the Republic and the blood of vengeance that flowed in the Civil War and beyond. The Church liked to remind Spaniards how much they had suffered during that war, but the clergy sought to forget how it was an important accomplice in the military and Fascist terror during both the war and the postwar period. As George Orwell wrote in the fervor of battle, "Everyone believes in the atrocities committed by the enemy and not in those carried out by his side" (144).

NOTES

1. A version of this essay first appeared in *Morir, matar, sobrevivir: La violencia en la dictadura de Franco*, edited by Julián Casanova and Santos Juliá.

2. The data was obtained from investigations carried out by the historians who appear in the collection *Víctimas de la Guerra Civil,* edited by Santos Juliá (411–12), which separate the executions into the war and the postwar period. See also Souto Blanco; D. Jiménez 691–705; I. Jiménez; and Pérez. Ángel David Martín Rubio provides data on nineteen provinces that does not always coincide with that found in *Víctimas de la guerra civil.* He puts the number of deaths from the "nationalist repression of the post-war" at 25,229, and clarifies that although one might investigate the rest of the provinces (Vizcaya, Badajoz, Toledo, etc.), "the total will not exceed by much that number."

3. As related by Ramón Serrano Suñer. The "coldness" of Franco "when faced with the responsibility of putting an end to human life" is quoted in Sáinz Rodríguez (335).

4. The Tribunals and Courts of Political Responsibilities were erected on the order of the vice president of the government on July 2, 1939.

5. The best studies about the application of the law are those of Conxita Mir, Fabiá Corretgé, Judit Farré, and Joan Sagués in Mir, *Repressió.* See also Vilanova i Vila-Abadal (511), who includes the statistics from the different regional tribunals.

6. This line of continuity is underlined by Marc Carrillo, whose work I also cite regarding information about the lack of judicial guarantees; see Carrillo 22–23, 27–30. See also Lanero.

7. Ricard Vinyes, "Territoris," has carried out one of the best studies on this subject. Data on the prison in Valencia comes from Gabarda (52). Information about the Modelo of Barcelona is found in Torrent. According to Vicente Comes, the book had actually been written by Luis Lucía Lucía, former leader of the Valencia Regional Right (Derecha Regional Valenciana). It had been commissioned by the chaplain of the Modelo jail in Barcelona, Father Martín Torrent, who signed the book as his own; see Comes.

8. The *Livre Blanc* (Paris in 1953) is analyzed in detail by Ricard Vinyes, "Territoris," 43–55.

9. See Richards 86–89 for the link between jails and factories in this repressive system; see also his extensive investigation into the idea of "purifying" Spain (24–70). Francisco Moreno (360–61) also insists that benefits arose from the work camps and the purging of the government carried out by the victors. The information about the Central Organization of Social Redemption through Work can be found in Torrent 98–105. One of the first studies that concentrated on the theme of the clergy's assistance to the prisoners was that of María Encarna Nicolás's *Instituciones murcianas en el franquismo (1939–1962),* 90–101.

10. For all the information about the prison Les Corts in Barcelona, see Vinyes, "'Nada.'" For testimonies about life and death in women's jails, see Cuevas, *Cárcel, Mujeres de la resistencia, Mujeres en las cárceles,* and *Testimonios;*

Doña. For information about the shaving of heads and the use of castor oil, see Richards 58–59.

11. For a study of the different modalities of this repression, see Mir, "Violencia." See also Moreno; Cenarro, "Muerte"; and Casanova, "Guerra."

12. The parallel between the postwar period in Finland and the one in Spain is suggestive. The political need for repression and "popular" support for the white terror after the civil war in Finland are studied by Anthony F. Upton, who calls the white terror a "democratic phenomenon" (519).

13. On Valencia, see Gabarda 36. On Málaga, see Eiroa 18. For similar examples in Cuenca, see D. Jiménez 703. The "usefulness" of the terror is emphasized by Antonio Cazorla Sánchez 98–110.

14. Lluís Companys (1883–1940), Catalan politician and leader of the Left-Wing Republican Party (Esquerra Republicana de Catalunya), served as president of the Catalan Generalitat from 1934 to 1939. In 1939, at the end of the Spanish Civil War, he left for France as an exile and was returned by German agents to Spain. He was shot at Montjuïc Castle in Barcelona in 1940.

15. In Mercedes Vilanova's words, "the reaction to the repression by the illiterate population was varied, subtle, and wise. The illiterate had the ability to keep quiet, pass unnoticed, and make themselves invisible. One could say that their distance from power and written culture freed them from the repression suffered by the lettered militants" ("Anarchism" 105–6). Vilanova i Vila-Abadal has explored this premise at length in *Les majories invisibles*. On the consequences of the loss in a factory and cooperative, see Carme Vega.

16. See Sánchez, Ortiz, and Ruiz. The study on Aragón, which is still unpublished, has been carried out by Ester Casanova and José Luis Ledesma. For information on the "General Cause" as an instrument of denouncements used by the state, see Cenarro, "Violence," a study that was presented at the third Social Control Conference, Lisbon, in February 2000. On the impossibility of creating a legal system of denunciation in Nazi Germany, see Toro Muñoz 121–22. The best study to date on social control and the wretchedness of social relations in those years is Conxita Mir's *Vivir es sobrevivir*.

17. I am not aware of another document that is as unique, reliable, and heart-wrenching about denouncements and forgiveness as this one, though there exist many other testimonies that have been cited by specialists on the Civil War. See, for example, Bahamonde y Sánchez de Castro; Ruiz Villaplana. Also notable is the informative and thoughtful testimony of a former priest, Marino Ayerra Redín; see Ayerra Redín. All of these testimonies, as well as many other less relevant ones, the numerous monographs about the *franquista* repression, various published and unpublished studies about Aragón and La Rioja that I directed, my studies on the Civil War and anticlericalism, and documents that Conxita Mir, Francisco Espinosa, Julio Prada, and Carlos Gil provided me constituted the basic support for my book *La Iglesia de Franco*, some

of the arguments of which I give a brief summary here. I also used, for the part dedicated to the Civil War, the abundant documental information (especially that provided by the different Ecclesiastic Bulletins) found in Álvarez Bolado's *Para ganar la guerra, para ganar la paz: Iglesia y guerra civil: 1936–1939*. Hilari Raguer Suñer, one of the scholars who knows most about the Church during the war, has recently synthesized his studies in *La pólvora y el incienso*.

18. The complete comment by Martín Torrent about spiritual assistance to the prisoners is, "They, who are going to die, and we, who have not given the power to free them from their death on earth, can at least save them from eternal death" (Torrent 71).

19. The purging of the schools has been investigated by Francisco Morente in *La escuela y el estado nuevo*, from whose study I also have cited references to Ibáñez Martín; see Morente 110–12. For the case of Lugo, see Souto Blanco 304–17. The Church's influence on education in Spain is also treated in Guy Hermet's *Los católicos en la España franquista II*; see Hermet 148–52. On the reconstruction of the universities after the war, see especially Pasamar 19–85.

20. Citations are from Casanova, "España," a translation of the chapter that José Casanova dedicates to Spain in his book *Public Religions in the Modern World*, in which he performs a comparative analysis between the Catholic Church in Brazil and the Church in Poland. (There is a version in Spanish published by PPC, Madrid, in 2000.) Stanley G. Payne also studies those changes, the impact of Vatican II, and the dissidences in the Basque and Catalan Church dating from the sixties in *El catolicismo español* (242–48). See also Ruiz Rico; Botti; and Lannon. For the earlier years the following studies are useful: José Angel Tello Lázaro's *Ideología y política* and Javier Tusell's *Franco y los católicos*.

21. See also Lannon 130. Javier Tusell wrote some years ago that the Church, "more than Spanish society itself and much more than the politicians, should have known how to take the country down a path of reconciliation that would consist of peace, piety, and forgiveness that Azaña would have liked" ("La Iglesia" 47). This is an opinion directly in contrast with my assertions here, but on this theme, everything is a question of emphasis.

Grand Narratives, Collective Memory, and Social History

PUBLIC USES OF THE PAST IN POSTWAR SPAIN

Michael Richards

Those who, on the plea of narrating history, bustle about as judges, condemning

here and giving absolution there, because they think that this is the office of

history . . . are generally recognized as devoid of historical sense.

—Benedetto Croce, *History as the Story of Liberty* (1941)

It is possible to speak of a "crisis of memory" in contemporary Spain, although the term is not used here to suggest a fundamental breach of state legitimacy. The democratic principles of the Transition to democracy, symbolized in the 1978 Constitution, are almost unanimously seen as fundamental and legitimate (Edles). A decisive turning point appears to have been reached, however, in formulating or renegotiating a shared sense of the past in Spain. There remains a problem with the post-Franco transitional settlement. Although not systemic, the current situation revolves around aspects of community life, *convivencia*, and state-society relations, based on what we could label "social memory" around which broad social cohesion is established and reproduced. This conjuncture can be summed up by a feeling of suspense about the relationship of the past to the present. At the root of this problem is the fact that the Civil War of the 1930s and its repressive aftermath have not yet been effectively absorbed and understood as a collective experience through the availability of adequate public space for representing collective memories and the dissemination of multiple historical discourses. Efforts, therefore, to view the Transition as an unproblematic and foundational site of memory continue to provoke considerable resistance.

Reflecting on the particular problems posed by writing the history of the first half of the twentieth century, Julian Jackson has recently written, "This period is now undeniably the 'past' but it is close enough for our perspective on it to be constantly shifting. As we move away from the events, different parts of the landscape come into sharper relief; as we try to answer questions, the very questions themselves seem to change. This is true of all history writing, but especially of a period which still inhabits a twilight zone between history and memory" (1). For historians—working at a "scientific" level of usage of the past—the question is how to achieve the necessary critical distance from a period whose contested meanings are still part of contemporary political and social debates: How do historians operate from a vantage point *between* memory and history when recollections are still alive?[1]

There is also a "lower" level of use of the past, however, more public and more "popular," which seeks to propagate a common understanding of history (Pavone 74). This can be witnessed in the much-debated resurgence of public representations in Spain of memories of the Civil War since around the turn of the millennium. Forgetting was a key element of the peaceful Transition to democracy in the 1970s and 1980s, but the recent movement to recover memories in Spain has mounted a sustained critique of the social and political "amnesia" after Franco's death and has provoked some profound questioning of the democratic Transition as the founding myth of contemporary state legitimacy. These memories and representations have focused largely on individuals, their experiences of the war, and their suffering in the postwar period and have offered a corrective to a previous predominance of structures and ideologies in historical analysis. The dialectic between academic history and popular movements to recapture memories therefore constitutes a potentially instructive field of inquiry and raises questions about uses of the past in Spain.

Given the symbolism of the millennium, it was not coincidental that the Spanish crisis of memory became evident as the year 2000 drew closer. This reflection on the past was encouraged by other, more immediately political, global factors. With the collapse of Communism in 1989, and the seeming acceleration of historical changes, Europeans were exhorted to *remember* (Nora). In an ideological sense, the triumph of liberalism signaled "the end of history," so it was argued (Fukuyama). Post–Cold War triumphalism was heralded through the mass media, and a series of anniversaries toward the end of the last century encouraged the production and dissemination of images about the past. At the same time, historical consciousness was (and is) shaped by misinformation and misinterpretation, mediated as it is by commercial organs of mass information and other institutions that wield power. Many of these channels depend for their effectiveness on reducing the past to something politically usable.

More positively, the end of the East-West geopolitical and ideological conflict simultaneously opened up a range of possibilities for history based on collective identities that went beyond narrow political and national allegiances and that could be developed within civil society. The political purpose of the exhortations to remember that came from above has usually been obscured. There was some overlap with popular historical movements in the level of attention paid to a human rights agenda, for example. The global culture of memory, developed from above and below with great immediacy through the rapid exchange of information facilitated by technology, has had the effect of compressing or telescoping time: in various ways, historical imagination has been constrained by this sometimes overwhelming sense of presentism. In Spain, for example, the Civil War appears publicly as simultaneously an episode about which there is widespread ignorance and as a reality that shapes (in a usually ill-defined way) present-day experience. This problem is encouraged by oversimplified representations both of history and of people's complex memories. The danger in the public thirst for history as a product sponsored by the media, attempting to engage the collective emotions of its audience, is of a passive "surrender to history" (something "dead," or at least static, rather than dynamic) at the expense of any meaningful understanding of the past in relation to the present and future (Maier).[2]

Memories can be appreciated most effectively when placed within a framework informed by social historical methods and forms of reasoning. The myths surrounding the civil war—as manifestations of social memories—are integral to the social history of the conflict and its long aftermath.[3] The recent wave of publication, production, and dissemination of collective memories in Spain does not always address the question of social and cultural context by placing testimony and other traces of the past between memory and history. A history of ordinary experience might be able to say something about the relationship of barbarity to normality; it may begin to explore the rationality of wartime activities (including revolutionary gestures and the rituals of violence) by placing them in a broad context, avoiding moral judgment and condemnation, and offering an understanding, resting on empathy, as in Wilhelm Dilthey's historical philosophy of Verstehen (Ermath). Memories tend to have all manner of off-stage manifestations that may only rarely be expressed publicly. They require a sympathetic, empathetic analysis carried out in the light of the lived experience of the subject and the social and political texture of the time. Personal testimony has to be interpreted through attention to the use of language, moreover, and in the omissions and silences that can be as meaningful as seemingly more decisive spoken articulations (Portelli). This privileges subjective accounts, but it could be argued that such empathetic understanding, even when dealing with totalitarianism and its historical agents as well as the victims, has to precede any effective explanation.

The iconic status of the Spanish Civil War as a symbol of the conflictive twentieth century was bound to come under scrutiny as struggles for the ownership of the events of that century gathered pace. The legendary nature of the war has to do with a number of more specific factors. The war represented a pivotal moment as the last of the battles of a European civil war begun in 1917 and as curtain raiser to the broader conflagration that was to engulf the continent from September 1939. The notion of Spain as a battleground of ideas was reinforced by the presence of international volunteers, overwhelmingly for the Republic, who seemed to embody a sense of political self-sacrifice and idealism that post-1950s consumerist societies tend to view with some disbelief. There was also a romantic element to the way Spain was perceived by European intellectuals and others. Much of the poetic imagery envisioned Spain as a place not quite European, "that arid square" in W. H. Auden's phrase, "that fragment nipped off from hot Africa, soldered so crudely to inventive Europe" (213). The stereotype was of a people that alternated between bouts of great creativity and frenzies of religiously motivated emotion and irrationality.[4] These perceptions are naturally part of what historians are interested in: they are part of the story and can be viewed as significant social facts. As such, however, they cannot serve in themselves as historical interpretations. Much of current historical debate continues to some extent to be shaped by the myths of the war, making a plausible route between history and memory as a way to understanding the war and its aftermath more difficult to work out.

The concerns of *l'histoire du temps présent*, the significance of generations, the relationship of events to processes, the meaning of the term "contemporary history" are also useful here (Aróstegui). Following these concerns, and locating memory as part of social history, we can combine the social and cultural history of the Civil War—focusing particularly on the *experience* of conflict—with an account of the evolution of postwar memory (Ealham and Richards). The genuinely *Spanish* roots of the war, located in the rhythms of daily life and social change in the prewar decades, and the lived experience of the conflicts of the 1930s— as social revolution as well as military conflict—help us to identify the myths *as* myths and explain their lasting resonance. An account of the ways in which postwar social changes have shaped memories might help us to position the Civil War within the broad contours of Spain's recent past and assess its importance for current historical consciousness.

These are clearly complex problems, and there is only space here to look at a few definable cognate elements. Three areas in particular can be connected usefully. First, the epic-tragic grand narratives of the Civil War can effectively be reduced to three "big stories": religious crusade or holy war, class war analysis, and fratricidal struggle ("war between brothers").[5] Second, the resurgence of representations of memories of the war since 2000 can be seen as a popular challenge to each of these grand narratives and therefore, in some ways, as shaped *by them*. Third, we can compare both the mythical constructs and these popular challenges to the condition of current historical ("codified" or "scientific") practice on the Civil War.

In his 1975 memoir about a constrained middle-class life in Barcelona during the early postwar years of the 1940s, published in the year of General Franco's death, the poet and liberal publisher Carlos Barral discusses what the imposition of a dominant memory or meta-narrative of the war meant. At one point he writes,

> Not only were virtue and shame imposed, and orthodox thinking and fear of God, but all record of a different life was wiped from consciences. Nobody felt obliged to understand those who had been mistaken. All the older people I knew in those days had either lived under the wing of the Nationalist army or had suffered the unrepeatable privations and humiliations of the war. In my family any allusion to Republican relatives was scrupulously avoided: influential people who had shared our table and were now on the other side of the frontier or had committed suicide in some political prison, and everyone, including the maid servants, who the day before yesterday had shouted "*no pasarán*," took part in the enthusiasm for the new era and wrapped themselves in the folds of delirious religiosity. (18)

This short passage suggests several areas which are worth discussion. To begin, empiricists could object (and this is so often the case in the historiography of the Civil War) that, as a liberal intellectual, Barral was sympathetic to the Republic and the Left in general and that therefore his testimony constitutes a subjective and unreliable source. As we know, however, there are no neutral sources for history: written and other oral traces of the past document aspects of that past in a great variety of complex ways—not merely "left" and "right"—that need, in each case, to be explained. When speaking of "unrepeatable privations and humiliations" Barral is critically confronting the left-wing social revolution that accompanied the Civil War and its human consequences, an underdeveloped theme because it has always constituted the main target of the state's official story of crusade and martyrdom. Condemnation has made confronting the revolution as a problem of social history problematic except from the position of groups, parties, and classes that attempted to implement the revolutionary program for the destruction of the existing order.

The balance between remembering and forgetting is particularly problematic in the aftermath of revolutions and civil wars.[6] In such wars a gulf is placed between opposed concepts of "the nation" and ideas of legitimacy, of society and citizenship. As Barral again suggests, there is no easily definable temporal frontier between "war" and "peace," especially when there is no formal cease-fire, no peace treaty, and no intervention by an international peacemaking force. The war effort of the defeated and their sacrifices and grief are denied public expression and representation. There were no memorials to bestow honor upon the sacrificed of the Republic. Unlike the experience of veterans in a national war against an external enemy, there was no "homecoming" in Spain in 1939 for those who fought for the Spanish state even to the extent of war pensions for the widows (Vega). The "homecoming" for Republicans with the death of Franco in 1975 would be silent and without public recognition, because of the tacit agreement to forget the past, which was the price of the peaceful Transition to democracy. The recent movement to identify and recover some of the Republican dead from anonymous burial pits is motivated by a desire to dignify the dead precisely by bringing bodies "home."

The primary theme in this passage from Barral's *Años de penitencia* is the hegemonic Francoist memory of postwar Spain and the way this attempted to forge identity according to the moral spirit of the Nationalist war effort.[7] This official memory was imposed at great cost and aimed to reach into the private sphere. The wartime social revolution was accorded no social legitimacy and was portrayed as something foreign and merely as a crime. The human results of the revolution were to be publicized and crudely quantified to bolster the Franco regime's legitimacy, and the "sin" of revolution was used as a pretext for redemption through punishment (*Causa general*).[8] The Barral extract also suggests how, with Franco's victory, the revolutionary slogans were replaced by outwardly expressed signs of religious devotion. The atmosphere of fear had real effects on social relations and on memory: for one thing, morality and solidarity were undermined in the rush to demonstrate loyalty. Divisions were kept alive: for the victors, the material fruits of victory, and for those who were desperate, plenty of motives for denouncing neighbors. So great was the fear that, within families, the generations were divided: children could not be told about their parents' recent past because they might speak to others. Only through silence— and the sacrifice of identity and a sense of self—could people associated with the Republic be relatively sure of avoiding imprisonment or the purge of employment. Barral's central concern is therefore the highly complex way that authoritarian memory interacted with individuals' complicity, their willingness to conform and desire to forget in a context of dismantled social and political relations. People in Spain were "forgetting"—rationally—long before the Transition to democracy.

GRAND NARRATIVES: CRUSADE, CLASS WAR, FRATRICIDAL CONFLICT

It is possible to unravel the web that knits together our myriad images of the Spanish war from what we refer to vaguely as "memory," "history," "nostalgia," "amnesia," and "forgetting" by exploring the grand narratives that have dominated public collective understanding for so long. These "great stories"—crusade, class war, fratricidal struggle—can be explored doctrinally, politically, and culturally. In other words, they were simultaneously ideological, mobilizing, and expressive of certain collective sentiments. This last point, to do with culture (collective mentalities, feelings, perceptions) and the ways historical actors understood what was happening around them and related events to prewar customs, shared ideas, and everyday life, has been largely neglected historiographically. These aspects are difficult to reduce to merely a part of the battle, whether military or political, but, because they are to do with group identities, are essential elements of the ways in which people *remember* the war.

Like all grand narratives, the "great stories" of the Civil War have been assigned labels (Berkhofer). Indeed "civil war" is a label that itself requires explanation, since both sides during the war sought scrupulously to avoid employing the term. Personal testimonies, the wartime press and official internal communications in both zones, and eyewitness reports of various kinds all indicate that ordinary people used other terms than *"guerra civil"* to describe the conflict. This is not the first such war where this has been the case: many people tended to speak simply of *"la guerra"* because it affected them primarily as bodily and psychological hardship, hunger and illness, and loss (of loved ones, of lives, and of a day-to-day sense of equilibrium), rather than primarily as something narrowly political. The main concerns were work, food, and the well-being of home and family. For some groups of people, particularly activists and militants of leftist organizations, the conflict was "*la revolución*"; others saw things in broadly similar terms, though they would be less obviously political and talk of the conflict as "the rising of the people against the *señoritos*" (Martínez-Alier).

Religious Crusade

Throughout the war and for some twenty years thereafter, the Nationalists and Francoists presented the conflict as a "crusade" against Bolshevism in defense of Christian civilization—an authoritarian remedy to "anarchic chaos" and the eradication of "agitators." The Franco regime then integrated this political Holy War against "Communist atheism" into a broader notion of religious crusade. By August 1936 the antiliberal rhetoric of Catholic traditionalism, exemplified by the Carlists of Navarra, which had the idea of a religious crusade at its heart, had been adopted by the embryonic Nationalist state (Caspístegui; Cruz). Spain, embodied ascetically by the rebel generals and their sacrifices, had received a sacred mission from God to battle against Communism, those "without God" and the "Judeo-Masonic conspiracy." In the postwar era Franco would become the preeminent repository of this official remembering of the war. The struggle—allegedly for freedom from Soviet imperialism—was imagined as a replaying of the centuries-long reconquest from Islam. The remarkable temporal distillation of this image seemed only to intensify its resonance—at least for those who wished to believe—as a universally abstract symbol of "good" combating (and even transforming) "evil." Franco relied on thousands of North African soldiers who, in fighting his crusade "against Godlessness," became "Christianised" (Balfour 279–85). Anti-Islamic sentiment was therefore played down, but the centuries-old myth of the Moorish threat lay at the root of the construction of the "Communist menace" as a modern-day Eastern plague. The officially prescribed position in the 1950s and for some part of the 1960s therefore portrayed the wartime Republic simply as a proto-Stalinist monolith and its leaders as willing collaborators in a project to establish a Spanish Soviet satellite.[9]

The anti-Communist crusade narrative is not quite dead. In the wake of the collapse of the Communist Eastern bloc, there has been a wave of post–Cold War triumphalist history—not at all restricted to accounts of Spain's past—that revived the argument that the rebellion of the generals in 1936 had been staged in order to prevent a Soviet takeover of Spain. There has been some overlap here between a minority academic history and equally tendentious but more media-friendly, politically oriented production. Some accounts have appeared in "popular" editions aimed at a mass market.[10]

The popularity of the anti-Communist crusading discourse requires further research, but there seems little doubt about the mobilizing potential of the religious crusade narrative that obscured the social roots of the war and impeded a sociological analysis of its origins (Southworth, *El mito*). The social dimensions of the war have only gradually and partially been recovered, being largely reduced to quantifying the physical violence and repression.

The adoption of the rhetoric of holy war was suggested by the episcopacy of the Church, arguing with some legitimacy in the face of the great anticlerical purge in the summer of 1936 that the existence of religion was at stake (Gomá, "Report"; Raguer Suñer, *La pólvora*).[11] This was the simple duality portrayed in historical textbooks of the postwar era (Cámara Villar).[12] It is not surprising that many Spanish children grew up believing that "*la guerra de España*" was fought by Spaniards against foreigners: Julián Grau Santos (born in 1937), for example, recalled how "gradually it was instilled in me and I always believed that Spain had won the war against foreign enemies of our historic greatness" (Borràs Betriu 481).

The many rituals and ceremonies in honor of those killed in combat for the Nationalists contributed to the patriotic and religious crusade against atheism so that there was an ideological and representational symbiosis between religion and war. This can be seen in illustrated form in the official published history of the war, the multivolume *Historia de la Cruzada*, assembled by Joaquín Arrarás and published between 1939 and 1941. To an extent this military-religious symbiosis occurs in most wars because there is a need for mourning and commemoration of those who have been sacrificed. Many people, like the servants of the family Barral, participated for appearance's sake, but there was also an important social and cultural element to the crusade that revolves around the notion of popular faith and religiosity (Richards, "'Presenting'"). The myth resonated because it related to popular perceptions and needs. The reestablishing of crucifixes in schoolrooms as part of the process of Francoist "liberation" was an opportunity for popular devotional rituals in strongly Catholic Castile and Navarre. The sentiment was inculcated from childhood. The front page of the *Diario de Navarra* on September 1, 1936, showed a picture of a teacher in Pamplona kissing a large crucifix in front of rapt rows of small children.

Class War

The great political mobilization of the 1930s in Spain reflected both an evolving set of class relations and a variety of other tensions, contradictions, and collective claims, based on community, neighborhood, gender, etc. Unlike interstate wars, which are essentially territorial, civil wars are social wars—they are like revolutions and have important determining social and cultural features. At the same time as expressing class divisions, each side draws on a range of social referents in order to demonize the other as "antinational"; one reason why the term "civil war" was avoided by the wartime protagonists was for fear of legitimizing the "foreign" enemy. The political authorities played on this sense of "invasion" and made the "invading" threat seem very personal because winning minds was more important than gaining territory (Núñez Seixas). Both sides therefore used the vocabulary of the *guerra de liberación nacional* as part of the rhetoric of mobilization for the fight. The Nationalists adopted this habit as part of the "crusade" strategy; the Republicans did so in an attempt to unite their disparate political forces. The Spanish Communist Party (PCE), following the line insisted upon by Moscow, wanted desperately to bring the working class together with sections of the middle classes and, therefore, to suppress the social revolution.

Nonetheless, the response to the military rebellion in July 1936 took a revolutionary form, and the land and factories were seized throughout large parts of the country. In Andalusia more than 100,000 landworkers seized control of some 500,000 hectares of land, in a process justified by the slogan "the land for those who work it" (Bernal 147). The hunt for collaborators of the "Fascist" rebels presaged the wave of murderous anticlerical violence. After the war, many political activists remembered the conflict as *"la revolución,"* while others who were not integrated into labor organizations remained ambivalent as to whether the war-revolution had been won or lost. Oral testimonies suggest that amid the hunger of the immediate postwar years it seemed to many as if they had never had much to win or lose in the first place.

Class analysis offered a "scientific" framework of explanation that seemed to be reinforced by the class oppression of the postwar dictatorship. Because the dictatorship was so labor repressive, much of the social history writing in the post-Francoist era focused on a narrow understanding of social class and on the workers' movement and encouraged rather simplistic functionalist accounts. The PCE, highly influential in intellectual circles, kept doggedly to theoretical orthodoxy (Claudín). The class enemy was deemed unworthy of historical analysis, and so the relational sense of the role of social class in history went unappreciated.

While class identity has not played much of a role in the recent upsurge of collective memory, several other forms of collective identity that were visible during and after the war have also only been vaguely discussed. Aside from Catalanism and Basqueness, the identity bound up with the "recovery of historical memory" has curiously been reduced to *Republican* identity. This is probably because social class is a less meaningful category, but also because Republican identity can be relatively all-encompassing and neutral, democratic, and vaguely non-ideological. Popular history finds negotiating multiple identities rather difficult, partly because of the political imperatives that push a single identity to the foreground.

Fratricidal Struggle

Because of the need for eventual reconciliation (without blame), civil wars are apt in the end to be constructed as "fratricidal" (a "brother against brother" struggle) that, in theory, helps to rejoin the divided society, though there is normally an intervening period of triumphalist repression. The problem in Spain, as recent movements to recover memories make clear, has been the balance between truth and reconciliation, because for two decades the Republic was officially blamed for the war through a highly tendentious narrative.

The official discourse on the war in Spain as fratricidal had a political function that met several regime demands in the 1960s. A strategy was adopted for the official normalization of history alongside the economic normalization of 1959–1964, which had been ushered in with the Stabilization Plan, producing delayed participation in European postwar mass consumption. The regime was attempting to keep pace with social change and generational evolution, not by liberating history but by devising a set of methodological norms for its production. This state strategy was implicitly historical since it played down the mythical time of the crusade discourse and called on a quasi–social history framework instead—although, for the most part, this was *not* the social history of the Civil War but that of the much less controversial nineteenth century. Manuel Fraga, the dictatorship's minister of information in the 1960s and professor of political science in Madrid, sought to demonstrate publicly, for example, how Spain had become modern during the early nineteenth century, following the Napoleonic invasion of 1808, and that this modernity could no longer be denied 150 years later.[13] In effect, Fraga was relativizing the place of the 1930s Civil War in Spain's past and placing it within a broader process of change (Fraga Iribarne 7–8).

The state bureaucrat-cum-historian Ricardo de la Cierva, himself a child of the war and whose father was killed during the conflict, was charged with renovating the official history and memory of the war through his post in Fraga's ministry. The by now burdensome label of the "crusade" was to be replaced with less epic terms such as *"la guerra de España," "la guerra española,"* and so on. The notion of the *guerra de liberación nacional* passed out of usage more gradually than the "crusade" and was stubbornly maintained even as the term "civil war," suggestive of some sense of internal bipolarity, finally became more officially acceptable and formed the basis for future, general perceptions. In this modernizing or forward-looking narrative, where the past is not confronted, a link can be made, for example, to the form of historical memory cultivated by the Partido Popular in power from 1996 to 2004, which largely provoked the current crisis of memory in Spain.

A more sober historical apparatus was constructed, relying on the state's domination of documentation—there were still no public archives. Empirical method was hoisted as justification in this normative version of history, and "the facts" were ordered and scripted by regime insiders (such as Larrazábal). Cierva became a great champion of "history" (though the shift could alternatively be seen as one from myth to propaganda), which is defined by methodological objectivity and empiricism, though the epistemological-ideological problems of empiricism were naturally bypassed completely. His "facts" were selected "through a balanced evaluation," and his "judgments were supported by verifiable facts" (Cierva, Dedicatoria). The officially sanctioned monopoly of primary sources by state officials effectively denied access and public expression of a great mass of "truths" that were not to be argued about and contested within civil society. For a while, during the 1980s, this left something of a fetishism of facts as a legacy in the post-Franco era as a product of an understandable desire to expose "what actually happened."

In answer to a question about the meaning and consequences in 1970 of the Civil War, Cierva maintained that July 18 had been the foundational moment of the Francoist state and society. At the same time, he did not advocate turning back the clock; the Alzamiento Nacional was "a point of departure, never a reference point for moving backwards" (Borràs Betriu 56). Significantly, Cierva's comments implicitly referred to the official version of history—how the war had been inserted into Spanish "traditions"; he did not address broader society's understanding of the past, which might well have challenged such assumed "traditions." Thus the significance of complex notions such as tradition and historic consciousness remained highly ambiguous: "The civil war is in the foundations and the structures of Spanish tradition. . . . The war cannot be wrenched from our past precisely because it *is* our past; it cannot be wrenched from our present because it lives within our tradition. Where I think it should never be is in our future, in the form of a reality or in the form of fear" (Borràs Betriu 55).[14]

In spite of this history work undertaken under control of the state, understanding the causes and nature of the war could hardly have been advanced very much. A vagueness that spoke about "the tragedies of the past," "collective madness," and "fratricidal struggle" seemed merely to conjure up an elemental naturalism to replace the crusading essentialism of the 1940s and 1950s, so that the war became something like a devastating earthquake, epidemic, or some other natural disaster. The 1960s myth of the economic miracle perfectly complimented the fratricidal conflict narrative: the "Spanish tragedy" could be forgotten as it became engulfed in the consumerism that was the basis for the celebrations of Franco's "25 years of peace" in 1964 (Junta Interministerial). By 1970, the director of publications at the Ministry of Information, Jesús Unciti Urniza, was able to declare, unofficially, that "development and demystification" had produced "citizens who are greatly sensitized to the value of peace and respectful of divergent attitudes"—and, he might *pact of silence* have added, not interested in digging up the past (Borràs Betriu 98).

Following the death of Franco in 1975, reconciliation was consummated—by silence—in order to avoid a violent rupture. The consensual strategy for peaceful Transition was an extension of the theory of fratricidal struggle, becoming the basis for the tacit pact of forgetting in the 1970s and 1980s (Aguilar Fernández, *Memory*). This would also have an effect on the writing of history. History was not confronted, let alone conquered—the official version appeared to be accepted for the sake of peace, but this was tantamount to ignoring history. People were reluctant to ask difficult questions about the recent past for fear of jeopardizing the restoration of liberal-democracy. Political and social explanation of the war was eliminated from public debate. No particular social or political group was to carry the moral responsibility for the war or the postwar repression. The "war as collective madness" thesis (a representation still bearing some resemblance to the "crusade" imagery) seemed generally to be accepted—all Spaniards were somehow to blame.[15] The postwar sense of shame over the Civil War, regularly mentioned in oral testimonies from the 1970s, although partly imposed as an effect of dictatorship, was often expressed in terms of a failure of the wartime generation, a collective category more or less undifferentiated in some memories by concepts of ideological differences, social class, or religious alignment. Thus, vacuous psychological characteristics to do with the "hot bloodedness" or inherent "badness" of Spaniards suppressed personal and public memories and, at the same time, provided no basis for a historical interpretation of the Civil War (Reig Tapia).

THE RETURN OF MEMORY AND "POPULAR HISTORY"

The movement for the recovery of memory and the questions historians would want to pose about it can only be addressed in the context of the grand narratives that have been discussed above, precisely because

they were largely imposed "from above": the old grand narratives—
the demonizing crusade that pretended the Republic had enjoyed no
social support and the "brother against brother" narrative that normalized history to fit with economic development and to silence all
dissident versions of the past—are now being publicly or implicitly
criticized. Although historical methods have not been dwelt upon—
scientific legitimacy is conferred to an extent by the participation of forensic archeologists—the process of the recovery of memory has therefore been important. It is driven by a range of significant concerns that
reflect a relatively new historical agenda, which is personal, humanitarian, and political and, perhaps inevitably, reflects very present concerns. This recovery also potentially offers some relief from relentless political history—defined narrowly—by the partisans of Left and
Right.

The recent manifestations of collective memory focus largely on individuals and their suffering, a sign of a move from the history of collectivities and structures toward individuals and human agency. Academic historians have been placed in a position of addressing a much
broader circle of consumers than they are accustomed to. Several issues
arise for historians. There is some risk of narrowing the necessary critical distance that Julian Jackson alluded to in identifying the particular problems of writing the history of events still (just) within living
memory. The issue of whether history can be simultaneously rigorous
and compatible with modern mass media represents an important problem that is addressed elsewhere in this volume.

The stories of lives in penal labor detachments, concentration camps,
soldiers "missing in action," and "disappeared" children—told through
books, memoirs, TV documentaries (as investigative journalism and personal testimony), and internet exchanges—constitute a form of popular history and are, perhaps, a channel toward "history from below."[16]
The stories of anonymous mass burial sites, the *fosas comunes* resulting
from Francoist political executions, which have been written about by
Spanish and foreign journalists, emerged in the year 2000 and have
been the most dramatic manifestations of the upsurge in memories
of the war. A process of recovery, recording conversations with townspeople, and collecting their old photographs has begun, in spite of many
people's reluctance to speak about the subject of the war and the repres-

sion (Silva Barrera and Macías; Armengou and Belis, *Las fosas*). There has, therefore, been some attempt to place suffering within a context of life histories and evolving social relations.

This popular recovery of memory is not, however, without problems. The revelatory style of some of the published accounts has encouraged publishers eager to profit from the exercise, and political conservatives, whose version of the past is under attack, have retaliated by resurrecting lurid anti-Communist tales that are also taken up with alacrity by certain publishing houses (for example, Moa, *El derrumbe*). The unquestioned moral clarity pushed to the forefront by both sides, in the context of a rather low level of general historical consciousness in society, can be unsettling and tends, in effect, to perpetuate the long story of competing versions from Left and Right.

Academic history cannot claim to own the past, and it is worth posing the difficult question of who should be granted sufficient authority to represent the past in modern democratic society. Much of what has recently been revealed is valuable, but there is not much sense of moving forward in terms of historical understanding (in the sense meant by Dilthey), which is a pity because popular history reaches a mass audience. This audience, in general, has a rather diffused awareness of the past and does not have the benefit of the historian's vantage point. Much of the discourse of the recent upsurge of memory revolves around concepts such as "atrocities," "war crimes," and "crimes against humanity," for example—categories that are difficult to fit within the conventions recognized by academic history. Some of the recent work by professional historians has seemed to take the bipolar framework and the explanatory category of "crimes" for granted and has neglected the social and broadly historical context of events.

PERSONAL NARRATIVES AND POSTWAR SOCIAL CHANGE: MEMORY AND SOCIAL HISTORY

The sense of recovering *historical* memory is underlined by the focus on the Second Republic and memories of social life and culture in the 1930s. History potentially has something important to say about the period in relation to people's internalization and assimilation of ideologies.

In relation to this, the current movement for memory has given life to a progressive tradition of the 1930s that had no voice during the dictatorship. The intensity of cultural and political activities during these years—the often festive atmosphere that pushed for a popularization of "the political"—has been recalled in many post-Franco testimonies. A woman from Málaga who was in her twenties during the years of the Republic affirmed, for example, that the Republic changed customs, people had more open minds, there was a rapid intensification; one could tell in the way people expressed themselves: in communication between individuals, people spoke more and about more things, about politics; when there were informal meetings in the canteen, women went along too (González Castillejo 427).

With the end of the Cold War—and the potential for reducing the influence of political ideologies over Civil War history—there has been an opportunity to return to such social and cultural perspectives. The insights of cultural anthropology and oral history suggest that "ordinary" people in the past can be understood "in the light of their own experience and their own reactions to that experience": history from below (Sharpe 26). Oral history has an indispensable role in integrating "ordinary" experience, moving away from formal politics and structuralism toward the war's lived effects, toward human agency and the rhythms of social life over decades, though the results are not without limitations (Fraser).

Memory has therefore to be a part of social history and the term "social memory" can be applied to the ways in which representations of the past have been articulated, spoken about, constructed, and understood (Fentress and Wickham). Reconstruction of the past takes place within an evolving present. The ways in which memories of the war and repression influenced social behavior in Spain since 1939 is an essential part of postwar history. There is a meaningful relationship, therefore, between the period of instability of the 1930s and 1940s and the migration and development of the 1950s and 1960s, a period, in turn, that relates to the Transition to democracy, and so on. Postwar social change can be charted as a continuum in which the focus is on lived experience and memories—parts of the story make more sense in the context of the whole.

Some examples may be explored in order to illustrate this point. Four channels of social disruption in the 1940s and 1950s affected (and were affected *by*) the production and flow of memory. First, the physical, cultural, and political dismantling of communities of solidarity and shared ideas associated with the Left and the Second Republic as a direct result of the Civil War and state-led repression in its aftermath. Second, there was an important social or "informal" aspect to the repression: acts carried out or assisted by "ordinary people" and based on a complex mixture of fear and revenge and the struggle to survive by "accommodating" the new official mentality and its ideological and clientalist networks, especially in the countryside and provinces. Third, the black market in the 1940s, which dominated everyday economic life, was often class-based, coercive, and exploitative and increased hunger, suffering, and levels of polarization. But the unofficial market operated on many levels, and new relationships were established in a quiet (and illegal) struggle for survival—many revolving around women. This was a form of resistance (using the term in the sense that a body might be *resistant* to a disease, rather than as collective public mobilization). The black market upset previous practices and patterns. By necessity it was based on individuals rather than groups and disruptive of former social networks and of postwar social solidarity.

The fourth area—mass migration—is particularly significant in terms of the evolution of memory and society in the late 1950s and 1960s. Long before the Transition to democracy there was, in effect, a social and psychological Transition "from below" in Spain that contributed substantially to the conversion of defeat into what the dictatorship labeled the "economic miracle." Collective resignation—well-practiced endurance of poverty—sublimated the end of revolutionary hopes and military and political defeat. Migration to the cities was provoked by the reversal of 1930s attempted land reform as, for example, landowners ("the victors") took land out of cultivation. Energy, expressed in material sacrifices, was diverted toward silent work, auto-didacticism, the family, and urban migration at any cost. This amounted to the sacrifice of one generation in the interests of the next and has been lost in the current debate about historical memory. The 1950s and 1960s saw millions of lives cut in two by migration or emigration as people sought a sustainable life—enough to eat, relatively secure employment, and shelter. Mass migration led to a process of cultural destructuration as a consequence of this demographic activity. A social history of the "miracle" would therefore include an assessment of the felt effects and social costs of forced mobility and the shift to consumerism and the consequences of this process for collective memories.

A nomadic existence provoked by war and its aftermath, and the liquidation of working-class organizations, meant that cultural ties were undone by factors like these: pressure on gender relations (the predominance of women in the migratory process); cultural difference (sociologists were shocked at the condition of country people in the 1950s, physically aged by privations and hard labor); old customs integrating with the radio and mass media; advertising; consumption patterns; a mix of self-sacrifice, solidarity, withdrawal into the self, etc. In the process, memory itself was sacrificed—and the next generation had aspirations directed at the future rather than at looking back.

In the place of amnesia the notion of "resignation" seems better to sum up a sense of the popular classes taking stock realistically of the scale of the defeat represented by the Civil War and the failure of the revolution, the losses it entailed (breaking the myth of "the land for those who work it"), and what this meant in terms of new directions. This was no surrender, and the term "resignation" is not used in a negative sense to infer passivity. Instead, it implies a wholesale political disillusionment, but also a conscious and active decision by millions of people (many of them migrants) to take on painful sacrifices in the interests of generations to come. This was social and cultural reproduction in the aftermath of and in the face of the worst defeat imaginable.

CONCLUSIONS

The problem of historical memory has become more evident as historians and others have attempted to reconcile the resurgence of memory with history—though this is obviously *not* an issue of accuracy or "bias" and whether memories are "true" or not. The originating source of the problem has to do with the polarization created by civil wars and revolutions and the nature and longevity of the dictatorship that appropriated

Spain's war—the regime's official construction of "historical memory."
Representation of the war as a *guerra fratricida* left a great deal buried
deep in the collective psyche, particularly the painful experiences of
individuals and families. What is remembered is affected by what happens to people's lives in the years between the event and the recollection.
It is therefore the process of thinking historically (of recognizing the
significance of change over time) that allows a multiplicity of memories
to be heard rather than to be resubmerged within such catch-all concepts as "the memory of the defeated" or "Republican memory."

Memory and history can be distinguished as different though overlapping forms of recovering the past. "History" suggests a methodo-
logically codified practice that, though not epistemologically unproblematic, is aimed at a value-free enquiry into processes in the past. "Memory"
presents greater difficulties because of its close relationship to such partial terms as "tradition," "nostalgia," and "progress." At the same time,
the formation of human collective attachments to myths and the shaping of subjectivity do themselves take place *through time* and potentially
tell us a lot about the construction of social groups in the past and in the
present. *Historical memory,* lately referred to as a "given," can, as a category of analysis, be situated *between* history and memory. The same can
be said of "social memory": memories placed within an explanatory
framework of historical knowledge—a framework concerned with the
process of change over time and the relationship of this change to the
causes of other processes and events and ways of life. The transmission
of memories is therefore a vital part of social history.

In order to evaluate the recent popular challenge to the established
narratives of the war—"crusade," "class war," "fratricidal struggle" (all
of them products of "presentist" political needs)—it is necessary to understand the process by which the narratives were produced and evolved
(for example, the evolution of the "crusade" construct into the "fratricidal struggle" image). Dismantling them is the task of historians *and*
broader movements for the recovery of memory.

The upsurge in memory since the end of the millennium has also to
be analyzed in relation to the civil, political, and cultural communities
in which it has arisen. Politics can be understood here as something
broader than official or party activities; popular initiatives in mobilizing
memory can be seen as political in several ways, but the range of ways in

which public use is made of the past (for example, in the construction and reconstruction of collective identities) also needs to be considered.

Within the interstices of the "great" ideological narratives and the claims of informal civil society groups and associations and those of "popular" media (commercialized) history, it is possible to discuss the place of social and cultural history and efforts to register claims for the historicization of the Civil War, drawing together remnants of the past in an account that is structured in some way. Postwar memory has therefore been embedded in social and cultural change and can only be charted effectively as a unified, intergenerational, social process rather than as disembodied political "moments" on the way to "progress."

Collective memories in Spain cannot be properly understood, therefore, without accounting for the totality of postwar experience. The way in which the Civil War years and the early years of the dictatorship are currently remembered fragments the unity of the Spanish twentieth-century past, which can, in fact, be reconstructed through the methods of social history.

The process of change from memory to history is complex and not unilinear. It is affected by influences other than the passage of time. Memory has a public use that is liable to be recycled over centuries, though there may, as Jackson argues, be particular difficulties for historians of the first half of the twentieth century. Shared memory may be observed within social relations and "normal" practices, particularly in an authoritarian context. Collective attitudes, the shaping of work and material conditions, relationships to the environment (everyday life is above all *situated,* and hundreds of thousands of people in Spain moved from place to place in the period from the 1950s to the 1970s), and the realm of family and private life were shaped by what was remembered of the hopes and trauma of the 1930s and 1940s. Recent research on the era of the war suggests that memory was inscribed upon bodies, within families, and in shaping a sense of the self. The field of social relations under scrutiny needs, therefore, to be broad, incorporating not only social classes or incipient nations but also generations, neighborhoods, families, and gender.

There is, perhaps, a price to be paid for focusing on subjectivity and the landscapes of memory. In critiquing what he perceives as the "moral" rather than analytical or structural narrative of the twentieth century that "continues to transfix intellectuals and the public alike," Charles S. Maier assesses the price rather well (albeit in the context of thoughts about the Jewish Holocaust and the Gulag): "With its 'moving chords of memory,' the locations of history tug at our heartstrings and allow us to debate endlessly over museums and memorials while accepting—whether realistically or from exhaustion, depending on the perspective of the observer—the continuing limits on public-policy responses to social problems" (829). Paradoxically, the current ahistorical approach to collective memory in Spain—focusing in isolation on the crimes of Francoism—also tends to weaken any argument suggesting continuity between those who hold power in Spain today and those who benefited from victory in 1939.

It is impossible to argue against the process of unearthing memories of the Civil War in Spain: though full of problems, the process of popular reclaiming seems both necessary and inevitable. Historians should not condemn such movements but confront them critically (being aware of the entrepreneurship connected to some of them). Popular history may well enrich or call into question the overly intellectualized offerings of professional historians.

The problem of the relationship between professional history and the cultural historical media—and the relationship of both of these to memory—is highly significant in the age of global communications. Just as history as a way of knowing is being questioned by postmodern thinking, public history is ever burgeoning with seemingly boundless self-confidence. There is a strong case, therefore, for more public activity by historians—*as social historians*—who want to understand people in the past on their own terms and constructively complicate popular images of the past, looking for ambiguities and contradictions—rather than, as Benedetto Croce warned, wanting to act as judges or to make political propaganda.

NOTES

1. This has been one of the questions that has motivated the movement for *l'histoire du temps présent* (history of the present), begun in France in the late 1970s.

2. Maier summarizes Lutz Niethammer on this point.

3. Maritain, writing in the 1930s, warned that "social memory and imagination naturally cause one's intelligence to run the risk of anachronistic ideation" (30).

4. Auden served as a stretcher-bearer for the Republic and wrote "Spain" in April 1937.

5. François Godicheau makes useful observations on the "naming" of the civil war.

6. We know this from the case of Ireland, South Africa, Argentina, Chile, etc. See, for example, Roniger and Sznajder.

7. See, for example, the preamble to the Law of Political Responsibilities (February 1939) defining how tribunals—composed of soldiers, judges, and Falangists—in hearing political cases would "bring to their activities a tone similar to that which inspires the Movement" (Díaz-Llanos y Lecuona).

8. The fourth edition of *Causa general* appeared unchanged as late as 1961 through the Dirección General de Información.

9. For Franco's own anti-Communism and the Francoist propaganda campaign based on forged "secret documents," allegedly proving that the Spanish Communist Party (PCE) was plotting to seize control on the eve of the military revolt in July 1936, see Southworth, *Conspiracy*.

10. See Payne, *Spanish Civil War*. For a corrective, see Skoutelsky. For media-oriented, political accounts, see Romano; Ruiz Portella; and Moa, *El derrumbe* 109–23, 387–407. See also the editorial commentary in Radosh et al.

11. See also the influential pastoral letter "The Two Cities" (Sept. 30, 1936) by Enrique Pla i Deniel, the bishop of Salamanca who would succeed Gomá as primate in 1940; the letter is reproduced in Montero Moreno 688–708. For a contemporary Catholic critique of the concept of holy war, see Maritain.

12. There were also a large number of books and pamphlets produced by the Falangist Movimiento and its organizations for women and youth, the SF and the Frente de Juventudes, as well as courses on *formación política* (instruction in political matters) and *formación familiary y social* (instruction in social and family matters—for women and girls), most of which included sections about Franco and the war.

13. Before becoming minister, Fraga was professor at Madrid University and director of the Instituto de Estudios Políticos.

14. See Cierva, Dedicatoria i. Cierva's claim that *Historia de la guerra civil española* was the first book to use the term "civil war" in its title is in line with the new official nomenclature and possibly signifies some kind of claim to definitive status. See also Cierva, Dedicatoria xv–xvi; and Borràs Betriu 55–56.

15. The notion of a "mental sickness" and the pathologization of revolution were also significant elements of the war *at the time,* either because of the desperation of the situation (as in the case of the final reflections of the philosopher Miguel de Unamuno—see Feal, especially 51, which is cited in Godicheau

138–39—or for propagandistic motives to divert attention from the social origins and dimensions of the war; see Richards, "Morality."

16. A recent addition to the historiography of the Civil War in the Republican zone claims to be a "social history" of the conflict, which is also concerned with "the personal" and "ordinary experience" and with a critique of the "Great Man" view of history. See Seidman. The work is seriously undermined, however, by an a priori reductive framework of "individualism" that, in fact, shows no interest at all in subjective experience and that goes so far as to suggest that there are *no* social relations beyond the naked pursuit of individual interests.

PART II

Documentary Filmmaking

and the Recovery of Historical Memory

"El documental es un arma cargada de pasado"

REPRESENTATION IN DOCUMENTARY AND TESTIMONY

Anne E. Hardcastle

In her essay in this section, Jo Labanyi points to a curious contradiction in the recent attention to the *pacto de olvido* regarding the Civil War and Francoist past that occurred during the Spanish Transition to democracy. This pact of silence or oblivion has been constructed as "fact" precisely through the process of denouncing it. Frequent references to the *pacto de olvido* in the last six years have somewhat paradoxically transformed its secret or forgotten nature. To whatever extent it was (or even still is) practiced by members of the Spanish government, media, and populace during the last quarter of the twentieth century, the new millennium has seen a flood of interest in opening up the pact and discovering or, as Labanyi suggests with insightful yet disquieting accuracy, constructing whatever has been concealed by it. Breaking the silence about the past, numerous and varied materials— from documentary films to testimonial novels—related to recovering the lost memories of the Civil War and Francoist era have flourished in the once barren landscape of national recollection. Such revisitations of traumatic national history can be compared to opening up a forgotten tomb and discovering whatever past

---

My title is a deliberate play on Gabriel Celayas's poem "La poesía es un arma cargada de futuro."

secrets it contains. Of course, this metaphor has been carried out literally in the location and excavation of Franco's mass graves.

Arguably, the mass graves are the most compelling aspect of a larger project of historical memory recovery in Spain today. However, this memory work, including that associated with the mass graves, forms the crux of two approaches to the past, one of discovery and one of construction, both essential and inseparable from the process of history. As Gina Herrmann points out in her chapter, corpses possess a certain dynamism that animates the public. Unlike talking-head testimonies or even archival records, corpses are present as visual evidence in a way that demands attention. And yet a corpse in itself has no readily available meaning. Contexts must be constructed to give it a time, place, cause of death, or significance. Here is where the mass graves become a central—because so very visible—point in a larger concern over not only *whether* the past be remembered but, more importantly, *how* to remember its violence and repression.

In our media-savvy age, when image is everything, it is not surprising that documentary film has become a flashpoint in the memory war, arising from varying views on how the Spanish past should be remembered. Different from the treatment of mass graves from the perspectives of psychology, criminal justice, or even traditional history, documentaries move the phenomenon into the cultural sphere and, more than any other field, make it available to a large community of potential viewers. Such documentary films shown on television may be the first exposure many people have to this controversial subject. Following Derrida, Herrmann links television spectatorship to the political through questions about how images have been made, who has chosen them, and with what relationship to ideological positions. This link between viewing and politics returns inexorably to the conjunction of discovery and construction when recovering the past—bringing forth new information, new images of historical reality, and yet simultaneously constructing a context in which those images are to be understood.

In his book *Representing Reality: Issues and Concepts in Documentary*, Bill Nichols notes that despite their appeal to realism and truth claims, documentaries are equally enmeshed in ideological conflicts that determine their central arguments. "What counts as a realistic representation of the historical world," he observes, "is not a simple matter of progress toward a final form of truth but of struggles for power and authority within the historical arena itself" (33). Still, the ideological power play at work in documentary does not counteract the reality of experiences and consequences in the world: "Material practices occur that are not entirely or totally discursive, even if their meanings and social value are" (Nichols 109). Documentary is grounded in these material practices and produces images that uncover new dimensions of our social, historical, economic, and cultural reality. At the same time, the context constructed for understanding those images shapes the interpretation of their meaning in the "real" world. The problem of interpreting the real, inherent to documentary and testimony, has convulsed the Spanish public in its search for appropriate, just, and meaningful ways to represent the Civil War and Francoist past.

The documentaries and testimonies studied here are cultural products constructed through discursive and filmic practices, and, consequently, are only representations of the past. "Representation" has become a somewhat suspicious word through its postmodern association with simulacra, performance, and replication of an eternally displaced and inaccessible real world. Nichols does not deny that documentaries are representations of the real world, and yet he argues for a more comprehensive understanding of representation. "Representation" also refers to the act of standing in for others and acting on their behalf—the basis of representative, democratic government (111). Furthermore, "to represent" is to place facts before others in the making of a case, "especially to convey a particular view or impression of the matter" (OED, qtd. in Nichols 111). These additional functions of representation are as important, if not more so, in nonfiction texts whose significance resides in appeals to social justice. The three essays of this chapter never lose sight of who is being represented by recent documentaries and testimonies of repression and what case is being made on their behalf. Their critiques of some texts arise particularly when the interests of those depicted are not respected—not represented adequately, fairly, or authentically. These authors' concern with how the past is remembered or constructed in these texts intersects directly with how well they achieve a just representation, in all senses of the word, of the victims of the Civil War and Francoist period.

In 2002, 2003, and 2004, Montse Armengou Martín and Ricard Belis produced three documentary films, *Los niños perdidos del franquismo* (*Franco's Forgotten Children*), *Las fosas del silencio* (*The Spanish Holocaust*), and *El convoy de los 927* (*927 on the Train to Hell*), respectively, for the Catalan television program *30 Minuts* on Televisió de Catalunya. These films each examine different aspects of repression and violence during the Spanish Civil War and the Franco dictatorship: the forced relocation of Republican children, disappearances and mass graves, and the 1940 deportation of Spanish Republicans to the Nazi concentration camp in Mauthausen, Austria. As Armengou points out in her essay, much of the information contained in these documentaries had been appearing sporadically in texts by historians throughout the 1990s. Nevertheless, the films, produced for television and broadcast first on Catalonian stations and later nationally, brought their subject matter new visibility. And visibility, of course, is crucial in the exchange between individual testimony and historical memory; it refers not only to increased awareness or cognizance of repression, but also to giving visual representation to these acts.

Armengou's essay describes at length the role of documentary film and investigative journalism in generating this visibility for the repressed and forgotten traumas of Spain's recent past. She conceives of the journalist as "history's explorer," whose task is to reveal discoveries to mass audiences. Furthermore, she argues that documentary journalism plays a number of important roles in the recovery of historical memory. First, it gives "voice to those who have never had the chance to speak out, whether in dictatorships or in democracies." Second, this kind of investigative journalism also helps give a larger political context to individual experiences and provides an outlet for collective grief. In this sense, she suggests that her films and others like them have social and psychological functions as important as their historical ones. Finally, she focuses on how screenings and broadcasts of these documentaries have helped to break the "wall of silence" that has blocked discussion of the past in Spain. Fear and silence have produced as much grief as the actual acts of violence or oppression and have affected families into the present generation. "The freedom to recall the past should be a basic human right," Armengou affirms; she sees a significant place for film to document the process of national recollection. And yet, as with so much of the work associated with historical memory recovery, the past exhumed from archives, mass graves, and testimonies has direct ties to the present and demands both acknowledgment of victims' experiences and restitution for their loss. Armengou's essay outlines the political and ethical commitments behind her own vision of Spain's past as expressed in the documentaries. Her commitment does not stop with revealing whatever truth is to be had from historical memory recovery, but also includes the importance of documentary journalism in making a case for present actions as recompense for past atrocities and in promoting a sustained, open reevaluation of history.

Armengou advocates an active, politically engaged role for Spanish investigative journalism in the reconstruction of historical memory and in current issues of justice. However, she only sparingly turns to examples from her own films and presents their ideological commitments based largely on other sources. Gina Herrmann's chapter in this section, on the other hand, directly examines how Armengou and Belis's *Las fosas del silencio* projects its message in filmic text through a comparative analysis with Alfonso Domingo and Itiziar Bernaola's *Las fosas del olvido,* an apparently similar documentary on mass graves produced by Spain's government-sponsored public television channel. The two documentaries were broadcast less than a year apart and, as Herrmann argues, present divergent attitudes toward memories of historical violence.

As suggested by her essay's first subheading , "Searching for Justice in a Virtual World," Herrmann is especially concerned with the way documentaries about the mass graves, and about the repressions of the Franco regime in general, participate or avoid participating in a discourse of justice and what Roy Brooks calls a "theory of redress." Herrmann asks of the two documentaries: "Do the films promote the possibility of a culture of restitution that prescribes the attribution of guilt, public apology, and institutionally funded reparation?" In this context Herrmann prefers Armengou and Belis's *Silencio* for its inclusion of the political and ideological dimensions of victims' histories and because it "lays bare its agenda by depositing the blame at the door of the Nationalists." She argues that in its depoliticization of mass grave contexts, the *Olvido* documentary obscures "crucial ethical, judicial, and memorial distinctions" among the victims that would explain *why* these people were killed. Her detailed examination of several sequences provides key examples of how each film does or does not commit to a political vision of the history that informs it.

The two films also diverge in their treatment of mourning and the ultimate journey of the bones themselves. Particularly troublesome, Herrmann states, is the facile equation of a "proper burial" with closure, a comparison which ultimately delegitimizes victims' right to continued mourning. The bones must be uncoupled from their memorial value so that history and justice do not get reburied with the bodies. From this perspective, Herrmann criticizes the *Olvido* film for moving toward a funeral as its narrative climax, suggesting that the primary obligation to victims is reburial. *Silencio* does not contain scenes of reburial or other funerary rights and thus resists the historical and ideological closure implied by such ceremonies.

Apart from ceremonies, all three authors in this chapter note that the Spanish government has been slow to organize Truth Commissions or other tribunals. According to Herrmann, documentaries like C. M. Hardt's *Death in El Valle* (*La muerte en El Valle*) and *Las fosas del silencio*, which pursue evidence of perpetrator guilt, name them openly, and interview them on camera, "constitute creative proxies for the absent official mechanisms of justice" and maintain the idea of justice in the public consciousness. Certainly holding a radical vision of documentary films, Herrmann nevertheless sees a place for them as "trials by simulacra," able to accomplish some measure of public awareness and, perhaps, justice. In her comparison of the two films, Herrmann looks beyond the mere documentation of Civil War repression and violence and advocates a political construction of documentary images that couples victims' dignity not only with ceremonial reburial but also with recovery of their ideological histories, identification of perpetrators, and demands for justice and reparation.

An important and fascinating element of all these documentaries is the inclusion of testimonies. Witness testimony can provide a personal view of past events that reveals details never recorded by official history. In her essay in this chapter, Jo Labanyi looks at testimony and its use in the current flood of books and films participating in the national, public recollection of the Civil War and Francoist period. Labanyi begins by noting the legal origin of the word "testimony," which associates it with judicial process and a certain truth value. The memories recounted in testimonial literature, however, are often solicited by an interviewer and pieced together by an editor who constructs a particular story from the raw material. Labanyi's analysis explores different ways these testimonies have been anthologized and draws attention to the problematic representation of the past and the participants that often results from the constructions of perspective within each text. Her concern is "not with the question of whether these testimonies are helpful to their narrators as a form of memory-work . . . but rather with the question of whether their presentation encourages contemporary Spanish readers to think about the war in helpful ways." Different from their role in establishing what happened in the past, these testimonies are powerful documents of political and emotional issues of the present that influence contemporary democratic tensions.

Labanyi argues for an appropriate treatment of testimony and explains how some anthologies construct a perspective that is at best a tricky interpretation and at worst a disturbing manipulation of the narrators' experiences. Testimonies, she observes, are sometimes presented in collections as having the same factual status as history and risk being "construed as material evidence in their own right." Testimony is best used in conjunction with or as illustration of historical evidence from archival research. According to Labanyi, less rigorous volumes of testimonies present their material in ways that diminish their narrators by excerpting their stories, mixing them with others, and arranging the whole by chronology or theme. These kinds of anthologies often reduce the narrators to the moment of their persecution, omitting other pieces of their stories and painting them solely as victims of tragic events rather than active participants in their own history. She especially argues against "the practice of reproducing only those excerpts from testimonies that recount atrocities," a disturbing tendency that tips dangerously close to a sensationalistic pleasure derived from others' pain rather than any historical recovery. Furthermore, Labanyi goes on to say, mixing the testimonies, especially among Republican and Nationalist victims, can reproduce the idea of a "collective madness" that erases the political specificity of the conflict and impedes a present-day coming to terms with what really happened.

Although she presents various problems of representation in some testimony anthologies, Labanyi ultimately determines that these personal histories have an important place beyond their conflicted access to "truth" about the past. Equally significant, she concludes, is their ability to show "what the narrators feel about the past at the present time of speaking," which may help deal with the present realities of living together. Her critique of testimony collections that do not respect and reveal a larger process of historical investigation warns against a naive reading of testimony that clouds the political issues of the past still influencing current-day attitudes.

The essays in this section point to the dimensions of constructed meaning within what might be perceived as intrinsically "true" accounts, documentary film and testimonies. These nonfictions present their visions of the experienced reality of the Civil War and Francoist period within a wide variety of ideological contexts, some original to the speaker, some constructed by interviewers, editors, or filmmakers. Armengou, Herrmann, and Labanyi assert the importance of these texts in giving voice to individuals and to the larger nation as Spain confronts its past and searches for both just and helpful ways to remember what happened in a still potent period of history. Simultaneously, though, the construction of these voices in discursive or filmic practice alters perception of their experiences and embeds ideological interpretations into what might be construed as "objective" depiction. What ultimately unites these essays is their shared sensitivity to ideology and meaning constructed within each text; they promote a vigorous documentary and testimony production that respects complete, multiple viewpoints with more apparent though no less authentic ideological constructions as a way to represent the complex memories of Spain's painful national history.

Investigative Journalism as a Tool for Recovering Historical Memory

Montse Armengou Martín

In discussing the role of investigative journalism as a weapon for recovering historical memory in Spain, I will focus on my documentaries *Franco's Forgotten Children* (2002), *The Spanish Holocaust* (2003), and *927 on the Train to Hell* (2004), which have all been published in book format.[1] Many television and feature film documentaries on recovering historical memory have been produced in recent years, but they have not reached mass audiences for lack of good distribution channels and institutional support.[2] *Franco's Forgotten Children* was a turning point in awakening public awareness of Franco's repression and the need to recover collective memory. It had been preceded by important research done by historians in the '80s and '90s, who had intended to bring their findings to the public eye, but obviously, their works never made the best-seller lists.[3] In the late '90s, many associations of missing people and victims of the repression had started mobilizing.[4] The appearance of *Franco's Forgotten Children* whipped up public interest for the first time, and the term "historic memory" and awareness of the need to restore it became widespread.

Historians have published research on the Spanish Civil War and the Franco dictatorship. Politicians who played a role in this period of Spain's history have given their opinions on the events. Even novelists, painters, and singers have used their art to express their feelings about it. But you may be wondering, Why a journalist? What kind of contribution can a journalist make?[5]

In my work as a television journalist I have used archival images when referring to the subject of missing children—kids who were torn away from their biological parents and placed illegally with families who sympathized with the Fascist regime, children whose parents were tortured and murdered and who were then stripped of their identities. In Spain what comes to mind when one sees these images is Argentina. In *Franco's Forgotten Children* we show that the very same thing happened in Spain.

When a documentary or a report showed families desperately looking for their missing loved ones, people in Spain associated these images with Chile, South Africa, and more recently Bosnia-Herzegovina in the heart of Europe. Our documentary *The Spanish Holocaust* shows that in twenty-first-century Spain—a European Union member nation, a signatory to international human rights treaties, and a major first-world country—every night thousands of people search the Internet trying to find traces of their missing loved ones who were victims of Franco's repression either during the Civil War or in the postwar era. And this is all they can do, because there is no public office in charge of this task, unlike in other poorer, less stable democracies, like Guatemala.[6]

In Spain, as nearly everywhere else in the world, when scenes of death trains heading toward Nazi concentration camps appear on television—especially in 2005, when the world commemorated the end of World War II and the liberation of the death camps—people automatically associate them with the Holocaust and the extermination of the Jewish people. In *927 on the Train to Hell* we show that the first death train in Europe to be packed with entire families was not filled with Jews but with Spanish Republicans who were in exile in France. They were deported from the French town Angouleme to Mauthausen. This took place in August 1940. The massive deportation of Jews from France did not start until 1942.

This is what we have done at Televisió de Catalunya, a small public television network in Barcelona, the capital of Catalonia. With a limited budget—and sometimes without the corporate and official backing we would have liked—we have created a benchmark in both Catalonia and Spain, and our reports have been broadcast around the world and have won a host of prizes and awards.[7] And what is more important is that we have shown the world that its cozy view of the Franco dictatorship as a worthy ally in the fight against Communism was terribly wrong.

Our works were censored by the Spanish public television network TVE.[8] At the time, the right-wing Popular Party, led by J. M. Aznar, was in power. In the elections of 2004, the center-left Socialist Party (Partido Socialista Obrero Español), led by José Luis Rodríguez Zapatero, was voted into office. Since then, our documentaries have been broadcast to all of Spain on public television.

Coming back to the journalist's role during the recovery of historical memory, we might say that the journalist is history's explorer, revealing her discoveries to mass audiences. The first broadcast of *Franco's Forgotten Children* was in Catalonia alone, which has a population of six million, and was viewed by an audience of almost one million. The film was later broadcast on several autonomous Spanish networks, on cable TV, and on public and private channels in other countries. It has also been sold as part of a collection, and pirated copies are downloaded from the Internet.

Here I would like to emphasize the ethical, activist commitment of the journalist, namely the journalist's obligation to give a voice to those who have never had the chance to speak out, whether in dictatorships or in democracies. The defeated Republicans were silenced physically—through execution—and ideologically—through imprisonment, exile, and repression by terror. They were forced into oblivion three times: killed during the war and postwar era, silenced during the dictatorship, and forgotten in democracy. When the Franco regime killed someone, not only did they take a life, but they also exterminated an ideology, a personal history, a person's values. And they also violated the legitimate right to existence of the Republican government, which had been democratically elected by the people.[9] Personal memories must surface and be contextualized in collective history. The victims' relatives suffer personal grief, but our job as journalists is to bring to the surface the tragedy of collective grief.[10]

An important part of our job is giving the silenced victims a voice. We give a voice to the anonymous heroes who have no monuments commemorating their death in a Spain where even today there are streets named after the dictator and his cruelest cohorts and ideologists, government-subsidized housing bearing signs with the yoke and arrows of the Falange Party, lists of names of the "fallen for God and country" on church façades, and Francoist monuments.[11] Even today, when the Socialist government decides to remove a statue of General Franco in Madrid, it must do it at two in the morning.[12] You can be sure you will not find the names of the silent, anonymous heroes on streets, squares, schools, libraries, or sports complexes. Acknowledgment in these places, where young people go every day, could help teach them about the silenced deeds of anonymous heroes and perhaps help build a more democratic model of a hero.

How do journalists make these silenced voices come to the surface? Our main tool is the interview. Some people question this resource, and other disciplines often look down their noses at it. Fortunately, this mistrust is becoming a thing of the past, as multidisciplinary approaches are yielding excellent results. In the case of *Franco's Forgotten Children*, the research could never have been as comprehensive without the help of historian Ricard Vinyes, from the University of Barcelona, nor would the people interviewed have spoken as openly as they did without our expertise as journalists.

How things are said is almost more important than what is said. Memory is fragile; it fades with the passage of time under the weight of silence and fear of the official version of history and of other viewpoints. For us, for example, the important thing is not whether Franco's coup took place on July 18 or 19, but how the people experienced the coup, what its consequences were, and how everyday life was affected by that event, things often ignored by official history. Afterwards we do our job as journalists, treating the facts as accurately as possible. That is why working with historians is often necessary.

The witnesses' advanced age was also important. In gathering accounts that have been stifled for so long, we had the feeling that it was now or never. We are talking about people in their eighties and nineties, and many of the witnesses have died without ever speaking out.[13] In some cases, these oral accounts allow us to prove the existence of a repressive policy. For example, in the case of *Franco's Forgotten Children*, it may well be that we will never find a document ordering the kidnapping of "the sons of Reds." We know the pseudoscientific theories of Dr. Vallejo Nágera about Marxism as an illness (apparently caused by a "Red" gene) and about the need to separate children from parents suffering from this illness.[14] We have seen decrees that allow the changing of the names of children and making kids wards of the state.[15] We have found unpublished documents that prove that children who were refugees in other countries were kidnapped and taken back to Spain but never returned to their biological families.[16] However, the most revealing proof has been the accounts of witnesses who explained the final goal of all those tactics: to separate children from their families, to brainwash them, and to turn them into model citizens of the new Francoist Spain. Women have told us how their children were taken away from them, sons and daughters of these women recalled how their names were changed and how they were given to adoptive parents, and elderly people told us they were still hurt by the way they were insulted for being children of the "Reds" and by the fact that they were never able to find their real parents. But above all, these people were hurt because they could never talk about their grief, neither during the forty years of dictatorship nor under democracy.

As journalists, we have discovered that many people are still afraid to talk because democracy has not established the corrective (not vindictive) measures that memory, justice, and redress demand. In many rural areas, victims live next door to murderers, and they have been running into each other on the streets all these years. The descendants of these murderers often wield considerable political and economic power. These oral accounts have a beneficial effect on society and on the victims as well, as they become aware of the scale of the repression and understand their status as victims in a political context. This is especially important in the case of those who have no political training to help them understand that their suffering was not just a case of bad luck, but the product of an elaborate, global plan to exterminate the enemy. In our documentaries, we try to include a wide range of witnesses. We do not only look for members of a particular political party or people from one region alone. Very often, when witnesses see themselves in the context of the documentary, sharing their voices with other victims, they are grateful not only because they have freed themselves from stifled suffering, but also because they have understood the reasons for what happened. They learn that it was not just because a particularly bloodthirsty soldier had come to their village or because their father's idealism had brought misfortune to the whole family. Their participation can help them relieve the guilt that often burdens victims of abuse.

Our aim is not simply to give a superficial, nostalgic, or overly sentimental approach to the accounts given by our interviewees, but to put them in context. We present them together with our research to reveal new findings. And it is precisely this combination that allows us to prove that the witnesses were not victims by chance. Ordinary women were killed or imprisoned just because they happened to be married or related to one of the regime's enemies. Let us remember that those "enemies" included teachers, mayors, trade union members, and generally anyone deemed to be subversive.

Many philosophers have considered the role of witnesses. Reyes Mate is a Spanish philosopher who specializes in memory. He wrote, "A witness's account carries great authority. Such accounts are not only intrinsically valuable but also serve to dispel the silence of those who never got the opportunity to tell their story."

I have already mentioned the research that needs to be done to piece together witnesses' accounts, as well as the difficulty in unearthing documentary proof of the Franco regime's crimes. Both journalists and researchers alike face serious hurdles in examining Spanish archives. Records are often badly catalogued and conserved. Some of the people in charge of archives do their best to thwart our research. Many documents have been destroyed by neglect (fires, floods, damp) or deliberately. A case in point is the Falange archives in Barcelona, which were burned on the orders of Rodolfo Martín Villa, civil governor under the dictatorship, minister during the Transition, and later holder of various important positions on the boards of major Spanish companies.

Our task as journalists is to piece together the jigsaw puzzle to reveal the full horror of the Franco years. Documentary evidence of the regime's resort to illegal "adoption" of children and the changing of their identities is not new. But accounts of these crimes were confined to dry works by historians and obscure books by the victims themselves. It was the screening of the documentaries that brought the story to the public's attention.

When the documentaries were broadcast, the reaction of older people was remarkable—for many it was the first time they had mustered the courage to talk about Spain's evil past. The fact that a public TV network broadcast the documentaries helped break the wall of silence. Many felt the time had come to talk without fear of reprisal. A host of witnesses volunteered their accounts after the program was aired.

Young people were shocked by the revelations—furious that their school and university textbooks avoided any mention of the subject. Young people were amazed that Spain's media could give them Milosevic's latest testimony before the International Court in the Hague but told them next to nothing about the scope of Franco's crimes. This is a third-generation phenomenon. The first generation was killed or imprisoned, and the second one was silenced by fear. Now the victims' grandchildren want to know the truth. These youngsters are understandably disenchanted with Spanish society and see the Republic as a symbol of the struggle for freedom (see Arnabat). The Civil War generation believed that a new, better world was possible, and their grandchildren share that belief.

Let me tell you what happened during the shooting of *The Spanish Holocaust*. We were in Zafra, Extremadura, a region in southern Spain where Franco's troops brutally repressed the civil population as a foretaste of what the rest of Spain could expect. We were filming an interview with the daughter of the last Republican mayor, a man who maintained law and order and saved right-wingers and priests from the mob. We were in the village square, which had a monument to a Francoist commander, Captain Castejón. This was the man who had ordered 1 percent of the village population to be shot. A young man, about twenty years old, asked what we were doing, and we told him. We asked him to read the inscription on the monument. He was stunned as he read out the words "Glory to Franco." The daughter of the mayor executed by Captain Castejón filled him in on the captain's deeds. The young man said he did not really understand which side was which. What he did know is that troops had taken away his grandfather to be shot. When the mayor's daughter told him it was all Castejón's doing, the man fell silent. Then he yelled, "This monument is to the man who murdered my grandfather! It's like having a monument to Hitler in the village! It should be torn down." This ignorance about the past is no exception in Spain. *El País* published a survey on October 19, 2002, with a chilling statistic. It turns out that nearly 40 percent of youths between the ages of twelve and eighteen thought that living under a dictatorship was no different from living in a democracy.

Journalism is vital for revealing the truth. In Spain successive "democratic" governments have always taken the line that the past was best buried and forgotten. They have also done their best to create the impression that both sides in the conflict were equally to blame. The perverse reasoning behind this policy is that remembrance equals bitterness and forgetting equals reconciliation.

The right-leaning media in Spain have now taken the offensive. One can say there is something of a media crusade underway. This began in the late 1990s as advocates of the historical memory movement began to clamor for attention, because the Right believes it can be harmful (see Tremlett).

Historical research has also made great strides since the '80s. This research refutes the arguments of those who say that Spain's "Reds" killed more people than or the same number of people as the Fascists. We now know, and it has been scientifically proven, that this is untrue and that Fascist terror was vastly greater in scale.

In modern Spain, the right wing and the Church still dominate the media, and they have reacted to these revelations by mounting a campaign to put a thick gloss on the Franco regime and Spanish history. The propaganda merchants include newspapers like *El Mundo* and *La Razón*, radio stations such as COPE, the Libertad Digital website, and authors like Pío Moa, a former GRAPO terrorist. They are all linked to the Foundation for Social Studies and Analysis—FAES—led by José María Aznar, the former president of Spain. This is quite a disturbing picture.[17]

Several things need to be remembered in order to grasp the present situation. First, Spain suffered almost forty years of brutal dictatorship. Few regimes were more relentless than Spain's in wreaking vengeance on its political enemies. The last death sentences were issued just a few weeks before Franco's death. Spain's case is also unique for the way the Catholic Church connived with the regime and aided and abetted its crimes. The media was muzzled, and the truth was stifled.

Second, Spain's Transition to democracy left a lot to be desired. Left-wing parties were too weak to demand more, and the media obediently did their part by persuading the public that the past was best swept under the carpet. The media stilled the voices of the repressed masses by simply ignoring them. The failed coup in 1981 only reinforced the idea that the past should be forgotten.

Third, perhaps it is best not to judge Spain's Transition from dictatorship, but the key issue concerns democracy. The freedom to recall the past should be a basic human right and the cornerstone of any society that claims to be free. As the philosopher Theodor Adorno put it, the media have neglected their duty, and this amounts to irresponsibility.

Fourth, one should consider the role played by left-wing media. The Spanish Socialist Party (PSOE) governed from 1982 to 1996. The Socialists inherited the pact made during the Transition years to bury the past. Even so, it is hard to excuse the way in which successive Socialist governments and their media allies so enthusiastically pursued this policy. They are largely to blame for the failure to link the Republic's struggle of yesteryear with today's efforts to turn Spain into a real democracy. They opened up a yawning chasm in Spanish society. The younger generations do not grasp that the country's present democracy owes a great deal to the Republicans of two generations ago. The Republic had its faults, but it was infinitely preferable to what followed. Spain's failure to recall and to learn from the past may yet exact a high price in the future.[18]

The debate is now wide open on Spain's Transition to democracy. The irony is that much of the media that connived in silencing the truth are now swift to criticize.

Spain is quick to prescribe its own Transition to democracy as a model for Latin America to follow. Yet the Spanish media's criticism of the amnesty laws in Chile and other countries conveniently overlooks the impact of Spain's 1977 Amnesty Law. While it released many freedom fighters, it also ensured that those responsible for crimes against humanity went unpunished. The media have also studiously ignored the truth commissions set up in other countries to heal the deep wounds left by the past. Amnesty is one thing, but amnesia is quite another. It seems that many in Spain remain unaware of the distinction.

Now is the time for the media to restore memory to its rightful place. Failure to treat the past in a frank and fearless manner has grave—even terminal—consequences for a country's democratic health.

To conclude, I should say that it is high time the media in general—and the Spanish media in particular—accepted terms like "Fascism" and "genocide" in recovering memory. When we showed the documentary *The Spanish Holocaust* for the Prix Europa in Berlin, the jury members said that they liked it, but they thought the term "Spanish holocaust" was a bit strong. I can tell you now that Paul Preston, the eminent British scholar and specialist on the Spanish Civil War, is going to call his next book *The Spanish Holocaust*.

This is not just a question of opinion. The term "genocide" was defined by the Polish jurist Rafael Lemkin for the Nuremberg trials of Nazi crimes as "the elimination of a social group on race, religion or political grounds." Between 1939 and 1944 alone (the first five years after Franco's victory), there were 200,000 executions in Spain.

The Jewish philosopher Walter Benjamin committed suicide in Portbou, Spain, when he realized the authorities were going to hand him over to the Nazis. On his grave, overlooking the Mediterranean Sea, there appear the following words written in German, Spanish Catalan, French, and English as a vivid reminder: "It is harder to honor the memory of anonymous people than that of celebrities. The construction of history has to be devoted to the memory of the nameless."

NOTES

1. The documentaries were produced by *30 Minuts*, a program from Televisió de Catalunya, S. A. (Barcelona, Spain). See *Els nens perduts, Les fosses del silenci,* and *El convoy de los 927.* The books were published in Catalan and Spanish by Plaza & Janés (Random House Mondadori). See Vinyes, Armengou, and Belis; Armengou and Belis, *El convoy*; and Armengou and Belis, *Las fosas.*

2. The following are just a few examples: *Operación Nikolai* (Dolors Genovès, 1992), *Los niños de Rusia* (Jaime Camino, 2001), *Asaltar los cielos* (Javier Rioyo and José Luis López Linares, 1997), *Rejas en la memoria* (Manuel Palacios, 2004), *Presos del silencio* (Mariano Agudo and Eduardo Montero, 2004), and *La guerrilla de la memoria* (Javier Corcuera, 2001).

3. Some of these books, such as *Víctimas de la guerra civil,* edited by Santos Juliá and *Morir, matar, sobrevivir: La violencia en la dictadura de Franco,* edited by Julián Casanova and Santos Juliá, have proven essential for research on Franco's repression.

4. Mention must be made of the work done by the *Asociación para la Recuperación de la Memoria Histórica,* led by Emilio Silva and Santiago Macías, which disinterred the first bodies at Priaranza del Bierzo (León) in 2000. Since then, it has carried out more than five hundred exhumations in Spain.

5. Many artistic works denounce the Franco dictatorship in Spain, and some were even created during the dictatorship, in defiance of censorship: from foundational works of art (like Picasso's *Gernika*) to protest songs by folk singers (like Paco Ibáñez, Lluís Llach, José Antonio Labordeta, and others) and plays. Today a boom in Spanish literature is producing books on the Civil War and postwar years, both essays and fiction. Novels like *Soldados de Salamina,* by Javier Cercas, and *La sombra del viento,* by Carlos Ruiz Zafón, have become national and international best sellers.

6. Not long ago, Amnesty International published a report called "Ending the Silence and Injustice: The Pending Debt to Victims of the Spanish Civil War and the Franco Regime" (July 18, 2005). The report denounces the government's reluctance to comply with the international treaties it signed, like the Declaration on the Protection of All Persons from Forced Disappearances, and the fact that Spain has not signed the Convention on the Non-Applicability of Statutory Limitations to War Crimes and Crimes Against Humanity. It also reports that there has not been a policy of redress for the victims and that the few very limited measures toward it have not originated from their condition as victims of serious breaches of human rights, but have been concessions aiming for reconciliation without justice. The report states that the government has not acted against those responsible for the breaches, that the measures of redress were tardy and were transferred to local administrations, that the government asked for documentary proofs (ignoring the fact that the dictatorship destroyed many archives), and that there were no measures to help the victims of torture. The report concludes, "The right to redress, which comprises compensation for damage, restitution, rehabilitation, satisfaction and the assurance that the damage will not be done again, was not overseen by the judicial system . . . , which constitutes a second breach of internationally recognized rights" ("España" 58).

7. Our awards include the Liberpress Prize, awarded for professional work in the search for historical truth (Paris, 2003); the Grand Prix FIGRA (France, 2003); Film that Has Changed the World (Amnesty International, Amsterdam, 2004); and Best Direction Award (Human Rights Film Festival, Barcelona, 2003). Our work was also a finalist for the New York Prize, Japan Prize, Prix Europa (Berlin), and Santiago Álvarez Prize (Cuba), among others.

8. Jordi Martí, a Catalan member of the Spanish parliament, made a petition to the government on February 19, 2002, to broadcast *Franco's Forgotten Children* to the whole of Spain, but the request was denied by Spanish Radio and Television.

9. The need to restore the values of the Republic was stressed by the lawyer Joan Garcés, who contributed to opening the case against General Augusto Pinochet. See Garcés.

10. Many specialists are starting to work on the effects of the grief from open wounds in Spain, on both a personal and a social level, similar to work being done in other countries, especially in South America, by people like Carlos Martín Beristain, Elizabeth Lira, and others. See Guillermo Fouce's "La necesaria recuperación la Memoria Histórica." He belongs to Psychologists Without Borders, an organization that has volunteered to offer psychological support during exhumations in Spain. The last Conference on Mental Health held in Barcelona in 2006 dealt for the first time with the impact of silence on mental health.

11. There are many Spanish websites and forums that deal with historical memory. Foro por la Memoria (close to the Spanish Communist Party) has launched a campaign to report the streets and places with Francoist inscriptions.

12. This took place on March 17, 2005. The monument was an equestrian statue of General Franco placed in front of the Ministry of the Environment.

13. There have been, however, many attempts made by schools, local governments, universities, and so forth to gather accounts of witnesses. There is no global project similar to the USC Shoah Foundation Institute, established by film director Steven Spielberg, which has gathered 52,000 accounts from victims of the Jewish holocaust in fifty-six countries around the world.

14. See the works of Antonio Vallejo Nágera, including *Eugenesia* and "Psiquismo," and Nadal Sánchez.

15. For the registration of repatriated and abandoned children see Ley de 23 de noviembre de 1940 and Ley de 4 de diciembre de 1941.

16. Report from the Falange's Department of the Exterior on work done to date toward the repatriation of Spanish minors who had been expatriated, November 26, 1949.

17. See the excellent work on this subject by Francisco Espinosa Maestre, *El fenómeno revisionista o los fantasmas de la derecha española.*

18. Alfons Cervera presents interesting arguments on this subject.

Mass Graves on Spanish TV

A TALE OF TWO DOCUMENTARIES

Gina Herrmann

"The Resurrection of the Dead"

We are buried below with everything we did, with our tears and our laughs.

—Yehuda Amichai

SEARCHING FOR JUSTICE IN A VIRTUAL WORLD

In his book *The Dominion of the Dead,* Robert Pogue Harrison offers a reflection on the societal role of corpses that resonates with Spain's recent engagement with restless memories of Francoist terror: "For all its grave stillness, there is nothing more dynamic than a corpse. . . . A corpse in itself is neither disquieting nor disclosive. Only in its genealogical, sentimental, or institutional relation to the surviving loved one does it become the personification of transcendence" (93). The dynamism of corpses, born from extrajudicial assassinations carried out during and after the Spanish Civil War and displayed in print media and television documentaries, has animated the Spanish political and cultural landscape over the last half decade. Every image that passes before our eyes on the television screen is a spectacle, a spectre, a trace of the intangible, of absence. When the image pressed into our consciousness is that of a corpse, the spectre represents a two-fold absence, that of the intangibility of the televised body and that of the unrecoverable life that once possessed the corpse. As we look at the spectre, it watches us and asks us to issue a response.

In his interviews collected in *Echographies of Television,* Jacques Derrida casts the Barthesian notion of "emanation" in an intersubjective, ethical light that brings specifically television spectatorship into the realm of the political. He says, "This flow of light which captures or possesses me, invades me, or envelopes me is not a ray of light, but the source of a possible view: from the point of view of the other" (Derrida and Stiegler 122–23). Spectatorship involves a "spectral oath" that links mutual apprehension between the viewer and the *revenant* to matters of respect and demands for justice (123–24). But watching television, Derrida quips, ought also to be an act of social dissection: It "is a political task. . . . Because of the effects it engenders on the political scene, but also because I should understand how this is done or made, how it is fabricated, who has the power, who chooses, what are the relations of forces" (138). This essay picks up these Derridian reflections on the production of televisual media, concern for the other, and spectator responsibility with the intention of tracing them through recent Spanish documentaries devoted to the spectral remnants of the Franco dictatorship.

In less than one calendar year, between March 2003 and late January 2004, television audiences in Spain could tune into two programs of investigative journalism about the opening of mass graves dating from the Spanish Civil War and the early postwar years. The first of these documentaries, the two-part *Les fosses del silenci,* which aired on Catalan television March 2 and 9, 2003, examines the social, political, and military contexts of three regions in Spain in which mass executions of Republicans were carried out by Nationalists, Falangists, and the civil guard. The film employs newsreel footage, testimonial interviews, legal documents of the era, analysis by well-known Spanish historians both liberal and conservative, and video coverage of the exhumation process and subsequent DNA testing in order to create a multilayered narrative. The spectator comes to understand the quality and the scope of what was a systematic Nationalist strategy for the ideological and, if necessary, corporeal repression or elimination of the Republican enemy. The filmmakers, Montse Armengou and Ricard Belis, won acclaim in the press and at various human rights film festivals, and yet the documentary initially received little attention from the Asociación para la recuperación de la memoria histórica (ARMH), the organization that is in large part responsible for the disinterment taking place in many regions of Spain since 2000, when the association's founder, Emilio Silva, led an effort to locate, identify, and give proper burial to the mortal remains of his own Republican grandfather. In January 2004, however, the Asociación sent out a mass transatlantic email that exhorted its recipients to tune into a new documentary about the opening of mass graves, *Las fosas del olvido,* directed by Alfonso Domingo and Itiziar Bernaola, scheduled to air on January 28, 2004, on the TVE series *Documentos.*[1] One sentence of the email reads: "Lo que os queremos proponer es que nos ayudéis a convertir la audiencia de dicho programa en un ejemplo del apoyo social que tiene la causa de estos republicanos desaparecidos. Se trata de convertirlo en una especie de referéndum oficioso: un espectador, un voto" (What we would like to propose is that you help us to convert the audience of this program into an example of social support that shares the cause of these disappeared Republicans. It's about turning it into a kind of unofficial referendum: one spectator, one vote) (Asociación para la recuperación). Emphasizing how visual media has paradoxically diffused and charged political processes (people "vote" by turning on the TV), the urge for viewership underscores the extent to which television, and particularly, the made-for-TV documentary genre has become a primary didactic tool of history. With this email, ARMH linked its mission with what would be a hastily composed and historically distorted television exposé for passive viewer consumption.

Some days after I received the email plea to tune into the program, I found another email from the Communist memorial organization, the Foro por la memoria, stating their regret for having recommended the documentary and expressing "consternación por el contenido del mismo . . . que contenía elementos muy negativos como la equiparación de las víctimas de los agresores y vencedores" (consternation regarding the content of the same . . . which contained very negative aspects such as the equivalence between the victims of the aggressors and the winners) (Pedreño). And in an attachment, José María Pedreño, the president of the Foro, lists—in a three-page, single-spaced, vituperative account—the ideological missteps of ARHM.[2] The Foro por la memoria is another vociferous human rights group in Spain carrying out efforts to locate, excavate, and identify the osseous remains and artifacts in mass graves. Pedreño conflates the problematic television documentary with the procedural and cultural errors of the Asociación, both of which function, according to Pedreño, outside of a rigorous *"referente ideológico"* (ideological referent) (Pedreño). Francisco Ferrándiz summarizes the significant ideological differences between the associations' respective protocols:

> ARMH identifies itself as an association of relatives of victims and sympathizers with no direct affiliation to any political party, and considers the relatives of victims to be autonomous and decisive in the organization of mourning. Foro por la Memoria works from within the Communist Party and supports the politicization of the exhumation and handling of the bones. In their ceremonies exhumations are often carried out under a Republican flag, and at times incorporate other elements of the traditional left-wing commemoration protocol, such as speeches by Communist Party leaders, references to the heroism of the victims, raised fists and singing hymns over the remains, etc. ("Return" 3)

It is beyond the scope of this essay, as well as out of my personal experiential reach, to analyze here the increasingly acerbic relations between the various memorial organizations, relations strained by struggles over control for the cultural, ideological, and geographic landscape of the mass graves phenomena.[3] I can nevertheless comment on my experience of the two counterposed documentaries: one, *Silenci,* that couches the stories of Republican dead within concrete historico-political contexts, and the other, *Olvido,* that turns on a fetishization of dead bodies at a troubling historical remove from the political circumstances that occasioned extrajudicial assassinations. Although Pedreño's excoriation devolves into such an exaggerated condemnation of ARMH that he risks undermining his own credibility, his articulation of the fundamental differences between the rival organizations echoes my reading of what people in the historical memory community have constructed as two rival documentaries: the acclaimed Catalan *Silenci* and the more criticized *Olvido*.[4]

Neither piece of television journalism moves beyond the model of nonfiction film characterized by "the four fundamental tendencies of documentary . . . to record, reveal or preserve/to persuade or promote/ to analyze or interrogate/ to express" (Renov 21). Each employs an authoritarian, off-screen "voice of God" narrator and is interview-based. Through the traditional codes and material processes of the interviews, archival footage, and representations of archival documents as the fundamental epistemological sources of the past, the filmmakers in both cases create the perception of a dialogic approach to their subject. In the case of TV2's *Olvido*, dependence on old newsreel footage parallels commentary by witnesses, default functions of documentary that align the viewer with the filmmaker. Whereas *Silenci* highlights the testimonies of respected Spanish historians of differing ideological persuasions, in *Olvido* the work of summarizing the historical record is left, oddly, to a group of well-known Spanish novelists (Javier Cercas, Julio Llamazares, Andrés Trapiello, Jesús Ferrero) who have recently published fiction in the vein of "historical memory," focusing on the Spanish Civil War and the Franco dictatorship.

Armengou and Belis's overarching expository strategy reveals that no one witness or historical analyst can provide the "whole truth." They thematize the possibility that each narrator possesses only a portion of the story, and that some actually lie, while the Domingo/Bernaola production does not even imagine the value of incorporating "unreliable" narrators into the film. In this way, the Catalan documentarists position evidence and argument in suspension, leaving room for the thinking spectator to do some work of the construction of meaning.

In the following pages, I analyze these documentaries by way of three interrelated themes, an analysis that aims to assess the function of television documentary and its reception within the larger projects for the dissemination of a pluralistic memory of Spain's history since 1939. The first is the degree to which the documentaries stand in the service of what Roy Brooks calls, in his edited volume on reparations titled *When Sorry Isn't Enough,* a "theory of redress." Do the films promote the possibility of a culture of restitution that prescribes the attribution of guilt, public apology, and institutionally funded reparation? The second concern considers how the films cast younger people as recipients of a complex and traumatic history and how, in turn, the spectator is interpolated in this dynamic of historical reception. In so far as television documentary acts as a didactic visual artifact, the viewer might contemplate what kind of education the viewing public receives. Finally, I investigate the epistemological status of the bones, framed by the first two issues; that is, what are the bones meant to mean in each documentary? How might we conceive of an endpoint for these bones on their symbolic and physical journey from their original improper burial site to the new consecrated space they may inhabit with equal unquiet?

Before I proceed, a digression is in order. My arguments below take as a given and a point of departure the belief, indeed, the conviction, that for many survivor families the exhumation and subsequent dignified ritual of reburial activate a cathartic response to what seemed to be a limitless temporal and affective expanse of uncertainty, shame, grief, rage. When excavations of mass grave sites incorporate systems of narrative support for the family members, including the collection of testimonies, acknowledgment of the victims' political activities, discussions about the period of repression, among other methods, the funerary rites become one part of a larger process of potential closure. As Ignacio Fernández de Mata points out in his chapter in this volume: "experience has consistently shown that the narration of these painful events in the context of the search for the localization and identification of the remains and the restoration of their family's dignity leads to relief. . . . Part of the pain contained in the memory generated by trauma is somehow exorcised when, like a skeleton in a grave, it is unearthed, brought to light, and shared—release and gratitude are evident when an interview is over and when exhumations are successful." No integral closure, no "cure," no definitive relief is ever forthcoming when the social fabric of the world is "ruptured," to cite Fernández de Mata again, by a statesponsored terror that leaves survivors economically, culturally, and emotionally bereft.

Unlike Chile, Argentina, Bosnia, South Africa, Rwanda, and other nations, where exhumations are only a piece of a larger project for social reconstruction in the aftermath of war and atrocities, Spain has not moved beyond the question of mass graves and into a realistic debate about the viability of truth commissions or other forms of judicial repair. But just as reburials do not guarantee personal or collective healing, tribunals likewise offer no assurances of accountability or an altered public consciousness about the past. Research conducted on state-sponsored terror, genocide, disappearances, and mass graves in other nations point to a variety of possible institutional, personal, and scientific strategies for social reconstruction and reclamation. Recent studies by Lessie Jo Frazier, working on postdictatorial memorial practices in Chile, and Eric Stover and Harvey Weinstein, the directors of the Human Rights Center at Berkeley, offer up multiple alternative platforms for dealing with the aftermaths of mass atrocities. Yet Stover and Weinstein, in their edited volume *My Neighbor, My Enemy*, hypothesize that the "performance of justice" particularly "tribunals, judgments and truth commissions . . . are not enough" (xiii). Though they come to the conclusion that such acts are necessary, they caution against the belief that these performances should serve as a social panacea.[5]

Even if we agree with Stover and Weinstein's depressing findings that "finally, we must dispense with the trope that justice can be healing" (12), much more time and effort needs to be spent asking why in Spain there appears to be no public debate about judicial responses to mass executions when many of the perpetrators are still alive. Another deliberation striking for its absence is any serious discussion of imaginative alternatives to private reburials, as I contemplate below. All of this is to say that Spain's projects for the dissemination of democratic memory tend to turn on assumptions that the right recipe—whatever combination of excavations, economic, and moral rehabilitation of victims, lustration programs, etc.—can effect reparatory and distributive justice (in the public sphere), take away the pain of the proverbial open wounds inflicted by the dictatorship (in individuals' psyches), or complete the still inaccessible historical record on the Franco regime.[6]

At stake in the following discussion is the role of just one small piece of this puzzle of memory politics: how filmic representations of projects to unearth bodies and memories embrace or resist the facile equation of "*entierro digno*" and "closure." Made-for-television documentaries potentially reach millions of viewers and persuade through the genre's "emphasis on replication of the historical real" and the persis-

tence of truth claims as "a defining condition" (Renov 25–26). Therefore the two films under discussion constitute rather easily consumed
cultural articles of "truth" about Spain's dictatorial past and the human
rights crimes of Francoism. Documentaries and exhumations of mass
graves resulting from terror have the same goal: to uncover truths not
meant to be revealed. While documentaries about mass graves express
an intensely metadocumentarist intention and aesthetic, they both push
up for viewing what Roland Barthes refers to as "that rather terrible
thing which there is in every photograph: the return of the dead" (qtd. in
Renov 25).[7] The discomfort produced by probing into Spain's cache of
bones explains why, during Aznar's presidency, the state-run television
station ("la 2") refused to purchase and air *Les fosses del silenci*.[8]

The Catalan documentary commences with an indictment. In the
opening sequence, an archival photo of General Mola, reproduced so
as to recall a page ripped out of a history book, appears with a voice off
screen reciting the general's famous declaration "hay que extender el
terror, hay que dejar sensación de dominio eliminando sin escrúpulos
a todos los que no piensen como nosotros" (we must extend the terror;
we must impose the impression of dominion while eliminating without scruples everyone who does not think as we do) (qtd. in Armengou
and Belis 28). The subsequent frame shows an archival photo of Republican dead. The following shots continue this dynamic of cause and effect between the highest Nationalist military leaders' proclaimed policies of annihilation and archival images of mass slaughter of what the
viewer assumes are Republican bodies. From the very first, *Silenci* lays
bare its agenda by depositing the blame at the door of the Nationalists.

Such clarity about the attribution of crimes against Republicans con-
founds the makers of *Las fosas del olvido*.[9] While it is hard to imagine
that the filmmakers consciously sought to equilibrate Nationalist and
Republican crimes, the result of the film is nevertheless a manipulation
of archival images, words spoken in interviews, and editing techniques
that suggest an even distribution of culpability among "*rojos y fachas*."
Although the narrating voice early on in the *Olvido* documentary does
claim that of the estimated 30,000 disappeared, the majority correspond
to Republican losses, the film's multiple and weakly developed plots, as
they unfold, increasingly undermine the meaning of this data. Tangling
up wartime battlefield deaths with extrajudicial executions and cases of

disappearances during the 1940s further limits the historical utility of *Olvido*. The narrative middle of the film shifts gears from a treatment of blood shed through Francoist repression to a long sequence dedicated to a 2003 commemorative celebration of the International Brigades at the Battle of the Ebro. This narrative interlude sandwiched between sequences about investigating disappearances and massacres effects a melding of all human tragedies occasioned by the Civil War and the subsequent reign of terror, obscuring the crucial ethical, judicial, and memorial distinctions between loss in war and loss in times of declared peace. The spectator comes away with the sense that the producers, anxious to capture on film any "happening" associated with the memory boom, allowed the available (and certainly emotively appealing) photo ops to dictate the shape of the final filmic product.

In *Silenci*, on the other hand, with the more complex presentation of the regional, community, and political circumstances in which each individual case of murdered or disappeared is embedded, the figure of 30,000 is enlivened and accorded memorial and material energy. Montse Armengou sees the work of investigative journalism as a labor of ideological retrieval: "When the Franco regime killed someone, not only did they take a life, but they also exterminated an ideology, a personal history, a person's values. . . . The victims' relatives suffer personal grief, but our job as journalists is to bring to the surface the tragedy of collective grief" (see her essay in this volume). A fundamental part of this labor of contextualization is the ascription of blame, a discourse of accountability woven into the film's narrative structure.

Two examples stand for the various ethically troubling ways Domingo and Bernaola's *Olvido* purports to bring history to memory and in the process evades a discourse of recrimination and guilt. Twice during the film, newsreel footage of a mass execution by firing squad appears in a narrative sequence that fails to identify the executioners or the dead; the result suggests an equivalency between the two groups.[10] What is perhaps the greatest oversight or indignity—it is difficult to extract the director's and screenwriter's agenda from the final product—is the lack of political, vocational, communal, socioeconomic, or ideological context in the presentation of the lives of the now unburied Republican dead. The audience never discovers *why* these people were targeted for elimination by the Nationalists. The film's hesitation to recognize the total defeat of the Republicans gets played out in a subtle instance of narrative preferential treatment: the only victim of Civil War executions who receives any form of character development is the Falangist journalist Manuel Fernández Varés. The spectator is presented with pages from the Falangist journals he founded and in which he published articles and political cartoons. His son tells the interviewer that through his cartoons his father "se metía con los republicanos y eso podía haberle granjeado una enemistad política" (made fun of the Republicans and that may have earned him some political enemies). Shockingly, this constitutes the single occasion in the film when a witness or surviving family member offers any contextual information about the motivations for disappearance or execution. To be clear, only the Nationalist victim becomes a narratable subject of history, a subject undone by left-wing extremism. All other victims, from both sides of the political divide, meet their violent deaths as a consequence of "civil war" fought by disembodied and de-ideologized perpetrators.

We can track this bias in yet another instance. While accounts of Francoist torture chambers are conspicuously absent from *Olvido*, the infamous Communist *chekas*—detention and torture centers—figure prominently in the story of the disappearance of Fernández Varés. Finally, he is the only victim around whom a full narrative of memorial recuperation is constructed: we follow his children in the various stages of their ultimately failed journey to find his remains. Filmed in what appears to be their upper-middle-class homes, the adult children of the journalist speak gently and with self-composure. These are "reasonable" people. This use of iconic authentication (choosing backgrounds of shots that seem to confirm the speaker's status—bookshelves, kitchens, laboratories, etc.), which in this case includes books, desks, a well-dressed window, stands as an index of their cultural and socioeconomic elitism, their education and corresponding access to fields of knowledge.

According to the visual and narrative logic of *Olvido* then, any discourse of responsibility and redress should address Falangist victims with equal recognition for their losses and their absences. The question is not whether Nationalist families deserve to have their experiences and pain woven into the memorial fabric of the Francoist past, but rather what kind of *care*—meaning both craft and solicitude—the aesthetic and historical materials are employed with in making the filmic narrative. As Linda Williams suggests in an essay about truth and history in documentary, "some form of truth is the always receding goal of documentary film. But the truth figured by documentary cannot be a simple unmasking or reflection. It is a careful construction, as intervention in the politics and the semiotics of representation" (324). One leaves the *Olvido* program wondering about the circumstances surrounding its production: Did TV2, the national television station that in 2003 still answered to the Aznar government, ask the directors to strive for a balance between Nationalist and Republican memories? Were the filmmakers in a hurry to bring the "hot" topic of mass graves to television, in such a rush that they compromised the visual and historical integrity of the project?

Documentaries and the opening of mass graves share a paradox. The exhumation of the mortal remains of the victims of organized terror echoes the documentary impulse, as Louis Menand explains with regard to the documentary genre: "Someone doesn't want us to see this" (95). Part of the effort to correct false memory through the recuperation of bones involves addressing just who this someone is who does not want us to see the product of his deeds, the perpetrator whose crime hinges on the evidentiary status of the skeleton. In socially committed documentary the spectator's education is often mirrored in the filmic frame by the presence of characters, in our two cases, younger men who appear to be seeing what was not meant to be seen, like us, for the first time. Both documentaries utilize this didactic trope whereby the spectator finds herself questioned by a young man seeking to uncover a family mystery of a disappeared guerrilla fighter (*maquis*) in the early 1940s.

In *Olvido*, the youth generation of Spain receives its singular expression in the shape of one handsome man, Manuel Ortega, probably in his mid-twenties, who claims he has been intrigued by the semi-occluded family stories of the disappearance of his great-grandfather, a *guerrillero* in the armed anti-Franco resistance. Ortega is not filmed interviewing family members or conducting research in archives, but rather wandering through a rural expanse, visiting the ruins of an old *maquis* safe house, and strumming his guitar. Accompanied by a historian, to whom he relates what little he knows about his relative, Ortega confesses that as a child he imagined his great-grandfather, "*un rojo,*" as a creature dressed in red, disappeared in the middle of the night. He had longed to discover, he claims, "a qué bando pertencía" (to which side he belonged) and what his fate had been. A thoroughly unreliable narrator, inappropriate and unconvincing in his affect, Ortega fails to demonstrate intellectual or cultural curiosity about his family's legacy of Communist activism and martyrdom. The aura of self-absorption (particularly in the shots of him playing the guitar) surrounding this supposed amateur historian interrupts our own investment in the investigation of the truth and, by association, divests other young Spaniards of an ethico-historical curiosity that the film purports to impart.

The Catalan documentary, meanwhile, handles the serious issue of the education of the postmemorial generations with greater complexity. Here designating perpetrators, *naming names,* connecting personal political trajectories to acts of violence are on the syllabus, so to speak. In one of the most moving sections of the film, Antonio Lama, a historian who has studied the Francoist repression in Zafra, accompanies an elderly man named Pablo Duque to the village graveyard. What is important to note in this sequence is how a discourse of attributing culpability meets up logically with the urgency to authorize younger generations with the stories of a past silenced by fear.

The episode opens with a shot of Lama (perhaps in his forties) walking alongside the white-haired Duque. The voice-over narrates details of the repression in Zafra in the first days after the Republican defeat. The spectator follows Lama and Duque to the interior wall of the cemetery, against which approximately two hundred civilians were killed by firing squad. Duque's voice is heard as his fingers run over the bullet holes. He leads Lama, the camera, and Armengou (at one point she asks a question although she does not appear in the frame) alongside the columbarium; he knows the gravesites well. Here is his cousin's niche: "la mataron embarazada" (they killed her while she was pregnant). Further down the line Duque identifies the resting places of other civilian victims of the brutal repression. At first macabre—there are so many murdered bodies in the cemetery—the scene turns heartbreaking when Duque pulls out a key and opens the door to his family's mausoleum.

Through the unstable movement of the filmic frame, the spectator senses the presence of the (handheld) camera and Armengou behind Lama and Duque, who turn to examine the photo of Duque's mother placed in the center of an altar. Duque breaks into heavy sobs, clutching the portrait of his mother: "Mi madre sufrió mucho por criarnos a los cuatro hermanos. La pelaron, le dieron medio litro de aceite de ricino, . . . pobrecita mía, lo que la hicieron sufrir" (My mother suffered a lot in order to care for the four of us brothers. They shaved her head; they gave her a liter of castor oil. . . . My poor mother, they really made her suffer). The historian and filmmaker (members of the so-called third generation) not only function as historical agents who register Pablo Duque's accusation but also accompany Duque in witnessing a flood of psychological pain of a traumatic personal trajectory released into their encounter, in front of the camera, before a community of other potential witnesses.[11] Duque weeps, as do most of the testimonial speakers featured in both *Silenci* and *Olvido,* the tears of his childhood self, frozen in the moment of childhood confusion and terror, still bound to an ineffable loss.[12]

The cathartic power of this chapter of the film resides not only in the moment of grief, for just before Duque enters the family crypt he beckons the camera toward the names emblazoned on a particular niche. His fingers touch the raised letters of the full names of the men who terrorized Zafra: "Mirad, éste era José Hernández Mancera, se dedicaba a matar a la gente" (Look. This was José Hernández Mancera. He killed people). Cutting to a close-up of the nameplate, the camera captures the names and then cuts back to Duque's face: "Era guardia civil. Su hermano, Antonio Hernández Mancera, mató a mi padre. Le ayudaron José Ortigosa y Francisco Críspulo" (He was a civil guard. His brother, Antonio Hernández Mancera, killed my father. They helped José Ortigosa and Francisco Crispulo). Armengou's voice sounds from outside the frame, asking Duque how well he knew these men. Duque responds that Hernández Mancera lived literally in "la casa de enfrente" (the house in front of ours); they crossed paths every day, for decades. We are transfixed by the sound of the names of suspected perpetrators, registered now through sound and image in the spectral televised archive that has no institutional correlative.

BEYOND THE ANTIGONE AGENDA

Consider that Antigone is trying to grieve, to grieve openly, publicly, under

conditions in which grief is explicitly prohibited by an edict, an edict that

assumes the criminality of grieving Polyneices and names as criminal anyone

who would call the authority of that edict into question.

—Judith Butler, *Antigone's Claim*

Let us shift now to the question of the epistemological and evidentiary status of bones projected by each documentary. By focusing on the recuperation and proper reburial of bones, the *Fosas del olvido* documentary operates under what we can think of as the "Antigone agenda." The film's plot from the beginning moves tenaciously toward what it purports to be the psychic, political, and spiritual closure encapsulated in a Catholic funeral for the victims of a collective execution in León. Once the ritual reinterment concludes (a rite many of the victims might have rejected, given their Communist or otherwise leftist ideals), the disembodied narrator closes the film with a declaration that Spain can finally turn the page on its painful past. Is the spectator to assume that injury has healed over, "*cicatrizado*" (scarred over), to use a favorite metaphor in the historical memory community? In the *Olvido* documentary, the evidentiary status of the bones is taken for granted as the reburial purportedly heals long-festering wounds. A previous sequence devoted to the process of DNA testing further limits the meaning of the osseous artifacts, for the goal of the scientific work is to determine whose bones belong to whom. The implication is that personal pertinence outweighs both the ideological context in which these crimes were committed and the politics of responsibility and restitution. Yet the funeral scene suggests (but never clarifies) that DNA identification was not carried out; survivor families never discovered which particular bones had inhabited the bodies of their individual loved ones.[13]

Silenci, in comparison, imagines the Spanish postdictatorial memorial condition in the same way historian Lessie Jo Frazier understands

Chile's: "Rather than politics as mourning, by allowing themselves to be haunted, these orphans of the regime Transition effect a countermourning that refuses to relinquish the past and gropes toward a politics that might allow their memories' integrity with a vision for the future" (105). Productive countermourning involves un-conjoining recovered bones from an imaginary memorial value. Human rights activists in Chile demonstrate and commemorate not at the new consecrated grave sites, but at the vacated killing fields. The Catalan documentary affirms that markers of memory (graves, monuments, plaques, and the like) constitute only one kind of restitution. Like Frazier, Montse Armengou and Ricard Belis campaign for a countermourning that has the potential to reconfigure national discourse about the memorial obligations of healthy democracies through the inclusion of the words "responsibility," "right," "justice," or even, as Frazier says, "vengeance and damnation" (116).

Les fosses del silenci reaches its full dramatic potential in a sequence involving the prolonged investigation of a young civil guard named José Antonio Landera to discover the circumstances of the brutal murder of his miner activist great uncle, a legendary *maquis* named José Landera Cachón but popularly known as Periquete.[14] Remarkable in this sequence is that the narrative originates only *after* Landera has located, exhumed, and given Periquete's remains *"un entierro digno."* The sequence then begins where *Olvido* leaves off, reminding the viewer that gravestones do not contain either memory or pain. Shot almost entirely outside, the sequence visually and narratively thematizes the exteriorization of local dirty secrets of revenge and murder. Having long suspected that Periquete met his end after having been detained and tortured by local Falangist thugs, Landera embarked on a mission of factual retrieval, conducting oral histories with the village residents and consulting historical archives. José Antonio, who knew scarcely the basic details about the Spanish Civil War, evolved into a "historical memory" activist focused on educating his own generation about the culture of repression in the 1940s and '50s. Like the Foro por la memoria, Landera views with suspicion decontextualized exhumations.

Periquete was a miner of libertarian beliefs who took refuge in *"el monte"* when the civil guard and local Falangistas took over his town soon after the outbreak of the war. Once discovered in their hideout, Periquete and his comrade Perfecto Álvarez González, "Carrero," were, according to multiple sources Landera interviewed, beaten, dragged from the back of a truck, and eventually shot. When Periquete still showed signs of life after the first bullet failed to kill him, the testimonies claim, he bellowed to his captors, "Asesinos, si me queréis matar, lo tendréis que hacer a palos, porque a tiros no me vais a matar" (Murderers, if you want to kill me, you will have to do it with blows because with bullets you are not going to be able to kill me) (Armengou and Belis 225). So his assassins beat him to death with the butts of their rifles. In the riveting chapter of Armengou and Belis's book dedicated to Landera's search for Periquete's killers, the authors recount how Landera located one of the implicated parties, an elderly Falangist named Arturón, with whom he managed to set up a meeting in 2001 by claiming he was interested in the history of the Falange in the region: "Arturón preguntó: '¿Qué, ya se está volviendo a reorganizar la Falange en la zona?' Fue en aquel momento cuando José Antonio decidió desvelarle que era guardia civil, pero no como los que había conocido Arturón: él era el sobrino nieto de Periquete; acto seguido le echó en cara su pasado asesino. Arturón se puso muy pálido. Tres días después, moría de un infarto" (Arturón asked, "What? The Falange is being organized again in this area?" It was in that moment that José Antonio decided to reveal to him that he was a civil guard, but not like those Arturón had known: he was the great nephew of Periquete. Immediately his murderous past was in front of him. Arturón became very pale. Three days later, he died of a heart attack) (226).

It would have been quite a coup on the part of Armengou's team to have captured this encounter on film. By the fall of 2002, Landera's investigative perseverance paid off. He identified another Falangist, one Nicandro Álvarez, who was reported (by Arturón himself) to have participated in the murder of Periquete and Carrero. This time the cameras were there to memorialize the confrontation. The documentary team and Landera decided to intercept Nicandro on "el típico paseo de jubilado" (the typical *paseo* of the retiree) on a rural road on the outskirts of the town Prado de Paradiña. The serious and soft-spoken Landera insists that witnesses have placed Nicandro with the victims on the night of their assassination. When no amount of evidence presented by Landera (including the rumor that Nicandro apparently wore Periquete's watch for many years) can persuade Nicandro to incriminate himself, Landera brings the conversation to closure by invoking the wrath of the victims' ghosts: "¿Qué tal tiene la conciencia?" (How is your conscience?). Nicandro responds: "¿Yo? Pues muy tranquila" (Me? Well, very calm). Landera: "¿No tiene miedo, si es que existe algo, a encontrarse a Carrero y Periquete allá arriba?" (Aren't you afraid, if there exists something beyond, of meeting Carrero and Periquete up there?) (Armengou and Belis 230).[15]

The nephew of Periquete, in his resolution to investigate, indict, and seek justice *beyond* the exhumation and proper burial of his great uncle, embodies a necessary skepticism about how the artifact, the trace, the memorial can naturalize versions of the past. Frazier says, "The remains of a few of the executed and disappeared may be recovered, identified, and placed on consecrated ground, but should they be mistaken for the recuperation of the lost person, of lost solidarities? Should we expect to mourn at their crypts?" (110–11). The *Silenci* documentary appears to instinctively understand the argument that James Young makes in his book about Holocaust memorials, namely that designated sites of memory and the material evidence contained or displayed within are not in and of themselves the events from which the traces were produced. Young points to the risk of having our memory-work displaced by claims of proof. Periquete's nephew approximates this Chilean model of countermourning that Frazier defines as "a perpetually oppositional dialogue with the dead for the pursuit of justice" (116). Landera echoes this model in his comments to Armengou: "Yo tengo miedo que todo esto se convierta en un desenterramiento masivo de cadáveres. Creo que es más importante recuperar la historia de esas personas que sacarlos de donde están" (I'm afraid that all this is going to turn into a massive disinterment of cadavers. I think it's more important to recover the history of these people than to dig them out of wherever they are) (Armengou and Belis 231). He does his research, accuses, and allows the accused the opportunity for self-defense. Through this simulation of judicial process, Landera—and the filmmakers— emulate a prosecutory process unlikely to ever take place in the courtrooms of Spain.

TRIALS BY SIMULACRA

Modern technology, contrary to appearances, although it is scientific,
increases tenfold the power of ghosts. The future belongs to ghosts.

—Jacques Derrida, *Echographies of Television*

One of the many pending issues in Spain's crisis of memory is not the risk of oblivion but the failure to redress. As I have been arguing, the ethos of the Armengou/Belis documentary warns against the assumption that "proper" reburial constitutes justice. I want to emphasize again that while the *Olvido* documentary moves precipitously toward the funeral as the point of narrative climax and historical and ideological closure, the Armengou/Belis film shows not a single funeral or burial. For its refusal to show burials, and particularly through the Landera sequence, the film subtly alludes to a suspicion of funerary rites, a resistance to burying justice and history along with corpses of the disappeared that led certain groups associated with the Mothers of the Plaza de Mayo in Argentina to come out against government-sponsored exhumations and reburials.

The exhumation of remains in mass graves has not been received in the international human rights community as an unquestionable good. One of the disturbing characteristics of programs for exhumation, identification, and reburial is that the efforts to dignify the dead risk being decoupled from efforts to bring perpetrators to justice through institutional channels. That is, while the victims ideally regain their identities, those responsible for their deaths remain in anonymity and thus continue to enjoy the impunity that has characterized so many postdictatorial transitions to democracy, including those in Spain, Argentina, and Chile. In Spain, the memorial activist group Asociación de Familiares y Amigos de la Fosa Común de Oviedo has come out against the exhumations because the recovery of corpses erases the evidence of "genocide," acting out a "second killing" of the victims. According to Ferrándiz,

A number of manifestos circulated on the internet suggested that the exhumations were being done for media attention and personal profit, undermining the powerful denunciation of injustice inscribed in the buried bones, silent witnesses of the atrocities. What was to be done with the bones? What about those bones that remained un-identified? These organizations maintain that the graves should re-main untouched as testimonies of the cruelty of the massacres and the sacrifice of the dead. They promote *above-ground* commemorative and symbolic markers—the identification of grave sites, the instal-lation of monuments, inscriptions and lists of names of those lying in the graves—and the organization of periodic rituals of remem-brance. (Ferrándiz, "Return" 3)

Anthropologist Zoe Crossland, in her article about forensic archae-ology and the disappeared in Argentina isolates another important point of resistance to the retrieval and reburial of mortal remains that bears citing at length:

Each burial and ceremony brings the nation as a whole closer to clo-sure, while leaving those responsible unchallenged. The memorial act implies tacit consensus through public participation in the ceremo-nies of the wake and funeral. It can therefore be seen as creating a sta-bilizing and dominant view of the dead disappeared as their relation-ship to the past is confirmed. . . . Not only do the exhumations locate disappeared individuals without truly "reappearing" them, but after burial and commemoration, the disappeared no longer exist in a pow-erfully liminal state. These interest groups (*Madres* and others) have therefore maintained and exaggerated the separation between the physi-cal remains of the dead and their lived histories [I think this is some-thing that the Armengou/Belis documentary alludes to], in order to contribute to the disembodiment of the disappeared. The problematic nature of this ghostliness plays a vital role in maintaining the memory of the abuses of the military, and in preventing the creation of a new national identity based on leaving the years of the "dirty war" behind in the past. ("Buried Lives" 155)

Victims retrieve their names, while those responsible remain anony-mous.

In 2005 the interministerial commission on the victims of the Span-ish Civil War and the Franco regime was due to make recommendations about moral rehabilitation and economic compensation. However, in September of that year, Vice President María Teresa Fernández de la Vega announced that the commission would take more time to contemplate a proposed law for historical memory, in order to consider the victimization of Republicans and Nationalists alike. While de la Vega attempted to reassure those lobbying for the law that investigations would concentrate primarily on Republican victims, she also insisted that the entire history of the Civil War and the Franco regime must be revisited. And in December 2005, the government released a ministerial order announcing that the state would consider providing subventions to associations carrying out the search for and exhumation of victims.[16] This order further divided the memorial organizations working on excavation of burial sites, with ARMH in favor of receiving the governmental support, while Equipo Nizkor and the Foro maintain that the state should shoulder the full financial and logistical responsibility of the work to locate the victims of violent or forced disappearances (see "Polémica"). The question of whether or not to subcontract this work remains still at a critical distance from that of tribunals or truth commissions.

While it is nearly impossible to imagine a sea change in Spain that would allow for the establishment of commissions or judicial indictments of Francoist officialdom or functionaries implicated in the killing of Republicans, individual acts of investigation into executions and disappearances represent simulated tribunals. One of the major strengths of the Armengou/Belis documentary, as well as its companion book, is that it constructs a narrative around individual efforts to put a name and a face to specific perpetrators. Such simulations should be welcome but viewed with caution. Moving the work of institutional justice into popular spheres (television, independent associations of relatives of victims that carry out their own investigations) is a perilous business. I maintain, nevertheless, that the televised judicial simulacra stimulate, in the minds of hundreds of thousands of viewers, the *idea* that the time for justice has not passed, that correction remains plausible. Herein lies the power of the Landera sequence.

An earlier documentary, C. M. Hardt's 1996 *Death in El Valle/Muerte en El Valle*, produced originally for Channel Four Television in England, also deals with a granddaughter's search for the men who killed her Republican grandfather, Francisco Redondo Pérez, a man who provided a safe house to members of the resistance (*Guerrilla*) in the region of El Bierzo (León). Placing herself at the narrative center of the film, she traces her own story as a dogged detective on the trail of suspects. So focused on the evidence and proof of the case, Hardt neglects to attend to the family stories surrounding the murder: Why did her grandparents harbor resisters? What were their political affiliations? Most importantly, how did Redondo Pérez's death change the lives of his wife and young children? Hardt's obsessive need to discover *who* pulled the trigger leads her too far afield from the *why*. The spectator, for example, realizes right away why Uncle Pablo does not want Hardt to make the film, a stance that baffles his niece: he was a boy of eleven when he and his sister went to collect the body of their father, dumped in front of a local church. Unlike Pablo Duque and other survivors interviewed in both *Olvido* and *Silenci,* who cry children's tears over children's memories, Uncle Pablo has remained "storyless" in the aftermath of the violence he witnessed. And the film does not place itself in his service, does not provide an opening through which he can become a narratable subject in Hardt's forensic plot.[17]

Muerte en El Valle merits separate analysis beyond the limitations of this essay. Suffice it to say for our purposes that despite the film's oversight of the social and affective history of the family's survivorship, it still contains an utterly chilling sequence in which Hardt manages to get invited into the house of one Ignacio Gil Perdigones, a former civil guard, and proceeds to accuse him of the extrajudicial assassination of her grandfather. Like Landera, she carried out archival research that helped her identify the men involved in her grandfather's death and subsequently fabricated a historical project far different from the one she has actually undertaken in order to gain access to her grandfather's executioner. And like both Pablo Duque and Landera, by repeating the names of the accused on camera, Hardt offers up her charges for public consumption.[18] When Hardt reveals her real intentions after showing him a photo of her grandfather, Gil Perdigones equivocates, insisting that he properly applied the "*Ley de fugas*," shooting the grandfather only after he tried to escape. Finally, the wife of Gil Perdigones interrupts, asking who exactly killed Redondo Pérez, to which C. M. responds, "*su marido*" ("your husband"), and the shot abruptly ends with a freeze frame on the image of the accused.

The filming and public dissemination of Landera's and Hardt's confrontations with the men they believe responsible for their respective relatives' deaths bring denunciation into the social sphere, releasing it from the limiting frame of private memory. In a political and social climate in which the state-sponsored judicial process of perpetrators remains outside of public debates, individual incriminations and reclamations, caught on camera, constitute creative proxies for the absent official mechanisms of justice. These acts of provocation serve as supplements, in the Derridian sense as both substitution and accretion, for the eternally deferred institutional mechanisms for accountability.

―― Katherine Verdery, in her groundbreaking *The Political Lives of Dead Bodies,* alerts us to the overwhelming proportions of the tasks of social repair pending in the afterlives of atrocity and dictatorship: "This is an immense topic. To do it even minimal justice requires attending to political symbolism; to death rituals and belief, such as ideas about what constitutes a 'proper burial'; to the connections between the particular corpses being manipulated and the wider national and international contexts of their manipulation; and to reassessing or rewriting the past and creating or retrieving 'memory.' Any student of dead-body politics (of which there is much, worldwide) should consider these subjects" (3).

To the extent that documentary film brings these "subjects" to public consciousness, thereby inviting viewers to become students of "dead-body politics," they circulate not merely as texts but function in the social arena as *acts*.[19] Perhaps, as ARMH's email I quoted at the beginning of this essay suggests, spectatorship can be a performative event, a referendum, that affects how the state grapples with its responsibility to legislate a coherent, compassionate, and comprehensive course of restitution to the human beings injured by Francoism. C. M. Hardt's and José Antonio Landera's determination to engage suspected assassins and even to invite their damnation resists the foreclosure on justice that is at risk when the memorial instrumentalization of dead bodies works in the service of a premature politics of reconciliation. Can documentaries instill fear in the hearts of the surviving perpetrators? If the future belongs to the ghosts, then perhaps Nicandro will, as Landera intimated to him when they met on that country road, "encontrarse a Carrero y Periquete allá arriba."

NOTES

1. For more information on the ever-evolving debates on exhumations, visit the website www.memoriahistorica.org. At the time this article was composed and under review, the Ley de memoria histórica was still a *"Proyecto de ley."* It became law in December 2007.

2. Emilio Silva and ARMH have distanced themselves from *Las fosas del olvido,* which they initially endorsed. Montse Armengou has commented that Silva now readily recommends *Les fosses del silenci.*

3. Francisco Ferrándiz, in his presentation at the *Franco's Mass Graves* symposium held at Notre Dame October 28–29, 2005, described the reciprocal recriminations of the two organizations.

4. For the full text of Pedreño's attack on ARMH, see Pedreño.

5. During the symposium at Notre Dame in October 2005 that led to the publication of this volume, the participants engaged in a spirited debate about the viability of establishing truth commissions and the relative value of punitive versus corrective justice. Notable in this discussion was historian Julián Casanova's view: "I do not think it is a good idea to ask for punitive justice now, almost thirty years after the death of Franco." Casanova, and others, lobby instead for historical studies, total access to archives, museums, and other contributions to the "social dimension of the memory."

6. The ethical dilemmas of post-atrocity societies involve both a correction of knowledge and a correction of behavior. McEvoy and Conway in "The Dead, the Law, and the Politics of the Past" write, "Forms of burial, methods of commemoration, and the achievement of emotional closure are important to many beyond those directly affected by death. In particular, in the highly charged political contexts discussed below, death disputes are of central societal importance in jurisdictions that are attempting to come to terms with their history. Legal control over the dead, the regulation of their memorialization, and the relationship between their fate and processes of postconflict healing in such societies are often key to what Nagel has described as the distinction between *knowledge* and *acknowledgement* (541)."

7. Both *Fosas* films fall into the rather traditional Griersonian category of documentary filmmaking characterized by the appeal of "direct address." C. M. Hardt's *Death in El Valle* falls somewhere near the intersection of the Griersonian model (direct address), cinema verité, and a more complex model where "aesthetic and epistemological assumptions become more visible," that is, self-reflexive. Hardt the filmmaker participates as maker, protagonist, and witness (Nichols 242).

8. Montse Armengou notes that since the PSOE came back into power in 2004, TVE picked up the film and it has been broadcast nationwide. Personal telephone communication, Nov. 15, 2005.

9. See articles by Herrmann and Loureiro in *Journal of Spanish Cultural Studies* 9.2 (2008) for differing assessments of the historical biases of the work of Armengou and Belis.

10. These blogs can be accessed through the Foro por la memoria website.

11. This episode is described, as are all of the film's various plotlines, in the documentary's companion book *Las fosas del silencio*. For the Pablo Duque encounter see Armengou and Belis 38–41. What the book does not describe is the heart-wrenching tenderness historian Antonio Lama extends to Duque on their visit to the Duque family mausoleum.

12. At other moments in the *Silenci* documentary, young people from Spain and abroad who have volunteered to participate in the excavation effort rehearse their (admittedly reductive) understanding of the Spanish Civil War and its aftermath with one another and, significantly, with the elderly survivors keeping vigil at the excavation sites, anxiously awaiting the first glimpse of bones.

13. The issue of DNA identification is extremely complex. Positive scientific identification of remains may well be impossible for the majority of bodies found in Spain's mass graves, especially in the larger sites. See forensic scientist Lorente Acosta's article.

14. The website dedicated to Periquete can be found at http://es.geocities .com/paisajes_gerrilla/periquete.html.

15. Although Landera has not found supporting documentation of Nicandro Álvarez's role in Periquete's death, the Civil Register of Vega de Espinareda (León) contains records of Álvarez's participation in the beating and shooting death of another man. See Armengou and Belis 230.

16. *El País* journalist Carlos Cué covers news about memorial work in Spain. See Works Cited for a list of his articles. Articles from *El País* can be easily accessed in the newspaper's online archive or by entering the full title of the article into an internet search engine.

17. The notion of a "narratable self," the sense of self that comes from knowing one's own story (part of which gets told by others) comes from the thinking of Italian philosopher Adriana Cavarero; see Cavarero.

18. Unlike Landera and Duque, Hardt did find official documents that name the two civil guards who shot Redondo.

19. Linda Williams describes this documentary value, one shared, in my estimation by Hardt as well as Armengou and Belis, in these terms: "there can be a historical depth to the notion of truth—not the depth of unearthing a coherent and unitary past, but the depth of the past's reverberation with the present" (325).

Testimonies of Repression

Methodological and Political Issues

Jo Labanyi

The number of historical studies on the Civil War and dictatorship published in Spain since General Franco's death in 1975 is
now massive; these have been published throughout the postdictatorship period. The mid-1980s additionally saw the emergence
of a number of novels and feature films on the war (Labanyi,
"Memory"), followed in the mid-1990s by a flurry of early Francoist memorabilia and related reminiscences (Harvey). It was only in
the late 1990s, however, that historical studies, novels, and documentary and feature films started to focus overwhelmingly on the
wartime and postwar Francoist repression.[1] A key text was Santos
Juliá's 1999 edited volume *Víctimas de la guerra civil,* which established a paradigm for discussing the Civil War and the dictatorship
in terms of victimhood. This emphasis on victimhood was given
additional impetus by the exhumations of victims of the Francoist
repression set in motion by Emilio Silva's first public excavation of
a mass grave in 2000 and his consequent founding of the Asociación para la Recuperación de la Memoria Histórica (ARMH).

In the wake of this new focus on victimhood, the years
2000–2003 saw the appearance, in rapid succession, of a number of collections of testimonies. Beginning in 2003, the year of
the first two documentaries by Montse Armengou and Richard
Belis on the victims of Francoist repression, *Els nens perduts del
franquisme* and *Les fosses del silenci,* made for Televisió de Catalunya, television largely took over responsibility for airing testimonies of victims. Since that date, only a trickle of print testimonies

have been published, contrasting with the production of an impressive body of documentary film, most of it made for television, based on interviews with eyewitnesses or surviving relatives of the wartime or postwar repression (Resina, "Window"; Herrmann).

This article discusses a selection of the testimonies issued in book form between 2000 and 2003. Passing reference will be made to the earlier collections of testimonies published in the late 1970s and 1980s by Fraser, Leguineche and Torbado, and Cuevas Gutiérrez and to the books that accompanied Armengou and Belis's above-mentioned television documentaries of 2003. I shall be concerned not with the question of whether these testimonies are helpful to their narrators as a form of memory-work—something that their compilers (with the exception of Armengou and Belis) have not seen fit to address in their eliciting or editing of the narratives—but rather with the question of whether their presentation encourages contemporary Spanish readers to think about the war in helpful ways. My argument will be that these edited collections, while valuable in making readers—especially the vast majority born after the war—appreciate the extent of the wartime and postwar repression, nonetheless help to construct a form of collective memory that obscures the key political issues about the past and about how we deal with it in the present. Memory is the afterlife of the past in the present.

We can bear in mind here the American feminist lawyer Bonnie Honig's suggestion, in her book *Democracy and the Foreigner,* that the most appropriate genre for narrating the nation is not the romance but the gothic novel, for democracy does not mean living happily ever after with those you love, but learning to live nonviolently with those you would rather not live with and who may fill you with terror (107–22). To do this, one needs to know about the events that have caused this terror, and to understand terror as an emotion. The current discourse on terrorism—as in "the war on terror"—encourages us to forget that terror is an emotion, and not an act or fact. In this essay I will argue that the main value of testimonies is not the legal function of establishing what happened (though that has to take place too), but the insight they give us into emotional attitudes toward the past in the present time of the speaker. Only if this is borne in mind can testimonies serve not only to recognize past injustices but also to work for a future that is not determined by them.

Testimony (*testimonio*) has become a privileged genre in Latin America for making state terror known to the public. It has mostly been promoted by Marxist critics, largely in the United States, who have seen in its first-person micro-histories a way of saving Marxist political commitment while also acknowledging the postmodern critique of "master narratives." The titles of the key critical works in the field are eloquent: John Beverley's 2004 *Testimonio: On the Politics of Truth* and Georg Gugelberg's 1996 edited volume *The Real Thing: Testimonial Discourse in Latin America.* The word *testimonio,* as is made even clearer by the English "testimony," has a legal origin: it is the eyewitness account of someone testifying to a court of law in order to establish who was guilty of a crime. In other words, its purpose is to establish the facts so that justice may prevail. This involves not only legal recognition of what was unjustly suffered by the victim but also the entitlement to reparation and, most importantly, punishment of the perpetrator of the crime. *Testimonio* became a literary genre in Latin American countries ruled by repressive regimes (especially Guatemala, Argentina, Uruguay, Chile) where such firsthand evidence could not be made public through the legal system. We may note that, in Spain, the 1977 Amnesty Law ruled out the possibility of bringing to trial perpetrators of violence during the Civil War and Francoist dictatorship—thus opening up a space for alternative forms of testimony.[2]

There are differences between *testimonio* and oral history, as all writers on the former insist, in that *testimonio* is denouncing an injustice and thus has a particular urgency. But there are also significant overlaps between the two. In both *testimonio* and oral history, the eyewitness report reaches us via the mediation of an interviewer, who presents it to the public in edited form. In both cases, it is usually the interviewer who solicits the account. And in both cases we have a form of memory-work. Memory is notoriously unreliable, but, as Felman and Laub have shown in their classic study of Holocaust testimonies, *Testimony: Crises of Witnessing in Literature, Psychoanalysis, and History,* what memories give us, especially when they are unreliable, is an insight into the emotions in the present attached to the past events that are recalled.

The volumes of testimonies of wartime and postwar atrocities published in Spain from 2000 to 2003 have been compiled by journalists, and sometimes historians, concerned—as befits their profession—with the truth value of these testimonies as historical evidence. It seems significant that such volumes escalated under the last years of the Partido Popular Government of 1996–2004, which consistently refused to support the excavation of mass graves or the opening of archives to the public. These testimonies function as a supplement to the demands by historians and activists for open access to material evidence. But in the process they risk becoming construed as material evidence in their own right. The works that use testimonies most responsibly are those in which the first-person memory narratives are backed by historical evidence.

Particularly impressive examples are Montse Armengou and Ricard Belis's two books based on their 2003 documentary films for Televisió de Catalunya's program *30 Minuts: Los niños perdidos del franquismo* (2003), coauthored with the historian Ricard Vinyes, which investigates the postwar separation of babies and young children from their Republican mothers in order to "save" them from "ideological contamination," and *Las fosas del silencio* (2004), which interviews eyewitnesses on the executions carried out by the Nationalists during and after the Civil War. In these documentaries, the testimonies are interspersed with accounts by historians based on archival research, as well as visits to the "scene of the crime." The accompanying books include a considerable amount of historical contextualization based on firsthand archival research. Another good example is the oral-history work done by the historian Ángela Cenarro in Aragón, where the testimonies are supported by meticulous historical research ("Memory").[3] In all of these cases, we are dealing with historical investigations that draw on testimonies, rather than the edited collections of testimonies that are the subject of this essay. A noticeable difference is that Armengou and Belis, and Cenarro, critically analyze the testimonies informing their investigation; no such analysis is found in the many other anthologies of testimonies that have appeared in democratic Spain. This lack of analysis is not only a wasted opportunity but encourages readers to take the stories narrated at face value.

This is not just a difference between the work of journalists and historians, not only because Armengou and Belis, although journalists by profession, engage in the firsthand research one expects of historians, but also because not all historians who draw on testimonies do so with an appreciation of the specific qualities of oral accounts. For example, the otherwise groundbreaking *Blood of Spain* (published in English and Spanish as early as 1979) by British historian Ronald Fraser is highly problematic in its mingling of historical narrative and first-person accounts such that one often is not sure who is speaking. Neither does Fraser tell us anything about the circumstances of the interviews or about the relation of the excerpts cited to the whole transcripts. The principal problem in Fraser's book is that the excerpts from the interviews are selected according to their subject matter and then inserted into a chronological historical narrative as if the informants' memories and the historian's account of the war's progress had a similar factual status. This is not how memory—notoriously nonchronological and nonfactual—works. Consequently, Fraser's intertwining into his historical account of excerpts from a mass of oral-history interviews brings the history to life and democratizes it by giving us a multiple view "from below," but it ignores the specificity of memory as a mental process.

This mining of firsthand testimonies as a "resource," so as to "recover" particular events, with the excerpts ordered either chronologically or thematically, is the norm in the collections of testimonies that appeared between 2000 and 2003. I am thinking of Alfonso Bullón de Mendoza and Álvaro de Diego's *Historias orales de la guerra civil* (2000); Jorge Martínez Reverte and Socorro Thomás's *Hijos de la guerra: testimonios y recuerdos* (2001); Carlos Elordi's *Los años difíciles: El testimonio de los protagonistas anónimos de la guerra civil y la posguerra* (2002), which published letters and documents sent, by invitation, to his radio program *Hoy por Hoy* (broadcast on Cadena SER) between September 2001 and June 2002; and José María Zavala's *Los horrores de la guerra civil* (2003). The notion of "recovering" the past is a problematic one: this is achieved when documents from the time are presented for publication—several radio listeners sent in farewell letters written from prison by their fathers on the eve of their execution—but not when we are given a memory narrative spoken or written in the present. Memory is not a slice of the past waiting hidden to be "recovered"; it is a process that operates in the present and cannot help but give a version of the past colored by present emotions and affected by all sorts of interferences from subsequent experiences and knowledge. As Elizabeth Jelin has stressed, writing about postdictatorship Argentina's handling of the "dirty war," memory is a form of "labor"—that is, a process of "working through" that takes place in the present.

Awareness of these characteristics of memory has been strong in the abundant historical and theoretical work on the Holocaust. Armengou and Belis provocatively subtitle their book *Las fosas del silencio* with the question: *"¿Hay un Holocausto español?"* and they title the English version of their documentary *The Spanish Holocaust,* answering their question in the affirmative. The question "Is there a Spanish Holocaust?" is an important one, not only because an affirmative answer would mean recognition that the victims should receive reparation and that the guilty should be brought to trial, but also because much can be learned in Spain from the debates about how the Holocaust is (or should be) remembered, at both a public and a private level. It is necessary that historians and journalists in Spain should first have concentrated on establishing what happened and who was responsible. But if there is to be a further stage of working through those memories of violence in order to achieve a democratic society where different groups agree to cohabit peacefully despite fearing or hating each other, there also needs to be a critical exploration of the feelings in the present of those who offer their testimonies. In his essay "On Forgiveness," Derrida notes that official "forgiveness" ceremonies serve the function of unifying the nation, enforcing homogeneity from above; such instrumental "forgiveness" is an economic transaction conditional on the repentance—and consequent conversion—of the guilty (31–35). This, of course, was the agenda behind the intermittent offers of pardon by the Franco dictatorship. Derrida argues for a concept of unconditional "forgiveness" whereby one pardons that which is unforgivable. Whether the victims of Francoist aggression should offer their aggressors unconditional forgiveness is debatable. We can, however, usefully relate Derrida's argument to Honig's insistence that democracy means not turning hatred and fear into love but agreeing to live nonviolently with those one hates and fears.

A positive feature of Derrida's notion of unconditional forgiveness is that it gives agency to the victims. In some respects, the parallel between the Francoist repression and the Holocaust is unhelpful, since the dominance of the Holocaust in memory studies sometimes risks tipping into an endorsement of victim culture, whereby only the stories of victims are found valid or interesting. Particularly problematic has been the privileging, in writing on Holocaust victims, of trauma: we need to ask why trauma is such a seductive concept, why the stories of trauma victims so often become best sellers. One cannot help feeling that the attraction may, in at least some cases, be less a desire to know the truth than a disturbing pleasure derived from "regarding the pain of others" (to cite the title of Susan Sontag's last book).

Trauma is generally defined as the blocking of memory by an event so horrific that it cannot be registered and thus recalled. Instead, the traumatic event keeps reenacting itself for the victim, who is unable to break free of its grip. More radically, Ernst van Alphen has argued that trauma occurs when the event so fails to fit any known category of thought that it cannot even be "experienced" in the first place, let alone remembered. By this he means that, in modern Western culture, sub-jecthood is defined in terms of autonomy and agency. Thus, if all autonomy and agency are taken away, it becomes impossible to conceive of oneself as a person. In such cases, one becomes the object of an event, rather than the subject of an experience: he notes how Holocaust survivors tend to recount their horrific experiences in the third person and talk of how they had to "kill the self" in order to survive. This denial of personhood to Jews, gypsies, homosexuals, and other "deviants" was precisely what the Holocaust was about. Such objectification both allowed the Holocaust to happen and was enacted in its genocidal regime.

I shall come back to this loss of personhood at the end of this essay. What I want to note at this point is that the recent proliferation of testimonies about the Civil War shows that we are not dealing here with trauma (blocked memory), for these firsthand accounts remember past events in the most graphic detail. I am not suggesting that there were no genuine trauma victims of the Spanish Civil War, but by definition they are not the authors of these testimonies. If these eyewitnesses did not tell their story before, the reason is evidently that, for the nearly forty years of the Franco dictatorship, there was not a public sphere—and often not even a private sphere—in which their accounts could be heard by willing listeners. And while censorship was abolished by the 1978 democratic constitution, Spaniards during the Transition were more concerned with the uncertainties of the future than with a repressive past that they wished to put behind them. This lack of interlocutors for some sixty years has created habits of silence that are hard to break. This is important since the emphasis on trauma, by attributing the failure to recount past atrocities to the internal psychic mechanisms of the victim, can stop us from looking for social and political explanations of this failure. One is struck by the number of cases when the stories of past atrocities are told not to children (still too close to events to want to know, or for their parents to want to pass the burden onto them), but to grandchildren (born late enough not to have inherited the legacy of humiliation, shame, and fear).[4]

While the best of these Spanish collections of *testimonios* do serve to give agency—a voice—to those who suffered, there is sometimes a stress on victimhood that, while eliciting sympathy, can encourage a view of Republican supporters as "helpless" objects of historical events beyond their control. This is tricky, because the "*víctimas de la guerra civil*" (to cite the title of Juliá's pioneering volume) were indeed victims and often reduced to the status of a thing, if not a corpse. But it is important not to create a landscape of perpetrators and victims as though those were the only historical positions. We need also to pay attention to the immense grey areas in between these two positions: for example, by examining the difficult subject of the responsibility not just of perpetrators, but of informers, or of those who simply turned a blind eye. This is an area that has barely been broached in Spain—unlike Germany, France, or Holland, where there has been considerable debate on the widespread complicity with Nazism of the population at large. We need also to show that those who were reduced to the status of victim by extreme repression were nevertheless, in other aspects of their lives, individuals with agency.

Here I am arguing against the practice of reproducing only those excerpts from testimonies that recount atrocities perpetrated against victims and in favor of printing the interview transcript in its entirety (or at least with minimal editing). In this respect, there is a striking contrast between earlier collections of testimonies published in democratic Spain and those that have been published since 2000. I refer here to Manuel Leguineche and Jesús Torbado's pioneering *Los topos*, published in 1977 and reissued in 1999 on the back of the recent "memory boom," and to Tomasa Cuevas's collections of testimonies of women activists imprisoned during the war and the Franco dictatorship, *Cárcel de mujeres* (1985) and *Mujeres en la Resistencia* (1986)—reprinted in a single volume in 2004 as *Testimonios de mujeres en las cárceles franquistas*. In both cases, the testimonies were mostly gathered before the end of the dictatorship. In both cases, too, the compilers give us full life histories, each one occupying a separate chapter. This allows their narrators to represent themselves as subjects and not just as victims, since their story is not limited to moments of persecution.[5] In *Los topos*, it is noticeable that the narrators give more space to their wartime exploits— which construct them as historical agents—than to their thirty or so years in hiding, when their agency was severely reduced. All of them stress how they kept mentally, if not physically, active in their hideouts. In the testimonies of female members of the Communist Party (including herself) collected by Cuevas, what strikes the reader is the courage of these women who did not abandon their political activism despite their repeated imprisonment and torture. That is, they depict themselves as women who refused to be reduced to object status, despite what was done to them. The narrative form of the testimonies compiled by Leguineche and Torbado, and by Cuevas, is that of the picaresque genre, which insists on the subaltern narrator-protagonist's ability to defy authority by mocking its rules. The result is an insight into the mentality of a series of individuals that impresses, not just because of what they have suffered, but above all because of their resourcefulness and capacity for survival.

By contrast, the testimonies published since 2000 are narrated in the mode of tragedy, for these are stories of victims, as the jacket blurbs stress. These volumes do not give full life histories[6] but are organized in thematic or chronological chapters, mixing testimonies from a number of narrators in each chapter in order to construct a composite account of a particular category of atrocity. In the most problematic cases, the interviews are chopped up into snippets, which are then spliced together with snippets on the same topic from other interviews (as previously noted, Ronald Fraser had done this in his 1979 *Blood of Spain*). Martínez Reverte and Thomás's *Hijos de la guerra* and Elordi's *Los años difíciles* do not go this far, but they arrange their testimonies in themed or chronologically ordered chapters, edited in such a way that they are devoted almost exclusively to accounts of atrocities.[7] Nonetheless, they print each individual's account (or personal documents submitted to the radio) one at a time, rather than plundering them for "highlights" that are then cut and pasted in different sections to illustrate different points. This allows them to contribute not just to an understanding of what happened but, at a more fundamental level, to the history of subjectivity.

This practice of organizing the testimonies into composite themed or chronological chapters is also used to mix accounts by both Republican and Nationalist victims. This is a striking feature of most of the collections of testimonies published from 2000 to 2003, the explicit aim being the avoidance of partisanship. There have, to my knowledge, been no attempts in Spain to record life stories of perpetrators—although Armengou and Belis make a good job of pursuing a perpetrator in *Les fosses del silenci,* and Manuel Rivas's 1998 novel in Galician, *O lapis do carpinteiro,* is noteworthy for making a perpetrator its narrator. The earlier 1977 *Los topos* throws in a small number of Nationalist survivors, interviewed at the last minute (one suspects at the request of the publishers). But in their compilation *Hijos de la guerra,* Martínez Reverte and Thomás make a point of mixing testimonies by people who suffered the war as children on both sides, on the grounds that, regardless of their parents' politics, they were equally innocent victims. Their explicit aim is to encourage "el reconocimiento del sufrimento de los demás" (the recognition of the suffering of others) (13): a noble sentiment that nevertheless ends up producing a depoliticized vision in which everyone is a victim. *Los años difíciles* respects the overwhelming predominance of Republican testimonies and documents submitted to Elordi's radio program (as he notes), but it includes several accounts of victims of Republican repression. This is right and proper, but the indiscriminate mixing in the same chapter of accounts by victims on both sides creates the impression that they were all the victims of a "collective madness" (the phrase is frequently used). Such a notion glosses over the fact that this was a conflict between radically different political visions.

This depoliticizing strategy becomes explicit in the collections of testimonies that overwhelmingly privilege atrocities committed in the Republican zone. *Historias orales de la guerra civil,* based on nearly a thousand family interviews undertaken by students at the Universidad de San Pablo-CEU in Madrid as an assignment for their history degree, claims to be impartial while admitting, "Claro que estamos hablando de una universidad católica y de élite" (Of course we are talking about an elite Catholic university) (10). Of the responses, 54.9 percent are pro-Nationalist, 12.7 percent are pro-Republican, and the rest are undeclared. The result is an overwhelming predominance of atrocities committed by Republicans, compounded by the editors' consistent use of the term "liberation" to refer to Nationalist territorial gains. This volume cuts and pastes snippets from a mass of interviews into its various themed chapters, so that one cannot build up a profile of any of the narrators, which would enable one to interpret what they say. In the absence of any picture of the individual narrators that would reveal their ideological positioning, the reader is encouraged to take the accumulation of snippets as "fact." The editors' claim to impartiality is belied by their practice of starting each chapter with accounts of Republican atrocities, plus the overall move of the chapters from the war and repression on both sides to "*Piedad y perdón*" (Piety and Pardon) and "*Guerra y religión*" (War and Religion, an account of persecution of Catholics).

It is important to have testimonies from Nationalist supporters, but this mix of depoliticization and blatant bias, while claiming objectivity, is dangerous. Much worse is José María Zavala's 2003 *Los horrores de la guerra civil*, which claims to be a "trabajo exhaustivo y ecuánime" (exhaustive and balanced work) while offering a lurid gallery of "fusilamientos, violaciones, mutilaciones y decapitaciones, infanticidios, enterramientos de vivos, cadáveres devorados por fieras" (executions, rapes, mutilations and decapitations, infanticides, burials of the living, cadavers devoured by wild animals) (back cover). The book's epigraphs from political figures of the Left and Right (Manuel Azaña and Dionisio Ridruejo) are chosen to suggest that both sides were equally guilty. The editor's preface, however, clarifies that the book's aim is to combat the pro-Republican bias of post-1975 Spanish historians, concluding that the panorama of "universal violence" it will offer is an illustration of Hobbes's dictum that "man is a wolf to man." This volume at least makes it blatantly obvious that the presentation of the Civil War as a collective madness is a strategy for avoiding Nationalist responsibility.[8]

Nevertheless, we need to find a way of tackling Nationalist memories if there is to be a working through of old hatreds. It is not surprising that there have been more Truth Commissions than Truth and Reconciliation Commissions, for reconciliation—if it is to be more than an enforced national unification—is not easy. The classic Truth and Reconciliation Commission is that of South Africa, which brought perpetrators and victims together in public, to try to work through their antagonistic feelings with the help of a professional "comforter." This process has been criticized as a state-sponsored public performance, which by definition skewed the testimonial accounts by forcing them into an overall narrative that had reconciliation as its predetermined end (Castillejo-Cuéllar). Indeed, exemption from prosecution was granted in advance to those who agreed to tell their story in public. Chile's Truth and Reconciliation Commission, which produced the Informe Rettig, attempted no such "working through" and has been dismissed by critics (Richard, Avelar) as an official mourning process designed to lay the past to rest as quickly as possible. The impact of official investigations into state repression in Latin America, and elsewhere in the world, on the current discourses of memory in Spain is evident, to the extent of providing a vocabulary for talking about repression.[9] Not only has Spain not attempted any such reconciliation process, but it has not even had a Truth Commission.

This is where testimonies can play a productive role. For what testimonies give us is not so much evidence of what happened as evidence of what the narrators feel about the past at the present time of speaking. A striking feature of the pro-Republican testimonies in most of the volumes I have mentioned, as the editors often note, is the lack of demand for retribution—though there is a strong demand for official recognition of the crimes committed. It seems that nearly four decades of not being able to voice publicly any demand for justice has led to an overwhelming desire, not to see the guilty brought to trial, but simply to have lifted the burden of humiliation and shame that was imposed on the defeated. But when we read pro-Nationalist testimonies—the volume *Historias orales de la guerra civil* is a frightening example—we cannot help but be struck by the virulence of the hatred for the Left that remains unabated to this day. Effectively, what emerges from these testimonies is that the Right continues to regard the Left as not fully human, as *"rojos"* denied any subjectivity.[10] In this sense, if we accept van Alphen's definition of the ultimate repression as the denial of personhood, the Right continues—at a figurative level—to exercise the denial of humanity that it enacted materially with the physical repression of the war and its aftermath.

It is perhaps impossible to change the mind-set of those who for nearly forty years had control over the way the Civil War was remembered. But what can be done is critical analysis of the many testimonies of the Civil War in the public domain, in order to try to understand— and produce public awareness of—the complex structures of present-day feeling that they reveal. This, I would argue, is just as important as using testimonies as evidence of what happened in the past. In saying this, I am arguing for a view of *testimonio* not so much as a "politics of truth" (Beverley's definition), but rather as a "politics of feeling."

NOTES

1. Loureiro notes how representations and studies of the Spanish Civil War prior to the late 1990s emphasized it as a heroic struggle, giving way in recent years to a stress on victimhood. As he points out, this shift in the last decade to a view of history of grievance is not limited to Spain.

2. Since the start of September 2008, Judge-Magistrate Baltasar Garzón has embarked on compiling a register of deaths as a result of reprisals during the wartime and postwar periods. This exercise has been undertaken in response to the many individuals who, appealing to the requirement of the December 27, 2007, Law of Historical Memory that official institutions provide information about victims of violence in the Civil War and Franco dictatorship to those requesting it, have filed such requests with the Audiencia Nacional over which Garzón presides. By September 25, 2008, Garzón had received from assorted associations a total of 130,137 names of victims of Francoist reprisals (the lists still have to be checked for possible duplications). However, none of the individuals requesting information about their "disappeared" relatives has asked for perpetrators to be brought to trial. See Altozano; Junquera and Gómez.

3. See also Cenarro's current oral history work with individuals institutionalized as children by the Francoist welfare institution Auxilio Social ("Memories of Repression").

4. For a thoughtful discussion of how the third generation (the grandchildren of those who experienced the war) has imbibed its meager knowledge of the wartime and postwar years, and the problems that are created by this, see Izquierdo Martín and Sánchez León.

5. The life histories published by Cuevas are very full and were collected by her personally from fellow Communist activists she had encountered in prison;

she allows them to stand with little interference from herself as editor. Leguineche and Torbado tell us little about the circumstances of the interviews they
conducted, apart from their time span (1969–1977) and frequently interrupt
the interviews to give information of their own. They have clearly edited the
transcripts but nevertheless present each life story as a discrete whole.

6. An exception is José Antonio Vidal Castaño's recent *La memoria reprimida: Historias orales del maquis* (2004), which gives full transcripts of extensive
life histories. Although the author's analysis of these unstructured interviews
tends to mine them for "proof" of what "really happened," their full reproduction allows insights into how key events have been processed psychologically.

7. The chapters in Martínez Reverte and Thomás's collection are "La victoria rápida," "Bombardeos, huída y exilio," and "En zona roja" (The Quick Victory; Bombings, Flight and Exile; In the Red Zone). Those in Elordi's book are
"La guerra," "La derrota" (despite including some pro-Nationalist testimonies),
and "La posguerra" (The War, Defeat, and The Postwar).

8. In fact the book, while claiming to present "más de doscientos testimonios" (more than two hundred testimonies), consists of a collage of quotes from
previously published sources, predominantly but not exclusively pro-Nationalist,
inserted into the author's own inflammatory account. Zavala's later book *Los
gángsters de la guerra civil* (2006) makes his political stance clear: the "gangsters"
are all Republican historical figures.

9. For example, Montse Armengou has worked as a journalist in Guatemala and Bosnia. Emilio Silva, founder and president of ARMH, has explained
how his contacts with Spanish lawyers involved in prosecutions concerning
human rights violations under military dictatorship in Chile and Argentina
facilitated ARMH's activities as a political pressure group (Labanyi, "Entrevista" 147).

10. Emilio Silva similarly concludes that national reconciliation is not possible in Spain since the Right does not recognize the suffering of those who
supported the Republic (Labanyi, "Entrevista" 154).

PART III

Speaking for the Dead

Literature and Memory

Toward a Pragmatic Version of Memory

WHAT COULD THE SPANISH CIVIL WAR MEAN TO CONTEMPORARY SPAIN?

Antonio Gómez López-Quiñones

In contemporary Spain, a double process is developing in relation to remembrance of the Civil War. On the one hand, there is a legitimate debate with political, legal, and economic repercussions about what would constitute a responsible, authentically democratic treatment of the legacy of the Civil War. On the other hand (and these two processes cannot be entirely separated), there is a new wave of interest in cultural products regarding the period 1936–1939 (documentaries, fiction films, television programs, new historiographical accounts, memoirs, novels, posters, oral history projects and exhibitions, among others). It would be fair to conclude that the contemporary Spanish cultural and political milieu cannot be properly understood without taking into consideration the Civil War's shadow. I purposely use the word "shadow" because, as Samuel Amago and Joan Ramon Resina claim, the relation between the Civil War and Spanish democracy, between Francoism and post-Francoism, has been camouflaged or veiled. In fact, Amago's and Resina's essays should be framed in a larger intellectual project that attempts a critical revision of the politics of memory in Spain. There are, at least, two relevant elements in this intricate interaction among politics, memory, and culture.

The first element is the relevance of memory for recent debates on collective and political identities. This is a well-documented phenomenon in which the work of some historians and theoreticians, such as Pierre Nora and Maurice Halbwachs, has been instrumental. Nora reinterprets memory in a positive light because, as Noa Gedi and Yigal Elam affirm, in his account, "memory is no longer a servant of history, a mere tool; it is, on the contrary, on a par with history. Memory has in fact become a separate significant corpus, an equal though 'antithetical' rival" (33). Memory is also regarded as a subjective, explicitly political and pluralizing tool with which to democratize unified, officially or academically controlled versions of the past. Memory's emotional, multiple, dynamic, and "alive" quality has played an essential role in our current understanding of the Spanish Civil War. Both Amago's and Resina's works assume memory ("collective memory," "public memory," "traumatized memory," "official memory," "repressed memory") as a privileged locus for resistance or contestation. In opposition to traditional historiography, memory "disrupts the facile linear progression of the narration, introduces alternative interpretations, questions any partial conclusion, withstands the need of closure" (Friedländer, *Memory* 53). In the Iberian context, attempts to create closure, imposing an official, postdemocratic, and also restrictive version of the Civil War, are being destabilized by a political and performative mobilization of memory.

The second element is the critical reexamination of the so-called pact of oblivion. For a couple of decades, any challenge to this rule of silence was postulated as an inconvenient or irresponsible attack on a peaceful, delicate, and finally successful process of negotiation between conflicting ideological forces. Moreover, breaking the consensus achieved during the mystified Spanish Transition demanded physical, emotional, political, and intellectual efforts that, for many years, have been too exhausting for a country "obsessed with creating the image of a brash, young, cosmopolitan nation . . . based on a rejection of the past" (Labanyi, "Engaging"). It would be difficult to accurately understand Amago's and Resina's articles if we do not keep in mind that they insist on an alternative political (and not only material) modernity that does not disseminate false images and comforting discourses about a traumatic past. Amago and Resina also agree on the fact that such an alternative modernity has necessarily to confront the Transition's deficits and simplifications. These two authors are also pointing out one of the main difficulties of cultural inquiry in contemporary Spain, namely the complex association between predemocratic and democratic institutions, figures, attitudes, and capitals. This disturbing association, which clearly shows that one of the main effects of the Transition was the reinscription of the old dictatorship onto the new democratic system, has created a growing discontent about Spanish democracy's fake and untrustworthy nature.

This is probably the reason for which, in these and many other approaches to contemporary Spain, there is a telling insistence on concepts such as treachery, myth, digression, surface appearances, putting aside, pretending, concealment, artificiality, manipulation, falsification, transvestism, and improvisation. In a recent essay (published in a compilation complementary to this one), Patrick Paul Garlinger reinterprets one of these concepts—namely "the recurrence of transgenderism as a discourse for describing the political transformation in Spain" (48). Garlinger's lucid approach focuses on the reactionary political implications of gender vocabulary when it is used to describe the inauthenticity of Spanish democracy. Although Garlinger considers a circumscribed lexical family, we could extend his logic to reclaim, with more positive connotations, all the vocabulary that underlines the inauthenticity of Spanish democracy. This is not very far, I would venture to say, from what Garlinger does in his own text, arguing that when we write about the conformation of subjectivities, collectivities, and/or political systems, we should conceive them not as a more or less stable substance but as a fluid and contradictory process. As a result, Spanish democracy and the Transition are inevitably inauthentic, bogus, or improvised in the sense that negotiating a political situation does not envisage characteristics such as authenticity or sameness. Spanish democracy is a difficult process of change and controversy in which we predictably find (it could not be otherwise) traces of multiple pasts and political aims. A complete rupture with the past and a total refoundation may sound appealing in theory but is pragmatically unfeasible.

Both Amago and Resina are keenly conscious of many of the main issues present in Garlinger's arguments. Garlinger's own ideas are consistent with a well-established school of postmodern thinking on the performative, partially discursive, impure, artificial, changing, incomplete, flexible, nonessentialist nature of identity. In relation to this model of identity, what we can conclude from Amago's and Resina's articles is that their authors adopt a different perspective on the politics of the inauthenticity of Spanish democracy, a perspective that insists on the political utility and ethical desirability of demanding a "true," "authentic," and "real" democracy. Quoting and reinterpreting Paul Ricoeur's opinion on the Vichy regime, Resina claims that "when a government accedes to the state, it accedes by virtue of national continuity." If, as Ricoeur claims, it would be impossible to understand institutional breaks and social discourse on rupture without national continuity, the "original sin" of the Spanish Transition would be its delusional attempts to fantasize an absolute refoundation, the new beginning of a (post)modern country, ignoring Francoism as if forty years of dictatorship were only a bad dream for which no one was responsible. It is from this perspective that the task of rethinking Spanish democracy's inauthenticity in a more positive light becomes more difficult.

Both Amago and Resina seem to conclude that Spanish democracy is still bogus and improvised not because Francoism was not dismantled but because it was transformed. This is likely (though perhaps not) the compromise required by the realpolitik for a nonviolent Transition to a formal democratic system. Today, this Transition remains bogus and improvised because, instead of facing this fact and its consequences, democracy was inaugurated in an act of joyful celebration and revelry, an abandoned moment of complete self-realization that Resina himself relates to the notion of *post-histoire*. What should have been (in geopolitical, social, economic, and institutional terms) merely a beginning was and is legitimized as a point of arrival. As a result, Spanish democracy is inauthentic because of its incapacity or unwillingness to address its authenticity. In other terms, the only way in which Spanish democracy could be truly authentic would be to recognize its bogus nature, its concealment, manipulations, diversions, and transvestisms and, of course, to take remedial action—to do something about it.[1] The importance of "doing something about it" should not be diminished because Amago's and Resina's essays do not defend a version of Spanish democracy as a system in which critical recognition of these inauthenticities would be enough. Both essays propose a prescriptive notion of what a legitimate Spanish democracy could and should be. Where the two authors differ from each other is in the specific measures Spain should adopt in order to provide a second Transition, as Amago suggests, or a permanent Transition, as Resina advocates.

Amago emphasizes notions of communicability, expression, and memory derived from the psychoanalytical theory of trauma. One thesis Amago correctly infers from the novels *Soldados de Salamina* and *La velocidad de la luz* is that "there must be some kind of self-conscious effort to acknowledge the past through reflexive contemplation and, ultimately, through communication." If this mourning process "functions not only as a therapeutic method for coming to terms with personal trauma but also as a way to memorialize the departed," then the absence of such a process produces several types of social and psychological pathologies. Amago claims that rational thought and speech about the Spanish Civil War can disperse specters and ghosts that would otherwise disturb and haunt individual subjectivities or even whole collectivities. The possibility of working through a trauma exists when there is appropriate dialogue, while silence and repression unleash compulsive reenactments that Frederick LaCapra has theorized under the rubric of "acting out."[2]

If real communication creates order, structure, perspective, distance, understanding, and control, then lack of communication or miscommunication are followed by disorder, ignorance, and disempowerment. Echoing the plot of the two novels, Amago highlights the meeting of rational individuals as a moment of epistemological enlightenment that strengthens the self and its coherent attachment to the world. It is through words and grammatical structures that a damaging relationship to the past can be reformulated. Telling and retelling to an "other" rebuild a world devastated by trauma.

Another thesis Amago infers from *Soldados de Salamina* and *La velocidad de la luz* is the transnational nature of war and of its psychological effects. The Latin American "dirty wars" of the 1970s and 1980s, the Vietnam conflict, and the Spanish Civil War have created similar traumas that a transnational analytical language (a new academic lingua franca) would allow us to comprehend and analyze. One could also add that the comparison between traumas is perhaps one of the most questionable aspects of Cercas's work because of its overemphasis on similarities.

It is important to note that Amago also distances himself from positivist conceptions of language, narration, and memory, stressing rather what language, narration, and memory cannot accomplish. These are some of the reasons for which Amago praises Cercas's recuperation of "lost accounts of historical happenings": his self-conscious narrators, his meta-narrative structures, his attention to the constructedness of historiography, his reflections on the incompleteness of historiographical accounts, and his insistence on the "contingent but nevertheless locally comprehensible meaning" of every narration about the past. If Amago's position has many empathic intersections with a postmodern understanding of history, it also shares with Habermas's philosophy a common faith in communication and rationality. The construction of a society where silenced or distorted voices abandon a repressed sphere to integrate into open communication presumes a common language that these voices can speak and a common public space where these voices can join in: "The lifeworld forms a horizon and at the same time offers a store of things taken for granted in the given culture from which communicative participants draw consensual interpretative patterns in their efforts at interpretation" (Habermas 298).

A "given culture," "a horizon," "a store of things," and a "consensual pattern" are precisely the factors required for a collective conversation among rational individuals about the Spanish Civil War, a conversation which could admit not only words but also acts. One of these acts would necessarily be the exhumations of Franco's victims deposited in mass graves. From a communicative perspective, these exhumations would clarify and extend the public forums where a society may talk about its past. It would be productive to consider Amago's ideas from the perspective, for example, of some of Habermas's most interesting commentators, such as Terry Eagleton or Jean Baudrillard.[3] Eagleton questions Habermas's idealistic confidence in the consensual and embracing powers of communicative structures, while Baudrillard challenges Habermas, pointing to the capitalist transformation of the public sphere of rational individuals into an incontrollable mass of consumers that reject political slogans and ideological messages. I mention Habermas's critics in order to highlight the questions implicitly and explicitly posed by Amago. Unearthing skeletons and buried voices is a task long overdue for which there is no longer any justified delay. Yet this urgency should not make us forget what kind of society is going to receive and assimilate these corpses and voices, a society galvanized by material modernization, consumerism, mass-media advertising, cultural performances, and a radical integration of intellectual activities into market laws.

It is at this point that returning to one of Cercas's novels can be quite informative. As Amago explains, Rodney Faulk, the main character of *La velocidad de la luz*, becomes "a walking, talking lacuna of history," "a walking phantasm, a ghost, or a zombie." Amago insightfully adds that this character's ghostlike state is due to his lack of communication and the impossibility of expressing his trauma. Even when he finally recounts his version of the massacre at My Khe, Amago concludes that "his tale has no depth, no reflexivity." I propose here the following hypothesis: that this "depth" mentioned by Amago, which makes a testimony truly therapeutic and healing, is a property intrinsic not to the narration itself, but to the context that receives, contextualizes, and gives social value to a particular testimony. Rodney's confession in front of a camera does not exorcise his personal demons because his public declaration is not valued by his political, social, and cultural context (the United States during the late 1980s).

In some junctures, incommunicability, isolation, or silence can be considered positive signs. They can, for example, indicate the unacceptable social character of some testimonies. Rodney's tormented, suicidal trajectory (that only a sadistic reader could celebrate) does not alter the fact that, in the social market of testimonies, his own narration was so devalued that it could not have any redeeming effect. In relation to Amago's essay, we could cite another example, the mass grave where Federico García Lorca was buried. In recent years, the Junta de Andalucía (the autonomous government of Andalucia) and Ayuntamiento de Granada (the local authority of Granada) have discussed the possibility of exhuming García Lorca's remains. García Lorca's family, which is deeply involved in the poet's legacy, has sided with the reticent voices that fear an opportunistic and political misappropriation of the poet.

Although I am aware of accredited voices that have questioned García Lorca's family and its true motives to adopt such a decision, I would like to propose a constructive political reading of this controversial choice. First, the appropriate social, political, and cultural atmosphere to receive the poet's corpse does not exist. Progressive political forces should not be intersected in a frivolous, self-justifying, pompous mega-party in which Lorca's image becomes a profitable fetish or a sanitized commodity with which everyone, even his ideological detractors, can identify. Second, the absence of a tomb or funeral monument perpetuates Lorca as the uncomfortable personification of the guilty conscience of a city, a social class, and a political movement. Lorca's unbodied status represents a critical exteriority: the impossibility of completely assimilating Lorca, of erasing the political implications of his death, and of paying off a debt that cannot be paid with marble and heartwarming speeches.[4]

Lorca's and Rodney Faulk's asymmetrical examples (and I am conscious of comparing a historical figure to a fictional character) should make us cautious about what we require of Spanish democracy. Demands that overemphasize the importance of recuperating testimonies or exhuming cadavers without paying close attention to the context that is to receive them will run the risk of ignoring certain key issues. Resina refers to these issues when he warns us against "the domestication of historical memory" by certain fictional accounts of the Civil War that "claim the freedom to indulge audiences' melodramatic proclivities." We should also take into consideration the fact that in a market society where nostalgia inspires a great variety of products and has even become a product itself, the Civil War is always on the verge of being commodified and/or becoming a source of profitable commodities. As Resina and Amago conclude, the point of this whole debate is not whether we remember the victims or whether we speak of them. The point is, rather, how and in what terms we regard the victims and the motives for why we talk about them. If the most legitimate reaction is not to be the profitable articulation of a melodramatic pathos around an inflated, good-for-all-purposes, politically reassuring victim, then it is more important than ever to rethink the ideological agenda behind our own demands of the handling of the legacy of the Spanish Civil War. This is the reason Resina, in his essay, disregards humanist, well-intended, or conciliatory positions about the politics of memory in Spain, demanding a type of remembrance with a clear and transformative ("pragmatic" or "action-oriented" we could add) political intention.

Using Harald Weinrich's classic book (*Lethe: The Art of Critique and Forgetting*) as a source of theoretical arguments, Resina links "the exhaustion of the Transition ethos" to recent exhumations of lost cadavers from Franco's violent repression. He argues against the historicization of the Spanish Civil War or, in other terms, against the sociopolitical consideration of the Spanish Civil War as a frozen fresco of illustrious but harmless figures and events, a distant past with which we safely relate through the lens of objectified, detached, impersonalized, and "scientific" information. He examines in detail several aspects of the Transition because this political process instituted the myth of a consensual refoundation through the "lesser evils" of amnesty and amnesia (that, as Resina reminds us, had the same original meaning in Latin and Greek). In fact, this essay could be read as an indictment against the Spanish democracy's falsification of its foundational documents, ideological genealogy, and geopolitical organization. Once we face a demythologized Transition, some quasi-naturalized public institutions and documents, such as the monarchy, the constitution, and even official historiography, need to be rethought. Rather than the venerated base of the so-called Spanish Miracle, they should be seen as extremely contradictory entities that tell us as much about democracy as about Franco's legacy.

One of the most appealing arguments in Resina's essay is that the Transition's shortfalls cannot be measured in only quantitative terms. He calls attention to the never-specified and sometimes-intangible distribution of social value that "determine[s] the·potential and restrictions of subsequent generations." From this perspective, it is impossible to accurately calculate how much damage and pain the dictatorship inflected upon some communities and how beneficial this dictatorship was for many others. Resina's point is that this institutionalized, socialized, and internalized distribution of damage and benefits, shame and prosperities, fear and pride, has never been discussed, confronted, or remedied by the new and improvised democratic society. Under these circumstances, Resina accepts that corpses from Francoist crimes are susceptible to semantic manipulation because their meaning is never self-evident. They are—from the beginning and perpetually—framed by social, ideological, and cultural interests. On the other hand, this author perceives an uncanny and "undeconstructible" element in these exhumations and these unburied bodies, "that abolish[es] the temporal gulf between *that* action and *this* feeling."

Resina also reflects on *Antigone* because this classical tragedy offers him the rhetorical tools and a theoretical context to interrogate the political and cultural implications of mass graves from the era of Fascist repression. Perhaps the most important lesson we can learn from *Antigone* is that "the dead who are not granted a safe passage into the cultural beyond remain politically alive" and that "a state that does not bury the dead decomposes alongside the corpses." Proper burials and funeral rituals are not only a form of granting death a symbolic status, but also a communal act of justice that should exceed any government's prerogatives. Although Resina's vocabulary is not so indebted to psychoanalytic or trauma theory as Amago's is, both of them concur in pointing at the politically degrading ("haunting," disquieting," "falsifying," "unsettling") effects of these improperly buried corpses.[5] For Resina, there is also a direct connection between the debate on mass graves and the multinational character of the Spanish state. He claims that if we do not want to disseminate false images of the past, the current recovery of corpses and testimonies needs to be framed in a precise geopolitical context.

Spain was in 1936 a multinational state in which a centralist, authoritarian movement reacted with violence against the country's so-called peripheral nationalities. Remembering the Spanish Civil War, Resina asserts, implies the recognition of national differences and alterities that seven decades ago were physically and symbolically attacked by reactionary forces with an economic and cultural interest in defending an illusory indivisible Spanish unity. In fact, the contemporary representations of the Civil War that, whether from a left-wing or a right-wing perspective, obviate this factor, implicitly postulating a "National (Hi)story" for the whole peninsula, should be observed with skepticism. In a crucial historical moment when the constitution is being used as an ahistorical straitjacket for necessary and overdue geopolitical reforms, Resina demands recollections of the Civil War with an incisive political edge— in other words, recollections that do not ignore crucial contributing factors of the war, factors that have not been properly addressed thirty years after the restoration of democracy.[6] It is precisely from this perspective that I would like to briefly comment on another vector of the Spanish Civil War that is being disregarded or ignored (as much, I would argue, as the multinational character of the Spanish state itself).

In relation to recent recuperations of silenced testimonies and corpses buried in mass graves, we should remember that many of these stories are directly linked to long-standing struggles against capitalism. In the 1930s, the struggle incorporated several purposes and political affiliations, but all shared a common concern for issues such as accumulation of capital, class conflict, exploitation, working-class rights, redistribution of wealth, and access to means of production. I am willing to accept that the mere mention of these concepts has acquired an outdated flavor; neoliberalism, globalization, and late capitalism seem so entrenched and incontestable that this vocabulary has acquired an obsolete, unfashionable aura. The paradox of this aura is that, in contemporary Spain, issues related to capitalist modernization are more relevant and pressing than ever. It is undeniable that Spain's historical situation in the 1930s should not and could not be mechanistically identified with the current state of affairs. It is also undeniable that confronting capitalism (of which Fascism can be considered, as Jeffry Frieden explains, an avant-garde manifestation) is one of those topics whose relevance, far from vanishing, has increased exponentially.[7] Politically relevant approaches to the Civil War (through new testimonies or excavations of mass graves) should not refrain from placing the trajectory of anticapitalist movements and their relevance to twenty-first-century Spain at the center of this debate.

In the case of the multinational reality of the Iberian Peninsula and the intensification of the capitalist logic in Spain, Resina's and Amago's essays (as well as my own remarks) emphasize both the particular content of contemporary politics of the past and, above all, the way we relate to this content. No other philosophical reflection has been more influential in this respect than Walter Benjamin's *Thesis on the Philosophy of History*. From this brief yet complex text, I would like to underline Benjamin's concept of historiographical knowledge, not as a closed, completed entity that perpetuates an epic of victories and humiliations, but as an unfinished process that admits radical reorientations and ruptures. If, as Benjamin affirms, "the past carries with it a temporal index by which it is referred to redemption," the Spanish Civil War has the potential to inspire new avenues of political thought and cultural reflections on a much more democratic, egalitarian, participatory, inclusive, and truly pluralist Iberian Peninsula in the future (254). This will be a difficult and tortuous task in a time when radical political proposals tend to be dismissed and caricaturized as 1960s-style myths, infantile nonconformity, late-romantic utopias, intellectual fixation on defeated causes, contra-factual dreams, or futile expressions of vague anti-system feelings. Beyond these criticisms (although they do need to be taken and answered seriously), if remembering the Spanish Civil War does not mobilize our political energies, opening new scope for debate and action, this past will be condemned to play a disgraceful role, becoming an eclectic, semi-empty, manipulable rubric with which to peddle a broad array of products (testimonies, films, novels, excavations, corpses, or objects) for the growing nostalgia market.

NOTES

1. Alberto Medina has referred to this political attitude as an "ética masoquista de la memoria" (a masochistic ethic of memory): "Los residuos de la historia, la incapacidad de olvidar, funcionan como una fuerza que obstaculiza o niega la clausura llevada a cabo por la ficción dominante creando un espacio de resistencia radical" (The residue of history, the incapacity of forgetting, functions as a force that makes difficult or impossible the closure proposed by the dominant fiction, thus creating a space for radical resistance) (190).

2. LaCapra affirms that "working through would thus seem to involve a mode of repetition offering a measure of critical purchase on problems and responsible control in action which would permit desirable change" (209). "Acting out" would imply a kind of compulsive repetition in which there is not that "measure of critical purchase on problems and responsible control" that creates a healing distance between past and present (209).

3. Eagleton partially disagrees with Habermas's philosophical proposal because "Habermas' discursive community must be absolved as far as possible from all distorting powers and interests, relying on the force of the better argument alone. This community 'virtualizes' the constraints of practical interests, suspends them, like the work of art, for a privileged moment, puts out of play all motives other than the will to a rationally grounded agreement" (405). In contrast, Jean Baudrillard concludes that "information dissolves meaning and the social into a sort of nebulous state leading not to a surfeit of innovation but to the very contrary, to total entropy" (100). It is difficult to imagine how a new

voice can participate in a rational public debate if what we call the "public" or "social" sphere has become a "total entropy."

4. Around this concept of challenging exteriority, Mari Paz Balibrea has articulated one of the most original interpretations of the Spanish Republican exile. In Balibrea's opinion, the insistence on integration and reincorporation does not take into consideration that the "Republican exile cannot and will never be totally contained nor exhausted within the Spain that was traumatically left behind" (6). Balibrea also states that "what gets crucially lost in the 'generosity' of such a democratic, pluralistic gesture (*'aquí cabemos todos'*), are the variety of political and ethical projects, what I have earlier called the alternative modernities, dead ends of Spanish modernity that those expelled in 1939 carried with them" (12). I would add to these fundamental arguments that those killed in 1939 also carried with them other alternative modernities (more inclusive and democratic) that should not be co-opted or neutralized.

5. It is also worth noting that in these and other critical approaches to Spain's contemporary culture, Derrida's postontological "hauntology" has been very influential. Derrida approaches "hauntology" as a logic that "would not be merely larger and more powerful than an ontology or a thinking of Being. . . . It would harbor within itself, but like circumscribed places or particular effects, eschatology and teleology" ("On Forgiveness" 10). I find particularly appealing in Derrida's essay his insistence on "[Marxism's] certain emancipatory and *messianic* affirmation, a certain experience of the promise . . . that is, not to remain 'spiritual' or 'abstract,' but to produce events, new effective forms of action, practice, organization, and so forth" (111–12). There is a strong historical and theoretical relation to be articulated between the legacy of the Spanish Civil War and Derrida's Marxist emancipatory and messianic affirmation that, as he explains, "one can try to liberate from any dogmatics and even from any metaphysico-religious determination" (111).

6. Adorno affirms that "since the law tends to assert itself more effectively than freedom, we have to stay on guard and be constantly vigilant in the face of fetishization of law, for example, of juridical norms that claim that decisions once taken are irrevocable" ("What" 122). This fetishization of the law becomes a stronger temptation during periods of crisis or transformation (like the Spanish Transition itself), when freedom and the law restructure their relationship, which "is not a well-balanced, rational compromise, but possesses dynamic elements on both sides" (122).

7. Frieden's essay on capitalism's fate during the 1940s is quite illuminating in this respect (253–329).

The Weight of Memory and the Lightness of Oblivion

THE DEAD OF THE SPANISH CIVIL WAR

Joan Ramon Resina

> Death is the most powerful agent of forgetting. But it is not all-powerful. From time immemorial men have erected barriers against forgetting in death, so that clues suggesting remembrance of the dead are considered by specialists in prehistory and archaeology to be the surest indications of the presence of human culture. The rituals of worship of the dead with their pleas for intercession, sacrificial acts, and burial objects no doubt serve in many cases primarily to ensure that the dead person enjoys a smooth journey into the beyond. But gravestones always also serve as "monuments" warning the living not to forget their dead—and yet people often forget all too easily, for "life goes on." (Weinrich 24)

Thus begins Harald Weinrich's discussion of Dante's restoration of the memory of the dead in his magisterial book on forgetting. In this paragraph Weinrich establishes three basic points that bear on the subject of historical memory. First, the link between memory and the human condition comes down, in essence, to the evidence that to be human is to fight not against death (which is a survival strategy common to all living creatures) but against extinction, which only humans are capable of comprehending. To struggle against extinction involves resisting obliteration after the catastrophe of death has taken place. And this is of course what the Dantean characters do in the beyond, when they entreat the Christian poet to remember their stories. Short of undoing death, the poet may hold back their disappearance at the cost of immortalizing their suffering. Thus they meet their punishment in their own desire to become images of horror for all eternity.

The second point is that the rituals of burial (and we should add, of mourning) are meant to ensure the smooth departure of the dead—in other words, to sever their emotional entanglement with the living and to secure their status as images in memory. And the third point is the role that certain public acts of memory fulfill in the body politic, warning the living not to forget, or vice versa, stimulating oblivion so that life, a certain quality of life, can go on.

THE STRUGGLE AGAINST FORGETTING

The first of these points refers to witnessing, an activity implying some form of presence at the events being witnessed and a moral stance that cannot be dissociated from sympathy with the suffering of victims. In Spain the recent run to open mass graves from the Civil War has given a new twist to the politics of memory, which now appears clearly as an extension of the perpetrators' success. Since the creation in December 2000 of the Asociación para la Recuperación de la Memoria Histórica (ARMH) by Emilio Silva and Santiago Macías Pérez, people all over Spain have stepped forward and pointed out the location of unmarked graves, where seventy years ago a sizable number of men and women were hastily buried. They were victims of purges undertaken by the rebel army and Falange death squads with the connivance of the religious authorities. Official support for the retrieval of bodies has not been forthcoming, except in the case of volunteers who fell on the Russian front while fighting alongside the German Wehrmacht in World War II.

In Catalonia, the Generalitat under Jordi Pujol established a pilot program that helped carry out the first exhumations in a region where fifty-four mass graves containing over four thousand bodies were excavated in the environs of Barcelona alone. And the Basque government has provided aid for the forensic activities that are crucial to the identification of bodies. But so far the Spanish governments have remained aloof if not averse to the growing demand to air the material memory of the repression. The anxieties induced in a majority of Spaniards by those who tenaciously follow the archival trail leading to the exhumation of disappeared loved ones, by the renewed debate around the Fascist symbols and monuments persisting in many Spanish towns, by high-strung incidents like the dispute about the destination of confiscated archives, or by the obstinacy of Basques and Catalans in reasserting their national specificity in the framework of the state indicate that the psychological wounds have not healed and that the social division created by Franco's unconditional victory continues to shape the collective behavior of Spaniards.

The beginning of the excavations coincided with the high point of a debate about historical memory that is not exclusively Spanish, but global in scope. Nonetheless, it is reasonable to ask: Why now? The answer to this question bears on the exhaustion of the Transition ethos, a depletion of conviction in the virtues of that political maneuver that is tangible today in many spheres of political life. One of the consequences of this exhaustion has been the appearance of an Antigone complex. The appeals to restore the memory of the dead and the implicit need to recall the circumstances of their disappearance challenge the desire, crucial to the Transition's strategy, to historicize the Civil War and its aftermath. By "historicize" I mean here to degrade memories into events that no longer claim the attention, much less arouse the passions, of anyone with the exception of professional historians—events that one is done with.

At odds with the desire for a hasty closure of the past, the exhumation of corpses in the presence of immediate relatives showed the impossibility of establishing a clear distinction between history and memory. This is so because past and present remain interwoven in the emotions of the survivors. When Katherine Verdery writes, "Bodies have the advantage of concreteness that nonetheless transcends time, making past immediately present," she hints at the uncanny feeling that presides over the retrieval of long-concealed graves (28). Uncanny, not in the sense of a gothic manifestation of past violence, but in that of an experience that abolishes the temporal gulf between *that* action and *this* feeling. Uncanny, not because the light and fresh air that tear into the opened grave defamiliarizes the bodies felled by violence and ruined by

organic processes, but on the contrary, because the rush of consciousness and the release of contained expectation turn those remains into
our contemporaries. Just as long-buried objects can turn to dust at the
slightest aeration, the reemergence of the "secret" dead annihilates at
once the meticulous work of mandated amnesia. But it is not only the
so-called peace of Francoism that crumbles with the return of the repressed. Those frail vestiges of past violence foul a quarter of a century
of cynical democracy.

Dead bodies not only mark a space and localize a claim. They not
only ground the assertion "it happened here" but also partake of the
present implied by the "hereness." Bodies have the quality of relics, of
what is left behind (*relinquere*), but retain the pastness of an event. As a
relic, the corpse displays a concrete temporality and displays it, paradoxically, through the visible corruption of the evidence: fleshless bones,
rotten garments, body fragments that cannot be easily matched or identified. The fascination of mass graves nearly three-quarters of a century
after their making implies a turning point in the collective memory with
undeniable consequences for historiography. In the wake of the exhumations it becomes harder to relativize the past, and all that revision-
ists can do in the face of such evidence is to confront bodies with bodies in a macabre count aimed at crafting a balance without cost to the
moral status quo. But although the materiality of bodies cannot be gain-
said, and their identity may be analytically established, they do not, for
all that, resist semantic manipulation. Bodies, says Verdery, present the
illusion of having "a single meaning that is solidly 'grounded,' even
though in fact they have no such single meaning" (29). This is always
the case when dead bodies are mobilized in support of the social body's
foundational myth.

The Valley of the Fallen, the postwar massive stonework that serves as
Franco and José Antonio Primo de Rivera's mausoleum in the Guadar-
rama Mountains north of Madrid, is a case in point. This granite dream
of enduring empire remains a place of Fascist pilgrimage through the
semantic manipulation of bodies. Hallowed with the body of the Falange's founder and wrapped in the anticipatory aura of Franco's earthly
remains, the Valley of the Fallen was conceived as a shrine in advance of
its relics. Later, when the regime began to camouflage its ideological origins, bodies were called on again to provide the alibi for the blatant dis-

play of power. It was in this way that a few bodies from the Republican side ended up among the nearly forty thousand bodies that turned the monument into a "mass grave" of the Fascist crusade. This is how the fiction of a memorial to the sacrifice of both sides arose. The regime never acknowledged that this alleged symbol of reconciliation claimed the lives of thousands of Republican prisoners, who worked on its construction reduced to the condition of slaves.

Calamities like the Civil War retain their divisive potential not only for those directly involved but also for the groups that are defined by the institutionalization of the outcome. After the tragic settling of differences, societies redistribute social value in ways that determine the potential and restrictions of subsequent generations. One of the shortcomings of the Transition may be the conspicuous inability of the parties representing the Republic's legacy to write the history of the democratic state on the tombstones of their dead. The grave of President Companys, Franco's most illustrious political victim, was officially honored only as late as October 15, 2004, in a ceremony from which the president of the government and the head of the state were conspicuously absent. To this date, the court martial that sentenced Companys to death in 1940 has not been revised; as a consequence, the democratic state de facto upholds Franco's liquidation of Catalonia's government in the body of its elected representative. The Civil War continues to be a central referent for the collective self-perception of Spanish citizens, in part because it was the last extended conflict affecting the entire population and in part because the values it polarized are set in motion every time the memory of the conflict resurfaces.

The notion of *post-histoire,* mobilized at the end of the Cold War to announce the end of the Hegelian dialectic, had its modest prelude in the Spanish attempt to dam up historical forces with a constitution. Shedding Franco's totalitarianism but retaining the substance of his nationalism, this document soon became a political fetish and, like the crown it legitimizes and relies on, an instrument of immobility. But retrenchment behind a constitution conceived as the last station of political evolution requires the dimming of the historical consciousness, which then acquires subversive potential. The deteriorating sense of the past is made worse by the fact that we now live in posttraditional society. Experience is no longer communicated through widely accepted social rituals or transmitted along with ancient lore but fabricated ad hoc and disseminated through a combination of state-sponsored events and the opportunism of the culture industry. Commercial exploitation of the past produces an ersatz knowledge. At the same time, real confrontation with the past appears redundant if not downright blameworthy. Never before has there been so much fascination with historical memory and so much resistance to its implications. Our relation to the past has become spectatorial, as if mediated witnessing of the atrocities and injustices of previous generations happened in a different moral planet and could not claim our moral response in the lived present.

Contemporary attempts to launch a historical novel and film can draw on reliable material, but, more often than not, they claim the freedom to indulge audiences' melodramatic proclivities. Much of this work studiously avoids the harsher aspects and lingering implications of the Civil War, or when it confronts them, it is generally through an aesthetic detour. But there is no reason to be surprised by the domestication of historical memory. November 22, 1975, was not the downfall of a tyranny but the self-transmogrification of a regime that could last as long as it did thanks to its adaptability but also to broad support and even broader passivity. It would be wrong to confuse such passivity with helplessness, for it borders on complicity. As Saul Friedlander asserts, "in a system whose very core is criminal from the beginning, passivity is, as such, system-supporting" (*Memory* 73).

Widespread complicity accounts for the remarkable tolerance of the censoring of memory well after the Franco era. Such tolerance was often condoned as the price of reconciliation, but the reason cannot really be fear of another conflagration. A more likely cause is the impregnation of society with Francoist values through the capillary dispersion of corruption. It was not just the Francoist elite but a considerable part of Spanish society that found it convenient to divest itself of its memory. Although much of the evidence was destroyed in the 60s, when police files and the records of the civil governments were made to disappear, later destructions could have been prevented by swift judiciary action. How, if not by rhyzomatic complicity, can we account for the social tolerance of military and police archives closed to researchers, of files classified until the death of all concerned, of threats against journalists and media, of the rehabilitation of Falange and the ultraviolent

Fuerza Nueva organization as legal contenders in the first democratic elections? Why, despite sustained "left-wing" majorities in the '80s and early '90s, did the Spanish parliament fail to condemn the dictatorship until 2001, and then only in a lackadaisical manner shorn of practical consequences? The answer to these questions is that the Transition was not the democratic reinvention of the state that officialdom has vaunted for decades. It was, in effect, an intergenerational handing over of institutions calculated to remain in the same hands for a long time. Few of those institutions were shut, some underwent cosmetic changes, and most remained unchanged. They embodied the Francoist principles at the time. From then on they would channel the evolution of those principles into a diffuse climate of opinion. Repression of memory would make it easier to uphold that opinion without avowing, or even being aware of, its origin.

During the Transition the myth of a consensual refoundation of the state replaced the myth of the providential Caudillo. "Consensual" implied that a balanced representation of all social groups crafted the new political framework in the course of unhindered debate. Consensus both presupposed and promised national reconciliation. As a token of reconciliation, the regime granted across-the-board amnesty, releasing thousands of people who were serving sentences for political activity considered subversive under Francoist law. But there was a catch, which the crowds clamoring for amnesty in the streets failed to grasp. Amnesty implied amnesia. Both words mean, of course, something different in contemporary English. But the semantic gap is only an effect of the modern distinction between the individual and the social. Amnesty is institutionalized oblivion, the deliberate erasure of a part of the civic past that otherwise would cling to the present. Thus, if amnesia is, at least since Freud, disingenuous inability to recall certain chapters from personal history, oblivion is, in the words of Nicole Loraux, "the shadow cast by the political on memory" (83). In the first case the ego fears the return of the repressed; in the second the state is threatened by the relevance of the past to its present organization. Obviously, individuals cannot forget on command, but amnesty ensures that they relegate the proscribed memories to the realm of their private conscience.

Amnesty, then, is amnesia by decree. As a means of surmounting civic strife, it has a long tradition in the West. Regimes based on civic participation have often availed themselves of this tool, and thus we find the first instance of amnesty in a transition to democracy after a dictatorship, that of the Thirty, in fifth century BCE Athens. In 403, the victorious democrats proclaimed a reconciliation involving a ban: *me mnesikakein*, "It is forbidden to recall the misfortunes" (Loraux 87). Isocrates explained the effect of the ban, which was implemented through an oath taken by each citizen and enforced with heavy penalties: "Since we mutually gave each other pledges . . . , we govern ourselves in a manner as beautiful as collective . . . as if no misfortune had happened to us" (91). The intention could not be clearer: to rebuild the state on the fiction that violence in the past left no traces in the present, that it had not befallen the very community on which the ban was imposed. Could there be more explicit proof that politics, as the art of governance, requires the state's custody of the collective memory? An indiscreet peek at its cradle reveals that politics is not the daughter of memory, of Mnemosyne, but of Lethe, oblivion.

"Amnesty" and "oblivion" are words of Greek and Latin origin meaning the same thing. Once these words entered the political sphere, they took on a prescriptive sense. It is with this sense that a directive of "amnesty and oblivion" (redundant for good measure) featured in peace treaties in seventeenth- and eighteenth-century Europe (Weinrich 171). This clause imposed on the signatories the obligation to renounce all assignment of blame and retribution for acts committed in the course of the previous war. Such obligation was remembered by the Franco officials during the Transition and came into play regardless of the hopes or intentions of their victims. By demanding political amnesty, opponents of the dictatorship in effect barred the way to future indictment of the perpetrators, unwittingly granting democratic status to totalitarian individuals and collectives.

A final line had been drawn on the recent past. Soon the Franco decades were no longer seen as a time of exception to be redressed but as a continuum with Spanish history. The year 1939 was not, in the emerging view, an interruption of the self-determining tradition inaugurated with the Republic, but the beginning of a period of crisis management in line with an overarching nation-building project going back to the fifteenth century, or earlier in the most ardent accounts. It is now possible to understand how the democratization of the regime after Franco's death brought about the latter's normalization. The Transition had in fact begun six years earlier, when the Generalissimo proclaimed Juan Carlos his successor on July 22, 1969. The dictator's decision became the cornerstone of the consensus that could be reached after his death. But that consensus implied reinscribing the Francoist refoundation of the monarchy through his Law of Succession of 1947.[1] And thus everything was done to obliterate Franco's disruption of the dynastic line, creating in the citizens a sense of historical continuity based on the crown. This manipulation of memory, assisting what was in effect an embezzlement of popular sovereignty, gave Francoism the status of a ripple in the broader stream of the national monarchy.

Canceling not just the regime's liability but even the memory of its guilt satisfied everyone, including outsiders. All remaining international exclusions imposed on Spain since 1939 were repealed after 1975. With the cancellation of the guilt, the social division between victors and vanquished disappeared by enchantment, and with it the distinction between victims and perpetrators. Dissolving the moral certainties of but a few years before opened the way to a relativism that would increase in the same proportion as the collective memory declined, making the roles of victims and perpetrators interchangeable. Self-awarded political amnesty permitted Francoists to retain their social and economic privileges, while the opposition, relying on a moral trump card that it had just thrown away, saw in the myth of reconciliation an opportunity for a gradual transformation of the state. Time was on their side, they believed, and Francoism would just wither away. But the myth of the consensual pact threw political culture into a deep freeze, and democratic progress was hindered by a constitution that, instead of adjusting to the country's complexity, proved to be a fetter on the pragmatic evolution of the state.

IMAGES OF THE DEAD

The second point in Weinrich's quotation bears on the process of mourning and the transition of the dead from material presences to mnemonic images. Rituals of remembrance facilitate the disentangling of the living from the departed. Such rituals are at the foundation of culture and at the origin of sedentary society—in other words, of the state. To lie in state is to be placed in public view for honors accorded prior to burial. Public honoring of the deceased sustains the transcendence that the state claims with respect to each subject, lifting bereavement from the private to the social sphere. In ancient Greece the dead were severed from the family and taken over by the city. The purpose of the public rites, which expressly forbid the presence of female survivors, may have been to curb subjective mourning and bring excess under control, but their obvious effect was to ground the public spirit in the socialization of mourning (Loraux 20). This being the case, the state undergoes a crisis when, neglecting the imperative of ritual justice, it fails to gather the grief of the entire community into its fold.

Antigone's tragedy is often read as a confrontation between the atavistic law of kinship and the higher law of the state or, alternatively, as the clash between ethics and pragmatics. But she seems more in character as spokesperson for the political legitimacy that Creon's arbitrariness threatens. Creon's authority rests on the successful deployment of force in civil war and on the threat of further violence made legal by his diktat. His interdiction of burial for his personal enemies undercuts the state's claim to rise above factions, institutionalizes the civil split, and, as Tiresias warns, endangers the city. More fundamentally, it transgresses the limits of humanity by regressing to a precultural stage. Thus the ruler's inhumanity comes out in his ban on inhumation. Culture is disrupted by the refusal of ritual and the veto on the work of mourning. The tyrant's puffed-up identification of his will with the public good contravenes the fundamental principle of culture, namely the sublimation of violence into reassuring mnemonic images. Creon drives out the soothing images associated with the work of mourning by producing alternative images meant to arouse powerful emotions.

> So for the good of Thebes her laws I frame:
> And such the proclamation I set forth . . .
> Therefore to all this city it is proclaimed
> That none may bury, none make moan for him,
> But leave him lying all ghastly where he fell,
> Till fowls o' the air and dogs have picked his bones. (Sophocles 218)

Although mothers were denied participation in the Athenian funerals, they had a right to the bones of the funeral pyre (Loraux 37). This pledge of the state to return a material trace of the beloved body as proof of the honors rendered to it is broken by Creon's bequest of Polynices' bones to the beasts. By reinserting the corpse into nature's cycle without ritual mediation, Creon subtracts it from the realm of culture, calling into question the very foundation of the state.

If the state wants to perpetuate itself, Creon's disarticulation of Polynices' body—the scattering and defiling of his bones—calls for a contrasting image of steadfast composure. With such a balancing image, achieved through her own sacrifice, Antigone aspires to repair the breach made by the tyrant in the ritual cycle:

> I'll bury him; doing this, so let me die.
> So with my loved one loved shall I abide,
> My crime a deed most holy: for the dead
> Longer have I to please than these on earth.
> There I shall dwell for ever. (215)

The longer time she reckons with is the time of collective memory—that is, the recurrent time of a cult that Creon may not proscribe or curtail without bringing about his own downfall. It is, in short, the time on which the state is founded. The ancient polis had its origin in ancestor worship, practiced separately by each family or clan. Later, when public worship displaced the Penates or household gods, belief in the permanence of the dead through the observance of the rites by the living was transferred to the pantheon and became the foundation of the city.

If the state sublimates death into culture, Creon offends it by organizing a culture of death. Under the aegis of horror, sovereignty is synonymous with the tyrant's death-bringing power, while the images of carnage that he spitefully calls forth become the cornerstones of the new state. Unlike Oedipus, Antigone is not driven by an epistemological passion. When she confronts Creon with the bones of Polynices, the question about the truth (which implicates the state's legitimacy) is not raised. What counts, what is decisive (and the source of renewed tragedy) is her loyalty to the dead. Her justice-rendering act is inevitably tragic because, by turning the scene of horror into one of culture, she not only reasserts humanity but in fact turns the state against itself. And in this way she reinvents it.

The dead who are not granted passage into the cultural beyond remain politically alive. Unable to go on living themselves, the survivors become permanent reminders of a past that no one wants to heed. Their broken lives are evidence that a state that does not bury the dead decomposes alongside the corpses. In this light, the refusal of post-Franco governments to accord symbolic burial to the victims by apologizing for the crimes committed in the name of the state is a fatal avoidance of responsibility. And no pretext will deflect the consequences of denied ritual—certainly not the pretext that the Civil War makes Spanish society both victim and perpetrator and therefore the state cannot apologize to itself. Such an argument, fairly current in the '90s, when demands for symbolic restitution were being voiced, willfully dissolves the distinction between state and society and between society as a whole and the individuals and groups that were victimized, often for the slightest association with the previous structure of governance, for lukewarm adherence to the new axis of values, or simply for belonging to a stigmatized social group. Above all, it ignores that the state qua state is the ultimate referent for action undertaken by the institutions.

On the matter of responsibility, the post-Franco governments would have done well to consider the wisdom of Paul Ricoeur's stance regarding the Fifth Republic. When asked what he thought about François Mitterrand's argument that the French state did not have to seek forgiveness for the crimes committed by the Vichy government, Ricoeur replied,

> The fact that there was an institutional break does not mean that there was not a continuity of the nation precisely as a historical community, incarnated in the vast network of the institutions of civil society that are framed by the state. This is why I had the feeling that there was an obligation for the state to take in hand the totality of our history. . . . We would not only be more honest but we would be freer if we were to pass judgment on ourselves. No one would relate to their own personal

history in the manner we have been asked to relate to our national history: no one would say, "I was not the same, I was someone else." Contrary to what is claimed, the continuity is beyond debate, in particular in the public sector: if you open the register of high officials in 1948, you will see that two-thirds of them were already in their positions in 1942. (122–23)

If you open the register of high officials in Spain in 1980, you will see that many of them were already in office in 1975. Even after 1982, the year when political power was transferred to the opposition, many predemocratic bureaucrats remained in key institutional positions. But Ricoeur's point is not that one (innocent) regime must shoulder the responsibility of another (guilty) one, but that when a party accedes to the state government, it accedes by virtue of national continuity. Ricoeur's regret at the narrow moral vision of President Mitterrand is consonant with Friedlander's observation that "democratization of political consciousness and moral sensitivization of historical consciousness are unavoidably linked" (99).

OF GRAVEYARDS AND CONSTITUTIONS

Weinrich's third point refers to the mnemonic role of monuments to the dead. He argues that such monuments are inefficient guarantees of memory, because people are inclined to forget. Nevertheless, gravestones are apt localizations of memory, centers for the organization of the past. Each slice of the past, says Halbwachs quoting Bergson, is articulated by certain dominant memories, which provide support for secondary ones. To locate a memory means either to recognize it as dominant, or to discover a dominant memory, to which the one we want to situate is attached (146). Mass graves dug up with the help of the memory of survivors establish new overriding memories, which reorganize the relevance of the past.

Such localizations affect the collective memory more immediately and comprehensively than historiography does. The reason is that memory is bound up with action, whereas analytical discourse relates to knowledge. The more intimately consciousness is involved in the present, the more vivid and compelling memory becomes. According to Halbwachs, "each time we come close to *action*, consciousness adheres more to those memories that resemble our current perception from the viewpoint of the action that we must undertake" (146). Because action relies on memory, the latter is selective and cannot dwell on the totality of past experience, or enter into excessive detail. Its inherent tendency to simplification makes memory vulnerable to historical critique, as well as to reversals brought about by a different course of action or an altered pragmatic intent. On the other hand, memory retains the ethical force of witnessing and in this way rises easily to the status of a political factor.

If proximity to action determines that the memories selected by consciousness will resemble our perception of the present situation, then the reverse also obtains, and reiteration of a given memory threatens the subject with a recurrence of action deemed consistent with the pattern of recall. We are not far from the psychoanalytical concept of "acting out," although here the terms are reversed, for it is not repression that leads to a recomposed theater of action, but on the contrary, it is the fear of action that compulsively pushes memory back to the preconscious. The constitution, drenched in tacit memories of the Civil War and the dictatorship, makes it easy to appeal to fear of renewed violence in order to keep history still.[2] Impassioned appeals to the foundational consensus as the supreme argument to keep this political charter shut betray a troubled awareness that "consensus" on the same terms could no longer be obtained today. But fear depends on images, and the Transition's inability to face the horror that remained under its surface robbed the dictatorship of its sting in the memory of the young. To compensate for the fading conditioning by fear, affective images are periodically projected on the social imaginary: for instance, warnings about the state's Balkanization, a dire reference to the latest European civil war.[3]

When people denounce the fading of historical memory, this does not mean that historical research or memoirist writing is lacking. If anything, there is a glut of writing on the Civil War and the dictatorship, but the sheer volume of writing draws attention away from the central issues, neutralizing their potential impact. The constitution was, in this regard, a watershed. Rejected by the most obdurate members of the Francoist establishment—among them the future premier José María Aznar—it was endorsed by other groups as a limited but potentially adaptable framework through which Spain could leave its autocratic tradition behind. It represented an unstable truce between the spirit of change and that of continuity, achieved at the price of substantial forgetting. Even under these conditions, the "consensus-based" constitution could not prevent conspiracy and military attempts to bring the democratic process to a halt, or, less publicized, the involution of the autonomic process in the wake of the coup of February 23, 1981.

Since then, the constitution has changed its sign. No longer symbolizing the spirit of compromise, it has become an emblem of inflexibility and an instrument of regression. H. Rosi Song observes that "Este documento se erige como destinatario de una obligada devoción porque encarna la vigencia de una coherencia y unidad nacional que antecede al reconocimiento de la pluralidad de España" (This document has come about as the result of a compulsory devotion because it embodies the validity of an idea of national coherence and unity that precedes the recognition of the plurality of Spain) (225–26). In other words, it subordinates the recognition of fact to the prescription of ideology. Song perceptively points out the contradiction inscribed in the constitution and even its subversion by its putative guardians: "Pero la fidelidad expresada en el concepto de 'patriotismo constitucional' no se aplica a los principios sostenidos por la Constitución" (But the fidelity expressed in the concept "constitutional patriotism" cannot be applied to the principles supported by the constitution) (225). She refers to the appropriation of this document by the Conservative Party, but she could have added that the two dominant parties share its fetishization. To judge from the uses to which it is put, it seems that the constitution's single most important job is to stem the flow of history and to set limits to reality. The constitution is in effect a screen memory, a displaced metaphor for knowledge that is censored and must be constantly repressed lest it gain admittance into public consciousness. But of course, what is repressed resurfaces in the form of anxiety and compulsive behavior. The mass graves coming to light all over Spain as on cue are at once a potent image and proof positive of what the Transition repressed.

THE HISTORIAN'S TRANSFERENTIAL RELATION TO THE PAST

In conclusion I will examine one instance of "historicizing" used to challenge the political uses of a moralized memory of the Civil War. In an essay written for an American audience, Paloma Aguilar Fernández, a Madrid-based historian, denounces "the use and abuse of the past" in the practices of "nationalist movements, which tend to legitimize current grievances with reference to historical events" ("Institutional Legacies" 128).[4] Thus, she specifies her target from the start. Despite her generalization of questionable historical practices to all "nationalist movements," she resorts to the devious Spanish convention of confining "nationalism" to the subject nationalities,[5] even though historically the term "movement" qualifies only the aggressive nationalism that captured and transformed the state.[6] As Hannah Arendt explains, the name "movement" alluded to the profound distrust for political parties that reached decisive proportions in the years of the Weimar Republic (*Imperialism* 131). Thus, Aguilar's first inaccuracy is to designate as movements what are in fact conventional parties with all their stakes in parliamentary democracy. The point is not to take issue with a disingenuous palming off of political tactics as epistemic categories, but to doubt the wisdom of contesting the connection between current grievances and historical events, especially when the former are denied validity by calling the latter into question.

Aguilar's pretense of steering clear of the pragmatic use of history would appear naive if it were not devious. No less than the discourses she attacks, her account of memory is determined by a set of values, which are hardly divisible from that "use and abuse of the past" that she attributes to the political other.

Past events are always debatable. The moment they enter into the symbolic domain, they are consigned to interpretation and made consistent with values that, being anchored in the interpreter's social context, are not falsifiable. For instance, Aguilar claims that the Republican Basque government "betrayed" the Spanish Republic by negotiating its surrender to the Italians, rather than to the Spanish rebels, in exchange for permission to evacuate the people most at risk of reprisals; she also characterizes the refusal by the Basques (the "nationalists" in Aguilar's text) to destroy Bilbao's industry before the city fell to the rebels as a "betrayal" (136). These are value judgments that cannot be resolved in the sphere of fact. The facts are indisputable, but they do not necessarily substantiate Aguilar's judgment. It is not obvious, except perhaps to a Spanish Nationalist, that the Basque government should have prioritized Spanish honor over Basque lives and surrendered to General Mola instead of General Roatta. And the same is true about the notion that Basques should have destroyed their industry for the sake of a doomed republic that had first begrudged them autonomy and then failed to defend their country.[7] The Republic passed away, but industry continued to supply the Basque people's livelihood after defeat, while Madrid, whether Republican or Fascist, would live off its traditional business.[8]

Ultimately the question of treason does not lie in the facts but in the historian's loyalties. Aguilar's parti pris dictates her conviction that Euskadi entered the war as a political appendage of the Spanish republic, and this pre-intellectual choice prevents her from countenancing the plausibility of decisions made by the Basque government in the face of impending catastrophe and when the state could not or would not protect Basque lives and interests. Basque nationalism has its reasons as well as its myths, both at variance from those of Spanish nationalism. Questions of value entailing different loyalties cannot be settled by pitting rational historiography against the mythical memory of factitious victims. The dichotomy is devious because all concerned with the Civil War and the Franco period are sucked into its eddying area of influence. In this matter, it is important to reckon with the transferential relation to the past that Dominick LaCapra considers unavoidable in every epistemic relation to traumatic events.

Historicization, Friedlander warned, may be misused as a pretext for collapsing the distinction between a more nuanced interpretation of the past and "increasingly apologetic readings of the events" (99). Aguilar's text keeps within the bounds of the facts but perilously approaches the apologetic terrain broached more frankly by others. "What we are seeking to demonstrate," she says, "is that, contrary to what Basque nationalism has maintained, first clandestinely and then openly, the overall situation in the Basque country (at least during the war years and immediately after) was not clearly worse than in the rest of Spain but, in terms of certain indicators, substantially better" ("Institutional Legacies" 148).

With the help of statistical data, she points out that the number of trials initiated in 1939 in the Basque provinces is below the "national average" (147). From this she infers a milder repression in Euzkadi.

The problems with this modus operandi are obvious. In the first place, the end of the war in the Basque Country came in 1937, anticipating the postbellum repression in other parts of Spain by more than one year. During this period, as in the early days of the war, executions often took place without trial; as a result court proceedings are a highly unreliable benchmark of the cruelty visited on villages or entire provinces. Above all, reliance on official records for assessing the repression's scope and intensity is compromised by the extensive destruction of such documents in the '50s and '60s. Even the method of comparing quantitative data assembled by provinces ignores the impression, entertained by many Basques, of having been the object of special ruthlessness.

While Aguilar's point that social memory can be inflected by politics is indisputable, quantitative data offer only a defective approximation of the scope of a phenomenon that was not exactly characterized by judicial guarantees and the rule of law. It was not untypical for prisoners to be interned outside their home provinces; hence the correlation between the convict's origin and the site of the court martial must be taken with caution. Contrasting statistically the repression in Navarre with that of the three Basque provinces, for instance, is hardly a neutral method, large tracts of Navarre being populated by ethnic Basques. An accurate assessment of the repression would need to control for ideology—who was executed or imprisoned and for what reasons—and it would need to take into account the volume of exile in relation to demography. The higher the number of exiles, the more significant the repression of the remaining population, because it can be assumed that those with no political or military responsibility were more likely to stay behind.

Finally, the "national average" against which Aguilar assesses Basque repression includes the figures for Catalonia, whose particularly intense victimization she also challenges with a blanket dismissal of nationalist grievances. In this way Catalonia's record does double duty: on the one hand it helps the historian to dispute the Basque memory of the war and the postwar period, and on the other hand it is also questioned through the general indictment of the "nationalist" abuse of history.[9]

Statistics brace Aguilar's argument in other ways too. She compares postwar infant mortality rates in the Basque Country with the national average, inferring a higher standard of living, which would belie Basque allegations of having suffered especial duress. But the argument is flawed by her failure to take prewar conditions into account. Comparing the postwar and prewar levels of well-being for the same community would provide a more reliable picture of the degree of *social* injury. Had she taken prewar conditions into account, Aguilar would have had to admit that long before the war the Basque country outstripped most Spanish regions in material well-being.

But beyond the pitfalls of interpreting data, there is a methodological problem with estimating political repression solely or primarily through economic indicators.[10] Mob psychology has often justified the oppression of certain groups by pointing the finger at their perceived superior comfort. But a more versatile analysis would show that health and economic standards are by themselves not a reliable gauge of the degree of political well-being a social group enjoys, or of the level of suffering inflicted on it. A more refined analysis would certainly reckon with group-specific variables, which are ultimately those that tend to decide the fate of minorities in the midst of intolerant majorities. And it would try to estimate, however qualitatively, the hard-to-establish cost of subtraction, of the violently imposed regression from the previous social and cultural status, and of its immediate and long-term repercussions throughout the social body. It would, that is, recognize the pain of the missing limb, of the empirical specter of the would-have-been, and factor the costs of the decapitated future into the comparison of flattened social data—that is, data analyzed without benefit of a temporal coordinate that would permit an estimation of the degree of truncation introduced by the crisis that is the object of evaluation.

Aguilar aims to debunk what she considers opportunistic uses of memory to constitute an imaginary community of suffering. But in doing so, she produces a countermemory based on social measuring of pain, showing that the Basque provinces endured average or below average repression under Franco. The result is an image of uniform misery underpinning a Spanish national community, which not only would not have victimized the Basques but might even have been too bighearted toward them in the Transition, overlooking their disloyalty to the Republic and their relative well-being under the dictatorship. She takes exception to the existence of different memories of what for her are national—that is, essentially homogeneous—events.

Different memories tend to underwrite diverging narratives, and diverging narratives imply a divided social body. In other words, they call into question the myth of unity underlying the nation-state and threaten to shatter the dominant memory's legitimation of asymmetric power. Thus Aguilar subscribes to an entirely different legend and pits myth against myth, endorsing the fiction that the Transition was the "recognition of collective culpability for crimes committed during the war" (129). Victims and perpetrators are thus homogenized in the baseness of universally shared criminality. In this view there is no room for redress or even for apologies. The nationalization of guilt protects each and every perpetrator. As a result no one need suffer from a public bad conscience. Nevertheless, the dead are still surfacing and casting their shadows on TV screens. After 2000, public television channels started to broadcast the stories of survivors who decided to pit their isolated memories against a regime that exists by purloining a past that will not go away. Even, or perhaps especially, when driven by private pain and intimate emotion, the recovery of the dead shows that in the long run regimes of oblivion cannot be normalized, despite explications that seek to reallocate responsibility by making the victims shoulder the guilt all over again.

NOTES

1. Franco insisted that his resolution of the succession problem was an "instauration" rather than the "restoration" of the monarchy (Carr and Fusi 169).

2. The constitution does this not only tacitly but more overtly in dispositions such as Article 8, outlining the army's role in preserving the territorial organization of the state, codified as its "territorial integrity."

3. Recourse to the Balkans in reference to the demands for a territorial reorganization of political power within the state has been made, among lesser figures, by two former premiers, first by Felipe González, while he was still in office, and recently by José María Aznar. The rhetorical coincidence is an important symptom of the ideological common ground.

4. She is also a member of the Instituto Juan March, a research center founded under the dictatorship by the tycoon who helped finance Franco's coup d'état. While membership does not in principle presuppose ideological co-option, one should not lose sight of the fact that neither this nor any other private or public foundation underwent political scrutiny in the Transition, and that the links between private research and public power were simply taken over into the constitutional regime.

5. Aguilar is guilty of this rhetorical abuse when she opposes "national Spanish parties" to "Basque nationalist parties" ("Institutional Legacies" 140) and when further along she refers to the former as "nonnationalist parliamentary groups" (141–42).

6. The Spanish National Movement appeared in the wake of Spain's loss of its overseas empire. It was a compensatory though illusory effort to reassert empire through a pan-Hispanic movement. With respect to early-twentieth-century pan-movements, Hannah Arendt observed, "While overseas imperialism had offered real enough panaceas for the residues of all classes, continental imperialism had nothing to offer except an ideology and a movement" (*Imperialism* 105).

7. Juan Manuel Epalza, who on PNV (Basque Nationalist Party) deposed the Santoña military commandant, has explained, "We had asked the central government to send warships to transport our army to Catalonia; we had been refused," a fact that belies Aguilar's denunciation of the PNV's unwillingness to continue the war effort (Fraser 410). And Pedro Basabilotra, speaking of the resentment among Basque troops, points out, "They felt betrayed by the republic which had constantly promised and failed to deliver weapons. While in Madrid we heard they had arms and planes" (Fraser, *Blood of Spain* 412).

8. The argument that Basque factories should have been destroyed to keep them from falling into Franco's hands ignores the fact that Franco counted on virtually unlimited supplies from his allies. Aguilar does not go so far as to accuse Basque workers of collaboration with the Fascists, but she appears to factor into the latter's victory the Basque output of materiel after the fall of Bilbao.

9. The repression in Catalonia is amply documented. For an insightful discussion about the "deconstruction" of memory in recent Spanish historiography, see Colomines.

10. One indicator that is surely not trivial is the extent to which groups are included or shut out of political representation (and thus given an equal opportunity to influence their own future through the legal channels of the state). The electoral law in force today in Spain's "representative" democracy was designed to guarantee the subordination of the national minorities. By privileging an obsolete territorial representation based on the province rather than on population, it ensures Catalonia's underrepresentation. Each deputy from the

province of Barcelona requires 129,268 votes, whereas one from the province of Soria requires only 26,177 votes—that is, 103,000 fewer votes. In other words, Soria is represented on a five-to-one ratio with respect to Barcelona. If instead of Soria we compare Toledo, the most populated province of Castilla-La Mancha, we find that, with 90,064 votes for each deputy, Toledo's representation is 1.4 that of Barcelona. Even worse is the marginalization of Basques and Catalans in the senate, where each province has four representatives regardless of population. Furthermore, Basques and Catalans have, as such, no representation in the Supreme Court, with the result that the constitution is systematically interpreted against their interests. Elections are regulated by an Organic Law of July 19, 1985. Since the Socialists enjoyed absolute majority in Parliament that year, this law cannot be attributed to Francoism. Nevertheless, its approval and permanence suggests the extent to which naturalized Francoist attitudes pervaded the opposition party.

Speaking for the Dead

HISTORY, NARRATIVE, AND THE GHOSTLY
IN JAVIER CERCAS'S WAR NOVELS

Samuel Amago

La literatura debe desobedecer pactos de silencio.

—Manuel Rivas (qtd. in Pérez Oliva)

Los muertos no mueren nunca.

—Pedro Almodóvar (qtd. in Harguindey)

A considerable number of novels dealing with the Spanish Civil War and its aftermath have appeared in recent years. Works such as Almudena Grandes's *El corazón helado* (2007), Benjamín Prado's *Mala gente que camina* (2006), Manuel Rivas's *Los libros arden mal* (2006), Dulce Chacón's *La voz dormida* (2002), Javier Marías's *Tu rostro mañana: Fiebre y lanza* (2002), and Andrés Trapiello's *Una historia de Maquis* (2001), along with Javier Cercas's tremendously successful *Soldados de Salamina* (2001), are just a few examples of how a generation of Spanish authors has revisited Spain's traumatic national history and explored through literature the recovery and reconstruction of historical memory. A significant number of film narratives dealing with this period have also been produced, such as Vicente Aranda's *Libertarias* (1996), Antonio Mercero's *La hora de los valientes* (1998), José Luis Cuerda's *La lengua de las mariposas* (1999), Guillermo del Toro's *El espinazo del diablo* (2001),

Jaime Camino's *Los niños de Rusia* (2001), and the film adaptation of Cercas's novel, also titled *Soldados de Salamina* (David Trueba, 2003).[1] The recent release of Guillermo del Toro's gothic fable *El laberinto del fauno* (2006), which powerfully links an archetypal fairy-tale structure to an idealized vision of the against-all-odds efforts of the maquis who continued to fight Franquism in northern Spain into the 1940s, shows that the Spanish Civil War and immediate postwar period continue to provide ripe inspirational material for the creation of memorializing narratives.

Two generations after the end of the Civil War and a generation after the death of Francisco Franco, this conflicted period of history appears again and again in popular modes of cultural production. As we can see in both of del Toro's Civil War films, Spain's Fascist legacy and the *pacto del silencio* that followed it provide a fertile ground for ghostly treatments of Spanish history. *El espinazo del diablo*, for example, begins with a voice off screen that asks, "¿Qué es un fantasma?" (What is a ghost?). The viewer later learns that the voice belongs to Doctor Casares (Federico Luppi), who runs the orphanage that is later destroyed by the villainous Jacinto (Eduardo Noriega), who stands symbolically for the Fascist rebels who will later win the Spanish Civil War. After he is dead, Casares will continue to inhabit the orphanage as a ghost, settling in to watch over Spain—the film suggests—during the long dictatorship that was to come. Thus, Casares's answer to his initial question is doubly significant. What is a ghost? He answers, "un asunto terrible condenado a repetirse una y otra vez. Un instante de dolor. Algo muerto que parece vivo por momentos aún. Un sentimiento sostenido en el tiempo. Como una fotografía borrosa, como un insecto atrapado en ámbar" (A terrible issue condemned to repeat itself over and over again. An instant of pain. Something dead that appears for a few moments to still be alive. A feeling suspended in time. Like a blurry photograph, like an insect trapped in amber).

It has now become something of a commonplace to refer to the cultural inheritance of the Spanish Civil War and Franco's dictatorship in ghostly terms. Three excellent recent studies exemplify how Derrida's formulation of "hauntology," which he developed in *Specters of Marx* (1994) as a symbolic alternative to ontology (ghosts, after all, exist somewhere beyond the ontological realm), has been fruitfully employed to describe a cultural milieu in which past traumas continue to haunt the cultural present: Jo Labanyi's "History and Hauntology; or, What Does One Do with the Ghosts of the Past?", Anne E. Hardcastle's "Ghosts of the Past and Present: Hauntology and the Spanish Civil War in Guillermo del Toro's *The Devil's Backbone*," and Antonio Gómez's "Fantasmagoría y violencia en *El espinazo del diablo*" (Gómez López-Quiñones, *La guerra persistente*) are fine examples of this trend.[2] Giles Tremlett's *Ghosts of Spain* (2006) represents yet another notable book-length study that has shown how, seventy years after the beginning of the Civil War, the traumatic history of the country (and particularly Franco's legacy of death and the subsequent *pacto del silencio*) continues to haunt the collective unconscious and thus goes on manifesting itself in a variety of cultural spheres. Spain, as the authors of the collected essays in *Disremembering the Dictatorship: The Politics of Memory since the Spanish Transition to Democracy* (2000) variously argue, continues to be "haunted by the spectres of a past it has tried to surmount by denying it" (Resina, book jacket).

While the purpose of this essay is not to explain the sociology or politics of Spain's Transition to democracy or the attendant *pacto del olvido* that arguably made it possible—indeed, several of the essays that comprise this collection illustrate these issues admirably—I am interested instead in exploring how contemporary writers of fiction have reflexively engaged in the task of recuperating lost accounts and memories of history. I take as my point of departure two novels by Javier Cercas, *Soldados de Salamina* (2001) and *La velocidad de la luz* (2005), which are noteworthy because of their self-conscious engagement with the historiographical enterprise and because in both novels the writing of history has important psychic ramifications for narrators who have become obsessed with giving a voice to the dead. While the first novel deals explicitly with the Spanish Civil War, *La velocidad de la luz* calls for attention not only because of the marked thematic and structural similarities it shares with *Soldados de Salamina*, but also because of its patent use of gothic terminology to describe the psychological effects of war and the personal trauma that it causes. Further, the novel subtly invites the reader to make connections between past traumas (the Vietnam War) and present ones (Iraq), in much the same way that *Soldados de Salamina* made connections between the Spanish Civil War and the oppressive Latin American dictatorships of the 1970s and '80s (Cercas, *Soldados*

147). Thus, both novels draw attention to the transnational reality of war and reflect on how violence past and present continues to haunt contemporary global society.

In a very general sense, this essay is about narrative and about how the stories that go untold inevitably haunt their potential tellers. Much like the unearthing of mass graves that has inspired the present volume, Cercas's recent fiction is self-consciously obsessed with digging up and giving meaning to the past. Indeed, both novels demonstrate the profound manifestations—physical and psychic—that untold histories can have on their narrators. Thus I will be dealing with the role of narrators—be they fictional or real—in recuperating lost accounts of historical happenings. I shall conclude by suggesting that self-conscious narratives offer the writer perhaps the most authentic method of engaging with the complexities implicit in the writing of history, and that in so doing these kinds of stories draw attention to the responsibility of novelists and historians to tell the tales that have not been told, especially those that have been silenced.

While *Soldados de Salamina* has received understandable criticism for its somewhat emphatic, somewhat exclusive insistence on themes of masculinity (Ellis) and has been censured for a perceived sexist reinforcement of patriarchal systems of representation (Antón), I have argued elsewhere that the novel nonetheless offers a compelling account of a narrator in search of the truth about a forgotten story from the Spanish Civil War (Amago 144–65).[3] The novel is about a (fictional) author named Javier Cercas who, having just lost his father and gone through a divorce, begins to write what he obstinately insists will be a *"relato real"* (true story) about a minor event that occurred during the final days of the Civil War. The text that he purports to write is, at first, about how Rafael Sánchez Mazas (the Fascist ideologue and founder of the Falange) flees a Republican firing squad and, most interestingly for the narrator, is allowed to escape when an unknown soldier finds him hiding in the underbrush but chooses not to alert his comrades. The identity and personal motivation of this mysterious soldier become the central focus of the narrator, and he becomes obsessed to the point that he travels by train from Girona to a retirement home in Dijon, France, where he hopes to interview an ex-soldier named Miralles, whom he is convinced must have been the soldier who allowed Sánchez Mazas to escape.

But while the narrator is never able to get the story straight, and although he is never able to get Miralles to admit that he is the man who allowed Sánchez Mazas to get away, the process of researching and writing *Soldados de Salamina* (for this is the title of his novelistic "*relato real,*" too) has important personal ramifications for the narrator. The novel's emphasis on this process functions as a metaphor for the ethical responsibility of the historian. As Robert Richmond Ellis concludes in his study of the novel, Cercas's text "is not only a *memento mori* but also a paean to the living, for as the example of his narrator plainly shows, it is only through remembering that we experience our own humanity most fully" (532). Thus, a very specific task for one writer—who researches and writes a "real" account of one forgotten hero of the Civil War—not only functions as a method of coming to terms with his own personal loss and loneliness, but also allows him to contemplate the greater humanistic issues implicit in any authentic ethical exercise in historiography.

Ellis argues persuasively that *Soldados de Salamina* "is not primarily about the Spanish Civil War but rather the search for a father . . . and, ultimately, the creation of a hero" (527). This hero, of course, is Miralles, who, having fought in defense of the Republic, later joined the French Foreign Legion under General Leclerc in France, continued his fight against the Fascists in Europe and Africa, and finally, at the end of the Second World War, stormed Utah Beach in Normandy with the Allies. The hero-making thrust of the novel is also emphasized by critics such as Satorras Pons and Yushimoto del Valle, who have analyzed *Soldados de Salamina* in terms of the novel's meditations on the symbolic importance of Miralles as an archetypal modern hero. In another essay, Antonio Gómez has suggested that the novel's meditations on heroes are of fundamental importance, as the current Spanish democracy was conceived without any foundational heroes or heroic historical models. Thus, Gómez remarks, the novel is significant because it "returns to the Civil War in order to harvest a tradition and a history within which Spanish democracy and its inhabitants might find some kind of ideological satisfaction" (Gómez López-Quiñones, "La guerra" 119). So, while Miralles may or may not have been the soldier who helped Sánchez Mazas escape the firing squad, he is nevertheless "the last representative of an army, of a set of ideals, of an inheritance," and as such, writes Gómez, Miralles represents "the last opportunity to seek justice for those who in 1936 were on the side of the Republic" (123).

The narrator acknowledges that it is perhaps because of his simple condition as a survivor that Miralles has acquired in his mind the special distinction of hero. In narrative terms, however, Miralles is of fundamental importance because he embodies the missing piece of the novel that will be *Soldados de Salamina*. It is for that reason, whether or not Miralles is the soldier he has been seeking, that the narrator sets off for Dijon in the hopes of discovering the truth behind this "*secreto esencial*" (essential secret; 180) of the Spanish Civil War. But the novel is not only about this essential secret, but more importantly about the process of researching and telling the story. The novel self-consciously draws attention to the contingency of historiography in general by emphasizing the narrator's reconstruction of the story and the "real" historical happenings behind it. This metafictional emphasis on process over product functions to highlight the essential dynamics that are implicit in the writing of any history: (1) there must be a subject who reconstructs the tale, be it a historian, a novelist, a witness, a filmmaker; (2) the account relies on that subject not only for its coherence but also for its very existence; and (3) through the narrative efforts of this subject, the past is thus understood in terms of its relationship to the present.

In the last of the novel's three sections, the narrator puts everything together, powerfully linking his search for historical truth to his own personal story. It is by combining the personal and the historical that he finally figures out what his book will be about:

> aunque en ningún lugar de ninguna ciudad de ninguna mierda de país fuera a haber nunca una calle que llevara el nombre de Miralles, mientras yo contase su historia Miralles seguiría de algún modo viviendo y seguirían viviendo también, siempre que yo hablase de ellos, los hermanos García Segués—Joan y Lela—y Miquel Cardos y Gabi Baldrich y Pipo Canal y el Gordo Odena y Santi Brugada y Jordi Gudayol, seguirían viviendo aunque llevaran muchos años muertos, muertos, muertos, muertos. (Cercas, *Soldados* 208)

> although nowhere in any city of any fucking country would there ever be a street named after Miralles, if I told his story, Miralles would

still be alive in some way and if I talked about them, his friends would still be alive too, the García Sequés brothers—Joan and Lela—and Miquel Cardos and Gabi Baldrich and Pipo Canal and el Gordo Odena and Santi Brugada and Jordi Gudayol would still be alive even though for many years they'd been dead, dead, dead, dead. (Cercas, *Soldiers* 207)

As Gómez has pointed out, the narrator's personal crisis is linked to his investigation of the "grand crisis" of Spain during the Civil War. Through the process of researching and writing his tale, the narrator also comes to terms with his father's death and finally realizes that, although it has been more than six years since his father died, "mi padre todavía no estaba muerto, porque todavía había alguien que se acordaba de él. Luego pensé que no era yo quien recordaba a mi padre, sino él quien se aferraba a mi recuerdo, para no morir del todo" (*Soldados* 187); "my father still wasn't dead, because there was still someone remembering him. Or maybe it wasn't me remembering my father, but he who clung to my memory, so as not to die completely" (*Soldiers* 184). Keeping in mind the ghostly terminology that over the last decade has acquired particular currency in the field of Spanish cultural production and analysis, I want to draw attention to how Cercas's narrator underscores the power that the dead (and the past) have to haunt the present, and how writing functions not only as a therapeutic method for coming to terms with personal trauma but also as a way to memorialize the departed. As the reader can see in the quotation above, the dead father continues to exercise a very real ghostly agency within the subjectivity of the narrator, clinging to the author's memory in order to avoid absolute oblivion. In a contemporary cultural context in which the dead of the losing side of the Spanish Civil War are refused their rightful memorialization, the role of the writer, here and in Cercas's subsequent novel, is to remember the deceased through narration.

Indeed, it is only as the narrator's conversation with Miralles concludes that he begins to understand that the living have a vital responsibility to the dead. After his climactic interview with Miralles, the narrator ruminates on why the living must remember the dead and why these memories are important to us. Apropos of Miralles's own memories, the narrator thinks to himself, se acuerda por lo mismo que yo me acuerdo de mi padre y Ferlosio del suyo y Miquel Aguirre del suyo y Jaume Figueras del suyo y Bolaño de sus amigos latinoamericanos, todos soldados muertos en guerras de antemano perdidas: se acuerda porque, aunque hace sesenta años que fallecieron, todavía no están muertos, precisamente porque él se acuerda de ellos. O quizá no es él quien se acuerda de ellos, sino ellos los que se aferran a él, para no estar del todo muertos. (*Soldados* 201)

He remembers for the same reason I remember my father and Ferlosio his and Miquel Aguirre his and Jaume Figueras his and Bolaño his Latin American friends, all of them soldiers killed in wars already lost: he remembers because, although they died sixty years ago, they're still not dead, precisely because he remembers them. Or perhaps it's not him remembering them, but the clinging to him, so they won't die off entirely. (*Soldiers* 199)

Thus the narrator not only links Miralles's memories of his friends to his own memories of his father but also draws other Civil War veterans together with Ferlosio and Bolaño in order to build a broader notion of remembering in general. In this way, the narrator turns a specific, decidedly reflexive account of one lost episode from the Spanish Civil War into a universally relevant effort to remember the dead of all wars.

As the writing of his text progresses, the narrator comes to grasp that when Miralles dies, all of his stories will die with him. And when Miralles is gone, the memory that he carries of the dead will disappear, "porque no habrá nadie que se acuerde de ellos para que no mueran" (*Soldados* 201); "because there won't be anyone to remember them, to keep them from dying" (*Soldiers* 200). Herein lies the ethical responsibility of the writer. As Jo Labanyi remarks in her essay in this volume, the *testimonio* (of which Cercas offers a sort of fictionalized version through Miralles) offers us an important insight "into emotional attitudes toward the past in the present time of the speaker." In her discussion of the various *testimonios* that have come out in recent years in Spain, Labanyi shows that, even when memories are unreliable, they still allow the speaker to engage with a personal experience of reality that has important ramifications for the collective present. Not only are these *testimonios* valuable for the speakers, but they also have significant implications for those of us who read them. Every time a witness to the Spanish Civil War dies, we lose his or her personal stories. Although his account is fictional, the narrator of *Soldados de Salamina* nevertheless comprehends that when these witnesses die, we shall lose an important account of what happened before, during, and after the Civil War. What is the role of the writer in the face of such high stakes? To write, of course.

While *Soldados de Salamina* is a novel that attempts to vindicate the memory of the forgotten heroes who fought in defense of the democratically elected Spanish Republic, Javier Cercas's subsequent novel, *La velocidad de la luz,* focuses on the darker side of heroism and explores how suppressed memories can eat away at the conscience and ultimately destroy the young soldiers society asks to fight for it. Like Cercas's previous novel, *La velocidad de la luz* self-consciously emphasizes the importance of storytelling as a method of exorcizing the ghosts of the past and of coming to terms with their ongoing influence in the present. The novel also invites the reader to make connections between past wars and those that continue to plague the present.[4]

The novel takes as its point of departure an eccentric, emotionally damaged Vietnam veteran named Rodney Faulk, whom the narrator meets during his time at the University of Illinois in Urbana. As in *Soldados de Salamina,* the narrator closely resembles Javier Cercas himself, representing part of the novel's metafictional structure that seeks to complicate the boundaries between reality and fiction in order to draw the reader's attention to the dynamic nature of narrative. Rodney's reticence about his personal traumatic history creates much of the novel's tension, and the plot centers on the narrator's efforts to discover and tell his story. Thus, while *Soldados de Salamina* is about Miralles, Sánchez Mazas, and the narrator's efforts to put their stories together, *La velocidad de la luz* is about Rodney Faulk and the narrator's attempts to document the personal legacy that continues to haunt him as a result of his participation in an especially violent event during the Vietnam War.

During one of several conversations about literature that appear in the novel's first part, Rodney expresses his belief that silence is more eloquent than words and that the art of a good narrator lies in his ability to keep quiet about certain things (63). Given his laconic reserve, a good portion of the novel deals with the efforts of the narrator to figure out what makes Rodney tick and to get him to verbalize his past. Rodney Faulk is a walking, talking lacuna of history. But the narrator believes that somehow Rodney holds a key to understanding what occurred during the war. What happened to him in Vietnam? What was his role in the massacre at My Khe? These are the questions that compel the narrator of *La velocidad de la luz* to travel to the small Illinois town of Rantoul, where he interviews Rodney's father after Rodney has mysteriously disappeared. It is in Rantoul that the narrator discovers more clues as to why Rodney has vanished and about what really happened to him in Vietnam.

Much of the novel's second part deals with the narrator's meeting with Rodney's father, who tells the narrator that his son returned from Vietnam a decayed shadow of the man he used to be (133) and that he had become "un fantasma ambulante o un zombi" (134) (a walking ghost or a zombie), spending entire days in bed, smoking marijuana, and watching classic films on television. While the novel is by no means a gothic work, Cercas's use of spectral terminology to refer to the effects that the traumatic past can have on the present is significant. Rodney's father describes the post-Vietnam Rodney as a walking phantasm, a ghost, or a zombie. This same verbal construction (to be like a ghost or a zombie) is repeated throughout the novel to portray both Rodney and, after he later loses his wife and child to a car accident, the narrator himself. After the narrator has left Urbana and returned to Spain (some time before he has married), he decides he must continue writing in order to "convertirme en un escritor de verdad y no en un fantasma o un zombi— como Rodney y como los personajes de mi novela y como algunos habitantes de Urbana" (146) (make myself into a real writer, not a ghost or a zombie—like Rodney and like the characters in my novel and like some of the inhabitants of Urbana). Thus narrative communication is described as a method of avoiding the partial death of the phantasm, ghost, or zombie. Little does the narrator know that he will soon suffer his own personal trauma, which will temporarily turn him into a "fantasma o un zombi," forcing him to exist for a while in an interstitial space between the worlds of the living and the dead.

After a few years spent teaching Spanish in Urbana, the narrator moves back to Spain to become a "real writer." He marries for the first time and achieves a huge literary success with the publication of a novel (a fact that further emphasizes the narrator's similarity to Javier Cercas himself).[5] He begins to forget about his friend until Rodney reappears in the novel's third part, literally emerging like a ghost from "la penumbra de la escalera" (the shadow of the staircase) in a café in Madrid (161). It is during this final meeting between the two men that the narrator is able to ask Rodney about the incident at My Khe during the Vietnam War. Rodney, who continues to resist engaging with his past, assures him that whatever he imagines to have happened is probably what really happened: "Lo que te imaginas es lo que ocurrió. Ocurrió lo que ocurre en todas las guerras. Ni más ni menos. My Khe es solo una anécdota. Además, en Vietnam no hubo un My Khe: hubo muchos. Lo que ocurrió en uno ocurrió más o menos en todos" (178) (Whatever you imagine is what happened. What happened is what happens in all wars. Nothing more and nothing less. My Khe is just an anecdote. Moreover, in Vietnam there was not just one My Khe: there were many. What happened in one happened more or less in all of them). The tragic reality of all wars, Rodney suggests, is that atrocities happened everywhere and that the efforts to reconstruct the events that occurred in any one town acquire the banality of the purely anecdotal when considered alongside the thousands of other events that may have occurred. The fact that the novel was written as Spain's Partido Popular government was preparing to participate in the 2003 invasion of Iraq gives *La velocidad de la luz* an added relevance that likely was not lost on Spanish readers.

Rodney's inability to metabolize his past is what ultimately destroys him. In the novel's fourth and final section, which is narrated after he has lost his wife and child to a car accident, the narrator seeks Rodney out, hoping that perhaps he might learn something from his friend about dealing with personal trauma (279). The narrator arrives too late, however, as Rodney has committed suicide. But he discovers that Rodney's Vietnam War secrets had been revealed just before his death in a documentary entitled *Secretos sepultados, verdades brutales*. Rodney's widow gives the narrator a copy of the video, in which Rodney comments on his experiences at My Khe. The narrator's friend says that for years he could not forget the faces of each and every person he saw die there. Once again, I should like to draw attention to Rodney's use of gothic imagery to describe his relationship to the dead:

Se me aparecían constantemente, igual que si estuvieran vivas y no quisieran morir, igual que si fueran fantasmas. Luego conseguí olvidarlas, o eso es lo que creí, aunque en el fondo sabía que no se habían marchado. Ahora han vuelto. No me piden cuentas, ni yo se las doy. No hay cuentas pendientes. Es sólo que no quieren morir, que quieren vivir en mí. No me quejo, porque sé que es justo. (283)

They used to appear to me constantly, as if they were alive and didn't want to die, like they were ghosts. Later I was able to forget about them, or at least that's what I thought, although deep down I knew that they had never left. Now they are back. They are not asking for anything, nor do I give them anything. There are no debts to be repaid. It's just that they do not want to die. They want to live in me. I don't complain because I know that this is just.

In her essay included in this volume, Labanyi writes that "memory is not a slice of the past waiting . . . to be 'recovered'" but rather, "it is a process that operates in the present and cannot help but give a version of the past colored by present emotions." The narrator, quite unlike Rodney, seems to accept the fact that memory, as Labanyi proposes, is an ongoing process of working through things that takes place in the present. In order to avoid turning into a phantasm, a ghost, or a zombie, the narrator appreciates that there must be some kind of self-conscious effort to acknowledge the past through reflexive contemplation and, ultimately, through communication.

Rodney, on the other hand, refuses to work through his memories. His present is so affected by his traumatic past that he cannot function in normal everyday life, and as a consequence he is constantly and resignedly running away from his past. The novel's self-conscious emphasis on working through past issues through narrative suggests that perhaps it is because Rodney was unable (or unwilling) to work through or even share his history that he is doomed to be destroyed by it. Though he recounts his version of the massacre at My Khe in the documentary, he never appears to come to terms with his memories of it. Rodney tells his story, but his tale has no depth, no reflexivity. He does not work through his traumatic past. This "working through" is a way of dealing with the influence of ghosts and of coming to terms with feelings of guilt and the powerful psychic effects of trauma. While *La velocidad de la luz* is by no means a fantastic ghost story, Cercas nonetheless makes use of gothic language to describe how people can be haunted by their past and how that past must be faced fully if we are to move forward.

The irony of Rodney's case is that even after he is finally able to give voice to the ghosts of his history, he is unable to overcome their negative influence on him. His experience exemplifies what Avery Gordon has argued in *Ghostly Matters: Haunting and the Sociological Imagination,* in which she observes that "haunting is the sociality of living with ghosts" (201). *La velocidad de la luz* explores how ghosts manifest themselves psychically and how they can also have a real presence in the present, even turning living persons into "fantasmas o zombis." As Rodney confesses in the quotation above, the dead began to appear to him as if they were still alive, as if they were unwilling to die; he is literally haunted by the dead, and thus his history becomes a story about trying to live with ghosts. This kind of haunting, writes Cathy Caruth, occurs when a traumatized person "carries an impossible history within" and when that person cannot entirely possess it (qtd. in Hardcastle 126). Silence is not an option, either. Hardcastle points out that "the magnitude of traumatic events" can overwhelm "an individual's ability to cope with the memory, and so trauma manifests itself through a distorted, phantasmal perception of reality" (126).

While the reader never finds out why Rodney has killed himself, it seems reasonable to assume that he was ultimately unable to reconcile himself with the ghosts of his past and that he is finally overwhelmed by his traumatic memories. Undone by his impossible story, Rodney succumbs to the nihilistic prayer that appears famously in Ernest Hemingway's tale, "A Clean, Well-Lighted Place" (1933). The prayer, a pessimistic reworking of the Lord's Prayer, is cited directly by the narrator as a perfect incantation in memory of his friend: "Nada nuestro que estás en la nada, nada es tu nombre, tu reino nada, tú serás nada en la nada como en la nada" (Cercas, *La velocidad* 247) (Our nothing who art in nothing, nothing is thy name, your kingdom nothing, thy nothing be nothing on nothing as it is in nothing). The narrator thinks of Hemingway's story again as he contemplates Rodney's tombstone.

Rodney's final decision to share his account of the massacre at My Khe in the documentary can perhaps be explained in terms of Derrida's conceptualization of hauntology, which requires that the traumatized person speak to his or her ghosts in order to exorcize them, "not in order to chase away the ghosts, but this time to grant them the right . . . to a hospitable memory . . . out of a concern for justice" (qtd. in Labanyi, "History" 66). Thus in *La velocidad de la luz* the ghostly terminology that appears throughout the text describes the memory that remains of the dead and the power that they exert on the living. Only after he has himself gone through a traumatic event—when his wife and child are killed in an automobile accident—is the narrator capable of the empathy required to understand what that haunting really means. Thus, even though he has no firsthand knowledge of the Vietnam War, the narrator's role, after Rodney's death, is to provide his friend's ghost with a vicarious hospitable memory. The narrator's specific experience of personal trauma allows him to better understand Rodney. In *La velocidad de la luz* Rodney becomes an example of what happens if you do not confront honestly your traumas: you become a phantasm, a ghost, or a zombie.

During one of their first conversations, Rodney mentions to the narrator that normal people either suffer reality or enjoy it, but that they typically can't do anything with it. The writer, meanwhile, *can* do something with reality, because his task is to "convertir la realidad en sentido, aunque ese sentido sea ilusorio; es decir, puede convertirla en belleza, y esa belleza o ese sentido son su escudo" (69) (turn reality into meaning, even if that meaning is illusory; that is to say, to turn it into beauty, and that beauty or meaning is his shield). In Javier Cercas's fiction, narrative gives order to the chaos of human memory and palliates the sometimes tragic impossibility of forgetting. In spite of the indeterminate nature of language and our inability to comprehend history in any complete way, narrative, like the best poetry, is capable of expressing elemental human issues and can serve as an object "of recognition between persons beyond the contexts of their creation" (Stewart 235). And even while Cercas draws attention to the fictionality and incompleteness of his historical narratives, the forms and structures of literary creation can give the reader a knowledge "of somatic, emotional, and social conditions beyond whatever meanings their language conveys" (Stewart 235).

Once he has left Rantoul, presumably for good, the narrator begins to reflect on the importance of narrative in making meaning of the past and on his own role in that process. The narrator recognizes that, in one way or another, all the specific stories that exist—the tales about Rodney, his wartime buddy Tommy Birban, the narrator's own deceased family—form part of the larger history (*historia*), and he takes upon himself the responsibility to infuse it with some kind of meaning. The novel stresses the interconnectedness of the many stories that comprise our understanding of history through its many intertextual references—Hemingway's short story, for example, along with a score of other literary allusions—and through its emphasis on the similarities between the many wars that have traumatized the modern world. This theme of interconnectedness is further accentuated by the novel's circular structure.[6]

The narrator locks himself away in Gerona to write his novel about his experiences in Urbana, Rodney, the Vietnam War, and the traumatic death of his wife and son. When the narrator finally comes out of hiding to have a drink with his old friend Marcos, he once again invokes the gothic image of the zombie that he had used to describe Rodney, but this time he uses it to describe himself. While he looks at Marcos, he wonders if his friend might not see him as "un fantasma o un zombi" (296). Indeed, the narrator has been struggling with his own traumatic memories after the death of his wife and child, and finds that the only way out of the tunnel is to finish writing this novel. Unlike Rodney, the narrator embraces narrative communication as an active method of dealing with his memories and of working through his experience of trauma, thus exorcizing the ghosts that haunt him and finally achieving the power to live in the present. He writes that "escribir era lo único que podía permitirme mirar a la realidad sin destruirme o sin que cayera sobre mí como una casa ardiendo, lo único que podía dotarla de un sentido o de una ilusión de sentido" (302) (writing was the only thing that would allow me to look at reality without it destroying me or without it falling on me like a burning house; it was the only thing that could give it some meaning or illusion of meaning).

Cercas, like many of his contemporaries, writes his fiction from a postmodern perspective that acknowledges the untenability of any one interpretive vision of reality. This does not mean that the author espouses a relativistic "death of history" that some critics would have us believe is at the heart of postmodernism. Instead, he self-consciously acknowledges the embeddedness of all histories, true or false, and recognizes how all of these accounts provide important perspectives on a real totality that will always escape definitive expression through language. In spite of the inevitable inexactness of all narrative accounts of history—be they personal, historical, political, or social—storytelling allows the writer to immortalize the dead in some way and create an admittedly contingent but nevertheless locally comprehensible meaning out of the past. In this way the writer responds to his or her debt to the past and contributes to the ongoing flow of historiographical production. Storytelling also allows the teller of the tale to propose—though it is but one incomplete historical perspective—the legitimacy of his or her own story within a wider historical context.

As the historian Hans Kellner points out, there can be "no 'straight' way to invent a history, regardless of the honesty and professionalism of the historian" because "all history, even the most long-term, quantified, synchronic description, is understood by competent readers as part of a story, an explicit or implicit narrative" (127). Indeed, as Kellner emphasizes, "the longing for the innocent, unprocessed *source* that will afford a fresher, truer vision" will always be "doomed to frustration" (127). If there is indeed no "straight" way to invent a history, and if facts, as Roland Barthes has suggested, "can only have a linguistic existence, as a term in a discourse" (121), then perhaps the most authentic way to write a history is to write the history of that history. In both *Soldados de Salamina* and *La velocidad de la luz*, the straightforward reflexivity of their narrators is linked poignantly to an effort to give a voice to the silenced and forgotten ghosts of history. Once their story has been told, these ghosts are no longer anonymous, and they are allowed to exist in the collective consciousness in narrative form where, in the best of cases, we may learn from their experiences. In this way, *La velocidad de la luz*, like *Soldados de Salamina*, is a moving testament to the power of narrative to help us come to terms with the things that haunt us— memories, ghosts, the dead, and their stories.

On the penultimate page of *La velocidad de la luz*, the narrator reaches a kind of epiphany during a conversation he has with his friend and

confidant Marcos (who in this respect is very similar to the fictionalized Roberto Bolaño, who appears in *Soldados de Salamina*). The narrator realizes that the writing of this book—which is in fact the very book
we have been reading—will not only immortalize his dead wife and
son but also have a soothing impact on his own psyche:

> terminaría el libro [. . .] porque terminarlo era también la única forma
> de que, aunque fuera encerrados en estas páginas, Gabriel y Paula
> permaneciesen de algún modo vivos, y de que yo dejase de ser quien
> había sido hasta entonces, quien fui con Rodney—mi semejante, mi
> hermano—, para convertirme en otro, para ser de alguna manera y en
> parte y para siempre Rodney. (303)

> I would finish the book . . . because finishing it was also the only way
> that, even though they would be enclosed in these pages, Gabriel and
> Paula would continue in some way to be alive, and thus I would cease
> being who I had been up to then, who I was with Rodney—my like-
> ness, my brother—to transform myself into someone else, to become
> in some way and in part and forever Rodney.

In telling his story, the narrator assumes some of Rodney's identity by absorbing his narrative and thus engaging more wholeheartedly
in a process that Rodney could not ultimately bring himself to undergo.
The novel ends cryptically, as the narrator explains to his friend Marcos
that he has finally discovered, in the process of telling him his story,
how his novel will end and how he will write it. He explains, once again
evoking the novel's first line, that it will be an apocryphal tale: "será
una novela apócrifa, como mi vida clandestina e invisible, una novela
falsa pero más verdadera que si fuera de verdad" (304) (it will be an
apocryphal novel, like my clandestine and invisible life, a false novel
but more truthful than if it were true). And when Marcos asks him
how the novel will end, he replies with the final sentence of the novel:
"Acaba así" (304) (it ends like this). The novel's self-reflexive conclusion once again draws attention to the arbitrary nature of endings in
general and emphasizes the fact that while stories must always end,
history is ongoing and will always transcend the limits of narrative
expression.

The novel, as a symbolic act of remembering and telling, produces meaning for the subject by drawing him or her into contact with others, living and dead. The skeletons that have begun to be exhumed from Franco's mass graves do not only haunt the perpetrators of their deaths or the families who have lost their loved ones. These ghosts of the past haunt all of Spain, and as more people begin to tell their stories—be they apocryphal, like Cercas's narrators' tales, or horrifyingly true, like those that have appeared in at least a dozen documentary films and testimonies produced in Spain during the last ten years—these ghosts form an all-too-real part of the present. But perhaps, by giving them a voice, we may grant these ghosts the memorialization that they silently seek. Like Santi in del Toro's *El espinazo del diablo*—the murdered boy whose ghost lurks in the pool, waiting for the moment when his story will be known—Franco's legacy lies just below the surface, awaiting a time when the *pacto de silencio* may officially be broken. While the Ley de la Memoria Histórica may not have the desired memorializing effects or please everyone involved in its creation and implementation (see Tremlett's essay in this volume), writers in Spain and elsewhere endeavor to give a voice to those who were never able to tell their tales. Stories, after all, can put us in touch with a greatness that transcends the few fragile bodies of those who tell them.

NOTES

1. Antonio Gómez's book *La guerra persistente: Memoria, violencia y utopía: Representaciones contemporáneas de la Guerra Civil española* (2006) offers a comprehensive analysis of the persistence of the Civil War in the contemporary Spanish cultural imagination. Gómez ably analyzes many of these novels and films, relating them to Spain's political and historical present.

2. Using Derrida's formulation from *Specters of Marx*, Labanyi posits that "ghosts, as the traces of those who have not been allowed to leave a trace . . . are by definition the victims of history who return to demand reparation; that is, that their name, instead of being erased, be honored" ("History" 66). Derrida's concept of hauntology (as it is used in all of these essays) is developed as "a new philosophical category of being—an alternative to ontology—appropriate to describe the status of history: that is, the past as that which is not and yet is there—or rather, here" (Labanyi, "History" 66).

3. Ellis analyzes the gendered discourse of the novel in terms of its status as a "memory text" that tries to recuperate "a repressed or obliterated historical memory" (515). He argues that the narrator, in the process of searching out a father figure, "asserts the values of masculinity that inform the political imaginaries of both the right and the left" (515).

4. *La velocidad de la luz* is narrated under the spectre of the Iraq War. When the narrator returns to Rantoul, Illinois, in search of Rodney, he notices among the numerous luminous advertisements for Budweiser and Miller Lite several signs saying "Pray for Peace" and "Support our Troops" (242). When he enters a bar looking for his friend, he speaks to a fictional Illinoisan who expresses his frustration with U.S. foreign policy: "todo era mentira, los políticos nos engañaron a todos, igual que ahora: todos esos chicos muriendo como conejos en Irak. Ya me contará usted qué se nos ha perdido en ese país de mierda. Y qué se nos había perdido en Vietnam" (248) (everything was a lie, the politicians fooled us all, just like they are doing now: all those kids dying like rabbits in Iraq. Maybe you can tell me what we are looking for in that piece of shit country. And what we were looking for in Vietnam). The novel can clearly be read as a subtle indictment of Spain's Partido Popular and its leader, José María Aznar, who supported the U.S. invasion of Iraq in 2003 as part of what President Bush called at the time the "Coalition of the Willing." Translations from *La velocidad de la luz* are my own.

5. Cercas achieved enormous commercial and critical success with *Soldados de Salamina*, which at this writing has sold more than a million copies and has been translated into thirteen languages.

6. When the narrator undertakes the writing of this story within the fictional narrative, he begins by repeating the ambiguous lines with which the novel begins: "siento que llevo una vida que no es de verdad, sino falsa, una vida clandestina y escondida y apócrifa pero más verdadera que si fuera de verdad" (290) (I feel that I have not been living a true life, but rather a false one: a clandestine, hidden, apocryphal life that is nevertheless more truthful than if it were true).

PART IV

Unearthing the Past

Anthropological Perspectives on Franco's Mass Graves

Memory Politics among Perpetrators and Bereaved Relatives about Spain's Mass Graves

Antonius C. G. M. Robben

Dozens of mass graves have been discovered and rediscovered in Spain since the much publicized exhumation in Priaranza del Bierzo, León, in 2000. These burial sites contain the skeletal remains of thousands of the seventy thousand to a hundred thousand Spaniards executed by Francoist troops during the 1936–1939 Civil War and in its aftermath. The significance of these mass graves has changed over the decades. Silenced during Franco's reign and ignored by subsequent democratic governments, they have recently become the center of national commemoration, historical debate, and public and private mourning. Francisco Ferrándiz and Ignacio Fernández de Mata reveal with much sensitivity and insight the complexities of exhumation practices, commemoration politics, and the suffering of relatives who were only small children or not yet born when their parents, grandparents, uncles, and aunts were led away to the firing squad. They mourn losses that they hardly understood then and that still remain incomprehensible for many today. In this commentary on the superb essays of the anthropologists Ferrándiz and Fernández de Mata, I want to elaborate on this incomprehensibility of the Civil War executions, discuss the contested memories surrounding the exhumations, and draw some more attention to the perspective of the perpetrators, partly in comparison with my own research on similar themes in Latin America.

FACING AN INCOMPREHENSIBLE PAST

The time lag between the summary execution of twelve Asturian men and five women in October 1937 and their exhumation in July 2003 is so great that attempts to recuperate the truth surrounding that tragic event seem futile. Perpetrators and eyewitnesses have died, are too old to remember, or refuse to speak about the past. Even more tantalizing than this inevitable loss of testimony is the awareness that every traumatic experience is ultimately incomprehensible because the violent event is so psychologically overwhelming and disorienting that it can never be grasped, remembered, or understood in full. There are always unknowns and unknowables at the heart of trauma (Caruth, Introduction), and what is known cannot be fully integrated into consciousness because the reality is too horrible to acknowledge (Gampel). Traumatized people will therefore protect themselves by keeping the terrifying experiences separate from their everyday lives, even though traumatic memories might intrude on consciousness in nightmares, disturbing daydreams, or compulsive thoughts.

Exhumations are intrusions from a different order. They may upset the fragile emotional balance reached by surviving relatives after decades of silent suffering and thus cause renewed distress, but they may also provide a historical understanding, a podium for recounting hardships, and possibly a personal closure that allows survivors to reconcile themselves with the course of their lives and that of their executed relatives' lives. Furthermore, as Ferrándiz says in his essay in this volume, the official condemnation of the killings "has a clear relevance in order to rescue and rehabilitate the memory of the victims for the present and the future and affects both the most public and the most intimate spaces of political action."

The significance of the exhumations is magnified among people who were small children when the executions occurred. Already unable to grasp the political complexity of a Spain at war with itself, they failed to understand how their communities became entangled in the violence and why relatives were assassinated. Fernández de Mata describes the humiliation, stigmatization, ostracism, and pauperization of victimized children as a personal rupture of the world. What precisely was ruptured for these children?

When Fernández de Mata observes that the assassination of parents or siblings, and the ensuing misery and social exclusion, "shattered what should have been the safe haven of childhood for the surviving relatives of the victims of the repression of 1936," he is indirectly referring to the damage inflicted on what psychologists have called their basic trust (Erikson). Basic trust is acquired during early childhood, when infants learn that they can rely on their parents for love, care, and protection against external threats. They eventually develop a strong enough ego to cope with life's discomforts and have sufficient trust in humankind that they do not feel threatened by outsiders (see Bowlby; Erikson). Spanish children with traumatic Civil War experiences learned that they could not rely unquestionably on their parents for safety and that the outside world was a dangerous environment in which hostile forces deprived them forever of the affection of their executed parents. This distrust was repeatedly fed by the official silencing of the executions, the public commemorations of Franco's victory, and the memorials erected in memory of fallen Nationalists.

Francisco Ferrándiz describes movingly how an aging Esther Cimadevilla had been searching for a father whose image, life, and predicament were kept from her by her mother. She only recovered a threadbare account from the fading memory of her ninety-year-old mother a few months before she died. Her father, Emilio Montoto, had been executed in Valdediós, Asturias, in October 1937 and interred in a mass grave. Esther traveled from the United States to Spain in 2003 to assist the exhumation "in order to rescue and vindicate his memory." This rescue mission must have had a heightened importance because of her mother's deliberate silence. Extrapolating from my own research among relatives of the Argentine disappeared, I suspect that Esther's determination to find and bury her father was a manifestation of a deep-seated reciprocal care that exists between parent and child (see Robben, "Assault"). This daughterly obligation was intensified by her mother's outward emotional neglect of her dead husband. Esther undid her mother's and her native country's silence and provided her father with a proper burial, even though the forensic identification of Emilio Montoto was inconclusive.

The personal rupture of the world and the incomprehensibility of the tragic events extend also to the collective level, albeit in an inverse manner. The Spanish state ignored the Civil War executions and the presence of mass graves between 1939 and 2000. Although understandable during the Franco dictatorship and even during Aznar's Partido Popular government, the silence of the Socialist government of Felipe González is harder to grasp. Common understanding from genocide and especially Holocaust studies has it that societies need to repress or at least silence major atrocities for an extended time because they are not ready to face the many dead or admit to their own complicity in the killings. The belated soul-searching about the Holocaust in Western Europe is taken as emblematic of a universal social reaction to mass violence, notwithstanding the ongoing private suffering of the survivors. As I have pointed out in an analysis of Argentina's compulsive remembering of the state repression of the 1976–1983 dictatorship, the European response was historically, politically, and psychologically specific (see Robben, "Traumatized"). Unlike in the case of the Holocaust, Argentine society did not silence the horrors of the so-called dirty war when the military regime fell in 1983, but immediately created a Truth Commission to determine the fate of more than ten thousand disappeared Argentines, opened mass graves, divulged the testimonies of torture victims, prosecuted perpetrators, and sentenced five junta members to lengthy prison terms.

The Spanish silence about the Civil War atrocities compares therefore neither to the Argentine nor to the Western European situation but resembles more closely the Chilean indifference to the horrors of its 1973–1990 military regime. Both Chile and Spain underwent negotiated transitions to democracy: Chile with General Pinochet remaining in power as commander in chief of the armed forces and Spain with the transformation of a dictatorship into a parliamentary monarchy. Both countries were unable to hold perpetrators accountable because of amnesty legislation, and, just as important, both countries reaped the benefits from the rapid economic growth begun during authoritarian rule.

The Chilean sociologists Moulian and Lechner argue that the three-decades-long indifference to the repressive past by large sectors of Chilean society was caused by a collective complicity with military rule. They even speak of a compulsion to forget, exactly the opposite of the compulsion to remember that has typified Argentina. The Chilean silence was fed by the country's economic success and safeguarded by a military that zealously protected their personal and institutional interests. The Chilean middle and upper classes drowned their guilt about this complicity in consumerism, argue Moulian and Lechner. The businessmen, technocrats, and neoliberal intellectuals pretended to be afraid of endangering the calm and economically successful transition from dictatorship to democracy if they raised the Chilean military's accountability. This fear was held responsible for the national silence, while in fact it served to cover up their collaboration with Pinochet's regime, from whose neoliberal policies they benefited most. Pinochet even turned from dictator into patriarch as time passed. He became seen as Chile's principal benefactor who had given the country peace and prosperity.

Thus Chile's past was silenced to avoid a critical self-examination about civil society's complicity with the military regime, to prevent the eruption of social fractures that might undermine the transition from dictatorship to democracy, and to protect the blooming economy from a political instability that might deter foreign investments. Chilean society was so geared toward the future that it buried the past. It was a collective conspiratorial silence. The sudden discovery of a mass grave or a public testimony by a survivor of torture might briefly move the nation, but these revelations were not assumed in full by either the subsequent democratic governments or large segments of Chilean society out of deep guilt feelings. Silence was bought off with consumer goods to fill the emotional gaps left by seventeen years of dictatorship, the guilt of complicity, and the guilt of failing to empathize with suffering fellow citizens.

Has such complicity also been at play in Spain? Fernández de Mata mentions the collective rupture with the world at the outbreak of the Civil War and the post–Civil War social reordering that affected norms, values, gender roles, and the country's socioeconomic organization. The spoils of war were reaped by a petty bourgeoisie who took the jobs of executed workers, defeated Republicans, and blacklisted neighbors. The Spanish middle class owes its current prosperity to the growing industrialization and tourism industry initiated during Franco's dictatorship since the 1960s. There seems a parallel here with the Chilean silence, the consumerism, and the fear of destabilizing the country and the booming economy by raking up traumatic memories. Another parallel appears in the recent reexamination of the past in Chile and Spain. Just as the exhumation in León in 2000 turned into an unstoppable confrontation with a past silenced for more than six decades, so the detention of General Pinochet after an indictment by Judge Garzón in 1998, and especially the 2004 revelation of the former dictator's secret foreign bank accounts, have finally broken the Chilean embargo on the past. Pinochet's betrayal undid the societal pact of silence and is engendering national soul-searching with a yet uncertain outcome.

THE PERPETRATORS' HIDDEN CARTOGRAPHY

The exhumations in Spain have made "a formerly neglected cartography of terror and repression" visible, so writes Francisco Ferrándiz perceptively, one "that encompasses many landscapes and localities throughout the country." Ferrándiz observes that each opening of a mass grave confronts Spain with violated human remains, resignifies the past through extensive media coverage, reorders national space through the creation of commemorative landmarks, and redraws collective memory with the testimonies of witnesses and survivors.

Still, what remained invisible for more than half a century had always been known to survivors and perpetrators. If the Valle de los Caídos (Valley of the Fallen) memorial publicly acknowledged "the memory of those who fell during our glorious Crusade," then the mass graves with executed Republicans were the hidden memorial sites of Franco's victory (*El Valle*). General Franco regarded the Civil War as a divine reconquest of Spain—reminiscent of the Reconquista by the fifteenth-century Catholic kings and queens—that reclaimed lost symbolic and national territory from the Republican atheists. A military victory became therefore measurable in cities conquered and enemies buried in mass graves.

The summary executions during the Civil War symbolized a lasting victory. The executioners outlived their enemies at the moment of killing, a powerful feeling that has been described as follows by Elias Canetti: "The moment of survival is the moment of power. Horror at the sight of death turns into satisfaction that it is someone else who is dead. . . . This feeling of superiority to the dead is known to everyone who has fought in a war. It may be masked by grief for comrades, but these are few and the dead are always many. The feeling of strength, of standing alone against the dead, is in the end stronger than any grief. It is a feeling of being chosen from amongst the many who manifestly shared the same fate" (227–28).

Canetti was not a soldier, and his interpretation lacks grounding in lived experience, but his intuition was right. The following quote from a retired American officer specialized in the psychology of killing says very much the same: "Mass murder and execution can be sources of mass empowerment. . . . The soldier who does kill must overcome that part of him that says that he is a murderer of women and children, a foul beast who has done the unforgivable. . . . He *must* believe that not only is this atrocity right, but it is proof that he is morally, socially, and culturally superior to those whom he has killed. It is the ultimate act of denial of their humanity. It is the ultimate act of affirmation of his superiority" (Grossman 208–10).

Franco's troops reappropriated Spain by occupying the country with mass graves. These graves were material proof of the military's superior force and gave the troops the confidence that they were winning the war against the atheist revolutionaries. Once again, Canetti has tried to verbalize the feelings of a victorious soldier in the presence of his slain enemies: "As he walks among the graves he feels that he is alone. Side by side at his feet lie the unknown dead, and they are many. How many is not known, but the number is very great and there will be more and more of them. They cannot move, but must remain there, crowded together. He alone comes and goes as he wishes; he alone stands upright" (277). The symbolic power of mass graves derives from their reference to the mass of enemies, so suggests Canetti, and to the diminishing ranks of opposition through death, thus imbuing perpetrators with omnipotence.

The unceremonial burial of the defeated was the final act of victory. The dead were not acknowledged as fellow Spaniards who deserved a proper burial to reincorporate them into society as deceased members. Their death was seen as a gain for, rather than a loss to, society. The dumping of their executed bodies symbolized their inhumanity. Unlike the dead on the Nationalist side, who were immortalized at the Valle de los Caídos memorial, the executed were considered unpatriotic.

Yet the dead were present in the Spanish collective memory, as both authors have shown convincingly. They remained alive not only in the suffering of the surviving relatives who were unable to express their anguish openly, but I suspect that the perpetrators also remembered the executions they had carried out. Some might have been troubled by remorse and regarded the executions as a stain on their victory. Others took refuge in Spain's official public silence, while still others privately rejoiced in their horrendous deeds. These perpetrators would be reminded frequently of the dark past as they drove by the secret burial sites on their way to work or on vacation. The hidden mass graves served as faceless monuments to the glorious victory. What for the bereaved relatives became "a road map linking the political production of terror with the intimate experiences of the victims of repression," according to Ferrándiz, was an itinerary of triumphs for the perpetrators.

My interpretation of mass graves as invisible monuments is less speculative than it might appear at first sight. The earliest Spanish meaning of the word *monumento* is a place of burial (*sepulcro*), a memorial to a heroic act. Here lies one meaning of the mass graves for the victorious Nationalist troops. The concealed burial grounds were a constant reminder of their victory over evil. The mass grave/monument was a commemoration of the slaying of the "Reds," the atheists who had violated in July 1936 the graves of Spanish nuns, priests, and saints and openly displayed the mummified remains (see Lincoln). Such desecration did not serve as a justification for the unceremonial burial of the executed Republicans but was certainly known to the executioners and might have increased already existing feelings of revenge.

The second symbolic meaning of the mass graves for the victors was that they represented the worthlessness of the dead. The slain enemies did not merit a proper burial place as one would accord the fallen in a conventional war. The Republican atheists were less than human in the eyes of the military and deserved nothing better than a dog's grave. They did not need to be remembered by Spanish society and had to be prevented from turning into martyrs for future generations.

The third meaning of the mass graves was that their hidden location heightened the dead person's fall from society's grace. Evil could only be buried in unhallowed soil, not in a cemetery that would provide them with an identifiable status in a Catholic universe. The executed had become outcasts whose place outside the new social order was emphasized by their unacknowledged presence in mass graves. This spiritual, social, and spatial exclusion of the undesirable dead is of symbolic importance in many societies but has an added relevance in a deeply Catholic society like Spain.

In the end, these diverse meanings of the Spanish mass graves revolve around memory construction. They diminish the recollection of the Republican dead and fill the collective memory with victorious Nationalists. Together with the silenced memories and hidden memorials of the vanquished, there is an implicit wish to close public space to the suffering of surviving relatives and enlarge the public recognition for the Nationalist losses as sacrifices for the glory of Spain.

CONFLICTING MEMORIES AND TESTIMONIES

Are the recent efforts to exhume mass graves, identify and rebury the dead, return stolen property to the heirs, record the testimonies of survivors and relatives, build memorials, reexamine and preserve archives, hold official commemorations, and rehabilitate the defeated the manifestations of a national trauma? Both Ferrándiz and Fernández de Mata believe it is too early to tell, and they point perceptively to the heterogeneity of the historical memory movement. There are a few aged perpetrators who have unburdened their conscience. There are sons and daughters who search for their parents, young adults who want to reconstruct the life histories of their grandparents, local and regional governments that commemorate the Civil War victims, and a national government that ponders about what to do with Franco's symbolic presence in Spanish public spaces. In addition, there are historians, anthropologists, psychologists, writers, filmmakers, and journalists who have a significant impact on Spanish society through their "production, circulation, and consumption of images and narratives of Civil War terror." Finally, there is a general public who takes notice of, empathizes with, participates in, ignores, or is indifferent to this memory movement.

Most public attention has been drawn to the bereaved families. Fernández de Mata addresses the motivation of these searching relatives.

His explanation points to personal suffering and a social trauma. It is unclear whether there are still relatives with a psychic trauma from the sequels to the Civil War, but Ferrándiz and Fernández de Mata present several examples of intense personal suffering. Persons such as Esther, Maricarmen, Rosa, and Rosita desire a forensic exhumation to finally rebury their relatives with ceremonial honor, fulfill a family and moral obligation fed by basic trust, and provide blood relatives with a place to mourn the losses and remember the dead. This personal motivation is entwined with a social need, found in every human society, to care for the dead, give them a ceremonial burial, accord them a place in the hereafter, and acknowledge the bereavement of the mourners (see Hertz, *Death*). Some relatives experience the exhumation and reburial as the release of a lifelong burden and feel they can now die peacefully, while others acquire renewed energies to set the historical record straight and memorialize the dead in a national context.

The emotional and social closure brought about by the reburials does not inevitably relegate the executed to historical memory. Many relatives share the social trauma of an interrupted family line and bear the burden of having dehumanized ancestors whose lives were considered so unworthy that they were executed without a trial, and buried without ceremony. The trauma continues as unfinished social mourning, a recurrent return to the suffering of the executed, the awareness of their social stigmatization, the incessant call for vindication, and the desire to symbolically undo the harm inflicted on their assassinated relatives. As Krystal has remarked about the social trauma of Holocaust survivors, "unmastered memories represent 'unhealed wounds,' which keep generating painful affects. Memories that cannot be accepted may have to be reinterpreted or modified in a kind of self-detoxification" (156). The exhumations and reburials, the commemorations, an official recognition of injustices, and a rewriting of history help heal those wounds and overcome the social trauma. Bereaved relatives want to restore the agency and protagonism of the executed and make them once again, after six decades of oblivion, full participants and even heroes in Spanish history.

The perpetrators of the war crimes and the crimes against humanity during the Spanish Civil War have a much more subdued public voice in the current memory debate, but their modest role is shored up by the many relics from Franco's dictatorship. The Valle de los Caídos memorial site is possibly the most visible manifestation of such Nationalist memory, but there are also street names, school names, cemeteries, statues, landmarks, foundations, history books, films, and songs that bear the partisan imprint of the Francoists. Tight-lipped perpetrators conceal the location of mass graves consciously, not just because they are afraid of possible prosecution and reprisals, but because their concealment marks an enduring victory over the defeated, as the slain remain trapped in oblivion. Even the transformation of the Valle de los Caídos into an educational center will not erase the architectural imprint of the Franco dictatorship or make visible the miserable working conditions of the Republican prisoners who built the mausoleum containing the remains of General Francisco Franco and the Falange leader José Antonio Primo de Rivera. Certain experiences remain unrecoverable, and others are imprinted forever on Spanish society.

THE FUTURE OF SPAIN'S EXHUMATIONS

Spain embarked in the year 2000 on an unpredictable journey into its past. Francisco Ferrándiz and Ignacio Fernández de Mata have demonstrated that the exhumations have become a Pandora's box. Fernández de Mata writes of "debates, issues, processes, and struggles that have been increasingly shaking Spanish society since the first mass grave exhumation in October 2000," while Francisco Ferrándiz observes that the "exhumations are bringing to Spanish society . . . rather disturbing information regarding our past, our present, and probably our future as well." Pandora, who was according to Greek mythology the first woman on earth, received a box from Jupiter that encased all human ills. The contents escaped into the world when Pandora opened the box. This metaphor applies also to Spain's exhumations. The recent opening of the Civil War mass graves released the previously silenced suffering, anguished memories, and secrets about the atrocities committed by Franco's insurgent troops into the public arena to be debated, contested, and made public. Decades of silence were broken with painful testimonies. Spanish society began to question the official rendition of the Civil

War, and the human and social costs of this collective fratricide were revealed to the Spanish people.

What will the future bring for the exhumations and Spain's collective soul-searching? The historical reappraisal of the Civil War is barely under way and will develop into many yet unknown directions. Still, some potential developments may be envisioned when we draw upon the experiences with the exhumation of victims of political violence in Latin America. Chile and Argentina have been exhuming mass graves for several decades. The first exhumations produced great commotion because the assassinations had occurred relatively recently and most bereaved relatives were still alive. The expectation among human rights organizations was that the exhumations would lead to the identification of the victims, the restitution of the remains to the relatives for a proper burial, the prosecution and conviction of the perpetrators, and an eventual return to normalcy after the dead had been mourned and society had assumed its responsibility and guilt for past atrocities. But the political reality of these deeply divided societies proved more unpredictable than imagined, and the social traumas more unmanageable than anticipated (see Robben, "Traumatized"). Extrapolating from the consequences of the exhumations in Chile and Argentina, the following six effects might also take place in Spain.

One, the positive identification of skeletal remains becomes increasingly more difficult as time passes. Clothing has disintegrated, dental and medical records are unavailable, and close relatives who may remember accidental bone fractures that help the forensic investigations are no longer alive, while DNA testing is considered either too expensive or impossible because relatives cannot be located. There have been several cases of misidentification in Chile and Argentina, which brought much suffering to the surviving relatives and made people refuse permission for future exhumations, thus expressing doubts about the reexamination of the past. More than seven decades have now passed since the first Civil War executions in Spain. The possibility of some misidentifications is therefore real, and society's reaction uncertain.

Two, the exhumations in Chile and Argentina became regarded as pointless by some when increasingly more mass graves were opened but the perpetrators were not held accountable. The political choice not to prosecute the executioners made several Argentine human rights organizations oppose the exhumations. Such retraction is less likely to happen in Spain because most perpetrators have died. Furthermore, there are other ways than criminal prosecution for a society to deal with victimizers. Honors and medals can be withdrawn. Streets, squares, and buildings can be renamed. Commemorations can be discontinued, and memorials may be disassembled or remodeled to account for the Republican dead.

Three, the Argentine and Chilean exhumations were regarded as undesirable by certain groups in society because they either caused or dampened political protest. Political groups supportive of the military coups argued that bygones were bygones, and that now Chileans and Argentines had to work toward national reconciliation and economic prosperity. Exhumations were considered counterproductive in achieving those aims, and mass graves should therefore be left alone. On the other side of the political spectrum, in particular in Argentina, there were organizations such as the Mothers of the Plaza de Mayo, which began opposing the exhumations because these were setting in motion a mourning process among relatives who had recuperated their dead and thus would cause the political demobilization of the human rights movement and end in a national forgetting of military repression. Some voices of opposition to the ongoing exhumations have also been raised in Spain. They argue that old wounds are opened that will damage Spain's social fabric. It is yet uncertain whether this will be the case, whether Spanish society has not already been torn since 1936, and whether the dignified ritual reburial of the executed and the current soul-searching will not help to pull the country together through a more balanced treatment of the past.

Four, a substantial group of veterans of Argentina's "dirty war" has been actively glorifying their victory over the revolutionary insurgents and denying any wrongdoing during military rule. The overruling of amnesties and presidential pardons by the Supreme Court has even led to a resurgence of such political vindication. Plaques are revealed, masses are said, roll calls of the dead are published, videos are produced to shore up words with images, and commemorations are organized in the memory of the victims of the leftist subversion. At the same time, there has been a growing opposition to this denial of gross human rights violations by self-critical Argentine officers who condemn their former comrades. Instead, Chilean officers have been remarkably quiet about their human rights abuses. They have enjoyed the protection of a self-declared amnesty, while Chilean society was for decades unwilling to examine its past and not interested in demanding the accountability of perpetrators. The international arrest warrants against General Pinochet, the disclosure of his secret bank accounts, and the 2005 election of a president who spent time in Chile's most notorious torture center are changing the political landscape. The passage of time has made the prosecution of Spain's executioners most unlikely and their vindication of less political urgency. Still, the recent appearance in Spanish newspapers of obituaries of persons executed by Nationalist and Republican forces, and especially the combative tone decrying the dead on the Nationalist side, is worrisome. Furthermore, just as the increasing distance from the Civil War has allowed for the exhumation of mass graves, so this time lag may make some people idealize Franco's regime and in particular his role in the economic expansion of the 1960s and 1970s.

Five, exhumed, identified, and reburied victims of state terror have resurrected old political ideals in Chile and especially Argentina. Their violent deaths have given them a political role in history, which continues to incite strong ideological feelings. The Chilean and Argentine disappeared and executed are increasingly seen as idealists whose objective was to improve the lives of their countrymen and whose political ideas continue to be relevant today. I doubt whether Spain will witness a future resurgence of Republicanism, but a historical reappraisal of the five-year pre–Civil War Republic is always a possibility.

Six, Chilean and Argentine sites of trauma are slowly transforming into sites of memory as experience turns into history. Former torture centers have become museums in which school children learn about the military dictatorship. Monuments and memorials are erected at former mass graves. Memory parks arise to remember the dead and symbolize the suffering in artistic forms. In Spain, some memorials and commemoration plaques related to the Civil War executions have recently been inaugurated. Their permanence and significance in Spain's collective memory cannot be foreseen, but the controversies over their existence will most likely be less intense than in Chile and Argentina, as Spanish society is taking responsibility for its past.

The exhumations in Spain are thus a Pandora's box with many unforeseen effects but not all of them disruptive. When Pandora opened her box and allowed the ills to escape, only hope remained inside. The Spanish exhumations may open wounds inflicted by the Civil War, but they harbor also the hope that a society that is brave enough to uncover an almost forgotten and painful past will finally be at peace after having honestly looked at itself and drawn valuable moral and historical lessons.

The Rupture of the World and the Conflicts of Memory

Ignacio Fernández de Mata

This essay addresses four main topics related with the repression of the defeated in the Spanish Civil War. First, it looks at the narration of the victims' traumatic memories and the problems faced by both the narrator and the interviewer when attempting to recover these memories. Second, it focuses on the actual violence of Francoist repression in the areas controlled by the so-called Nationalists upon the breakout of the insurgency. Third, it analyzes the explanations constructed by different social sectors regarding the assassination of thousands of persons and their interment in mass graves, combined with information gleaned from the available historical record. And finally, it examines the conflicts of memory unleashed by the relatively recent wave of exhumations promulgated by the relatives of the assassinated victims, focusing on those in the province of Burgos, where I have conducted my research.

A YEAR OF MEMORY FOR SPAIN

On June 23, 2006, the Spanish Congress of Deputies declared the year 2006 as the Year of Historical Memory. This year thus commemorates the seventy-fifth anniversary of the founding of the Second Spanish Republic, and the seventieth anniversary of the start of the Spanish Civil War. The initiative, approved in the last congressional session before summer holidays started, came from the ranks of the minority coalition formed by the Green Party and United Left (the revamped Communist Party). The conservative Popular Party, the main opposition group to the government of Socialist José Luis Rodríguez Zapatero, was the only one that voted against the measure. They proposed to call the year 2006 the Year of Concord, commemorating the Transition instead, because it represented a time when the Spanish were willing and ready to come together and harmoniously build a common future. In the Popular Party's reading, the Spain of today seems to be floundering in the midst of fruitless debates and reopening of old wounds that tear at the social fabric and the very essence of the nation.

In this same context of memorialist vindications and passing judgment on the Spanish past, on July 3 the European Parliament issued a condemnation of Franco's regime, again with the sole opposition of the Spanish Popular Party members.

The proclamation of the year 2006 as the Year of Historical Memory goes beyond the aforementioned anniversaries, however. It condenses at the highest institutional level the types of debates, issues, processes, and struggles that have been increasingly shaking Spanish society since the first mass grave exhumation in October 2000.[1] The opening of Franco's mass graves has brought the intimate experience of defeat—the history of the vanquished—into the open, challenging the hegemonic history of the victors. Bones, visible and palpable and imprinted with violence, testify that Francoist repression was virulent and widespread—something that many Spaniards had as yet refused to accept. It is therefore not surprising that recent years have witnessed a bitter struggle over the representation of the recent Spanish past, from the establishment and development of the Second Republic in 1931, through the Civil War and the Francoist regime. The Right has generally opposed exhumations, refused to acknowledge new historical data about the past, and initiated a revisionist historiography that underlines the fatal flaws of the Left during the Second Republic and the Civil War and in fact blames the Left for its defeat and the violence unleashed. This vituperative conservative reaction against the emerging memory of the vanquished is not misplaced: memory in contemporary Spain is a major social, political, and moral issue that is leading to more than simply redefining the past.[2] It is at the heart of contemporary redefinitions of nationhood, civil society, citizenship, and democracy.

REMEMBERING THE IMPOSSIBLE, NARRATING THE INEXPRESSIBLE

"I talk now because nobody wanted to listen before" (Ascención G.).[3] Sixty-seven years after the first of the crimes took place, this was the explanation given by an informant to the anthropologist who interviewed her, a lapidary phrase that points at a crucial fact: the silence and incomprehension best represented by the old adage "There is no worse deafer man than he who refuses to listen." The victims' silence was imposed through the exercise of terror and power, as well as the complicit deafness by those who were not directly affected. Spanish society thus alienated a part of itself and accepted the hegemonic theses of the dictatorship, silencing its guilt and misgivings about consenting to the violence. To know, to speak, would become problematic, a certain source of social as well as personal conflicts that nobody wanted. The disclaimers that "it happened so long ago," "it's better to not look back," and "we must turn the page" are knee-jerk answers that often mask guilt and unclear consciences and that seek to end all discussion.

Remembering—*recordar*, in Spanish—implies returning through feeling, through the heart—*cor*, in Latin. Its meaning is therefore related to reliving, for although it is impossible to repeat a past experience, the act of *recordar* evokes the sensations produced by that experience. To remember is to feel again.

When studying the experiences of violence and terror suffered since 1936 through the memories of those who lived them, we face the problem that these traumatic memories were made socially invisible for more than six decades and have therefore remained unarticulated and often suppressed. A sudden, incomprehensible, and terrifying experience made all aspects of the Spanish surviving victims' lives precarious; it fragmented possible sources of warmth and support and created an environment of hostility that made every moment of their daily lives insecure and fearsome. Transmitting this experience is difficult not only because it is incomprehensible to a listener who did not live through it, but because the ruptured social fabric has remained torn, especially for those who continued to live under the weight of a hegemonic memory that silenced their experience.

Another problem of recovering these memories in the present seems to arise because the narratives told by old men and women recount experiences lived in their childhood. As they give their testimonies, informants' gestures and expressions reveal the pain of the children they were—the tears, fear, hopelessness, and disorientation felt at the loss of a parent or an older sibling.

A third pervasive problem lies in the difficulty of articulating through language experiences of suffering, horror, and panic. Michael Richards argues that "awful experiences, especially of loss, are impossible to forget because they are beyond normal human comprehension or existing schemata and cannot be assimilated into personal and collective narratives." He asks, rhetorically, "How is the inexpressible to be expressed?" ("From War" 94), and the answer lies in the diversity of strategies used by narrators that facilitate the articulation of their experiences. Some resources are narrative. Tomasa C. recalls, "I was sitting on my father's lap when they came to get him." Valentín C. says, "My father went to the store to get some pickled fish for supper, and he never came back." And Ascención G. remembers, "We were sleeping after dinner when they knocked on the door asking for my father." These narrative formulas that underline the rupture of the quotidian routine and then leave the action unfinished transmit the uncertainty that descended upon these men and women who were then children—the insecurity and, above all, the unexpectedness of what happened.

Elaine Scarry uses the notion of pre-language to describe nondiscursive resources used by individuals when recounting extremely painful experiences that include performance, gestures, and actions that involve the interlocutor who listens and is witness to the pain: "Pain does not simply resist language but actively destroys it, bringing about an immediate reversion to a state anterior to language, to the sounds and cries a human being makes before language is learned" (*The Body* 4).[4] The recourse to pre-language was clearly present in the conversations sustained with many of my informants when the pain of the experience they had lived spilled into their memories as they recalled and attempted to narrate them. The process of recording these memories and using them as a means to construct a historic-anthropological understanding of the events themselves is complicated by the difficulty experienced by the victims to use words in their narration. This situation is a constant in studies of traumatic memory. Authors such as Frankl, Semprún, Levi, and others make constant allusions to the incommunicability of horror.[5]

A memory can be vivid and detailed, but just as often it is shrouded by a cloud of dull pain and is therefore hard to verbalize. Many promising and intense conversations that we thought would yield exceptional data finally ended in nothing but general notes, for the facts that our informants wanted to share had receded and practically vanished behind the memory of the intense pain that was suffered and that was still present. When in August 2003 I visited Dominga E. in her house in a small village near Aranda, she was with her friend Mari Carmen R. During the interview, Mari Carmen kept muttering under her breath, "Oh, if only *I* spoke, if only *I* spoke." When I finished taking Dominga's testimony, I asked Mari Carmen to tell me her story. Suddenly, before an attentive listener, all she could say was that they had been very, very afraid and that the men had been taken away. Frustrated, she broke into tears, unable to transmit significant information, even though she knew that what she had lived through was significant and worth telling. When a space to speak and be listened to has finally come, the surviving victims are faced with the nonnarrativity of their pain. Gaining the empathy of their listener through the recourse to pre-language is the only way that expression feels sincere and useful.

Another example clarifies the notion of pre-language. Benilde S. lost two brothers between August and October 1936. A third brother was imprisoned. Ninety years old today, she cannot remember the details about her brothers' lives, their militancy, their relations, their dreams.[6] In her testimonies, she cried more often in moments of doubt, absence, or fragmentation of memory than when she recounted the capture and disappearance of her brothers. It is not precisely general pain or sadness that brought tears, but the incapacity to fully express the magnitude of the memory through words. Her recourse to pre-language is a strategy to repair the damage done by the passage of time. Listening came too late.

RUPTURE OF THE WORLD

The eruption of extreme violence in the summer of 1936[7]—which has been referred to as a holocaust by some authors—was experienced as what I refer to as a rupture of the world. This took place on two interrelated levels: on the one hand individual and on the other hand collective.

The life of apprehension, suffering, and alienation that would pervade the entire period of Francoism for many Spanish families could be described using Michael Taussig's expression "culture of terror": "From Timmerman's chronicle and texts like Miguel Angel Asturias' *El señor presidente*, it is abundantly clear that 'cultures of terror' are based on and nourished by silence and myth in which the fanatical stress on the mysterious flourishes by means of rumor and fantasy woven in a dense web of magical realism. It is also clear that the victimizer needs the victim for the purpose of making truth, objectifying the victimizer's fantasies in the discourse of the other" (Taussig, "Culture" 40). Although it came without warning, terror installed itself permanently. Testimonies are fraught with expressions of trepidation. The phrase "we have been afraid, very, very afraid," repeated by several informants, shows the anxiety and unease that continue to this day. As late as 2003, some of them set up secret appointments for interviews away from home; others received us at home but closed the curtains and made sure the doors were locked, and even then they lowered their voices to speak.

Personal Rupture

Pain can break an individual's world, especially a child's world. The brutal experience of the unexplainable—the murder of parents or siblings, sudden and increasing pauperization, destructuring of family life, constant humiliation and alienation, psychoses—all of these shattered what should have been the safe haven of childhood for the surviving relatives of the victims of the repression of 1936. These experiences marked the end of what had been "normal," everyday life, thus constituting a personal rupture of the world. As the wave of arrests and the rumor of assassinations spread, an environment of fear pervaded the lives of many who still did not believe that they would be directly affected (given the irrelevance of past military pronouncements in their personal lives) until the impossible also struck at their door. "We saw that they were detaining people, but we didn't think of running away. Why should we, when we hadn't done anything wrong?" declared Samuel G., whose brother was among those summarily executed (*fusilados*).

Children's descent into terror and insecurity was preceded and accompanied by the abuse heaped upon the women of their families. Female relatives of so-called Reds (*rojos*) were given degrading haircuts (the *pelonas*), were paraded around with their shaved heads through the streets, had their clothes torn, were taunted through songs. Beyond these initial vexations, they were constantly mortified and insulted for years. Incarcerated women and others were forced to assume the tasks associated with cleaning the barracks, hospitals, or officers' homes. It is not surprising that a significant part of the testimonies are stories of childhood humiliations and vexations.[8] According to his own testimony, Samuel G.'s father was assassinated in September 1936, when Samuel was seven years old, and he had to leave school in order to work along with his brothers. Among all the stories of hardship and suffering that he could have told us, he spoke of how he was forced to take his first communion dressed as a Falangist and was then excluded from the small celebration where the rest of the children were having cookies and sweet wine. This anecdote condenses the frustration and humiliation of a child in a world of cruel adults who insist on excluding the son in order to reproduce the stigma of his murdered father. His experience coincides with that of many other victims, whose exclusion was reproduced by the children of the victors, who insulted the victims at school and in the streets, perhaps with doses of oblivion that nonetheless did not reduce the cruelty perceived by the stigmatized children.

Childhood in fact ended with the disappearance of the assassinated father, an experience that not only caused emotional pain but led to the total pauperization of these people whose lives were often already precarious and who lost their head of household—sometimes the major, and often the only, source of income. The children of these severed households, some as young as seven or eight years old, engaged in labor that was often difficult for their age: they became a generation marked by an early entrance into the workforce, curtailed from pursuing schooling and with limited possibilities for improving their socioeconomic position in the future. The surviving victims were subalternized: they were orphaned by the law, excluded from public space, and sometimes directly or indirectly expelled from their communities. My own research shows how networks of support and sociability were reconfigured among them, reproducing in many ways a sort of culture of the vanquished, as they constituted social collectives within the towns and villages in a clear status of submission to the new conditions of life imposed upon society. I encountered numerous marriages among children of the executed, which reveal not only their search for community but the degree and endurance of their alienation. Especially in small towns, surviving "Reds" were snubbed in regular society decades after the war was over, and relatives of known "Reds" were accepted insofar as they rejected the ideology of their loved ones and openly embraced the regime. Members of these communities of pain were among the first to migrate in the 1940s, as they escaped dismal conditions of life and extreme pauperization, further abetting the hegemony of "non-Reds" in their communities.

Collective Rupture and New Social (Dis)Order

But the society that excluded relatives of "Reds" was also undergoing a general rupture of the world, as the norms and values that were until then considered natural and unquestionable were invalidated upon the outbreak of the war and the social fragmentation that preceded and surrounded it. This favored the eruption of repressed desires, the revindication of new social spaces, and the alteration of gender roles.

In 1936, Manuela B. worked as a domestic servant in Madrid. By mid-July, she returned to her parents' home for her vacation and was there when the war reached her hometown. Her father was assassinated in August, and her mother, who was publicly disgraced, suffered a mental crisis, leaving Manuela to support the family. In her free time, she kept a diary on the notebooks of the syndicate that her father had founded in the 1900s (ascribed to the UGT—the General Union of Workers).[9] Besides revealing an often confusing mix of her father's leftist utopianism and her own profound Catholic principles, her journal narrates the most painful and significant events of her community.

One of the elements that Manuela found noteworthy was the behavior of those she identified as "fascist women." In October 1936, these women "sing to, jump around, laugh at, and insult those whose hair has been shaved. . . . All their effort is put into parading them around." In

February 1937, Manuela writes of struggle and turmoil, for "five women signed a petition for the Captain [of the civil guard] of Aranda to have 25 men of the town executed, saying that they had heard them yelling, 'Long live Russia!'" In March, she describes ruthless women who accused their neighbors of what constituted deadly dissent.

> There is a band of women that spends its time denouncing whoever they find convenient. They kept denouncing people without thinking about it. And some of them were so keen that they screwed up, because they made an unfair denouncement that the Mayor followed through, and then on the 29th, a pair of civil guards in a little car came for a man who had never been mixed up in politics and also made him a prisoner. Who can be safe these days? There is no reason to be safe as long as petty hatreds (*malos quereres*) and revenges continue.

Come mid-June 1938, Manuela wrote that some of the "social prisoners" were released, "poor souls who had been suffering for 22 months. . . . Among them was a man of this town, and what madness! Seeing that some were *rojillos*, which is how they called them, the women tried to go to the Captains and the Commanders to say that they should execute all of them because they were all worse than those who had already died."

Traditional views of war portray men as the sole protagonists because they officially brandish and use firepower. But war, and the social relations and roles of war, go beyond the battlefield. When men go off to war, social roles are profoundly altered, as women are often incorporated into realms normally reserved for the masculine universe, including political action.[10] In the case of the Spanish Civil War, the transformation of gendered spaces was even more complicated and contradictory. On the Republican side, collective women's actions intended to effect societal change, but in the areas controlled by the insurgents, Fascist women acting in groups sought to reinvent a pre-Republican social order without representing or attempting to construct a "new woman."[11] Like an ancient Greek choir, they represented themselves as the angry voice of the community in the absence of men, and they wielded great power over the "Red" women, whom they shamed and vexed, and the men whom they accused based on gossip and rumor. This was their particular way of cleansing society from the moral decrepitude that had been introduced by—and was embodied in—the "Reds."[12] It was a type of sui generis empowerment of the feminine in which tensions and frustrations inherent in unequal gender relations could also be surreptitiously addressed, as women publicly exercised power over men, even "respectable men" (*hombres de respeto*).

These altered gender relations, the ideological polarization, the extermination of community members, the climate of fear and insecurity, and the unprecedented political importance of personal differences and problems—the deadly importance that made life precarious—signal just how deeply the world of social relations had been ruptured.

THE LOGICS OF VIOLENCE

Who Benefited?

Gender was not the only variable and social hierarchy affected by the coup and during the war, and women were not the only group to obtain a new social protagonism. The corporate world of the Spanish class system was also shaken and restructured. The interested calculation of the lower middle classes in the military coup was related to the possibility that it would provide job opportunities and spaces for political affirmation that had been usually reserved for the wealthier classes. In the end, the final triumph of the insurrection encouraged the emergence of a new petite bourgeoisie in these local spaces. I argue that, ideologically characterized by respect for traditional values, this new class hoped that so-called national regeneration would allow them to gain access to local power, and most were willing to ally with those who espoused the most exclusivist and violent discourses.

There was a redistribution of opportunities from those classified as "Reds" to those whose political activities (or lack thereof) coincided with the victorious side. These opportunities most often took the form of relatively unskilled jobs, which could be important in an impoverished economy characterized by high unemployment. In the neglected

municipal archive of Aranda de Duero names that would later be associated with the repression—of perpetrators as well as victims—show
up in claims, firings, and job transfers. Moreover, many survivors explain that the reason their relatives were denounced or placed on black-
lists of some sort is found in these conflicts between neighbors, which
are in fact evident in the documentary record.

Malos quereres versus Extermination Orders

The individual benefits that accrued to some, and the quarrels between
townspeople and community members that tore at the social fabric,
led many to accept the thesis that the assassinations were entirely the
product of envies and petty hatreds, *malos quereres*. We saw a similar
interpretation in Manuela B.'s personal journal. The Francoist regime
never acknowledged the massacres perpetrated by its adherents, much
less that they had taken place as part of a political program; indeed, it
encouraged the idea that rural villagers and peasants had acted on their
own wild impulses.[13]

Recent research has unequivocally shown that there were express orders to eliminate all individuals considered leftists in the zones where
the rebels had wrested power from the hands of the Republican government.[14] The instructions given by General Emilio Mola Vidal, director of the coup, lent an almost eugenicist character to the persecution
of "Reds," who were considered more than merely ideological enemies:
they were immoral; they were traitorous; they were anti-Spanish; they
were atheists; they went against all that was good.[15] In a conversation
with *Chicago Daily Tribune* correspondent Jay Allen—published by the
Tribune on July 28, 1936—Franco said that a truce between the warring
sides was impossible, because Republicans "fought against Spain," and
were thus to be stopped "at any cost" (qtd. in Luzán; my translation).[16]
Unfortunately for historians and researchers, there were both ample
time and motives during the Francoist regime and the anesthetizing
Transition to empty the major archives of compromising documents.
Nevertheless, a wave of new research that studies local sources more
deeply—municipal and provincial archives, prison documents, survivors' testimonies, archaeological evidence from the mass graves, and

overlooked documents in major archives and other sources—reveals the wider structural plan to eliminate all individuals considered leftists in the uniformity of the modus operandi followed by the rebels in diverse locales.

But the new historiographic tendency has insisted so much on the external origin of the repressive violence that some studies and even some associations dedicated to the recovery of historic memory now myopically deny the role of intracommunity tensions and local dynamics in the execution of violence. For some associations for the recovery of historic memory and for amateur historians, seeing the assassinations exclusively as the consequence of superior orders carried out by obedient villagers turns the individuals who were murdered into truly innocent victims. Their victimization is categorical because it is the product of military intelligence that procured the victims' names from lists of affiliation with parties, syndicates, or other associations, or mistakenly included them, whether or not the victims were politically and ideologically active. It is as if these amateur historians and activists portray victims' political activity or community conflicts as nonissues in order to stress the wrongness of their assassination. It should not be necessary to deny from the onset the role of local tensions and politics in order to deflect accusations that there were "reasons" why each victim was killed. After all, intracommunity tensions and political activism—even Communist militancy!—do not justify assassination, let alone interment in unmarked mass graves and the humiliation and exploitation of surviving relatives.

Moreover, despite the fact that orders did come "from above," the effects they had and their execution cannot be explained without taking into account the entanglement of these external demands with the internal conflicts of the community (see Bax; Seidman). It is clear from Manuela B.'s diary that village societies were enveloped in fear and animosity and fraught with tension; external orders and pressures mixed with internal tensions in a deadly dialectic. Furthermore, local explanations grant a sort of agency to the dead. By underlining the reasons why local envies and conflicts erupted, informants remember and in a sense honor their dead, many of whom were active in trying to change the status quo and invariably incurred the wrath of those who clung to it. Considering the execution of "superior orders" to eliminate all leftists as the only explanation for their assassination completely nullifies the individuality of the victims and the agency of community people in general—victims, perpetrators, collaborators, and bystanders alike. Emotions, hatreds, envy, tensions, and arguments embed the victim of repression in a world in which he or she was an agent, co-protagonist of his or her own history.

THE CONFLICT OF MEMORIES

Informed by an international framework of studies on memory, the analysis of traumatic experience and genocide, as well as a growing global acceptance of the principles associated with human rights since the end of the Cold War, Spain has seen the emergence of a social movement that seeks to "recover historic memory" encouraged by the opening of the mass graves of the Franco regime.[17] The Walter Benjamin–type "eruption" of this historic conflict in the present, in which a significant social sector demands attention and analysis of "the past" has come as a surprise (especially for international observers), for it has caused quite a stir on what appeared to be lethargic consciences. Relatives of the men and women whose bodies were buried in unmarked mass graves have led the social movement that seeks to reinstall these direct victims of repression into the political and social life of the country, even as they themselves are indirect victims and survivors.

Why are the bereaved families so concerned with the exhumations? Primarily they want to resolve the difficult trauma of having their loved ones buried in a field, "as if they were animals"—a common expression among the relatives of the victims. The issue of reinterment has a strong symbolic appeal.[18] The dead have culturally defined places where they should lie and where the living can relate to them, spaces that are adequate for remembering and honoring them through rituals and prayers that also allow closure. Family members want to close the cultural circle of personhood of their deceased loved ones by reintroducing them in the social sphere of the community. Not only was the exact location of the graves kept from them, they were also forbidden to visit them and leave flowers—the *guardia civil* kept surveillance—and widows, mothers, and next of kin were forbidden from making their mourning public (such as wearing black). In many cases, attempts were made to erase the very existence of the murdered victims by ripping the pages of the civil registry where they were recorded.

But despite their definite materiality and impartial existence, once bones are in the open they are not neutral scripts. Digging up a grave entails digging up the past—reencountering buried feelings of fear, pain, frustration, shame, and guilt. Although the exhumation process has been generally positive for the communities involved, deeply felt tensions and debates always surround them, especially during the initial stages. Old fears are rekindled; guilt is brought to the fore, shame for things done and things not done, regrets. Exhumations make these emotions urgent by revealing the hard evidence of death in the midst of communities used to the silent and often complicit cover-up of the past.

The victims are enjoying a new social protagonism, especially among the so-called third generation. The exhumed remains possess a symbolic capital (see Verdery) that reconfigures the dead men and women into heroes, and they and their surviving relatives thus participate in the construction of new social discourses from an advantageous position. Such symbolic capital is clearly made manifest in the multiple public services of homage paid to the victims. These ceremonies are usually neither as conflictive nor as multitudinous in locales where repression was numerically less deadly than in Aranda de Duero and its neighboring villages, where more than two hundred residents from a population of nearly ten thousand were assassinated.[19] Ceremonies in Aranda serve as perfect occasions for politicians to make an appearance, especially since the creation of the Interministerial Commission for the Support and Study of the Victims of the Civil War and Francoism made this topic fashionable among government officials. In the homage we organized when exhumation labors at La Lobera were over, provincial and local politicians among those present were eager to make press declarations.

In the service and reinterment of the recovered bodies that took place on September 1, 2005, national and regional-level politicians of the Spanish Socialist Party (PSOE), such as Diego López Garrido, speaker for the Socialists in Congress; Ángel Villalba, regional secretary of the PSOE of Castilla and León; José María Jiménez, PSOE's provincial sec-

retary; Julián Juez, provincial secretary of the UGT, as well as a slew of
regional, provincial, and local party leaders attracted a lot of media attention. The act was noteworthy because more remains had been exhumed in Aranda than in any other town in Spain till that moment. In
personal communications, many families complained about the political manipulation of the activity, noting that organizers had been more
concerned with facilitating the assistance of these politicians than that
of interested relatives of those to be reinterred. As a matter of fact, many
families were indeed missing, partly because of confusion regarding the
date of the activity, which had been changed three times. Politicians
made declarations and promises about their support for relatives, the
pursuit of truth and historic memory, symbolic reparations, and so
forth, and had their pictures taken next to the coffins.

Moreover, this new reading of the past is not lost on the few surviving
perpetrators, most of whom have closed ranks against the identification
and opening of the mass graves. Some have expressed fear of violent
reprisals, while others fear possible judicial proceedings. Still others
think that they would be forced to somehow compensate their victims'
families for the goods and property they stole. In the area where our research team works there has been no direct confrontation between perpetrators or their descendants and the relatives of the exhumed, but fear
exists nonetheless. In Aranda, a ninety-year-old Falangist who according to local hearsay "pulled a trigger," actually moved to Madrid when
the process of opening the graves of Monte Costaján was initiated in
2003—perhaps afraid of possible reprisals, perhaps to avoid questions.

This is one of the multiple significant questions that arise from the
conflict of memories: How do we negotiate the past and the discomfort
of guilt? What should be done—or remembered—in the cases where
people did things they knew to be wrong, under the conviction that it
was fair and necessary to do these things? What about those who were
carried away by the heat of the moment and participated in events that
they then regretted for the rest of their lives? These perpetrators often
feel remorse and live with guilty consciences, but few accept the responsibility of their participation in the events and ask for forgiveness.
As they negotiate and rewrite their past in accordance with the change
in the times, assuaging their guilt by placing themselves on the side of

the victims, helping locate the graves, and condemning the abuses in which they themselves partook, they nonetheless bear what I call "sick memories."[20]

An old guard from the Ribera of Valladolid and a former Falangist from Aranda are concrete examples. The guard narrated an execution in great detail and collaborated in the localization of the grave. He told the exhumation team that he had witnessed the killings silently perched on a tree, trying to avoid discovery in fear for his own life. But according to various testimonies, he was in fact one of the perpetrators. As a matter of fact, cartridges found in the exhumation grounds are compatible with his double-barreled shotgun, which informants had previously described as the weapon he used.[21] The former Falangist left an anonymous note—although everybody knew his identity—in the house of the sister of one of those assassinated in Aranda de Duero. In the note he expressed discomfort regarding the murders. He said that he did not participate in them and that he actually quit the Falange immediately after they took place. Moreover, he provided information about the "true" perpetrators—four individuals, three of whom had already died—saying that the sole survivor could give more information on the location of the graves and the identity of each body.[22] Both the guard and the Falangist reveal with their actions that they want to remove part of their guilt by cooperating with the relatives of the assassinated victims, while simultaneously denying that they in fact have any guilt to remove. According to a renowned Spanish psychiatrist, "the incapacity of integrating little by little the traumatic experience with the rest of our autobiography is a sign of danger, a sign that the emotional wound will worsen or become chronic."[23]

Obviously, the physical opening of a grave generates various reactions and discourses among those most closely involved. Some of the older family members voiced their desire to die peacefully now that the exhumations had been done. There are various cases in Aranda of people who promised their elders they would bury their murdered father or uncle or husband properly, with dignity. Our ninety-year-old Benilde S., whose two murdered brothers were supposedly in one of the graves at La Lobera, had promised her parents that she would disinter the bodies of her brothers and give them proper burial in the cemetery. This was also the case with the principal promoter of these particular exhumations, Restituto Velasco. He had promised his aunt on her deathbed that he would get his uncle—her husband—out of the mass grave. For these people, exhumation is a moral issue, and the restitution of the remains to the cemetery is an invaluable solace, as such more important than their identification.

Some of the younger relatives—often the children of the survivors, also indirect victims of the repression—try to spare their elders from suffering the pain associated with the eruption of this traumatic memory. But experience has consistently shown that the narration of these painful events in the context of the search for the localization and identification of the remains and the restoration of their family's dignity leads to relief (Ovejero Bernal). Part of the pain contained in the memory generated by trauma is somehow exorcised when, like a skeleton in a grave, it is unearthed, brought to light, and shared—release and gratitude are evident when an interview is over and when exhumations are successful. In Víktor Frankl's words, a true logotherapy takes place (see Frankl 139).

Obviously, exhumations do not affect all of the victims' surviving relatives in the same way. Different memories and emotions are intimately related with the lived experience of Francoism: the way the relatives came to terms with the assassinations of their loved ones and with their own social victimization. Exhumations are particularly problematic for those relatives who had accommodated themselves to the conditions imposed by the victors. Many of them had accepted the regime's logic that blamed their murdered parents not only for their deaths but for the problems they caused for the surviving family members. Some even held jobs in the Francoist political structure.[24] This is part of the drama and transformative power of suffering, as some people go from victims to collaborators with the perpetrators.[25] The surfacing of the bones of the dead into the open is a deep personal conflict for these persons, as it unsettles their efforts and struggles to construct an identity that distanced them from the "Reds" and was valued positively by Francoism. The orphaned children of "Reds" suffered immense psychological pressure under the ideological edifice of Francoism, principally by the priests and nuns who ran orphanages. There the children learned that their parents had committed great sins that they could help expiate, for which many were incited to serve the Church.[26]

In the exhumation at Villamayor de los Montes (Burgos), in July 2004, there was a clear example of a revamped identity, based on the denial of painful memories, one that was destabilized by the exhumation process. A man whose father was buried in the mass grave showed up with his three sons and tried to prevent the opening of the grave, arguing that the people concerned had not consented to the exhumation, that the process had not been carried out seriously, and that instead of digging up the dead, a memorial in stone should be built over the site—which was in the middle of the forest. This man had been mayor of a neighboring town as an active member of the conservative Partido Popular.[27]

A smaller number of relatives of the exhumed includes those who welcomed the exhumations but during their testimonies admitted to having signed death certificates that literally said that their parent had died because of the war (*por causas de la Guerra*) without giving another, more detailed, explanation—this, given the "pacified" character of Aranda when the executions took place, was not true—or had inexplicably disappeared. Having these certificates, they could collect the pitiful aid given by the government during the postwar period as well as perform other legal transactions that required this paperwork, such as remarry. The families that never accepted the signing of these documents today brandish what they see as their moral integrity with pride, leaving those who did sign in the uncomfortable position of moral corruptibility and betrayal of their victimized relative. For them, pain is transformed into a proud, vindicating identity.

Some sectors oppose the exhumations, including at least one pro-memory association, the Association of the Friends of the Grave of Oviedo. This association believes that historic memory is better served by identifying and preserving the mass graves in situ instead of opening them up and dispersing the remains of Francoism's victims. But in the cases I have studied, except for the incident of Villamayor de los Montes, those who oppose the exhumations belonged to the victorious side of the war. They are the ones who most vehemently declare that "stirring the ghosts of the past" will provoke divisions and problems that have already been overcome. This sector is protected by the Amnesty Law of 1977 that supported the discourse of "turning the page" during the Transition.[28] The problems of the Civil War were declared a thing of the past from the privileged position of their own victory. In many cases, they somatized the propaganda of the Francoist regime and its Church—*memoria rerum gestarum*—regarding the fairness of the struggle against the barbarity of the "Reds" (see Casanova, *La iglesia*; Raguer Suñer, *La pólvora*). And many who were not direct perpetrators of the extreme violence of 1936 but were affected by the psychological legacies of Francoism are convinced of the reasons and justifications of their cause.

Finally, multiple and varied reactions to the exhumations also come from those born during the democratic regime, the generation of the grandchildren and great-grandchildren of the war, who have been relatively free of the conditioning experienced by their parents and grandparents.[29] Some of these grandchildren have become the protagonists of the movement for the recovery of historic memory. The rest, self-identified as apolitical, embody a clear legacy of the *mesocracia* encouraged under Francoism: rule by petty middling sectors with no ideological inclinations. They ignore or are indifferent to the horrors experienced by their grandparents' generation, and they are the key factor in the definitive national reconciliation, which must begin in the recognition of others' pain and respect for others' suffering. Their reaction before the reality of the mass graves is often of surprise, as their views on their own nation or society are shaken. Many turn to artistic imagery, particularly film, to understand and explain that unknown reality that they can then approach through fiction—and the comparisons with what they know of Nazi extermination are constant. They must negotiate a past that they did not know belonged to them.

The bones of the assassinated men and women found in mass graves are undisputable witnesses to the extreme violence committed against them—a violence that went beyond summary execution into social erasure and absolute disrespect. Given the visibility of violence and suffering embodied in the bones, they also mediate between perpetrators and victims. They are a site of negotiation for traumatic memories and experiences of denial that need social recognition as a moral compensation for suffering. Faced with the absence of other policies, such as Truth Commissions or governmental investigations, the exhumations of the mass graves of Francoism, which led to the almost immediate involvement of academia, are one of the most significant social processes of contemporary Spain. They are necessary for the democratic, scientific, and social health of the country, for we are responsible for negotiating a past that must first be known and can then serve to construct a true history, without exclusions, a history for all sides—a history of suffering.

Just how necessary and how intimate such a historic recovery has become can be seen in my own family. My father is a conservative shopkeeper from Burgos, which is an eminently conservative city (it was the capital of the self-proclaimed crusade). He has been predictably very uncomfortable with my work, not only because of his own personal ideals and conservatism but because of the comments and pressure he endures in his social circle regarding his son's "questionable politics." To these, he always replies that his son was given this assignment, as if the chancellor of the university went around assigning each faculty member with particular homework. But his discomfort remains, and if I ever mention anything about the exhumations, he changes the subject, or waves me off, or gets into an argument about why I have to do this, why not let things be?—without actually continuing the discussion. He does not stomp out of the room because he has a very bad limp. But on one occasion, I cornered him in a conversation about the exhumation at Aranda. I showed him a piece of paper that we had found on the ground more or less over the mass grave—it had been attached to a bunch of flowers from the last All Saints Day, when families usually leave flowers for their dead. I read him the note, which said, "Even though you are many kilometers away from here, even if we do not know where . . . you have always been and you will always be with us. . . . A hug, and many many kisses from the whole family. We love you and we do not forget you, Grandfather, neither you nor the rest of the family that is with you, somewhere." When I looked up, my father was crying, and he said, "This has to be done" (*esto hay que hacerlo*).

NOTES

1. The exhumation developed in El Bierzo (León) was the first one conducted with expert forensic advice and rigorous identification of the remains in the context of the so-called movement for the recovery of historic memory. See Silva Barrera and Macías. Upon the advent of democratic rule, several exhumations were performed by relatives who gathered the remains, without in-

stitutional or academic support amid a political climate that officially discouraged digging up the past. But even these exhumations stopped after the failed coup d'état of 1981.

2. For a scathing critique of this revisionist tendency see Tusell, "El revisionismo"; Casanova, "Mentiras."

3. All interviews cited were conducted between May and September 2003 in Aranda de Duero and neighboring towns as part of my work in the exhumation of multiple mass graves as a member of the research team Violencia, Conflictos Civiles y Guerra of the Universidad de Burgos. The names of interviewees have been changed to protect their privacy.

4. See also Scarry, *Resisting*. As part of what has been called the anthropology of pain, see Morris.

5. See Frankl; Levi, *Si*; Levi, *La tregua*; Levi, *Los hundidos*; Semprún, *El largo*; Semprún, *La escritura*; and Semprún, *Viviré*. See also the novel *My First Sony* by Benny Barbash, whose child-protagonist explains why his father, a ghostwriter of Holocaust memoirs, stopped writing them:

> These poor people . . . want to translate their experiences into a language which hasn't yet been invented and will probably never be invented, and they rummage in the meager and narrow lexicon of words available to us, trying to find the formula which will express what they've been through, and in the end, the gap between what gets written and what they feel gives rise to frustration and resentment, and the entire project is doomed to failure from the word go, and Grandma's continuing silence is apparently the only language which can tell that story, and Dad, who knows how to put words together but doesn't know how to make sentences out of silence, decided to stop doing it. (qtd. in Milner 91)

6. Information or memories are not lost only because of the passage of time—in *I Remember Julia*, Eric Stener Carlson captures the conflict faced by relatives and friends of a disappeared Argentinean woman when they try to define exactly who she was, because the total meaning of the life of a person is not apprehensible.

7. The label "extreme violence" is applied using qualitative criteria that underline cruel or atrocious conduct regarding particular acts of violence and quantitative criteria related to the massive destruction of civilian populations. According to Jacques Semelin, "whatever the degree of its enormity, [extreme violence] is the prototypical expression of the negation of humanity, for its victims are animalized or objectified before being annihilated. We must go beyond moral judgments, to the political, economic and cultural circumstances which are capable of engendering such collective behaviors" (4).

8. "The word *vexation* conveys the idea about an external power, foreign to this world that agitates the body, severing the ties to others, and in this way

disturbing the internal being. To say that one has been vexed means that a powerful external force is causing internal problems that the filaments of the former extend deep inside the latter" (Kleinman and Kleinman 20).

9. A photocopy of this diary was given to the author by Manuela B.'s family. There are no page numbers.

10. Interviews done by Ackelsberg (130–31) are good examples of this: "The times that we lived during the war, six months were like three years in another context . . . so that, for me, the three years of war, all that I lived through, were like . . . ten years of my life. . . . When I was fourteen and fifteen I had experiences that would stay with me all my life engraved in my mind, such a flowering of ideas-made-reality that happened during this period! Even if I had died, I wouldn't have wanted not to have had that experience" (Pepita Carpena). Or in the words of another, "it was an incredible life, the life of a young activist. A life dedicated to struggling, to learning, renewing society. It was characterized, almost, by a kind of effervescence, constant activity. . . . It was a very busy life, got eight hours—or sometimes ten, if we got overtime—and going everywhere on foot to save money for the organization."

11. This "new woman"—whom I so name as a referential counterpoint to the "new man" of the 1960s international Left—was what Ackelberg's *mujeres libres* sought to become.

12. People's testimonies contain an ample collection of eugenicist terms, often linked to the vegetable-agrarian world. For instance, a common threat made regarding the children of the assassinated was "you must pull weeds by their roots" (*la mala hierba hay que arrancarla de raíz*); new rounds of assassinations after the hot terror was over were said to "glean" (*la rebusca*). According to Elaine Scarry,

> the recurrence here of language from the realm of vegetation occurs because vegetable tissue, though alive, is perceived to be immune to pain; thus the inflicting of damage can be registered in language without permitting the reality of suffering into the description. Live vegetable tissue occupies a peculiar category of sentience that is close to, perhaps is, non-sentience; more often, the language is drawn from the unequivocal non-sentience of steel, wood, iron, and aluminium, the metals and materials out of which weapons are made and which can be invoked so that an event entailing two deeply traumatic occurrences, the inflicting of an injury and the receiving of an injury, is thus neutralized. "Neutralization" or "neutering" (or their many variants such as "cleaning," "cleaning out," "cleaning up" or other phrases indicating an alternation in an essential characteristic of the metal, such as "liquefaction") is itself a major vocabulary invoked in the redescription of injuring. It begins by being applied only to weapons: it is the other peoples' firepower (guns, rockets, tanks) that must be "neutralized," but it is then

transferred to the holder of the gun, the firer of the rocket, the driver of the tank, as well as to the civilian sister of the holder, the uncle of the firer, the child of the driver, the human beings who must be (not injured or burned or dismembered or killed but) "neutralized," "cleaned out," "liquidated." ("Injury," 4–5)

13. This discourse reveals inherent contradictions in one of the principal elements of Francoist ideology: paradoxical invocations to the traditional peasant as bearer of the purest essence of the *patria* (the fatherland)—with a clear resonance of the German *volkgeist*—coexisted with the notion that these very peasants were primeval and violent. Francoist ideology inherited the bucolic search for the medieval peasant as the reservoir of Spanish national identity from nineteenth-century Romanticism, which gained currency throughout the early twentieth century with the influential Generation of 1898. (For an example of early twentieth-century interest in the rural world, see Fernández de Mata, "En este"). Francoist folklorization and idealization of "the peasant" and "the people" (*el pueblo*) was embodied in the dance and choral groups of the Spanish Falange, which were emulated by innumerable local folkloric associations throughout the country. But the emphasis on peasant savagery and virulence displaced the regime's responsibility for the massacres and the disappearance of thousands of Spaniards, as townsfolk were made suspect for murdering and secretly burying a few dozen neighbors in each village despite the regime's supposed attempts to control such extremes. Regardless of the contradictory character of these discourses, they were successful in the construction of Spanish public opinion. In fact, upon the opening of the first mass graves and the uncovering of historical—and forensic—evidence that pointed to the existence of plans of extermination and what some authors have referred to as a "Spanish Holocaust" (Armengou and Belis), many Spaniards still refused to believe that the relatives of those murdered or summarily executed in 1936–1937 were indeed telling the truth. The dark veil woven by the regime to conceal the reality of its deadly brutality was thick enough to last for over sixty years.

14. In the First Circular of July 1936 (Madrid, July 19), soon after the beginning of the military coup, Gen. Emilio Mola said, "We must sow terror. . . . We must set forth a sensation of dominion, eliminating without scruples and without vacillation all those who do not think like us."

15. Such ideas are evident in almost all of General Mola's allocutions and writings (see Mola Vidal). For a firsthand representation of General Francisco Franco's imaginary, see de Andrade's *Raza*. This text was turned into the film *Raza*, directed by José Luis Sáenz de Heredia, which premiered in Madrid on January 5, 1942.

16. This fragment of the interview, reproduced in Luzán, is worth quoting at length (my translation):

ALLEN: Isn't there any possibility of a truce, or a compromise?
FRANCO: No. No, definitely not. We fight for Spain. They fight against Spain.
          We are determined to go ahead at any cost.
ALLEN: You will have to kill half of Spain! . . .
FRANCO: I said at any cost.

17. For a lengthier discussion of this historic development, see Fernández de Mata, "El surgimiento."

18. A classic study with relevant comparative data regarding the meaning of these reburials can be found in Robert Hertz's 1907 essay, "Contribution à une étude sur la représéntation collective de la mort." A fragment of this work is included under the title "A Contribution to the Study of the Collective Representation of Death" in *Death, Mourning, and Burial: A Cross-Cultural Reader,* edited by Antonius C. G. M. Robben. In this same anthology see also Robben, "State."

19. When it took place, this was the largest single-town exhumation in Spain: 127 bodies were recovered by our research team, Violencia, Conflictos Civiles y Guerra, from various mass graves in La Lobera and Monte Costaján and in Aranda de Duero, where there are remaining mass graves to be exhumed. The team, made up of archeologists, forensic scientists, historians, and myself as a cultural anthropologist, tries to integrate the recovery and identification of the bodies with various sociohistoric projects. Such projects are circumscribed by the zone that was under the control of the insurgent military in June 1936, an area that underwent much more repression than actual battles. The members of the team are also part of Burgos's Asociación para la Recuperación de la Memoria Histórica (ARMH), and we actively collaborate in the exhumations that this organization sponsors in our province. We also participate in the Regional Coordinator for the Recovery of Historic Memory, which brings together the different associations that work on this topic in the autonomous community of Castilla y León, which are linked to the national ARMH, the Forum for Memory, and Amnesty International, trying to inform public policy and the responsibilities of local governments regarding this subject.

20. For a brief but interesting analysis of psychological and psychosocial traumas associated with guilt and memory generated by Francoism and state repression, see Ovejero.

21. This story was given as part of an interview by Ricardo Bedera, of Valladolid's ARMH, and related to the author in a personal communication.

22. The sole survivor, identified by name and address in the note, is the old man who left for Madrid as soon as work on the exhumations began.

23. Luis Rojas Marcos is writing about the surviving relatives of the terrorist attacks of March 11, 2004, but it is worth reading the following excerpt thinking of perpetrators who committed atrocious crimes nearly seventy years ago and are still guilt-ridden: "Burying distressing memories can cause great anguish or depression and stop the process of recovery. Moreover, by hiding how

we feel, we distance ourselves physically and emotionally from others precisely when we most need human touch, support, and consolation. What is worse, the persistence of these symptoms—which in the beginning are normal—*during more than four or five weeks,* and the incapacity of integrating little by little the traumatic experience with the rest of our autobiography is a sign of danger, a sign that the emotional wound will worsen or become chronic" (emphasis mine). My added emphasis underlines the length of time that both bereaved relatives and guilt-ridden executioners have gone without being able to seek consolation and support or talk freely, as the title of Rojas Marcos's article, "Please, Talk," suggests.

24. These attitudes are perceived as treacherous by those who refused to give up the social and political beliefs of their elders and who kept a sense of familial loyalty to their murdered relatives until today. These victims, who lived under the scornful labels of "red," "son of red," etc., are usually the ones who most avidly support the exhumations.

25. One case, which is hard to accept but which best reveals the complexity of this psychological conflict, is that of Chilean survivor Luz Arce, who wrote an autobiographical testimony; see Arce.

26. Encouraged by the nuns at her school, the daughter of Eduardo de Ontañón—an intellectual from Burgos who was exiled in Mexico after the war while his family stayed behind in Spain—became a nun to pray for her father's soul. Jacinto de Ontañón, personal communication. Similar cases are related in Vinyes et al.

27. Like him, many persons who hold higher administrative positions experience similar conflicts of memory that affect the institutional support needed to continue with the process of dignifying the victims and their relatives.

28. The Amnesty Law is no longer a source of comfort, however, given the precedents set in Argentina, where certain elements of their own amnesties have been repealed.

29. In fact, Ovejero (73–74, 77) cites studies that have shown that at least in Chile, and among Holocaust survivors, psychological and psychosocial traumas related to state repression have multiplied *under democratic regimes.*

The Intimacy of Defeat

EXHUMATIONS IN CONTEMPORARY SPAIN

Francisco Ferrándiz

A MASSACRE AT VALDEDIÓS

Valdediós, Asturias, October 27, 1937. Just a few days after the city of Gijón was taken by the Nationals and the region of Asturias surrendered to Franco's troops, a tragic event took place in a monastery that was at the time being used as a psychiatric hospital. It was only one in thousands of similar incidents taking place in the recently defeated Asturias and all throughout Spain, as part of a systematic repressive policy involving "the annihilation of the defeated," a policy carefully designed to produce and extend a regime of terror necessary to consolidate the emerging political and military power (Juliá, "De la 'Guerra'" 13).[1] Seventeen members of the hospital staff, twelve women and five men, many of them nurses, were shot to death by soldiers in the outskirts of the monastery-hospital, after a "death list" reached the hands of the military authority that was positioned there. The list was read aloud, and those named were separated from the rest. Emilio Montoto, thirty-eight years old, was one of those listed. When they were taken away to be shot, Emilia Carolina Ricca, age thirty-two, ran after them.[2] According to what her then two-year-old daughter Esther Cimadevilla was told by her aunts many years later, Emilia managed to see "something" of what happened in a neighboring meadow— something that "traumatized" her to the point of leaving Spain for Cuba about one year later with her three-year-old daughter.[3] Emilia's mother and her two sisters lived in Cuba, where Emilia had met her husband in 1933 before both moved back to Asturias in search of better employment possibilities.

According to Esther, the Valdediós killing condemned her family to "stumble around the world." Six years after arriving in Cuba, Esther's mother married again. Later, in 1962, as a result of the "political problems" in Cuba, they moved to the United States (Cimadevilla, Esther's interview). Esther told me that her mother barely talked about her time in Valdediós or about the killing of her father, and that during a period of about eight years, her aunts told Esther, Emilia had not even mentioned it. "She did not want to talk about it." She wanted to "block it out" from her memory, "as if it had never happened." "I could only get occasional glimpses that something strange had happened to my father, scattered in conversations here and there. . . . Even the letters we got from my aunts in Asturias were hidden by my mom," said Esther (Graveside interview). Until she got married at eighteen, she did not even know that her father had been shot; that her mother and grandfather had managed to obtain in Villaviciosa, home of the monastery of Valdediós, a death certificate for her father, which alleged that he had died in a "war accident"; or that her mother had a picture of her father she had never shown Esther. "Before one of my aunts gave me that picture after I married, I did not even know how he was [what he looked like]."

Yet her father's death became an obsession for Esther. Sixty-six years after the shooting, she had traveled all the way from Tomball, Texas, to be present at the exhumation of the mass grave where her father had been dumped in 1937 along with sixteen others. "When I learned that this was going to take place, I had to come. If I had stayed there in the US while this was going on, I would have been agonizing about it forever. I had to make this effort and be present, even if they do not find him, if they do not identify him, in order to rescue and vindicate his memory." Even after all those years, the traumatic event was neatly inscribed in the landscape. When Esther got to Valdediós in July 2003, the path that came down the hill from the upper meadows made a noticeable turn to the right, avoiding the reasonable, straight line, to prevent passing people and cattle from stepping over what turned out to be the location of the mass grave.[4]

According to recent historiographical research, the number of people executed by Franco's troops and collaborators during and after the

Emilio Montoto, La Habana, Cuba, before his marriage.
Courtesy of Esther Montoto.

Spanish Civil War has been estimated at between seventy thousand and a hundred thousand, or even more.[5] Methods of execution included occasional massacres, such as the one that took place in Badajoz's bull-ring in 1936, where between 1,000 and 1,500 prisoners were allegedly shot, and the so-called *sacas* or *paseos* ("strolls"), a generalized and well-designed terror and death technique where prisoners, drawn from jails and concentration camps, or citizens deemed collaborators of the defeated Republican government and therefore included in execution lists by local Franco agents were driven in trucks at dawn and shot in isolated places and abandoned on the spot or dumped into ditches.[6] Extreme forms of vengeful violence took place on both sides of the Civil War. The debate surrounding who was first, who was reacting, who was more systematic and cruel, and what were the different logics behind both "extermination machineries" are not unusual in Spanish historiography (Juliá, "De la 'Guerra'" 25–29).

A good deal of the numerous war victims on the winning side, the *caídos por España* (fallen for Spain), including those illegally executed either by irregulars or by popular tribunals on the Republican side, were for the most part named, located, exhumed, and commemorated in due course during the first years of Franco's dictatorial rule—the peak of which was the building with forced labor, between 1940 and 1959, of the monumental and currently extremely controversial Valley of the Fallen or Valle de los Caídos, where Franco's body now rests. Meanwhile, the corpses of many of the defeated still remain in unmarked graves by roadsides, cemeteries, shooting walls—often right outside of the cemetery's perimeter—mining galleries, sunken submarines, or battlefields, transforming many of them into "disappeared," who in complex ways still disturb the country's social, political, and symbolic foundation.[7] Burials range from individual graves to full-scale mass graves with more than 1,500 individuals in them, such as the Fosa Común de Oviedo in Asturias.[8]

Many of the graves have themselves disappeared below urban developments or freeways, along with the traces of the massacres. Yet numerous others, like the one in Valdediós, are still preserved and spread throughout Spain. Until recently, with the exception of exhumations that had mostly regional, local, or just family impact, a screen of silence has surrounded Spain's mass graves. Politically, the repression that took place during the war and the dictatorship had been neutralized—it now seems only partially and temporarily—with the 1977 Amnesty Law issued during Spain's prestigious Transition to democracy (see Ferrándiz, "La Memoria" and "Return"). According to Santos Juliá, with this crucial law, excesses by both sides of the conflict were not forgotten but rather "thrown into oblivion" ("Echar" 14–24; see also Ranzato 63–65). Thus, by this logic, for the generations who had lived through the war and its aftermath, Civil War massacres and their associated mass graves would remain as a sort of public secret that had been successfully blocked out from the grandchildren of the conflict, in order to consolidate Spain's emerging democracy.

During Francoism, especially during the early postwar years, many of the mass graves of nationalists, which appeared as a consequence of the violence perpetrated by Republicans, were located, commemorated, and opened by the dictatorship under a hegemonic ideological framework of "Martyrdom for God and Spain"; then, in the late fifties, there was an astonishing number of corpses flowing from mass graves across the country with the destination of Valle de los Caídos, where Franco built his megalomaniac shrine to the "martyrs" of the Civil War (Sueiro; Aguilar Fernández, *Memory* 116–29). Relatives of victims of the Francoist repression had also organized exhumations, particularly in the late 1970s and early 1980s in regions such as Navarre and La Rioja, although they had no relevant political or technical support, their media impact was limited, and the work did not trigger a chain reaction like the one provoked by the most recent exhumation cycle. Then, in October 2000, with the opening of a mass grave in Priaranza del Bierzo, León, containing thirteen bodies, a new chapter of Spain's memory politics regarding the Civil War was set in motion, with still unknown consequences. This is no small operation. Since Priaranza, which started the latest wave of exhumations, more than 171 graves have been opened, containing over four thousand bodies (see Gómez).

In what follows, I will reflect on the impact that the production, circulation, and consumption of images and narratives of Civil War terror— especially as it relates to the opening of mass graves containing corpses of disappeared persons resulting from Franco's repression but including also many other scenarios (González-Ruibal 206–7)—are having in contemporary Spain, as part of a broader process of revision of the traumatic past. I will argue that the current exhumations are bringing to Spanish society, which is fully engaged in important debates regarding the uniqueness or multiplicity of our identity and the structure of our territorial organization, rather disturbing information regarding our past, our present, and probably our future as well. The revelation of what might be called "crime scenarios" in diverse parts of the country is provoking heated debates in politics, historiography, and the media, as well as in civil society at large. The public exposition of skeletons, skulls, and bone fragments bearing the marks of violence—from "perimortem" tortures to bullet wounds to coups de grâce—is powerfully bringing back tragic stories that were largely silenced or only whispered for decades.

The meaning and social impact of these exhumed remains depend, in turn, on the cluster of narrative plots that organize and compete around them, from political initiatives to expert discourses, to media reports, to artistic expressions, to the local, fragmented, and fugitive memories that barely survived silence and fear in the interstices of the hegemonic versions of the Nationalist victory (Steedly 119–43). Exhumations can also be understood and interpreted as a road map linking the political production of terror with the intimate experiences of the victims of repression.

THE REEMERGENCE OF TRAUMATIC MEMORIES

Writer Luis Mateo Díez called *Fantasmas del invierno* (winter ghosts) the characters of the tragic social, symbolic, and emotional landscape of Spain's postwar years. A landscape saturated with hallucinations, suspicion, fear, blood, silence, madness, lies, tortures, murders, orphans, disappeared, etc. The ghosts of the victory were recovered, honored, and glorified in the postwar years. Others, those of the defeated, partially vanished in the accumulations of years of silence and were blurred by time, repression, stigma, and the authoritarian commemorations and narratives of the war victors. Yet if we are to analyze what has been happening in the country in the last few years, especially the strong rebound of the images, narratives, experiences, and places of defeat, these memories never stopped roaming the scarce spaces left for them to articulate and evolve during the dictatorship.

In an interesting contribution to the reevaluation of formerly disregarded aspects of social life in social sciences, Avery Gordon has emphasized the importance of haunting by ghosts to the understanding of social life. To Gordon, the pressure exerted by traumatic memories is a "constituent element of modern social life" (7). Ghosts are "social figures" that lead to "that dense site where history and subjectivity make social life" (8). The tension and uncertainty provoked by "systematic injury" offers the analyst a privileged space to explore the relationship among power, knowledge, and experience, an entryway to what Caruth called "unclaimed experience" (*Unclaimed* 10–24). The swift reemergence of the defeated of the Civil War, after decades of repression and forgetfulness and after what many are now considering the false exorcism of the Spanish Transition to democracy, is not accidental or capricious. The juggling of debates regarding the nature and meaning of the traumatic past, such as the one Spain is undergoing now, reveals important shortcomings in the collective management of the "dirty linen" of the past. Although this was predictable during the dictatorship, it seems less so during the Transition to democracy and the following decades. The major political pacts, such as the Amnesty Law of 1977, and the abundant historiographical work critical of the Francoist versions of the events do not seem to have been enough to contain this impulse.

According to Jeffrey Alexander, when a given society reaches a historical moment when a revisit of a particularly painful event of the past becomes necessary, this is the beginning of a "social process of cultural trauma," with the "trauma process" being the gap between "event and representation" (10–11). Within this framework, societies generate fresh narrative plots on the nature of social suffering in the past, which influence the identity politics of the community affected. The success of this social process of memory upsurge depends on the efficacy with which it resonates with the public sphere and on the presence of attentive and sympathetic—as well as refractory—audiences. The process results in the reallocation of the hegemonic and subaltern narrative plots of the past, of the nature of social suffering and the profile of the "victims," and of the perceived convenience for possible reparations and attributions of responsibility. It is important to establish that this is a complex and controversial process that evolves over time, that it is possible to identify phases in the memory-work, and that each society has its own rhythms of absorption, overdose, and saturation of the traumatic past. This is also a delicate process, politically, symbolically, and emotionally charged, which mobilizes many different social collectives and agents in different points in time and with different "horizons of expectations," from the state and its institutions to small local associations or even individual initiatives, and has as a foreseeable consequence the consolidation of a competitive as well as transformative "meaning industry" around the traumatic past and the nature of social suffering in the context of the Civil War (Jelin 4, Sztompka 455).

Is it fair to say that Spain is immersed in such a trauma process? I believe it is, although it is still too soon to evaluate its scale, and, it seems reasonable to believe that the process does not affect all social and political collectives uniformly and with the same intensity, if at all. There have been important efforts to keep alive the memory of the defeated since the moment the events took place. These efforts were made in spite of the tough repression and the cascade of historiographical, commemorative, and propagandist work produced during the dictatorship—especially during the early years—to establish and nourish the authoritative versions of the victors in parallel to the prosecution, stigmatization, and asphyxiation of any spaces of articulation of the defeated at all levels, from political organization to the public and even private expression of mourning. The latest sprouting of the memory of the defeated, which anchors its roots in all these previous efforts and challenges the political and legal closure agreed on during the Transition to democracy, cannot be dissociated from the wave of grave exhumations, closely linked to the emergence of the movement for the recovery of historical memory, in good part led by the generation of grandsons and granddaughters of those defeated (President Zapatero being one of them). Although heterogeneous and not exempt of internal controversies, this social movement is based on the commonly shared perception that victims on the Republican side—already crushed during the war and the postwar years—had been abandoned and betrayed again during the Transition in exchange for political stability. Then, during the following thirty years, little was done to address the problem, and it is not uncommon to hear deeply felt complaints about Felipe González's political inaction regarding the war and dictatorship victims even when he was invested with an absolute majority in 1986 and 1989.

THE INTIMACY OF DEFEAT

The memory-work taking place around mass graves, whether they are exhumed or not, has been progressively making visible a formerly neglected cartography of terror and repression that encompasses many landscapes and localities throughout the country. Exhumations, in particular, have thrown into the face of Spanish society a series of uncomfortable and dramatic images of skeletons bearing the imprint of violent death. These images have swiftly circulated throughout Spain and also internationally. Media reprocessing of the diverse components of the memories of defeat—as expressed in exhumations, narratives, personal objects, bodily effects, art exhibitions, commemorations, academic acts, and so on—reframe and resignify them through different media formats and through the consolidation of a horizon of consumers of social suffering associated with the war. Some authors have issued a word of caution regarding this process by noting how the "clash among globalizing discourses and localized social realities so often ends up prolonging personal and collective tragedy" (Kleinman, Das, and Lock xi), and some associations linked to the memory recovery effort in Spain consider that media coverage mostly encourages a commercial "televisual pathos" and a "mushy" manipulation of suffering.[9] Nevertheless, not all media expressions are the same, and without the media impact, the trauma process would perhaps have run a much slower course (see Armengou, this volume; Ferrándiz and Baer; Herrmann).

In parallel to the media flow of social trauma and linked to the location of mass graves, the establishment of commemorative landmarks and rituals, and the exhuming of graves, there has been a rush to record the voices and narratives of the defeated, which have increasingly come into high demand. For many in the memory recovery movement, the progressive death of the oldest generation of victims means the disappearance of the mostly unrecorded and "unclaimed" yet crucial experiences of those defeated in the war, thus impoverishing the quality of Spanish democracy (Ferrándiz, "Return" and "Cries"; Aguilar Fernández, *Memoria*). The resulting revaluation of the suffering of the victims and witnesses of Franco's repressive actions has transformed the recording of testimonies into one of the principal aims of the recovery of historical memory. In this process, the thick silence inscribed by Franco's regime on its terror victims in the postwar years was definitely shaken.

We should pay attention to the many expressions of suffering and social trauma, and not only to the testimonies. Yet these narratives, commonly expressed in local idioms of distress and entangled in culturally bound emotions and feelings, have increasingly acquired special relevance as necessary companions of the exhumed bones (see Jelin). Stories that were voiced rarely if at all, and then mostly in whispers, hints, or passing references—in family settings and civil society alike—suddenly found in the exhumations and the disturbing caches of bones the resonance they had lacked during more than six decades. For example, the postwar narrative genre known in Spain as the *batallita del abuelo* (grandfather's battle), which symbolized the lack of communication between generations as expressed in the disinterest of the younger generation in their elders' tales of the war, has been increasingly transforming into a first-rate form of social knowledge bearing a renewed legitimacy. This is particularly true for the story of the defeated grandparent, the incarcerated grandparent, the traumatized grandparent, the short-on-words-out-of-necessity grandparent.[10]

Anthropology has long been interested in recording and deciphering the "memory of the vanquished," including prominently the indigenous forms of social memory (León-Portilla; Wachtel).[11] There is a general consensus among many of the authors devoted to this task that each cultural group has specific entryways and plots for the management of their social memory, including culturally relative rituals, languages, and other tangible and intangible mediums—places, artifacts, songs and music, food, daydreaming, emotions, diseases, and so on. The interest in the "memory of the subaltern" also encompasses the analysis of the way in which they manage to endure in the interstices of dominant versions of the past, whether colonial, postcolonial, or, in this case, interstate- and Civil War–related. Above, following Steedly, I referred to the memories of the Civil War—particularly what I might term "first-wave memories"—as "fugitive" (43). This term was used by Steedly to capture the slippery and unstructured nature of a kind of narrative—I expand the use here to include all means of memory flow—that can be better depicted as unsteady conglomerates of partial voices necessarily characterized by their indeterminacy. Their emergence, circulation, and interpretation, usually intertwined with personal, intimate stories, objects, and feelings as well as local contexts of reception and deciphering, do not rely on a globalizing interpretive framework. Rather, these kinds of narratives produce meaning only in their fragmentation and lack of closure.[12]

By "first-wave memories of defeat" I refer to those accounts and expressions of the past traumatic experience that have not yet entered into a full-fledged feedback relationship with other memories and discourses of the Civil War defeat within the memory industry that is taking shape in contemporary Spain. That is, I refer to memories on the wane. Although this topic is only noted here and requires further research, it is clear that, for example, once the initially fugitive memories circulate in the media in the form of narratives, landscapes, bodily plots,[13] personal objects, and so forth, they become a different kind of commodity available for massive consumption. By being exposed to larger audiences while being inserted in more cohesive interpretive frameworks, they are transformed in nature and lose a good part of their "fugitiveness."[14] This is not good or bad; it is just inevitable. Although in the context of this analysis all expressions of defeat are of undoubted interest if their context and circumstances of emergence, circulation, and consumption are properly understood, I argue that the first-wave examples reflect best the long-lasting effects of fear and terror, as a clear illustration of the shortage of proper and articulated languages and memory-anchors bearing public legitimacy to express suffering in contexts of extreme social, political, and symbolic repression.

Following Norbert Elias I consider violence and fear as two fundamental political operators linking the repressive activities of the state with the most intimate spaces of experience, particularly in the context of harsh repression of those defeated in a fratricidal war. In Elias's model, external social coercion steadily transforms into internal coercions (social constraint toward self-constraint), resulting in a continuous process of fear-based self-control, both conscious and unconscious—"automatic" or "blind" (443). The stability of the self-repressive apparatus is linked to the crystallization of monopolies of violence and other parallel forms of coercion. In this context, when we refer to the Civil War and to the social modeling of the "intimacy of defeat," including anaesthetized or mutilated emotions, screams or silences, hidden pictures and letters, silent tears and self-contained mourning, sickness and emotional disability, a traumatic vision or anguish for the disappeared, a song or a sound, a poem or a nightmare, a flavor or a scent, we are also referring to complex spaces of political action. Political structures have enormous power to infiltrate, colonize, injure, and disable the intimate structure of an important sector of the population, to "ruin the collective and intersubjective connections of experience," gravely damaging subjectivity (Kleinman, Das, and Lock x). Yet, in many cases, multiple acts of more or less clandestine resistance and survival strategies range from tiny domestic routines to protective silence, fugitive telling, decisions to join the resistance or proscribed political parties, and going into exile.

Esther was barely three years old when she left Spain for Cuba. Her mother, Emilia, tried to block her from the memories of the tragedy that took place in Valdediós while starting a new life for herself and her child. In 1996, Esther, who had been struggling to get more information throughout her life, trying to fill what she calls "an immense emotional hunger" for her past and her homeland, interviewed in New Orleans her then ninety-year-old mother on tape. This mother-daughter conversation, a family tape intended to record Emilia's faint voice and recollections at the end of her life, is paradigmatic of the "fugitive memories" of the Civil War. It is an example of the waning memories of Emilia's generation, as she herself passed away a few months after the recording was made. On the tape Esther managed to "pull out of her just a little bit more" of what they had "suffered" in Valdediós. In a testimony filled with unanswered questions and memory fissures, she recalls that Asturias had fallen, some soldiers came, there was a Mass, there was a meal, and then "there was death." The closest Emilia gets to the killing is when recalling that her husband told her, when his name was called, "Do not worry. Nothing is going to happen to me just for taking care of mad people."

Esther herself has faded memories of her firsthand experience in Asturias before leaving for Cuba, and none of her father. After returning to the United States from the Valdediós exhumation, she was so anguished at having no reminiscences of her father that, after watching a TV program on hypnosis, she considered the possibility of resorting to it in a last attempt at reaching this black hole of her early childhood experience. She remembers, "I was there with him and my mother. I must have heard or seen something" (Personal email, Oct. 5, 2006). Then later she recalls, "Maybe what I need is a psychiatrist to explain to me why I have always missed him so much. I was a girl who did not overcome not having a father" (Graveside interview). Her family dissuaded her from pursuing this option. Although her father is blocked out from her childhood memories, she can remember her grandparents: a man with a big moustache always wearing a beret and a tall and strong peasant woman. She also recalls a little stool that her father had carved for her so she could sit and see the rain falling outside of the window with her grandfather. The Asturias of her early childhood was, for her, falling rain. Then there was exile. She and her mother went to Portugal and took a ship to Cuba. Esther can recall some of the journey and especially the ship's arrival in the harbor at La Habana, where her grandmother and her two aunts were "waving their hands at them to show their happiness. I was three years old at the time, and I wondered who these cheerful people are. I was only three at the time" (Personal email, May 5, 2006). Throughout her childhood in Cuba and until her marriage, she only knew that there was something strange regarding her father's disappearance from their lives. Responding to her perplexity, she resented her mother's new marriage and "imagined things created by my childish mind," like the recurrent daydream of her father ringing their home's bell to reclaim his wife (Personal email, Aug. 5, 2006).

Others in her generation stayed in the Valdediós area and grew up with the fantasies, rumors, and stories emanating from the shooting and the grave in the war and postwar years. One important aspect of many of the narratives of the war that have been registered in the last few years is that many of them convey childhood or early youth memories. A child's imagination is a toolbox full of powerful metaphors that act as vehicles for fear and suffering. One important challenge for research in the Spanish case is the recollection and deciphering of these childhood memories. Rosa, an old woman I met on the exhumation scene in Valdediós, who was also a child when the shooting took place, conveyed to me a number of stories that still terrified her.[15] Rosa remembers that the bodies were only superficially buried, and that people in the vicinity realized that there were dogs pulling parts of the bodies out of the grave and feeding on them. Her father went to the site and buried them deeper. She also told me three interconnected stories that show the ways in which a traumatic event such as the one in Valdediós penetrates the fantasy world and the play repertoire of children, a clear example of how regimes of terror bluntly infiltrate these emerging spaces of creativity and action.

All of her stories referred to elaborations of the fear of death associated with the ghosts of those massacred, which both attracted and kept children away from the grave. When they played in the area, children would always run quickly when passing the grave site, particularly if it was at nighttime. Stories were circulated that claimed that hands of those murdered in the shooting would come out of the grave to grab passing people by the ankles. One also ran the risk of running into a rising corpse. A second story talked about a puzzling river of blood that some had claimed to have seen sprouting and flowing downhill from the grave. A third story claimed that, during certain years, the place gave off a terrible smell. The childhood stories emanating from this "space of death" (Taussig 3–36) or "gray zone" (Levi, *The Drowned* chapter 8) metaphorically contained some fugitive clues to a massacre that was intended to remain confusing and politically, socially, symbolically, and emotionally paralyzing.

Robben has noted the important amount of disorder, anxiety, and division that the very existence of mass graves and collectives of "disappeared," in all their forms, have in the social fabric ("State Terror"). On the one hand, the quality of being hidden, anonymous, covered by the scorn of the victors and the silence imposed on victims, all prevent the emergence of socially legitimate narratives and spaces of mourning. On the other, their exemplary quality is demonstrated in a full-scale criminal machine of death and fear. Yet childhood stories, emerging from within this ambiguity of the mass grave as a space of death, managed to keep alive the memory of the massacre in a political regime based on the imposition of obedience, silence, and fear on the defeated. As is the case with Rosa, some of these stories have lingered in the memory of those who were children in 1937 and still live in the valley, investing the grave with a mysterious attribute that protected it from possible intentional damage as well as potentially intrusive rural paths.

COMMEMORATING THE VICTIMS

Let's move now from the intimacy of defeat, as expressed in childhood fears, to more public spaces of political action. Elsewhere, I have outlined the current process of institutionalization of historical memory and the impact that it may have on the way in which Spain confronts the ghosts of the Civil War (see Ferrándiz, "Memoria," "Cries," and "Return"). Let me just briefly review what is a complex and multifaceted issue that is rapidly evolving and responds to a "continuous refinement of the understanding of the consequences of state terror," requiring further long-term research (Robben, "State Terror" 107).

Initially, exhumations were mostly organized by relatives and NGOs with little institutional support. Yet gradually different initiatives coming from institutions at the local, regional, autonomic, and national levels have been put in place to provide political and economic frameworks for the many and diverse actions related to the memory of the Civil War, mostly the memory of the defeated. Among other actions, funding has gone to academic research into those who disappeared during the war or to the exhumation process itself (a call for projects was opened in January 2006 by the Ministry of the Presidency with a €2 million fund attached to it); working groups designing full-scale and complex political projects for the management of the memory of the war (such as the Memorial Democràtic in Cataluña); the creation of archival and research centers (like the one in Andalucía); political actions by Congress;[16] and even an Interdepartmental Commission constituted in October 2004 and presided over by the vice president of the Spanish government, María Teresa Fernández de la Vega, which committed to issuing a wide-ranging political proposition to coordinate efforts nationwide in order to "honor those who suffered imprisonment, repression or death of liberties during the Civil War and Franco's dictatorship."[17]

Under fire by many NGOs and some parties on the Left, the government promoted some spectacular initiatives, like the return of the controversial *papeles de Salamanca* (Salamanca papers) to the autonomous government of Catalonia in 2005[18] or the nighttime and pseudo-clandestine removal of one equestrian statue of Franco in Madrid in March 2005.[19] These efforts were too little and too timid for parties on the Left, too much and unnecessary for the main party on the Right, the Partido Popular.

In this cascade of schemes, on April 27, 2006, Congress declared, after a law proposed by IU-ICV (United Left) and opposed only by Partido Popular with ERC (Catalan Republican Left) abstaining, the year

2006 the Year of Historical Memory and also the year of the victims of the Civil War and Franco's dictatorship. In this declaration, the Second Republic is also recognized as the "first truly democratic regime of Spain" and thus the direct precursor to the constitution of 1978 (see *Boletín*). Finally, after difficult negotiations and tough controversies, on October 31, 2007, the "Law for the recognition and widening of rights, and the establishment of measures in favor of those undergoing prosecution and violence during the Civil War and the Dictatorship" (popularly known as the Historical Memory Law) was approved by Parliament, although its unfolding in normatives and rules is still quite behind.

On October 16, 2008, Judge Baltasar Garzón issued a judicial decree declaring himself competent to judge the "crimes against humanity" committed by Franco and the leaders of the rebel forces and later ruling elite during the war and the postwar years. As this essay was being written, in October 2008, the Fiscal had issued a judicial remedy against Garzon's decree, which is still to be resolved in court. At the very least, even if Garzón's decree is finally filed away, the mediatic, symbolic, and political effect of starting a legal case against Franco and his military and political allies for "crimes against humanity" is not to be dismissed.

The appearance of these official commissions, working groups, and legal provisions specializing in the management of the memory of the Civil War and the dictatorship may, with the support of academics and technicians, have incorporated into the "memory recover" agenda initiatives (inevitably controversial and problematic) difficult to achieve in civil society alone. These include the judicial and economic—not only "moral"—rehabilitation of the defeated; the systematic support and standardization of processes of localization, commemoration, and, if appropriate, exhumation of mass graves, including the management of the remains; the official sponsorship of diverse commemorative actions celebrating the memory of the victims of the war; the erasure of symbols and monuments of the dictatorship and the repression—the most controversial being the fate of the colossal Valle de los Caídos; the return of public and private property pillaged during the war; and the commodification of memory by museums. Yet this institutional impulse necessarily has as a counterpart attempts—from the different political parties behind the initiatives—at the instrumentalization and control of the diverse measures taken, the budget allocations, the social trauma plots in all formats, and, more generally, the important social, cultural, and political capital now stemming from the memory of the victims of the Civil War.

The Valdediós killings have also been touched by this process. The grave opening activated a crucial connection between massacres, silences and childhood fears, the intimacy of defeat, and official celebrations of those murdered in 1937. On October 10, 2005, the president of the Principado de Asturias (principality of Asturias), Álvarez Areces, a member of the Socialist Party, presided over the inauguration of a monolith created by Asturian sculptor Joaquín Rubio Camín near where the mass grave lay unmarked and unnoticed for decades. Along with the monolith, a brand new sign reading "Valdediós mass grave" was placed in the parking lot next to the monastery access road.

The act of inauguration and homage was part of the events linked to the celebration of the fourteenth World Day of Mental Health. The president of the principality was accompanied by relatives of the victims, different political representatives, and members of associations linked to the recovery of historical memory, along with a sizeable escort of TV cameras and journalists. The open condemnation of the killings in 1937 by top-ranking public officials, after decades of fear, forgetfulness, and indifference, has a clear relevance in order to rescue and rehabilitate the memory of the victims for the present and the future and affects both the most public and the most intimate spaces of political action.

In his speech, Antonio Piedrafita, representing the relatives of the victims, recognized that the monolith and the act "symbolized, honored, and praised" those killed on that "fateful date."[20] Justo Rodríguez, from the Socialist trade union UGT, representing many associations behind the initiative, remarked how important it was to be able to transmit to children "the true history of the Spanish Uncivil War," uncivil precisely because of acts as horrific as the one that took place in Valdediós.[21] President Álvarez Areces, on his part, defined the act as one important piece of "historical justice" that, in coordination with similar acts that should be celebrated throughout Spain, was intended to honor the victims and show society's rejection of acts of terror and the politics of fear. The four-ton monolith was for him a monument to freedom and solidarity expressing the "respectful and blunt" collective will to remember past injustices but also to look forward. After almost seventy years, for many these political claims and commemorations had already come too late. For those on the Right, they are divisive, vengeful, and rancid.[22]

To conclude, let us move back again from high-level autonomic political acts and discourses to transverse processes taking place within the intimacy of defeat, a space that is a crossing point for individual biographies, evolving social and political processes, and a dictatorial regime founded on the systematic production of silence, fear, and repression for the war's losers. Before the inauguration of the monolith that would provide some kind of closure to a long memory recovery process, in August 2004, when the bodies of the seventeen people shot in Valdediós were returned from the laboratory of Francisco Etxeberria (professor of forensic and legal medicine at the University of the Basque Country), some relatives and associates decided that fifteen bodies were to be buried together—although in separate boxes—in a niche in a neighboring cemetery in Valeri, overlooking the monastery. The list of those killed was not definitively closed, and some families decided not to claim the remains of their relatives or attend any ceremony. Two other victims—including Antonio Piedrafita's father, who, according to local versions of the events, tried to escape the shooting by running uphill and was hunted to death—were taken away to be reburied in family pantheons elsewhere near Oviedo and in Gijón.

Even before the bodies appeared, when efforts to locate the grave were at a standstill in July 2003, Esther had already decided that, in case they were found, she did not want to bury her father in the United States. He had never shown any interest in that country. Her residence there was, in fact, the unintended endpoint of an exile that was a direct product of his killing. Furthermore, the identification of the body by the forensic team was inconclusive for her father, who could be one of two corpses with similar age and characteristics. Esther went to Valeri's cemetery two months after the bodies were placed in the niche, which was not sealed, waiting for her to make a final decision regarding her father's body. As she wrote to me in an email, "once in the cemetery, Antonio Piedrafita gave me the plastic box that supposedly contained the remains of my father. That was a very difficult moment for me . . . to have in my hands the remains of that person I have always loved and I barely knew. Can you imagine? Yet I say 'supposedly' because I do have every imaginable doubt that those were with all certainty the bones of my father" (Personal email, Apr. 29, 2006). Finally, Esther dropped the possibility of incinerating the body of her father and carrying the ashes with her, and her father was buried in Valeri along with most of those he died with in the neighboring monastery of Valdediós. The plaque closing the niche reads, below a reproduction of Picasso's dove, "Remains of Claudia Alonso Moyano, Luz Álvarez Flores, Rosa Flórez Martínez, Emilio Montoto Suero, Soledad Nieto Arias, Oliva Fernández Valle, and nine more. PEACE. Valdediós, October 27, 1937."

Esther left her father's body back in Asturias, but she was anxious to recover some objects that might have belonged to him. "A watch, a wedding ring, a shoe . . . even the bullets. The ones that might appear in his body, I do want them!" (Graveside interview). In the emails we exchanged after the exhumation, she insisted on having a bullet from the shooting, perhaps her childhood's most terrifying and slippery treasure, no matter how deteriorated it was. I had no access to the objects recovered in the exhumation, so I finally sent her via email a picture of one of the detonated bullets.

In a paper on the importance of understanding the evolving nature of the imaginary networks of political terror, Roger Bartra stressed the crucial importance of deciphering the "black boxes" of fear, like the ones belonging to the planes that were crashed as part of the 9/11 terrorist attacks. And the same can be said of the rest of the "black holes" and objects linked to the production of mass violence and terror, such as the SIM cards of the mobile phones that detonated the bombs in Madrid on March 11, 2004 (see Ferrándiz and Feixa), or even the mass graves. It is a reasonable guess that this bullet exchanged in digital format, one among hundreds of thousands of bullets of the repression, is an entryway to the intimacy of the defeat of the Civil War victims and their mutilated structure of feelings. Leaving a ripping trace through a space of death, it surely represents and expresses the tragedy and the suffering that shot though the lives of generations of Spaniards, in both the internal and the external exile, from the cruel and repressive political will behind the trigger to the deepest sentiments of the defeated.

NOTES

1. See also Casanova's contribution to this volume. For an account of post-war repression in Asturias, see Solé i Sabaté and Villaroya 208–20.

2. My ethnographic fieldwork in the Valdediós exhumation, including interviews with relatives and neighbors, took place in July 2003. I had a long interview with Esther during the exhumation process before the bodies were found. After she left for the United States, I continued to have email correspondence with her. The testimonies by Esther transcribed in this text come from three sources: the interview that I conducted in Valdediós on July 23, 2003, a day before the grave was located ("Graveside interview"); the email correspondence we exchanged when I was writing the first version of this paper, from April 29 to June 1, 2006 ("Personal email"); and a short, taperecorded conversation that she had with her sick mother in the summer of 1996 ("Esther's interview"). Emilia finally died on February 1997. I transcribed this latter interview from a copy of the original tape recording, although it was later published in de la Rubia and de la Rubia 95–102. The expressions in this paragraph come from the graveside interview. I would like to specially thank Esther Cimadevilla, Pedro de la Rubia, and Antonio Piedrafita for their invaluable help during the exhumation in 2003, and also during the process of writing this paper, swiftly responding to my telephone calls and emails.

3. In Fernández de Mata's expression (in his essay in this volume), that would be the moment of convergence in Emilia of the double "rupture of the world," individual and collective, as a result of the direct experience of extreme violence during the Civil War.

4. Cimadevilla, Graveside interview. The full report on the circumstances leading to the shooting according to historical reports, witnesses, and relatives of the victims, written by P. de la Rubia and J. A. Landera, can be found here: http://www.memoriahistorica.org/alojados/periquete/paginas/valdedios.html. The same account, as well as the archaeological and forensic report on the exhumation and the analysis of the remains of the seventeen people found in the mass grave, written by Francisco Etxeberria, Lourdes Herrasti, and Javier Ortiz, can be found here: http://www.sc.ehu.es/scrwwwsr/Medicina-Legal/valdedios/valde.htm.

5. See Juliá, "De la 'Guerra.'" Pío Moa, who is currently leading a revisionist approach underlying the inevitability and constraint of Franco's rebellion, an approach expressed in best-selling books, has denounced what he calls "myths" about Franco's repression and follows organic historian Ramón Salas Larrázabal in proposing much more conservative figures for Franco's repressive policies (Salas Larrázabal, *Pérdidas* 183–215). For Salas, the total number of victims of the war was around 625,000, including 159,000 from postwar hunger and sickness, 23,000 from postwar shootings, and 10,000 related to the activities of

the maquis—guerrillas—and to the participation of Spaniards in the Second World War. Thus, the total for the Civil War is 433,000. Out of these, 165,000 were related to sickness, so violent deaths were about 268,000. About 160,000 died in combat and 108,000 in repression. This would be the total for all sides. According to Salas, 72,500 were shot by Republicans and 58,000 by Franco, including the 23,000 shootings in the postwar period. However, in *Víctimas de la Guerra Civil*, Republican shootings are calculated at around 50,000, whereas the list of those repressed by Franco's troops might rise to 150,000, considering that at least half of them went unregistered in the civil registers during the war.

6. The scope of this massacre in the bullring is one of the most contentious aspects of the conflicting memories of the Civil War. For the winning side, it was just a legend. In some versions cherished by the losing side, it was a horrendous "bloody party." See Espinosa Maestre, *La columna* 205–50.

7. The controversy regarding the identification of the victims of Franco's repression as "disappeared," both during the war and afterwards, has raged since October 16, 2008, when Judge Baltasar Garzón legally defined these forced disappearances as crimes against humanity. For a comparison with the case of Argentine's disappeared and the intense social and political debates taking place around them and their exhumation, see Robben, "State Terror."

8. The memory of these individuals has been kept and commemorated by the Asociación de Familiares y Amigos de la Fosa Común de Oviedo (AFAFC), an association opposed to exhumations and in favor of the location, preservation, and commemoration of the mass grave sites.

9. As expressed, for example, in a manifesto by the association Archivo Guerra Civil y Exilio (AGE). See http://www.galeon.com/agenoticias/. See also Loureiro, for a more recent claim made by many in the recovery of the historical memory movement against the use of "pathetic arguments" as a replacement for knowledge and reflection (233).

10. For an evaluation of the political importance of this testimony-giving process, see Ferrándiz, "Cries."

11. For some classic examples, see León-Portilla; Wachtel; Price; Rosaldo; Hill; Rappaport.

12. See also Jelin 16–20. She emphasizes also the central role of forgetting and silence in narrative memory.

13. For the body as a crucial site for the crystallizing of social memory, see White.

14. It is also important to note that once these fugitive memories have circulated widely in the media, they may become secondhand or thirdhand memory plots to be used by other victims or relatives. On the incorporation of secondhand experiences into lived experiences, see Jelin 4.

15. She was around nine. She later worked as a guide in the monastery from 1965 to 1973. It was difficult for her even to show up at the exhumation site,

for she had been receiving threatening telephone calls since she started to co-operate with ARMH in locating the grave site.

16. For example, in November 2002, the Spanish parliament unanimously passed an unprecedented proposition condemning Franco's uprising in 1936 as an illegal rebellion against a legitimate government.

17. See Fernández de la Vega's declarations at the press conference follow-ing the Consejo de Ministros at http://www.la-moncloa.es/ConsejodeMinistros/Ruedas/_2004/r2307040.htm.

18. These are documents confiscated after the fall of Cataluña by Franco's regime, some of which were used in the subsequent repression. They were kept in Salamanca's Archive, and amounted to 5 percent of the total collection. Par-tido Popular defended the "unity" of the archive, resisting the transfer of the documents, and the mayor of Salamanca, from this same political party, orga-nized demonstrations and even changed the name of the street where the ar-chive is located to "Street of the Pillaging."

19. During the midterm celebration of his time in office, on April 23, 2006, President Zapatero challenged the opposition party Partido Popular, whose of-ficial line regarding this process is that it represents the unacceptable opening of old wounds, the breaking up of the consensus of the Transition, and an at-tempt at establishing a new hegemony of the defeated—to put them back on their pedestal when they return to office (Díez).

20. I videorecorded this commemorative act in full. All testimonies in the text are direct transcriptions from this videorecording.

21. The executive director of the Health Service in Asturias, who intro-duced the act, named the following entities behind the lobbying for the monu-ment and the act: the Federación de Servicios Públicos de UGT, the Asociación de Enfermería Comunitaria, la Asociación de Descendientes del Exilio Espa-ñol, la Asociación para la Memoria Histórica Asturiana, the Asociación As-turias por la Memoria, the Archivo Guerra y Exilio (AGE), the Monumento de la Colladiella, la Asociación de Amigos y Familiares de la Fosa Común de Oviedo, and the Asociación de Amigos y Familares de Represaliados de la II Re-pública. He stressed also the importance of historical research carried out by Pedro de la Rosa and J. A. Landera, and the forensic and archaeological research carried out by Francisco Etxeberria, Lourdes Herrasti, and Javier Ortiz.

22. An important challenge for future analysis is the long-lasting effects for the nation of Spain of these institutional revisits of the landscapes of traumatic memory in the framework of conflicting memory politics, including victim-hood politics.

The Grandsons
of Their Grandfathers

An Afterword

Giles Tremlett

THE PRIME MINISTER'S GRANDFATHER

On August 17, 1936, in the early days of the Spanish Civil War, Spanish army captain Juan Rodríguez Lozano sat in a prison cell in or near the northwestern city of León, awaiting his own death. Captain Lozano had remained loyal to the elected Republican government as it fought against the right-wing military rebels who had risen against it. Captured in the first few weeks of war, he had time, that day, to write a will that would be handed to his wife and children after his death. This, among other things, asked his family to forgive his executioners and begged them to clear his name when they could. His guiding principles, he said, had been to seek peace, to do good, and to improve the lives of those at the bottom of Spain's social scale. *"Muero inocente y perdono"* (I die an innocent man, and I also pardon), he said ("Un líder"). The next morning, at dawn, he was shot by a firing squad.

Some fifty-eight years after his death, the Spanish Socialist Party (PSOE) came to power. The party leader, a forty-three-year-old from León called José Luis Rodríguez Zapatero, became prime minister. He was the fifth democratically elected prime minister of Spain since democracy was restored following the 1975 death of General Francisco Franco, the Civil War victor—and leader of those who shot Captain Lozano—who ruled as dictator for thirty-six years.

Among other measures promised by the Socialists before they came to power was a new law to deal with what Spaniards had come to call *recuperación de la memoria histórica,* or "the recovery of historical memory." The memory that, according to Zapatero and others, needed recovering was precisely that of Lozano and tens of thousands more like him who had been shot by Francoist firing squads during the Civil War. All the other victims of the Civil War, be they prisoners, exiles, gays, gypsies, Freemasons, or Protestants, would also be dealt with in this law, as would the victims of Franco's dictatorship and those of the period known as *la Transición,* the Transition to democracy immediately after the dictator's death.

The man who was to lead this *memoria histórica* process, Prime Minister Zapatero, was Lozano's grandson.

While Zapatero led a minority government (with 164 of the 350 deputies in the main parliamentary chamber, el Congreso—eleven short of a majority), there were numerous small parties that also felt strongly that the victims needed recognition. These included the following: the Communist-led Izquierda Unida (IU-ICV, or United Left) coalition, with five deputies; the separatist Esquerra Republicana de Catalunya (ERC, or Catalan Republican Left), with eight deputies; the moderate Catalan nationalist group, Convergencia i Unio (CiU, or Convergence and Union), with ten deputies; and the Partido Nacionalista Vasco (PNV, or Basque Nationalist Party), with seven deputies. The support of these four groups looked set, initially, to guarantee an easy passage for the new law through the Spanish parliament, las Cortes.

This, however, was not to be. *Memoria histórica* turned out to be one of the thorniest issues tackled by a Zapatero government. A draft law, published in July 2006, provoked loud complaints from many quarters and was passed by the Congreso de Diputados on October 31, 2007. Below I look at the text of the draft law itself, as well as at the criticisms of it made specifically by several organizations: the NGO Amnesty International (AI), which thought it did not go far enough; the independent Asociación para la Recuperación de la Memoria Histórica (ARMH), which agreed with AI; the center-right *El Mundo* newspaper, which thought it went too far; and the Spanish Roman Catholic Church's Bishops Conference, which also thought it went too far.

The political debate has seen the main opposition party (the conservative People's Party, or PP, with 148 deputies at the time) alone opposing the law on the basis that it went too far. Both IU-IVC and ERC, meanwhile, have claimed that it falls well short of their expectations. Some of that debate is discussed below.

THE BACKGROUND TO THE POLITICAL DEBATE ON *MEMORIA HISTÓRICA*

Memoria histórica entered the Spanish political arena well before Zapatero came to power. He won the election on March 14, 2004, and took office on April 17. The previous prime minister was the PP's José María Aznar. He governed with an absolute majority in Parliament from 2000 to 2004. Previously, from 1996 to 2000, he led a minority government supported by moderate Catalan and Basque nationalists. Aznar's election in 1996 was a historic event in the sense that it was the first time since before the Civil War that a right-wing government had been elected to power democratically. He defined his political stance as that of the "reforming center" and, despite his party's historical antagonism to regional nationalists in Catalonia and the Basque Country, managed to ensure their support—finding common ground in the right-of-center Christian Democrat ideas shared by all three parties.

In his second term in office, however, Aznar had no need for political alliances, and the natural antagonism his party felt for regional nationalists quickly shone through. His government drifted increasingly to the right as Aznar declared that he would stand down after his second term. He personally chose his interior minister, Mariano Rajoy, to succeed him as party leader and candidate for prime minister in 2004—when the PP lost power.

The *memoria histórica* debate first raised its head in Parliament during the PP's second term (though there had been a number of previous laws that, without provoking much public debate, provided financial compensation to some victims). The work of ARMH, which had begun exhuming mass graves of Francoist Civil War victims in 2000, had much to do with the eruption of *memoria histórica* into the public sphere. So also, however, did the increasing desire of the other political parties in Parliament to find political ammunition against the PP. *Memoria histórica* offered them a weapon that could be used to associate the party that represented Spain's modern, democratic Right with the old, anti-democratic Right of Francisco Franco. In simple terms, the message they wanted to put across was that the PP was the natural heir—and protector—of Francoism. Early attempts by ARMH to prevent the whole debate becoming a party political issue proved ineffectual.

On November, 20, 2002—the twenty-seventh anniversary of Franco's death—the opposition parties managed to persuade the PP to sign a declaration condemning the military uprising of Franco and other generals that started the Civil War. The PP also agreed that local authorities should be called on to support attempts by victims' families to honor their dead, "making sure that this does not serve to reopen old wounds or stir the embers of civil confrontation."[1]

ARMH, which had petitioned Parliament to do something about the mass graves, was a key player in bringing this issue to Parliament. This, however, was as far as the PP was prepared to go. On December 1, 2003, all the opposition parties together organized a parliamentary homage to the "fighters for freedom against Francoism" (*luchadores por la libertad contra el franquismo;* M. Sánchez). Stirring speeches were made about the bravery of those who dared to oppose the dictatorship. Only the PP refused to attend.

THE ZAPATERO GOVERNMENT TUSSLES WITH THE PAST

After the Zapatero government came to power, a committee was set up to study the *memoria histórica* issue. The Comisión Interministerial para el Estudio de la Situación de las Víctimas de la Guerra Civil y el Franquismo was formed on September 10, 2004. It was overseen by Deputy Prime Minister María Teresa Fernández de la Vega, a former judge who generally acted as Zapatero's chief political troubleshooter. The committee was charged with coming up with measures to rehabilitate the victims "morally and judicially" while also providing them with "moral, social and financial" compensation (Cué, "El Gobierno").

Groups campaigning for the law were told that it would be ready by January 2005 (see Amnesty International, "Víctimas"). The government, however, began to stumble. The deadline passed, and a second date was given, for June 30. This was also missed. Asked in Parliament about this delay, in May, September, October, and December 2005 (in a series of questions from Catalan and Basque deputies) the government said that the commission was sifting through some eight hundred documents sent to it—and this was what was slowing things down (see Amnesty International, "Víctimas" 6). Those close to Zapatero, however, admitted there were other reasons. "The time is not right," one close advisor told me, referring to other, more pressing political problems that the government needed to overcome before the thorny issue of *memoria histórica* could be safely dealt with.

AMNESTY INTERNATIONAL GETS INVOLVED IN THE DEBATE

In the meantime, both Amnesty International and *El Mundo* got involved in the debate. On July 18, 2005, AI issued a report called "Spain: Putting an End to Silence and Injustice" (*España, poner fin al silencio y a la injusticia*). It reminded the government that Amnesty International Secretary General Irene Khan had personally urged Zapatero to tackle this issue on a visit in 2004, when she declared that "the government must not forget other victims. It should recuperate the memory, dignity, and remains of the forgotten victims of the Civil War and Franco's regime" (Amnesty International, "Spain").

"Spain has produced numerous victims of political, religious and racial persecution as well as victims of extrajudicial executions, disappearances, torture, arbitrary imprisonment and cruel, unjust court sentences," AI's report said. Crimes against international law committed during the Civil War and the Francoist period "were not dealt with during the *Transición*, nor were the rights of victims—who were denied truth, justice and compensation—dealt with either" (Amnesty International, "España").

AI went on to point out that the amnesties handed out between 1975 and 1977 had not only freed the political prisoners of Franco's regime but had also prevented the prosecution of those people who had taken part in the systematic repression practiced by the regime. The amnesties, AI said, "included measures to pardon and forget acts which, under international law, are considered crimes against humanity" ("España").[2] The "crimes" to which AI was referring had been committed by police officers, prosecutors, members of the armed forces, judges, and other Francoist officials who were, effectively, freed of any criminal liability for their acts.

The NGO called on the government to find and, where requested, dig up the mass graves of the Civil War. It also wanted Zapatero to establish a special section of the attorney general's office to investigate unsolved disappearances and extrajudicial killings from the Civil War (*desparaciones forzadas y ejecuciones extrajudiciales*). It also, more polemically, called for Francoist court sentences passed for political "crimes" to be formally overturned and declared null.[3]

EL MUNDO DEFENDS THE TRANSICIÓN

The report provoked an angry reaction from *El Mundo* newspaper (at least one of whose senior editors told this author that he had relatives buried at Paracuellos del Jarama, where several thousand victims of extrajudicial Republican firing squads operating in and around Madrid had been buried in mass graves during the Civil War).[4] Two days later it published an editorial entitled, "No to the Partial Revision of History."

El Mundo started by rapping Amnesty International over the knuckles for only concentrating on the victims of one side of the Civil War. "There are events from those terrible years that still have not been made fully clear, like the slaughter at Paracuellos," it said. "During the war all sorts of atrocities were committed by both sides. Since the arrival of the Zapatero government, however, there has been a climate of skewed historical revisionism aimed at remembering the past in an unfair and selective manner." "The Civil War and the Francoist repression that followed are painful episodes of our history," *El Mundo* went on to say. "Some of the protagonists, from both sides, are still alive. The Spanish Transition is envied the world over precisely because of the efforts made toward avoiding the reopening of old wounds and toward achieving reconciliation. The events of that period can be studied and analyzed by historians, but in no way should they be allowed to become used for debate or political agitation by the government or by the opposition. That way, we would all lose" ("Revisión").

El Mundo identified what, for many who were angered by it, was one of the main problems of the *memoria histórica* debate, namely that it was mostly about the memory of those who lost the war. Campaigners argued, in reply, that the winners had spent forty years investigating and commemorating those who died as a result of the excesses of the Republican (losing) side of the war. Wherever possible, they had exercised justice, trying, sentencing, and sometimes executing those deemed guilty of Civil War crimes.

Criticism of the *Transición* was something that *El Mundo* found especially hard to stomach. Indeed, criticism of the *Transición* was one relatively new element that the whole *memoria histórica* debate was introducing into public discourse. Up until now the *Transición* had been widely revered as a hallowed moment in Spanish history. To suggest that it may have had faults not only meant breaking that consensus but also threatened to encourage those who had always maintained that the *Transición* was imperfect—principally separatists or nationalists in the Basque Country and Catalonia. These felt that certain elements of the *Transición*, especially an article of the 1978 constitution that gives the armed services the mission of "guaranteeing the sovereignty and independence of Spain, [and] defending its geographical integrity and constitutional order" (Título Preliminar, Article 8.1) were the result of threats applied at the time by former Francoists, especially in the military. This article, they argued, could be interpreted by the armed services as giving them the right to act against any movement, including peaceful independence movements, whose aim was to break up Spain and thereby change its "geographical integrity." Such critics had always claimed that the *Transición* had been conditioned by what was commonly known as "the sound of saber-rattling" (*el ruido de sables*)—in other words, the threat of a pro-Francoist coup d'état and a return to military dictatorship.

El Mundo's reaction provoked concern in the government. It did not want to be seen as dividing Spaniards. The families of those killed by Republican death squads, meanwhile, began to publish *esquelas* ("in memoriam" notices) in *El Mundo* recalling the deaths of loved ones at the hands of, among others, "the Marxist hordes." Similar *esquelas* began to appear in left-wing newspapers, recalling those killed by Franco's Nationalists. The government was aware of the influence that *El Mundo* had over certain wavering voters. This particular editorial was widely blamed by *memoria histórica* campaigners—notably by Emilio Silva, the head of ARMH—for a further delay to the law.

AI, angered by the delays, replied with a second report called "Victims of the Civil War and Francoist Repression: The Disaster of the Archives and the Privatization of the Truth" (*Victimas de la Guerra civil y el régimen franquista: El desastre de los archivos, la privatización de la verdad*), in which it condemned the government's slowness in coming up with a new law and reminded it that, in the meantime, it was failing to do anything else to help the *memoria histórica* process move along— referring especially to the difficulties of accessing archival material about Civil War victims. It also repeated its earlier demands for "unjust sentences passed as part of the Francoist repression to be declared null and void" ("Víctimas" 16).

That the government was nervous about its proposals could be seen from the timing of its release of the draft law. This came out on July 28, 2006, in the dog days of the summer, when Spaniards were already concentrating on their summer vacation (which traditionally are taken in the month of August) and thinking about the weeks they would spend at the beach. Most politicians had already disappeared from Madrid on their vacation, and newspapers were publishing, or preparing to publish, their lightweight summer editions.

The law's long-winded name—La Ley de extensión de derechos a los afectados por la Guerra Civil y la dictadura (Law for extending the rights of those affected by the Civil War and the dictatorship) was another sign of the government trying to play the scale of the law down. The expression *memoria histórica*, which was already becoming controversial in itself, was absent. In my view the aim of the government was to look as though it was not rocking the boat, suggesting instead that this was simply a "continuation" of previous laws—including the amnesties of the 1970s—which had gone some way to compensating Franco's victims.

THE DRAFT LAW

The introduction to the draft law spoke of the "spirit of reconciliation and concord" that "guided the *Transición*" and led to the passing of Spain's 1978 constitution. It also spoke of previous laws that had dealt with some of the issues involved but claimed that there were "legitimate and just" petitions from the *memoria histórica* groups and several political parties to "honor, once and for all, those who suffered injustice and grievances." Among the victim groups it mentioned were the dead, the imprisoned, forced laborers, and exiles. The main aim of the law was to recognize "an individual right to the personal and family memory of each citizen" (*un derecho individual a la memoria personal y familiar de cada ciudadano*). This was to be achieved by issuing what would be called *Declaraciones de reparación y reconocimiento personal*—and which I will call "victims' certificates"—to victims or their families. The certificates would be handed out by a committee of experts set up by Parliament. They would also be published in the Spanish state's official bulletin.

Public monuments and symbols commemorating the Civil War and the dictatorship would be dealt with by measures based on "the principle of avoiding the exaltation of conflict between Spaniards" so that "public symbols become a point of encounter and not of confrontation, offense or grievance" (*símbolos públicos sean ocasión de encuentro y no de enfrentamiento, ofensa o agravio*). Those digging up graves were also to be offered help, though, as both AI and ARMH would point out later, this help was severely restricted.

The introduction to the law concluded that it sought to "help close wounds that are still open among Spaniards and to give satisfaction to those citizens who suffered, either directly or through their families, the consequences of the tragedy of the civil war and the repression of the dictatorship." The law itself, it added, was not about fixing a particular version of Spain's *memoria histórica*: "It is not the legislators' job to construct or reconstruct a supposed 'collective memory.'" The aim was, rather, to "recognize and widen the rights of those who suffered persecution or violence, for political or ideological reasons, during the Civil War and the dictatorship, promoting . . . the recovery of personal and family memory, and adopting supplementary measures aimed at overcoming the division between citizens with the objective of increasing cohesion and solidarity between different generations of Spaniards on the basis of the principles, values and freedoms of the Constitution."

There followed a general condemnation of punishments meted out—by either side in the Civil War or, later, during the dictatorship—for "belonging to political parties, trade unions, religious or military organizations, ethnic minorities, secret societies, Masonic lodges and resistance groups or for behavior related to cultural and linguistic choices or sexual orientation." Anyone who had suffered, or believed a family member had suffered, any of these circumstances during the Civil War or dictatorship had the right to ask for a victim's certificate, the so-called *Declaración de reparación y reconocimiento personal*. These would be handed out by a committee of five wise men and women, "of recognized prestige in the field of social sciences, chosen by a majority of three-fifths of Parliament."

The victims' certificates "will have as their only aim the verification of executions, sentences or sanctions which were manifestly unjust and contrary to those rights and freedoms that underpin today's constitutional order and which are the basis of society's [peaceful] coexistence." The certificates would not, however, give the victims or their relatives any right to "compensation of an economic or professional nature." They would also "omit any reference to whoever took part in the events or in the judicial processes that led to sanctions or sentences," by which it meant the perpetrators of the crimes or the public officials involved in Francoist repression.

There followed a series of measures to improve the pensions and other monetary compensation already on offer to different groups of victims, be they widows and orphans or former political prisoners. Compensation was also offered to a new group of people, the so-called victims of the *Transición*. Families of those who died "in defense of or while demanding democratic freedoms and rights" between January 1, 1968, and October 6, 1977 (two years after Franco's death) would receive €135,000 euros compensation. Most of these victims had died as result of police beatings, shootings by far-right terror gangs, or being shot by police officers.

Local authorities were to be obliged to "facilitate" (*facilitar*) attempts by the descendants of victims to locate those who "disappeared violently during the civil war or in the repression that followed it." They would also be obliged to "facilitate" the work of any organization founded before June 1, 2004, dedicated to the same task (ARMH, for example, would qualify). These branches of local administration "will be able to give grants to help meet the cost of these activities." The "relevant" public authorities would also put together and make available "maps which show the land where the remains" of such people lie. The government, for its part, would produce a similar map "of all Spain." Land containing victims' graves would have (an unspecified) special protection order applied to it.

Local authorities would have to elaborate protocols for those wishing to exhume graves and would be responsible for handing out permits. When they did this, however, they would be obliged "to take into account any opposition among the direct descendants of those in the grave." (This reflected the controversy over the grave of poet and playwright Federico García Lorca, which is believed to lie in a mass grave at Víznar, outside Granada. Lorca's descendants opposed its disturbance, while the families of two other men buried with him campaigned for it to be dug up.) Where landowners refused to let people onto their land, they could be obliged to do so, but the gravediggers would have to indemnify them for losses.

Francoist symbols and those devoted to "one side of the confrontation" on public buildings would be removed unless there were artistic or architectural reasons for them to stay. Political acts (like the homage to Franco on the November 20 anniversary of his death, which I witnessed and described in my book, *Ghosts of Spain*) would be expressly banned in the underground basilica at the Valle de los Caídos (which contains the tombs of both Franco and Falange founder José Antonio Primo de Rivera). The foundation that runs the site would be obliged to "honor the memory" of all those who died in the Civil War and to "exalt peace and democratic values." A new Civil War archive, the Memoria Histórica Archive, would be based at Salamanca and would expand its collection to include documents relating to Francoism, anti-Franco guerrilla movements, exiles, concentration camps for Spaniards during the Second World War, and the *Transición*.

ARMH DISAPPOINTED BY THE DRAFT LAW

For ARMH the draft law was a huge disappointment. The state had not pledged to dig up mass graves itself, leaving the job to volunteers, relatives, and any local authority who felt like it. It meant, the group claimed, that "incomprehensibly, human rights have to be guaranteed by volunteers from NGOs rather than by the state." The victims of the Republic, it observed, would get the same treatment as the victims of the Nationalist side in the Civil War. That meant equal treatment was being given to "those who defended a democratic regime [during the Civil War] and those who acted against it, supporting a coup d'état that ushered in a dictatorship which squashed democracy for forty years." ARMH called on the government to find a way to formally overturn the summary sentences handed down by Franco's military tribunals "that led thousands of Spaniards to the firing squad, concentration camps, prisons or exile." It also demanded that Spanish schoolchildren be taught properly about the period, pointing to a University of Leipzig report that showed that only between 2.5 and 9 percent of the space devoted to the twentieth century in Spanish history books covered the forty-four-year period of the Republic, the Civil War, and Francoism. A poll in *El País* newspaper had shown, it said, that 36 percent of Spaniards did not recall receiving any information at all about the Civil War and the dictatorship while at school.[5]

AMNESTY INTERNATIONAL SEES THE LAW AS A STEP BACKWARDS

Amnesty International responded to the proposed law with a thirty-five-page critique. This started off with a quotation from Louis Joinet's 1997 Report to the UN High Commission for Human Rights on the "Question of the Impunity of Perpetrators of Human Rights Violations (Civil and Political)." "Before turning over a new leaf one must have read the old one," Joinet said.[6] AI was damning of the government's draft law. "Some measures represent a step backwards," it said ("España" 5). "This draft law not only ignores human rights and international law but actually puts into place [new] obstacles to the rights of the victims. . . .

They are more appropriate to a 'full stop' law," it said, referring here to the Ley de Punto Final passed, though later overturned, in Argentina in an attempt to prevent further prosecutions of human rights crimes by the military juntas of the 1980s. Crimes against humanity and war crimes "cannot be wiped out by acts of pardon or forgetting," it added.

AI identified three principal concerns: first, that the draft law ignored human rights and international law; second, that by covering up the names of perpetrators it was guaranteeing impunity and therefore was a "full stop" law; and finally, that the Spanish state itself declined to accept any form of responsibility. The second point seemed to be of most concern. By protecting the identities of perpetrators, the law created an obstacle to "establishing individual criminal or civil responsibilities." "In this sense the draft law helps to cover up the responsibility of the main criminals and their leaders," it added (28). The government should also, it said, have established a legal protocol for exhuming, identifying, and reburying bodies from mass graves. Above all, it said, the draft law had not even bothered to mention "the right of victims to justice." Although it was not explicit in this criticism, AI was pointing to the fact that Francoist officials—and officials from either side in the Civil War—who had committed human rights abuses would still be protected from prosecution by the terms of the 1970s amnesties.

AI also disputed the government's reasons for turning down its earlier petition that sentences be declared null and void. A separate report that accompanied the draft law, it pointed out, had claimed that this would endanger the Spanish legal principal of "the security of something already judged." The victims' certificates, AI said, did not "aim to clarify the truth," especially where they blocked access to the names of the perpetrators of crimes. Amnesty International's conclusions were damning of the Zapatero government. "The government, with this draft law, has not tried to move toward clearing the truth about crimes which formed part of a systematic methodology of widespread repression that used state resources to violate human rights, legislated to repress, denied judicial protection to the victims and employed the courts to pursue opponents, placing Spanish society in a state of absolute defenselessness and creating an atmosphere of terror and control," it said (35).

EL MUNDO HITS BACK

The day after the draft law was published, *El Mundo* headlined its editorial: "Historical Memory that Pleases No One" (*Una memoria histórica que no contenta a nadie*). It claimed that the timing and naming of the law were signs that there was "a certain air of shame" surrounding it. "Zapatero has tried to keep everyone happy but has upset everyone," it said. *El Mundo* considered the victims' certificates—which it called "diplomas"—to be "a joke," pointing out that the candidates to receive them could be numbered in the millions. The government, it felt, had backed down from its original plans but should have dropped the matter entirely. "The fact that the project could have been worse—by revising court sentences or obliging the church to retire plaques commemorating its own dead—does not mean that it is any good. It is still a grave error for Mr. Zapatero to keep fuelling his well-earned fame for playing with the past as if the spirit of the *Transición* had nothing to do with him."

THE CHURCH ACCUSES ZAPATERO OF REOPENING CIVIL WAR WOUNDS

Spain's Roman Catholic bishops were incensed by the proposed law. The Roman Catholic Church hierarchy had supported Francoism, whose guiding philosophy was, after all, known as National Catholicism. More than 6,500 bishops, priests, monks, and nuns had been killed by the Republican side during the war. A number of these had been canonized by the Vatican, many of them during the papacy of John Paul II (1978–2005). Benedict XVI and the Vatican received criticism for the beatification of 498 Roman Catholics executed during the Civil War. The Spanish Church also had a long history of individual priests with anti-Francoist tendencies (Franco's police estimated the total, in the dying days of the regime, at around 10 percent and operated a special prison for them in Zamora), but—while backing democracy—it remained broadly conservative after his death.

The church had openly opposed several Zapatero policies (ranging from same-sex marriage and easier divorce to a weakening of the grip of the Roman Catholic Church on religious education in schools). In November 2006 the Spanish Church's most senior body, the Plenary Assembly of the Spanish Bishops' Conference, met. *Memoria histórica* was high on the agenda and was damned as part of a "strong new wave of laicism." The first point the bishops wished to make in the pastoral letter they issued after their meeting was, as the topic heading ran, that "Reconciliation Is Under Threat" (*Orientaciones morales ante la situación actual de España*). Spain had changed greatly over the past few decades, the bishops said, and recent history had been "more agitated and convulsed than was desirable." In order to understand the present, they said, Spaniards had to view it "through the perspective of events over the previous century, serenely respecting the whole truth of a complex set of facts."

In the years after Franco's death, they said, the Church had "overcome any nostalgia for the past and collaborated robustly to make democracy, and the full recognition of fundamental rights for everyone—without religious discrimination—possible. . . . This 'robust' attitude of the Church and of Roman Catholics helped bring about a *Transición* based on consensus and reconciliation among Spaniards. Pardon, reconciliation, peace, and coexistence were the great moral values proclaimed by the Church and which most Catholics and Spaniards in general experienced intensely in those moments." The letter continues,

> Between us all we should make sure that the achievements of that time are not lost. A society which seemed to have found a way forward through reconciliation and distension is, once more, divided and confrontational. The selective use of *memoria histórica* is reopening old Civil War wounds and bringing back to life sentiments that had seemed to have been overcome. These measures cannot be considered a form of social progress. They are, rather, a historical and civic step backwards, with the obvious risk of provoking tension and discrimination as well as the alteration of a tranquil coexistence.

THE POLITICAL DEBATE

The church's line was very much that being followed by the People's Party—with which it was allied on several other issues against the

Zapatero government (see "Una ley"). The draft law was not debated in Parliament until December 14, 2006. It provoked angry reactions from almost all sides, though the government managed to force it through to the next stage of the parliamentary procedure (during which it can still be withdrawn or altered), thanks to the Catalan votes of CiU and the abstention of the Basques in the PNV party.

Deputy Prime Minister María Teresa Fernández de la Vega said the law was not designed to divide. The law had inherited "the best of the spirit of the *Transición* and the principle that led us to a stable, consolidated democracy: concord," she said ("El Congreso"). "Far from being against anyone, what it aims to do is justice," she added. The government did not want to write or rewrite history, she insisted. That was still a job for historians.

The PP said the law was revisionist and unnecessary. PP Deputy Manuel Atencia called it false, hypocritical, erroneous, and irrelevant. The council of wise men and women would, he said, become the "tribunal of the official memory Inquisition" (Díez and Cué, "El proyecto"). He said that eight laws and three royal decrees had already dealt with the question of rehabilitating and compensating victims. "This has been dressed up as an initiative that seeks concord, but, really, it is nothing less than another step in the strategy of breaking the great pact of [peaceful] coexistence between Spaniards agreed to during the *Transición* and in the Constitution," he said, before comparing the proposed archive in Salamanca with the Ministry of Truth in George Orwell's *1984* (Díez and Cué, "La primera ley"). The law would, he said, "stir up the mud" of Spain's past.

Socialist José Andrés Torres Mora asked why the PP was so offended by the law when "the only mud that is being moved is that which covers the bones" of the victims (Díez and Cué, "La primera ley"). ERC and IU-ICV continued to demand that political sentences handed down by Francoist tribunals should be formally overturned. ERC also demanded that King Juan Carlos should formally ask forgiveness from the victims on behalf of the Spanish state for "the consequences of the military uprising against the Republican constitution." ERC deputy Joan Tardá brought Captain Lozano, the prime minister's grandfather, into the debate. "You should be hoping that, in seventy years' time, a grandson of yours could quote this law with the same pride that you quote the political testament of your murdered grandfather. But that will only be possible if you change this law to conform with people's human rights" (Díez and Cué, "La primera ley"). Torres Mora replied, "The prime minister's grandfather, aware of the awful fact that he was going to be killed, was able to look into the future and look forward to concord, saying: 'I die an innocent man and I also pardon.' . . . I lament the fact that you are using the memory of a grandfather who suffered the injustices of 1936 and now suffers them again in the name of ERC" (Díez and Cué, "La primera ley").

While the draft law was voted through to the next stage of parliamentary debate, CiU and the PNV both made clear that their future support could not be guaranteed. The draft law had not gone far enough. They wanted changes before allowing it to pass onto the statute books. After the parliamentary debate, *El Mundo* again turned on the government: "The victims of Francoism do not need rehabilitation at all, given that there was an amnesty followed by financial compensation and that historians themselves have made sufficiently clear exactly what happened in that sad moment [of history]," it said in an editorial ("Una ley").

While recognizing that the government had tried to be moderate, *El Mundo* said that the main problem with the law was that, unlike the amnesties and other previous laws dealing with victims, it had not been born out of a consensus with the opposition People's Party. Even some senior Socialists, it claimed, had come to rue the government's decision to pass a *memoria histórica* law. "We have already seen the result [of this law]: old wounds have been reopened and have caused social confrontation as can be seen from the *in memoriam* notices published in the papers in recent months," it said ("Una ley").

So what happens next? While victims and their advocates have suggested that the law does not go far enough, and the political Right has continued to characterize the law as a dangerous move toward opening old wounds, it has nevertheless "generated an atmosphere of debate, ferment, and *inquietude* over the past" that Stephanie Golob suggests "may be the Law's lasting legacy" (Golob 138). Whatever happens in the future, this debate looks increasingly like the last act—or, alternatively, the death throes—of a period that Spaniards will always idealize but have never properly defined, *la Transición*.

NOTES

1. The BLAH document continues, "el congreso de los diputados reafirma una vez mas, el deber de nuestra sociedad democrática proceder al reconocimiento moral de todos los hombres y mujeres que fueron víctimas de la guerra civil española, así como de cuantos padecieron mas tarde la represión de la dictadura franquista. Instamos a que cualquier iniciativa promovida por las familias de los afectados que se lleve a cabo en tal sentido, sobre todo en el ámbito local, reciba el apoyo de las instituciones evitando, en todo caso, que sirva para reavivar viejas heridas o remover el rescoldo de la confrontación civil" (the congress reaffirms once again that the duty of our democratic society is the moral recognition of all men and women who were victims of the Spanish Civil War, as well as those who later suffered repression at the hands of the Francoist dictatorship. We insist that any initiative promoted by the families of the victims should be enacted, above all at the local level, in such a way as to avoid the opening of old wounds or the fanning of the embers of civil confrontation).

2. AI went on to say, "incluyeron dispociones de pretendido perdón y olvido respeto de actos, considerados por el derecho internacional como crímenes contra la humanidad" (they included laws intended to grant forgiveness and forgetting for acts that international law considers crimes against humanity) ("España").

3. In their words, "adoptar las medidas legislativas necesarias dirigidas a la Nulidad de tales sentencias" (to adopt the necessary legislative means directed to the nullification of these decisions) ("España" 67).

4. The figures available are estimates and run from four thousand to seven thousand.

5. For more information on this, see the following website: http://www.memoriahistorica.es.

6. The full text of Joinet's UN report for the Commission on Human Rights is available at http://www.law.duke.edu/shell/cite.pl?59+Law+&+Contemp.+Probs.+249+(Fall+1996).

Works Cited

Abella, Rafael. *Por el Imperio hacia Dios: Crónica de una posguerra (1939–1955)*. Barcelona: Planeta, 1978.

Ackelsberg, Martha. " 'Mujeres libres': The Preservation of Memory under the Politics of Repression in Spain." *Memory and Totalitarianism*. Vol. 1. Ed. Luisa Passerini. New York: Oxford University Press, 1992. 125–44.

Adorno, Theodor. *Problems of Moral Philosophy*. Stanford: Stanford University Press, 2001.

———. "What Does Coming to Terms with the Past Mean?" *Bitburg in Moral and Political Perspectives*. Ed. Geoffrey H. Hartman. Bloomington: Indiana University Press, 1986. 114–29.

Aguilar Fernández, Paloma. "Agents of Memory: Spanish Civil War Veterans and Disabled Soldiers." Winter and Sivan, *War* 84–103.

———. "Institutional Legacies and Collective Memories: The Case of the Spanish Transition to Democracy." *States of Memory: Continuities, Conflicts, and Transformations in National Retrospection*. Ed. Jeffrey K. Olick. Durham: Duke University Press, 2003. 128–60.

———. *Memory and Amnesia: The Role of the Spanish Civil War in the Transition to Democracy*. Trans. Mark Oakley. New York: Berghahn Books, 2002. Translation of *Memoria y olvido de la guerra civil española*. Madrid: Alianza, 1996.

Aizpeolea, L. R. "Las víctimas de la Guerra Civil y de la dictadura serán rehabilitadas por ley." *El País* Sept. 11, 2004.

Albar, Manuel. "Sobre unos sucesos: El verdadero culpable." *El Socialista* Jan. 2, 1932.

Alcala-Zamora y Castillo, Niceto. *Memorias: Medio siglo de vida política española visto por el primer Presidente de la 2a. República*. Barcelona: Planeta, 1998.

Alexander, Jeffrey C. "Toward a Theory of Cultural Trauma." *Cultural Trauma and Collective Identity*. Ed. Jeffrey C. Alexander et al. Berkeley: University of California Press, 2004. 1–30.

Alfonsi, Adela. "La recatolización de los obreros en Málaga, 1937–1966: El nacional-catolicismo de los obispos Santos Olivera y Herrera Oria." *Historia Social* 35 (1999): 119–34.

Alphen, Ernst van. "Symptoms of Discursivity: Experience, Memory, and Trauma." Bal, Crew, and Spitzer 24–38.

Altozano, Manuel. "Garzón lanza la mayor investigación sobre los desapareci-dos del régimen de Franco." *El País* Sept. 2, 2008: 1, 10.

Álvarez Bolado, Alfonso. "Guerra civil y universo religioso: Fenomenología de una implicación (I)." *Miscelánea Comillas* 44 (1986): 233–300.

———. *Para ganar la guerra, para ganar la paz: Iglesia y guerra civil: 1936–1939.* Madrid: Universidad Pontificia de Comillas, 1995.

Álvarez Chillida, Gonzalo. *El antisemitismo en España: La imagen del judío (1812–2002).* Madrid: Marcial Pons, 2002.

Álvarez Puga, Eduardo. *Historia de la Falange.* Barcelona: Dopesa, 1969.

Amago, Samuel. *True Lies: Narrative Self-Consciousness in the Contemporary Spanish Novel.* Lewisburg, PA: Bucknell University Press, 2006.

Amichai, Yehuda. "The Resurrection of the Dead." Trans. from Hebrew by Leon Wieseltier. *New Yorker* Nov. 29, 2004: 149.

Amnesty International. "España, poner fin al silencio y a la injusticia." July 18, 2005. http://www.es.amnesty.org/uploads/tx_useraitypdb/victimas_fran-quismo_05.pdf.

———. "Spain: Window of Opportunity for a Fresh Start on Human Rights." June 11, 2004. http://www.amnesty.org/en/library/info/EUR41/007/2004/en.

———. "Víctimas de la Guerra civil y el régimen franquista: El desastre de los archivos, la privatización de la verdad." March 30, 2006. http://www.es.amnesty.org/uploads/tx_useraitypdb/victimas_franquismo_30marzo2006_05.pdf.

Andrade, Jamie de (pseudonym, Francisco Franco). *Raza: Anecdotario para el guión de una película.* Madrid: Numancia, 1942.

Andrés-Gallego, José, and Antón M. Pazos, eds. *Archivo Gomá: Documentos de la Guerra Civil.* Vol. 5. Madrid: Consejo Superior de Investigaciones Científi-cas, 2001.

Antón, Eva. "*Soldados de Salamina*: Guerra y sexismo: Otro ejemplo narrativo de la reacción patriarcal." *Mujeres en Red.* May 9, 2003. http://www.nodo50.org/mujeresred/cultura/soldados_de_salamina.html.

Arce, Luz. *El infierno.* Santiago de Chile: Planeta, 1993.

Archivo Histórico Nacional. "Declaración del testigo Francesc Casanova a la Causa General, Provincia de Barcelona, 8 June 1942." Barcelona, 1942.

Arendt, Hannah. *Imperialism.* New York: Harcourt, Brace and World, 1968.

———. "'The Jewish Question' (1937 or 1938)." *The Jewish Writings.* Ed. Jerome Kohn and Ron H. Feldman. New York: Shocken Books, 2007. 42–45.

Armengou, Montse, and Ricard Belis. *El convoy de los 927.* Barcelona: Plaza & Janes, 2005.

———. *Las fosas del silencio: Hay un holocausto español?* Barcelona: Plaza & Janes, 2004.

Arnabat, Ramon. "I vosaltres, ¿què vau fer?" Suplement *Quadern*. *El País* Sept. 15, 2005: 2–3.

Aróstegui, Julio. *La historia vivida: Sobre la historia del presente*. Madrid: Alianza, 2004.

Arrarás, Joaquín. *Franco*. 7th ed. Valladolid: Librería Santarén, 1939.

———. *Historia de la Cruzada española*. 8 vols. Madrid: Ediciones Españolas, 1939–1943.

Asamblea Conjunta Obispos-Sacerdotes. Ed. Secretariado Nacional del Clero. Madrid: Biblioteca de Autores Cristianos, 1971.

Asociación Católica Nacional de Propagandistas de Oviedo. *Asturias roja: Sacerdotes y religiosos perseguidos y martirizados (octubre de 1934)*. Oviedo: Imprenta Trufero, n.d. [1935].

Asociación para la recuperación de la memoria histórica (ARMH). "La Asociación para la recuperación de la memoria histórica quiere convertir su audiencia en un referéndum oficioso." Email sent to ARMH Listserv. Jan. 20, 2004.

Auden, W. H. "Spain." *Voices Against Tyranny*. Ed. John Miller. New York: Scribner's, 1986. 17–32.

"Aún quedan tribus." *El Pueblo Manchego* (Ciudad Real), Jan. 4, 1932.

Avelar, Idelber. *The Untimely Present: Postdictatorial Latin American Fiction and the Task of Mourning*. Durham: Duke University Press, 1999.

Ayerra Redín, Marino. *No me avergoncé del Evangelio (desde mi parroquia)*. Buenos Aires: Ed. Periplo, 1958.

Aznárez, Juan Jesús. "Crimen sin castigo en América Latina." *El País* Mar. 25, 2007: 10–11.

B., Manuela. Personal journal, 1936–1937. Private collection of Ignacio Fernández de Mata.

Bahamonde y Sánchez de Castro, Antonio. *1 año con Queipo memorias de un nacionalista*. Barcelona: Ediciones Españolas, 1938.

Bal, Mieke. Introduction. Bal, Crew, and Spitzer vii–xvii.

———, Jonathan Crew, and Leo Spitzer, eds. *Acts of Memory: Cultural Recall in the Present*. Hanover, NH: University Press of New England, 1999.

Balfour, Sebastian. *Deadly Embrace: Morocco and the Road to the Spanish Civil War*. Oxford: Oxford University Press, 2002.

Balibrea, Mari Paz. "Rethinking Spanish Republican Exile." *Journal of Spanish Cultural Studies* 6.1 (2005): 3–24.

Ballester Domingo, Vicente, S. D. B. *Marcelino Olaechea*. Unpublished manuscript.

Barbash, Benny. *My First Sony*. Trans. Dalya Bilu. London: Review, 1999.

Barbero, Edmundo. *El infierno azul (Seis meses en el feudo de Queipo)*. Madrid: Talleres del SUIG (CNT), 1937.

Barral, Carlos. *Años de penitencia: Memorias.* Barcelona: Tusquets, 1975.

Barrio, Antonio Marquina. "Los bombardeos aéreos de poblaciones civiles en 1938." *La Guerra y la paz cincuenta años después.* Ed. Francisco Aguado Sánchez. Madrid: Campillo-Nevado, 1990. 531–47.

Barthes, Roland. "The Discourse of History." *The Postmodern History Reader.* Ed. Keith Jenkins. New York: Routledge, 1997. 120–23.

Bartra, Roger. "Las Redes Imaginarias del Terror Político." *Claves de Razón Práctica* 133 (2003): 4–9.

Baudrillard, Jean. *In the Shadow of the Silent Majorities.* New York: Semiotext(e), 1983.

Bax, Mart. "Planned Policy or Primitive Balkanism? A Local Contribution to the Ethnography of the War in Bosnia-Herzegovina?" *Ethnos* 65 (2000): 317–40.

Bayle, Constantino. Introduction. *Por Dios y por España* by Isidro Gomá. Ed. Constantino Bayle. Barcelona: Casulleras, 1940. 489–520.

Benjamin, Walter. "Critique of Violence." *Selected Writings.* Vol. 1: 1913–1926. Ed. Marcus Bullock and Michael W. Jennings. Cambridge: Cambridge University Press, 1996. 236–52.

———. "Theses on the Philosophy of History." *Illuminations.* Ed. Hannah Arendt. New York: Schocken Books, 1985: 253–64.

Berkhofer, Robert. *Beyond the Great Story: History as Text and Discourse.* Cambridge: Harvard University Press, 1995.

Bernal, Antonio-Miguel. "Resignación de los campesinos andaluces: La resistencia pasiva durante el franquismo." *España franquista: Causa general y actitudes sociales ante la dictadura.* Ed. Isidro Sánchez Sánchez, Miguel Ortiz Heras, and David Ruiz. [Cuenca]: Ediciones de la Universidad de Castilla La Mancha, Servicio de Publicaciones, 1993.

Bernanos, Georges. *Les grands cimetières sous la lune.* Paris: Plon, 1938.

Bertrán Güell, Felipe. *Preparación y desarrollo del alzamiento nacional.* Valladolid: Librería Santarén, 1939.

Beverley, John. *Testimonio: On the Politics of Truth.* Minneapolis: University of Minnesota Press, 2004.

Blanco Escolá, Carlos. *General Mola: Elególatra que provocó la guerra civil.* Madrid: La Esfera de los Libros, 2002.

Blinkhorn, Martin. *Carlism and Crisis in Spain 1931–1939.* Cambridge: Cambridge University Press, 1975.

———. *Para ganar la guerra, para ganar la paz: Iglesia y guerra civil: 1936–1939.* Madrid: Universidad Pontificia de Comillas, 1995.

Boletín Oficial de las Cortes Generales. Congreso de los Diputados. 7th Term, no. 221–13. May 4, 2006: 39–40.

Bonada, Lluís. Interview. *Avui.* February 28, 1990.

Borràs Betriu, Rafael. *Los que no hicimos la guerra*. Barcelona: Ediciones Nauta, 1971.

Botti, Alfonso. *Cielo y dinero: El nacional-catolicismo en España (1881–1975)*. Madrid: Alianza Editorial, 1993.

Bowlby, John. *Attachment and Loss*. Vol. 1. Harmondsworth, UK: Penguin, 1991.

Brooks, Roy. *When Sorry Isn't Enough: The Controversy over Apologies and Reparations for Human Injustice*. New York: New York University Press, 1999.

Bullón de Mendoza, Alfonso, and Álvaro de Diego. *Historias orales de la guerra civil*. Barcelona: Ariel, 2000.

Butler, Judith. *Antigone's Claim: Kinship Between Life and Death*. New York: Columbia University Press, 2000.

C., Tomasa (pseudonym). Personal interview conducted by Ignacio Fernández de Mata. March 29, 2003.

C., Valentín (pseudonym). Personal interview conducted by Ignacio Fernández de Mata. March 29, 2003.

Cabanellas, Guillermo. *Los cuatro generales*. 2 vols. Barcelona: Planeta, 1977.

Calleja, J. J. *Yagüe, un corazón al rojo*. Barcelona: Juventud, 1963.

Calvo Sotelo, José. *La voz de un perseguido*. 2 vols. Madrid: Librería de San Martín, 1933, 1934.

Cámara Villar, Gregorio. *Nacional-catolicismo y escuela: La socialización política del franquismo (1936–1951)*. Madrid: Editorial Hesperia, 1984.

Canal, Jordi. "Las campañas antisectarias de Juan Tusquets (1927–1939): Una aproximación a los orígenes del contuberio judeo-masónico-comunista en España." *La masonería en la España del siglo XX*. 2 vols. Ed. Antonio Ferrer Benimeli. Toledo: Universidad de Catilla-La Mancha, 1996. 1193–1214.

Canetti, Elias. *Crowds and Power*. New York: Viking Press, 1966.

Carlavilla, Mauricio. *Anti-España 1959: Autores, cómplices y encubridores del comunismo*. Madrid: Editorial NOS, 1959.

———. *Asesinos de España: Marxismo, anarquismo, masonería: Continuación de El enemigo*. Madrid: Ediciones Bergua, 1935.

———. *Sodomitas*. [Madrid]: Editorial NOS, 1956.

Carlson, Eric Stener. *I Remember Julia: Voices of the Disappeared*. Philadelphia: Temple University Press, 1996.

Carme Vega, Monjo. *Els treballadors i la guerra civil: Història d'una indústria catalana collectivitzada*. Barcelona: Emúries, 1986.

Carr, Raymond, and Juan Pablo Fusi. *Spain: Dictatorship to Democracy*. 2nd ed. London: Allen & Unwin, 1981.

Carrillo, Marc. "El marc legal de la repressió de la dictadura franquista en el període 1939–1959." VVAA, *Notícia de la negra nit: Vide i veus a les presons franquistas (1939–1959)*. Barcelona: Associació Catalana d'Expresos Polítics, 2001.

Caruth, Cathy. Introduction to Part II. *Trauma: Explorations in Memory*. Ed. Cathy Caruth. Baltimore: Johns Hopkins University Press, 1995. 151–57.

——. *Unclaimed Experience: Trauma, Narrative, and History*. Baltimore: Johns Hopkins University Press, 1996.

Casanova, José. "España: De la Iglesia estatal a la separación de la Iglesia y Estado." *Historia Social* 35 (1999): 135–52.

——. *Public Religions in the Modern World*. Chicago: University of Chicago Press, 1994.

Casanova, Julián. "Guerra de exterminio, paz incivil: los fundamentos de la dictadura franquista." *El franquismo: El régimen y la oposición. Actas de las IV Jornadas de Castilla-La Mancha sobre investigaciones en Archivos. Archivo Histórico Provincial de Guadalajara, Guadalajara, 9–12 noviembre 1999*. Vol. 2. Guadalajara: Anabad Castilla-La Mancha, 2000. 579–88.

——. *La iglesia de Franco*. Barcelona: Crítica, 2005.

——. "Mentiras convincentes." *El País* June 14, 2005. http://www.elpais.com/.

——. "Otras memorias: Chile, Uruguay, Argentina." *El País* Sept. 14, 2008. http://www.elpais.com/.

——, and Santos Juliá, eds. *Morir, matar, sobrevivir: La violencia en la dictadura de Franco*. Barcelona: Crítica, 2004.

Caspístegui, Francisco Javier. "'Spain's Vendée': Carlist identity in Navarre as a Mobilizing Model." Ealham and Richards 177–95.

Castillejo-Cuéllar, Alejandro. "Knowledge, Experience, and South Africa's Scenarios of Forgiveness." *Truth Commissions: State Terror, History, and Memory*. Ed. Greg Grandin and Thomas Miller Klubock. Special issue of *Radical History Review* 97 (2007): 11–42.

Causa general: La dominación roja en España, avance de la información instruída por el Ministerio público. [Madrid]: Ministerio de Justicia, 1943.

Cavarero, Adriana. *Relating Narratives: Storytelling and Selfhood*. Trans. Paul A. Kottman. London: Routledge, 2000.

Cazorla Sanchez, Antonio. *Las políticas de la victoria: La consolidación del Nuevo Estado franquista, 1938–1953*. Madrid: Marcial Pons, 2000.

Celaya, Miguel. *Cantos Íberos: Poesías completas*. Barcelona: Laia, 1977.

Cenarro, Angela. "Memories of Repression and Resistance: Narratives of Children Institutionalized by Auxilio Social in Postwar Spain." *Remembering and Forgetting on Europe's Southern Periphery*. Ed. Yannis Hamilakis and Jo Labanyi. Special issue of *History & Memory* 20.2 (2008): 39–59.

——. "Memory Beyond the Public Sphere: The Francoist Repression Remembered in Aragon." *Spanish Memories: Images of a Contested Past*. Special issue of *History & Memory* 14 (2002): 165–88.

——. "Muerte y subordinación en la España franquista: el imperio de la violencia como base del 'Nuevo Estado.'" *Historia Social* 30 (1998): 5–22.

————. "Violence, Surveillance and Denunciation: Social Cleavage in the Spanish Civil War and Francoism, 1936–1950." *Social Control in Europe: 1800–2000*. Ed. Clive Emsley, Eric Johnson, and Pieter Spierenburg. Columbus: Ohio State University Press, 2004. 281–300.

Cercas, Javier. *Soldados de Salamina*. Barcelona: Tusquets, 2001.

————. *Soldiers of Salamis*. Trans. A. McLean. New York: Bloomsbury, 2004.

————. *La velocidad de la luz*. Barcelona: Tusquets, 2005.

Cervera, Alfons. "Relato más allá de la zona oscura y prohibida." *La memoria de los olvidados: Un debate sobre el silencio de la represión franquista*. Ed. Asunción Álvarez and Emilio Silva. Valladolid: Ámbito, 2004. 153–62.

Churchill, Winston. "Speech to the House of Commons." *Daily Telegraph* June 19, 1940.

Cierva, Ricardo de la. *Bibliografía sobre la guerra de España (1936–1939) y sus antecedentes*. Barcelona: Ariel, 1968.

————. Dedicatoria. *Historia de la guerra civil española*. Vol. 1. Madrid: Editorial San Martín, 1969.

————. *Francisco Franco: biografía histórica*. 6 vols. Barcelona: Editorial Planeta, 1982.

Cimadevilla, Esther. Esther's interview with her mother, Emilia Carolina Ricca. Summer 1996.

————. Graveside interview conducted by Francisco Ferrándiz. July 23, 2003.

————. Personal email correspondence with Francisco Ferrándiz. April 29– June 1, 2006.

Claudín, Fernando. "Dos concepciones de la vía española al socialismo." *Horizonte Español* 2 (1966): 59–100.

Cohen, Stanley. *States of Denial: Knowing about Atrocities and Suffering*. Malden, MA: Blackwell, 2002.

Cohn, Norman. *Warrant for Genocide: The Myth of the Jewish World-Conspiracy and the Protocols of the Elders of Zion*. Harmondsworth, UK: Penguin, 1970.

Colomines, Agustí. "La deconstrucción de la memoria: El argumento perverso sobre la represión franquista." *Casa encantada: Lugares de memoria en la España constitucional (1978–2004)*. Ed. Joan Ramon Resina and Ulrich Winter. Frankfurt am Main: Vervuert, 2005. 207–21.

Comes, Vicente. "Un secreto de Luis Lucia y el engaño del capellán Martín Torrent." *Historia 16* (1998): 28–35.

"El Congreso rechaza todas las enmiendas al proyecto de Memoria Histórica presentada por el Gobierno." *El País* Dec. 14, 2006. http://www.elpais.com/.

Connerton, Paul. *How Societies Remember*. Cambridge: Cambridge University Press, 1989.

Conolly, Eduardo. "Mauricio Carlavilla: El encanto de la conspiración." *HIBRIS: Revista de Bibliofilia* 23 (2004): 4–19.

El convoy de los 927. 30 Minuts. Dir. Montserrat Armengou and Ricard Belis. Televisió de Catalunya, S. A. Barcelona. March 7, 2004.

Cortés Cavanillas, Julián. *La caída de Alfonso XIII: Causas y episodios de una revolución.* 7th ed. Madrid: Librería de San Martín, 1933.

Croce, Benedetto. *History as the Story of Liberty.* London: Allen & Unwin, 1941.

Crossland, Zoe. "Buried Lives: Forensic Archaeology and the Disappeared in Argentina." *Archaeological Dialogues* 7.2 (2000): 146–159.

———. "Violent Spaces: Conflict over the Reappearance of Argentina's Disappeared." *Matériel Culture: The Archaeology of Twentieth-Century Conflict.* Ed. John Schofield, William Gray Johnson, and Colleen M. Beck. London: Routledge, 2002. 115–31.

Crozier, Brian. *Franco: A Biographical History.* London: Eyre & Spottiswoode, 1967.

Cruz, Rafael. "Old Symbols, New Meanings: Mobilizing the Rebellion in the Summer of 1936." Ealham and Richards 159–76.

Cué, Carlos. "Las asociaciones se impacientan y exigen una solución definitiva." *El País* Sept. 12, 2005. http://www.elpais.com/.

———. "De la Vega frena la ley de memoria histórica para acoger a ambos bandos." *El País* Sept. 12, 2005. http://www.elpais.com/.

———. "Las fosas de Franco se abren poco a poco." *El País* Sept. 12, 2005. http://www.elpais.com/.

———. "El Gobierno habilitará 'jurídica y moralmente' a las víctimas del franquismo." *El País* Sept. 10, 2004. http://www.elpais.com/.

———. "La Junta crea una comisión interdepartamental para la reparación de las víctimas del franquismo." *El País* (version Andalucía) Nov. 10, 2004. http://www.elpais.com/.

———. "La última cuenta pendiente de la democracia." *El País* Sept. 20, 2004. http://www.elpais.com/.

Cuevas Gutiérrez, Tomasa. *Cárcel de mujeres.* 2 vols. Barcelona: Sirocco, 1985.

———. *Mujeres de la resistencia.* Barcelona: Sirocco, 1986.

———. *Mujeres en las cárceles franquistas.* Madrid: Casa de Campo, 1979.

———. *Testimonios de mujeres en las cárceles franquistas.* Ed. Jorge J. Montes Salguera. Huesca: Instituto de Estudios Altoaragoneses, 2004.

Davis, Madeleine. "Is Spain Recovering its Memory? Breaking the Pacto del Olvido." *Human Rights Quarterly* 27 (2005): 858–80.

Death in El Valle/Muerte en El Valle. Dir. C. M. Hardt. CM Pictures Production for Channel Four Television (UK), 2005. http://www.deathinelvalle.com.

De la Rubia, Ángel, and Pedro de la Rubia. *La fosa de Valdediós.* Gijón: Fundación Municipal de Cultura, Educación y Universidad Popular del Ayuntamiento de Gijón, 2006.

Derrida, Jacques. "On Forgiveness." *On Cosmopolitanism and Forgiveness.* New York: Routledge, 2001.

————. *Specters of Marx: The State of the Debt, the Work of Mourning, and the New International*. Trans. Peggy Kamuf. London: Routledge, 1994.

————, and Bernard Stiegler. *Echographies of Television*. London: Polity, 2002.

Díaz-Llanos y Lecuona, Rafael. *Responsabilidades Políticas (Ley de 9 de febrero de 1939, Comentarios, Notas, Disposiciones Complementarias y Formularios)*. Zaragoza: Librería General, 1939.

Díaz Nosty, Bernardo. *La Comuna asturiana: Revolución de octubre de 1934*. Bilbao: ZYX, 1974.

Díez, Anabel. "El líder socialista augura que el PP no derogará sus reformas." *El País* Apr. 24, 2006. http://www.elpais.com/.

————, and Carlos Cué. "El proyecto de Ley de Memoria Histórica divide al Congreso." *El País* Dec. 14, 2006. http://www.elpais.com/.

————. "La primera ley que honra a los represaliados por Franco salva el principal escollo en el Congreso." *El País* Dec. 15, 2006. http://www.elpais.com/.

Dijkstra, Bram. *Evil Sisters: The Threat of Female Sexuality and the Cult of Manhood*. New York: Knopf, 1996.

Doering, Bernard. "Jacques Maritain and the Spanish Civil War." *Review of Politics* 44 (1982): 489–522.

Doña, Juana. *Desde la noche y la niebla (mujeres en las cárceles franquistas)*. Madrid: La Torre, 1978.

E., Dominga (pseudonym). Personal interview conducted by Ignacio Fernández de Mata. May 9, 2003.

Eagleton, Terry. *The Ideology of the Aesthetic*. Oxford: Blackwell, 1995.

Ealham, Chris, and Michael Richards, eds. *The Splintering of Spain: Cultural History and the Spanish Civil War, 1936–1939*. Cambridge: Cambridge University Press, 2005.

Edles, Laura Desfor. *Symbol and Ritual in the New Spain*. Cambridge: Cambridge University Press, 1998.

Eiroa, Matilde. *Viva Franco: Hambre, racionamiento, falangismo: Málaga, 1939–1942*. Málaga: Artes Gráficas, 1995.

Elias, Norbert. *The Civilizing Process*. Oxford: Blackwell, 1994.

Ellis, Robert Richmond. "Memory, Masculinity, and Mourning in Javier Cercas's *Soldados de Salamina*." *Revista de Estudios Hispánicos* 39 (2005): 515–35.

Elordi, Carlos. *Los años difíciles: El testimonio de los protagonistas anónimos de la guerra civil y la posguerra*. Madrid: Aguilar, 2002.

Elsaesser, Thomas. "Europe in Cinema, Cinema in Europe." Paper presented at the European Science Foundation Exploratory Workshop, University of Southampton, Sept. 16–18, 2005.

Ericksen, Robert P., and Susannah Heschel. Introduction. *Betrayal: German Churches and the Holocaust*. Ed. Robert P. Ericksen and Susannah Heschel. Minneapolis: Fortress Press, 1999. 1–21.

Erikson, Erik H. *Childhood and Society*. London: Imago Publishing, 1951.

Ermath, Michael. *Wilhelm Dilthey: The Critique of Historical Reason*. Chicago: University of Chicago Press, 1978.

Espinosa Maestre, Francisco. *La columna de la muerte: El avance del ejército franquista de Sevilla a Badajoz*. Barcelona: Editorial Crítica, 2003.

———. *El fenómeno revisionista o los fantasmas de la derecha española: Sobre la matanza de Badajoz y la lucha en torno a la interpretación del pasado*. Badajoz: Libros del Oeste, 2005.

de Estella, Gumersindo. *Fusilados en Zaragoza, 1936–1939: Tres años de asistencia espiritual a los reos*. Zaragoza: Mira, 2003.

Falange Tradicionalista y de las JONS, Secretaría General. Informe sobre la labor desarrollada hasta la fecha para la repatriación de menores españoles expatriados. Archivo General de la Administración. Nov. 26, 1949.

Feal, Carlos. *El resentimiento trágico de la vida: Notas sobre la revolución y la guerra civil españolas*. Madrid: Alianza, 1991.

Felman, Shoshana, and Dori Laub. *Testimony: Crises of Witnessing in Literature, Psychoanalysis, and History*. New York: Routledge, 1992.

Fentress, James, and Chris Wickham. *Social Memory*. Oxford: Blackwell, 1992.

Fernández de Mata, Ignacio. "En este portal barrido, barrido sobre mojado . . . *Estampa* y los inicios de la etnografía castellana." *Estampa de Burgos: Artículos de Eduardo de Ontañón en la revista Estampa (1928–1936)*. Ed. Ignacio Fernández de Mata and Juan Carlos Estébanez Gil. Burgos: IMC Ayuntamiento de Burgos-Diputación Provincial de Burgos, 2006. xxiii–xliii.

———. "El surgimiento de la memoria histórica: Sentidos, malentendidos y disputas." *La tradición como reclamo: Antropología en Castilla y León*. Ed. Luis Díaz Viana and Pedro Tomé Martín. Salamanca: Junta de Castilla y León, Consejería de Cultura y Turismo, 2007. 195–208.

Feros, Antonio. "Civil War Still Haunts Spanish Politics." *New York Times* Mar. 20, 2004: 9.

Ferrándiz, Francisco. "Cries and Whispers: Exhuming and Narrating Defeat in Spain Today." *Journal of Spanish Cultural Studies* 9.2 (2008): 177–92.

———. "The Intimacy of Defeat: An Anthropological Analysis of Testimonies Recovered Around Mass Grave Exhumations from the Spanish Civil War." Unpublished lecture delivered at University of Notre Dame. October 2005.

———. "La Memoria de los Vencidos de la Guerra Civil: El Impacto de las Exhumaciones de Fosas Comunes en la España Contemporánea." *Las políticas de la memoria en los sistemas democráticos: Poder, cultura y mercado*. Ed. Susana Narotzky and José María Valcuende. Sevilla: ASANA-FAAEE, 2005. 109–32.

———. "The Return of Civil War Ghosts: The Ethnography of Exhumations in Contemporary Spain." *Anthropology Today* 22.3 (2006): 2–8.

———, and Alex Baer. "Digital Memory: The Visual Recording of Mass Grave Exhumations in Contemporary Spain." *Forum Qualitative Sozialforschung /*

Forum: Qualitative Social Research 9.3 (2008): Art. 35. http://www.qualitative-research.net.

——, and Carles Feixa. "An Anthropological View on Violence." *Multidisciplinary Perspectives on Peace and Conflict Research: A View from Europe*. Ed. Francisco Ferrándiz and Antonius C. G. M. Robben. Bilbao: Humanitarian-Net, 2007. 51–76. http://www.humanitariannet.deusto.es/publica/PUBLICACIONES_PDF/Multidisciplinary%20Persp.pdf.

Ferrer Benimelli, José Antonio. *El contubernio judeo-masónico-comunista: Del Satanismo al escándolo del P-2*. Madrid: Ediciones Istmo, 1982.

Fouce, Guillermo. "La necesaria recuperación de la Memoria Histórica desde la psicología social." *Psicología sin fronteras: Revista electrónica de intervención psicosocial y psicología comunitaria* 206, 1.2: 58–76.

Fraga Iribarne, Manuel. *Las transformaciones de la sociedad española contemporánea*. Madrid: Ediciones del Movimiento, 1959.

Franco Bahamonde, Francisco. *Apuntes personales sobre la República y la guerra civil*. Madrid: Fundación Nacional Francisco Franco, 1987.

Franco Salgado-Araujo, Francisco. *Mi vida junto a Franco*. Barcelona: Editorial Planeta, 1977.

Frankl, Víktor. *El hombre en busca de sentido*. Barcelona: Herder, 1989.

El franquismo: El régimen y la oposición. Actas de las IV Jornadas de Castilla-La Mancha sobre investigaciones en Archivos. Archivo Histórico Provincial de Guadalajara, Guadalajara, 9–12 noviembre 1999. Vol. 2. Guadalajara: Anabad Castilla-La Mancha, 2000.

Fraser, Ronald. *Blood of Spain: The Experience of Civil War*. London: Allen Lane, 1979.

——. "Historia oral, historia social." *Historia Social* 17 (1993): 131–39.

Frazier, Lessie Jo. "'Subverted Memories': Countermourning as Political Action in Chile." *Acts of Memory*. Ed. Mieke Bal, Jonathan Crewe, and Leo Spitzer. Hanover, NH: University of New England Press, 1999. 105–19.

Frieden, Jeffry. *Global Capitalism: Its Fall and Rise in the Twentieth Century*. New York: W. W. Norton, 2006.

Friedländer, Saul. *Memory, History, and the Extermination of the Jews of Europe*. Bloomington: Indiana University Press, 1993.

——. "Trauma, Transference, and 'Working Through' in Writing the History of Shoa." *History and Memory* 4.1 (1992): 39–52.

Fukuyama, Francis. *The End of History and the Last Man*. London: Penguin Books, 1992.

G., Ascención (pseudonym). Personal interview conducted by Ignacio Fernández de Mata. Sep. 25, 2003.

G., Samuel (pseudonym). Personal interview conducted by Ignacio Fernández de Mata. Apr. 4, 2003.

Gabarda, Vincent. *Els afusellaments al País Valencià (1938–1956)*. Valencia: Edicions Alfons el Magnànim, 1993.

Galarza, Ramón de. *Diario de un gudari condenado a muerte*. San Sebastián: Ediciones Vascas, 1977.

Gampel, Yolanda. "Reflections on the Prevalence of the Uncanny in Social Violence." *Cultures Under Siege: Collective Violence and Trauma*. Ed. Antonius C. G. M. Robben and Marcelo M. Suárez-Orozco. Cambridge: Cambridge University Press, 2000. 48–69.

Garcés, Joan. "Experiencias ejemplares en la recuperación de la memoria histórica." *Jornades per a la Universitat Progressista d'Estiu* (JUPEC), Barcelona, July 2005.

García Lorca, Federico. *Obras completas*. Ed. Arturo del Hoyo. 3 vols. Madrid: Aguilar, 1989.

García Venero, Maximiano. *La Falange en la guerra de España: La unificación y Hedilla*. Paris: Ruedo Ibérico, 1967.

Garlinger, Patrick Paul. "Sex Changes and Political Transitions; or, What Bibi Andersen Can't Tell Us about Democracy in Spain." *Traces of Contamination: Unearthing the Francoist Legacy in Contemporary Spanish Discourse*. Ed. Eloy E. Merino and H. Rosi Song. Lewisburg, PA: Bucknell University Press, 2005. 27–52.

Gedi, Noa, and Yigal Elam. "Collective Memory: What Is It?" *History and Memory* 8.1 (1996): 30–50.

Gibson, Ian. "Escritor Ian Gibson dicta cátedra en España." Aug. 8, 2007. http://www.eluniverso.com/2007/08/08/.

Gil Robles, José María, and Pablo Beltrán de Heredia. *No fue posible la paz*. Barcelona: Ediciones Ariel, 1968.

Girard, René. *The Scapegoat*. Trans. Yvonne Freccero. Baltimore: Johns Hopkins University Press, 1989.

Godicheau, François. "Guerra civil, guerra incivil: La pacificación por el nombre." *Guerra civil: Mito y memoria*. Ed. Julio Aróstegui and Godicheau. Madrid: Marcial Pons, 2006. 137–66.

Goldin, Vladislav I., and John W. Long. "Resistance and Retribution: The Life and Fate of General E. K. Miller." *Revolutionary Russia* 12 (1999): 19–40.

Golob, Stephanie R. "*Volver*: The Return of/to Transitional Justice Politics in Spain." *The Politics of Memory in Contemporary Spain*. Ed. Jo Labanyi. Special issue of *Journal of Spanish Cultural Studies* 9.2 (2008): 127–41.

Gomá, Isidro. "Carta Colectiva." July 1, 1937.

———. Report of Spain's Catholic Cardinal Primate, Isidro Gomá, to the Holy See. Aug. 13, 1936.

———. "To Alberto Onaindia." May 5, 1937. Andrés-Gallego and Pazos 357.

Gómez, Luis, and Natalia Junquera. "¿Dónde acabaron?" *El País* Sept. 14, 2008: 1–4.

Gómez López-Quiñones, Antonio. "La guerra civil española: *Soldados de Salamina* de Javier Cercas." *Palabra y el Hombre* 127 (2003): 115–29.

———. *La guerra persistente: Memoria, violencia y utopía: Representaciones contemporáneas de la Guerra Civil española*. Madrid: Vervuert/Iberoamericana, 2006.

Gómez Pérez, Rafael. *Política y religión en el régimen de Franco*. Barcelona: Dopesa, 1976.

González Castillejo, María José. "Realidad social de la mujer: Vida cotidiana y esfera pública en Málaga (1931–1936)." *La mujer en Andalucía*. Ed. Pilar Ballarín and Teresa Ortiz. Vol. 1. Granada: Universidad de Granada, 1990. 417–31.

González Cuevas, Carlos. *Acción Española: Teología política y nacionalismo autoritario en España (1913–1936)*. Madrid: Editorial Tecnos, 1998.

González-Ruibal, Alfredo. "Making Things Public: Archaeologies of the Spanish Civil War." *Public Archaeology* 6.4 (2007): 203–26.

Gorboff, Marina. *La Russie fantôme: L'Émigration russe de 1920 à 1950*. Lausanne: Editions L'Age d'Homme, 1995.

Gordon, Avery. *Ghostly Matters: Haunting and the Sociological Imagination*. Minneapolis: University of Minnesota Press, 1997.

Graham, Helen. *The Spanish Civil War: A Very Short Introduction*. Oxford: Oxford University Press, 2005.

———, and Jo Labanyi. Introduction. *Spanish Cultural Studies*. Ed. Helen Graham and Jo Labanyi. Oxford: Oxford University Press, 1995. 1–23.

Grossman, Dave. *On Killing: The Psychological Cost of Learning to Kill in War and Society*. Boston: Little, Brown, 1996.

"La guerra contra la Guardia Civil." *ABC* Jan. 2, 1932.

Gugelberger, George M. *The Real Thing: Testimonial Discourse and Latin America*. Durham: Duke University Press, 1996.

Habermas, Jürgen. *The Philosophical Discourse of Modernity*. Cambridge: Polity, 1987.

Halbwachs, Maurice. *Los marcos sociales de la memoria*. Trans. Manuel Antonio Baeza and Michel Mujica. Barcelona: Anthropos, 2004.

Hardcastle, Anne E. "Ghosts of the Past and Present: Hauntology and the Spanish Civil War in Guillermo del Toro's *The Devil's Backbone*." *Journal of the Fantastic in the Arts* 15.2 (2005): 119–31.

Harguindey, Ángel S. "Entrevista: Pedro Almodóvar." *El País* Mar. 17, 2003. http://www.elpais.com/.

Harrison, Robert Pogue. *The Dominion of the Dead*. Chicago: University of Chicago Press, 2003.

Harvey, Jessamy. "The Value of Nostalgia: Reviving Memories of National-Catholic Childhoods." *Journal of Spanish Cultural Studies* 2.1 (2001): 109–18.

Heras, Agustín Martínez de las. "El discurso antimasónico de *Los Hijos del Pueblo*." *La masonería en la España del siglo XX*. Ed. José Antonio Ferrer Benimeli. 2 vols. Toledo: Universidad de Castilla-La Mancha, 1996. 713–50.

Hermet, Guy. *Los católicos en la España franquista II: Crónica de una dictadura*. Madrid: CIS-Siglo XXI, 1986.

Herrera Oria, Enrique. *Los cautivos de Vizcaya: Memorias del P. Enrique Herrera Oria, S.J., preso durante cuatro meses y medio en la cárcel de Bilbao y condenado a ocho años y un día de prisión*. Bilbao: Aldus S. A., 1938.

Herrmann, Gina. "Documentary's Labours of Law: The Television Journalism of Montse Armengou and Ricard Belis." *The Politics of Memory in Contemporary Spain*. Ed. Jo Labanyi. Special issue of *Journal of Spanish Cultural Studies* 9.2 (2008): 193–212.

Hertz, Robert. "Contribution à une étude sur la représéntation collective de la mort." *L'Année Sociologique* 10 (1905–1906): 48–137.

———. *Death and the Right Hand*. Aberdeen: Cohen and West, 1960.

Hill, Jonathan D., ed. *Rethinking History and Myth*. Chicago: University of Illinois Press, 1988.

Hills, George. *Franco: The Man and His Nation*. New York: Macmillan, 1967.

Honig, Bonnie. *Democracy and the Foreigner*. Princeton: Princeton University Press, 2001.

Iglesia, Vincent Comes. *En el filo de la navaja: Biografía política de Luis Lucía Lucía (1888–1943)*. Madrid: Biblioteca Nueva, 2002.

Iranzu, Xavier de [Manuel de Irujo]. "The Republic in the Church." *Euzkadi* May 26, 1938.

Iribarren, José María. *El general Mola*. Madrid: Editorial Bullón, 1963.

Irujo, Manuel de. Unpublished Letter to Vidal i Barraquer. July 4, 1938. Archivo Vidal i Barraquer. Barcelona: Abadía de Montserrat, 1971–1977.

Iturralde, Juan. *El catolicismo y la cruzada de Franco*. Vol. 3. [Bayonne]: Editorial Egui-Indarra, 1955.

Izquierdo Martín, Jesús, and Pablo Sánchez León. *La guerra que nos han contado: 1936 y nosotros*. Madrid: Alianza, 2006.

Jackson, Julian. Introduction. *Europe 1900–1945*. Ed. Julian Jackson. Oxford: Oxford University Press, 2002. 1–15.

Jelin, Elizabeth. *State Repression and the Labors of Memory*. Minneapolis: University of Minnesota Press, 2003.

Jiménez, David Prieto. "Aproximación a la represión física durante la posguerra en Cuenca capital (1939–1945)." *El franquismo: El régimen y la oposición. Actas de las IV Jornadas de Castilla-La Mancha sobre investigaciones en Archivos*. Vol. 2. Guadalajara: Anabad Castilla-La Mancha, 2000.

Jiménez, Ignacio Martín. *La guerra civil en Valladolid (1936–1939)*. Valladolid: Ambito, 2000.

Jiménez Asúa, Luis, Juan-Simeón Vidarte, Antonio Rodríguez Sastre, and Anselmo Trejo. *Castilblanco*. Madrid: Editorial España, 1933.

Jiménez Campo, Javier. *El fascismo en la crisis de la Segunda República española*. Madrid: Centro de Investigaciones Sociológicas, 1979.

Juliá, Santos. "De la 'Guerra Contra el Invasor' a la 'Guerra Fratricida.'" Juliá, *Victimas* 11–54.

———. "Echar al olvido: Memoria y amnistía en la transición." *Claves de Razón Práctica* 129 (2003): 14–25.

———. "Toda la historia." *El País* Sept. 19, 2004. http://www.elpais.com/.

———, ed. *Víctimas de la guerra civil.* 1999. Madrid: Ediciones Temas de Hoy, 2006.

Junquera, Natalia, and Luis Gómez. "Juicio a la barbarie." *El País* Sept. 14, 2008: 2–4.

Junta Interministerial para la Conmemoración del XXV Aniversario de la Paz Española. *25 Aniversario de la paz española: El gobierno informa.* Madrid: Junta Interministerial Conmemoradora, 1964.

Karl, Mauricio. *Asesinos de España: Marxismo, Anarquismo, Masonería.* Madrid: Ediciones Bergua, 1935.

Kellner, Hans. "Language and Historical Representation." *The Postmodern History Reader.* Ed. Keith Jenkins. New York: Routledge, 1997. 127–38.

Kleinman, Arthur, Veena Das, and Margaret Lock. Introduction. *Social Suffering.* Ed. Arthur Kleinman, Veena Das, and Margaret Lock. Berkeley: University of California Press, 1997. ix–xxvii.

———, and Joan Kleinman. "Lo moral, lo político y lo médico: Una visión socio-somática del sufrimiento." *Psiquiatría transcultural.* Ed. E. González and J. M. Comelles. Madrid: Asociación Española de Neuropsiquiatría, 2000. 13–35.

Kolbert, Elizabeth. "Looking for Lorca." *New Yorker* Dec. 22, 2003: 64–75.

Krystal, Henry. "Studies of Concentration-Camp Survivors." *Massive Psychic Trauma.* Ed. Henry Krystal. New York: International Universities Press, 1968. 23–46.

Labanyi, Jo. "Engaging with Ghosts; or, Theorizing Culture in Modern Spain." *Constructing Identity in Contemporary Spain: Theoretical Debates and Cultural Practices.* Ed. Jo Labanyi. Oxford: Oxford University Press, 2002. 1–14.

———. "Entrevista con Emilio Silva." *The Politics of Memory in Contemporary Spain.* Ed. Jo Labanyi. Special issue of *Journal of Spanish Cultural Studies* 9.2 (2008): 143–55.

———. "History and Hauntology; or, What Does One Do with the Ghosts of the Past? Reflections on Spanish Film and Fiction of the Post-Franco Period." *Disremembering the Dictatorship: The Politics of Memory since the Spanish Transition to Democracy.* Ed. Joan Ramon Resina. Amsterdam: Rodopi, 2000. 65–82.

———. "Memory and Modernity in Democratic Spain: The Difficulty of Coming to Terms with the Spanish Civil War." *Poetics Today* 28.1 (2007): 89–116.

———. "The Politics of Memory in Contemporary Spain." *Journal of Spanish Cultural Studies* 9.2 (2008): 119–125.

LaCapra, Frederick. "Acting-Out and Working-Through." *Representing the Holocaust: History, Theory, Trauma.* Ithaca: Cornell University Press, 1994. 205–23.

Lanero, Mónica. *Una milicia de justicia: La política judicial del franquismo (1936–1945).* Madrid: Centro de Estudios Constitucionales, 1996.

Langdon-Davies, John. *Air Raid: The Technique of Silent Approach, High Explosive, Panic.* London: Routledge and Sons, 1938.

Lannon, Frances. *Privilege, Persecution, and Prophecy: The Catholic Church in Spain, 1875–1975.* Oxford: Clarendon Press, 1987.

Las fosas del olvido. Dir. Alfonso Domingo and Itziar Bernaola. Realización de Israel Sánchez Prieto. TV2 Documentos. 2004.

Lechner, Norbert. *Las sombras del mañana: La dimensión subjetiva de la política.* Santiago: LOM Ediciones, 2002.

Ledesma Ramos, Ramiro. "El 'caso' Valladolid." *La Patria Libre* (1935). Rpt. in *Escritos políticos 1935–1936* by Ramiro Ledesma Ramos. Madrid: Herederos de Ramiro Ledesma Ramos, 1988.

Leguineche, Manuel, and Jesús Torbado. *Los topos.* Barcelona: Argos, 1977.

Lemkin, Rafael. Nuremberg Trials of Nazi Crimes. Resolution 96(1), General Assembly of the United Nations, Convention on the Prevention and Punishment of the Crime of Genocide. Resolution 260A III. Dec. 9, 1948.

León-Portilla, Miguel. *The Broken Spears: The Aztec Account of the Conquest of Mexico.* Boston: Beacon Press, 1962.

Les fosses del silenci I & II (Las fosas del silencio). 30 Minuts. Dir. Monste Armengou and Ricard Belis. TV3, Televisió de Cataluyna, S. A. March 2003.

Levi, Primo. *Los hundidos y los salvados.* Barcelona: Muchnik Editores, 1989.

———. *La tregua.* Barcelona: El Aleph Editores, 1988.

———. *Si esto es un hombre.* Barcelona: El Aleph Editores, 1987.

Ley de 4 de diciembre de 1941 sobre Inscripción en Registro Civil de niños repatriados y abandonados. Jefatura del estado. *BOE* Dec. 16, 1941, núm. 350, p. 9819.

Ley de 23 de noviembre de 1940 sobre Protección de huérfanos de la revolución y la guerra. Decreto del Ministerio de Gobernación *BOE* Dec. 1, 1940, núm. 336, p. 8253.

"Una ley que enfrenta a los españoles sin reparar nada." *El Mundo* Dec. 15, 2006. http://www.elmundo.es/papel/2006/12/15/opinion/2061387.html.

"Un líder de optimismo blindado y con un profundo compromiso socialista." *El Mundo* March 10, 2008. http://www.clarin.com/diario/2008/03/10/elmundo/i-02201.htm.

Una memoria histórica que no contenta a nadie." *El Mundo* July 29, 2006. http://www.elmundo.es/papel/2006/07/29/opinion/2005634.html.

Lincoln, Bruce. "Revolutionary Exhumations in Spain, July 1936." *Comparative Studies in Society and History* 27 (1985): 241–60.

Lopategui, José Ignacio, ed. *Aita Patxi: Testimonio*. 2 vols. Bilboa: Gráficas Bilbao, 1978 and 1984.

López Fernández, Antonio. *Defensa de Madrid*. México D. F.: Editorial A. P. Márquez, 1945.

Loraux, Nicole. *Mothers in Mourning*. Trans. Corinne Pache. Ithaca: Cornell University Press, 1998.

Lorente Acosta, José Antonio. "Exhumar no es identificar." *El País* Oct. 6, 2008. http://www.elpais.com/.

Loureiro, Ángel. "Pathetic Arguments." *The Politics of Memory in Contemporary Spain*. Ed. Jo Labanyi. Special issue of *Journal of Spanish Cultural Studies* 9.2 (2008): 225–37.

Luis, Francisco de. *La masonería contra España*. Burgos: Imprenta Aldecoa, 1935.

Luzán, Julia. "La guerra en primera plana." *El País* Nov. 12, 2006. http://www.elpais.com/.

Maeztu, Ramiro de. *Defensa de la Hispanidad*. 4th ed. Madrid: Editorial Cultura Española, 1941.

Maier, Charles S. "Consigning the Twentieth Century to History: Alternative Narratives for the Modern Era." *American Historical Review* 105 (2000): 807–31.

Mainer, José-Carlos. "Cadáveres en el armario." *El País* Oct. 14, 2006: 3.

Maíz, B. Félix. *Alzamiento en España, de un diario de la conspiración*. Pamplona: [Editorial Gomez], 1952.

———. *Mola, aquel hombre*. Barcelona: Planeta, 1976.

Marías, Javier. "Un país grotesco." *El País semanal* Sept. 10, 2006: n.p.

Maritain, Jacques. Preface. *The Martyrdom of Spain*. By Alfred Mendizábal. London: Geoffrey Bles, 1938. 1–48.

Martin, Claude. *Franco, soldado y estadista*. Madrid: Fermín Uriarte, 1966.

Martín Rubio, Ángel David. *Paz, Piedad, Perdón . . . y Verdad: La represión en la guerra civil: Una síntesis definitiva*. Madrid: Editorial Fénix, 1997.

Martínez-Alier, Juan. *La estabilidad del latifundismo, análisis de la interdependencia entre relaciones de producción y conciencia social en la agricultura latifundista de la Campiña de Córboba [sic pour Córdoba]*. Paris: Ediciones Ruedo Ibérico, 1968.

[Martínez de Bedoya, Javier]. *Onésimo Redondo Caudillo de Castilla*. Valladolid: Ediciones Libertad, 1937.

Martínez de Campos, Carlos. *Ayer 1931–1953*. Madrid: Instituto de Estudios Políticos, 1970.

Martínez Reverte, Jorge, and Socorro Thomás. *Hijos de la guerra: Testimonios y recuerdos*. Madrid: Temas de Hoy, 2001.

Mate, Reyes. "Lugares de memoria." *El País*. Apr. 12, 2004: 12.

Mateo Díez, Luis. *Fantasmas del Invierno*. Madrid: Alfaguara, 2004.

McEvoy, Kieran, and Heather Conway. "The Dead, the Law, and the Politics of the Past." *Journal of Law and Society* 31.4 (2004): 539–62.

Medina, Alberto. *Exorcismos de la memoria: Política y poética de la memoria en la España de la transición*. Madrid: Libertarias-Prodhui, 2001.

Menand, Louis. "Nanook and Me: 'Fahrenheit 9/11' and the Documentary Tradition." *New Yorker* Aug. 9, 2004. http://www.newyorker.com/archive/2004/08/09/040809crat_atlarge.

Milner, Irish. "Writing and the Holocaust: Problematics of Representation in the Second-Generation Literature in Israel." *Journal of Israeli History* 22.1 (Mar. 2003): 91–108.

Minguez Goyanes, Jose Luis. *Onésimo Redondo (1905–1936): Precursor sindicalista*. Madrid: Editorial San Martin, 1990.

Mir, Conxita, ed. *Repressió econòmica i franquisme: L'actuació del tribunal de responsabilitats polítiques a la província de Lleida*. Barcelona: Publicacions de l'Abadia de Montserrat, 1997.

———. "Violencia política, coacción legal y oposición interior." *El primer franquismo (1936–1959)*. Ed. Glicerio Sánchez Recio. *Ayer* 33 (1999): 115–45.

———. *Vivir es sobrevivir: Justicia, orden y marginación en la Cataluña rural de posguerra*. Lérida: Milenio, 2000.

Moa, Pío. *Los crímenes de la guerra civil y otras polémicas*. Madrid: La Esfera de los Libros, 2004.

———. *El derrumbe de la segunda república y la guerra civil*. Madrid: Encuentro Ediciones, 2001.

———. "Un Consejo a Gibson." Oct. 9, 2007. http://www.libertaddigital.com/opiniones/opinion_38787.html.

Mola Vidal, Emilio. *Obras completas*. Valladolid: Librería Santarén, 1940.

Molinero, Carme, and Pere Ysàs. *"Patria, Justicia y Pan." Nivel de vida i condicions de treball a Catalunya, 1939–1959*. Barcelona: Edicions de la Magrana, 1985.

Monge i Bernal, José. *Acción Popular (Estudios de biología política)*. Madrid: Imp. Sáez Hermanos, 1936.

Montero, José R. *La CEDA: El catolicismo social y político en la II República*. Madrid: Ediciones de la Revista de Trabajo, 1977.

Montero Moreno, Antonio. *Historia de la Persecución Religiosa en España, 1936–1939*. Madrid: Biblioteca de Autores Cristianos, 1961.

Mora, Antoni. "Joan Tusquets, en els 90 anys d'un home d'estudi i de combat." *Anuari 1990–1991 de la Societat d'Història Eclesiàstica Moderna i Contemporània de Catalunya*. Ed. Institut d'Estudis Tarraconenses Ramón Berenguer IV. Tarragona: Diputació de Tarragona, 1992.

Moradiellos, Enrique. *La España de Franco (1939–1975): Política y sociedad*. Madrid: Síntesis, 2000.

Moreno, Francisco. "La represión en la posguerra." Juliá, *Víctimas* 277–405.

Morente Valero, Francisco. *La escuela y el estado nuevo: La depuración del Magisterio Nacional (1936–1943)*. Valladolid: Ámbito, 1997.

Morris, David B. *The Culture of Pain*. Berkeley: University of California Press, 1991.

Moulian, Tomás. *Chile actual: Anatomía de un mito*. 3rd ed. Santiago: LOM Ediciones, 2002.

Nadal, Joaquín María de. *Seis años con don Francisco Cambó (1930–1936): Memorias de un secretario político*. Barcelona: Editorial Alpha, 1957.

Nadal Sánchez, Antonio. "Experiencias psíquicas sobre mujeres marxistas malagueñas. Málaga, 1939." *Baética: Estudios de Arte, Geografía e Historia* 10 (1987): 365–83. Reprinted in *Las mujeres y la guerra civil española*. Madrid: Ministerio de Trabajo y Asuntos Sociales, Instituto de la Mujer, 1991. 340–50.

Els nens perduts del franquisme (Los niños perdidos del franquismo) I & II. 30 Minuts. Dir. Ricard Vinyes, Montserrat Armengou, and Ricard Belis. Televisió de Catalunya, S. A. Barcelona. January 20, 27, 2002.

Nichols, Bill. *Representing Reality: Issues and Concepts in Documentary*. Bloomington: Indiana University Press, 1991.

———. "The Voice of Documentary." *Film Quarterly* 36.3 (Spring 1983): 17–30. Rpt. in *Film Quarterly: Forty Years, a Selection*. Ed. Bill Henderson and Ann Martin. Berkeley: University of California Press, 1999. 246–67.

Nicolás, María Encarna. *Instituciones murcianas en el franquismo (1939–1962)*. Murcia: Editora Regional de Murcia, 1982.

Niethammer, Lutz. *Posthistoire: Has History Come to an End?* Trans. Patrick Camiller. London: Verso, 1992.

"No a la Revisión Parcial de la Historia." *El Mundo* July 20, 2005.

Nora, Pierre. *Les Lieux de Mémoire*. 7 vols. Paris: Gallimard, 1983–1994.

Núñez Seixas, Xosé-Manoel. "Nations in Arms Against the Invader: On Nationalist Discourses during the Spanish Civil War." Ealham and Richards 45–67.

Olaechea Loizaga, Marcelino. *BOE de Pamplona* Dec. 12, 1936: 429–31.

Onaindia, Alberto. "Letter to Cardinal Gomá." Apr. 28, 1937. Andrés and Pazos 382–84.

Ortiz Villalba, Juan. *Sevilla 1936: Del golpe militar a la guerra civil*. Sevilla: Diputación Provincial, 1997.

Orwell, George. *Mi guerra civil española*. Barcelona: Destino, 1978.

Ovejero Bernal, Anastasio. "Memoria, emoción y afectos: traumas psicosociales en las víctimas del franquismo." *La Represión Franquista: Mito, olvido y memoria*. Asociación para la Recuperación de la Memoria Histórica de Valladolid y Palencia. Valladolid: Universidad de Valladolid, Centro Buendía, 2006. 67–83.

Pasamar, Gonzalo. *Historiografía e ideología en la postguerra española: La ruptura de la tradición liberal*. Zaragoza: Prensas Universitarias de Zaragoza, 1991.

Pavone, Claudio. "The Two Levels of Public Use of the Past." *Mediterranean Historical Review* 16 (2001): 74–86.

Payne, Stanley G. *El catolicismo español.* Barcelona: Planeta, 1984.

———. *The Spanish Civil War, the Soviet Union and Communism.* New Haven: Yale University Press, 2004.

Pedreño, José María. "Apoyar a la ARMH es enterrar la memoria." Jan. 23, 2004. Foro por la Memoria. http://www.nodo50.org/foroporlamemoria/documentos/jmpedreno_23012004.htm.

Peiró, Francisco X. *Fernando Huidobro, jesuita y legionario.* Madrid: Espasa-Calpe, 1951.

Pemán, José María. *El hecho y la idea de la Unión Patriótica.* Madrid: Imprenta Artística Sáez Hermanos, 1929.

Pérez, Isaac Rilova. *Guerra civil y violencia política en Burgos (1936–1943).* Burgos: Editorial Dossoles, 2001.

Pérez del Pulgar, José Antonio. *La solución que España da al problema de sus presos.* 1939.

Pérez Oliva, Milagros. "Manuel Rivas: El guardián de la memoria." *El País semanal* Nov. 5, 2006: 12–18.

Pingree, Geoff, and Lisa Abend. "Homage to Catalonia." *Nation* Mar. 28, 2005: 20–24.

Plenary Assembly of the Spanish Bishops' Conference. "Orientaciones morales ante la situación actual de España." Nov. 23, 2006. http://www.conferencia episcopal.es/DOCUMENTOS/Conferencia/OrientacionesSituacionActual .htm.

"Polémica propuesta del gobierno para los restos de los fusilado por el Franquismo." *El periódico de Catalunya* Jan. 23, 2006. http://www.elperiodico.com.

Portelli, Alessandro. "What Makes Oral History different?" *The Oral History Reader.* Ed. R. Perks and A. Thomson. London: Routledge, 1998. 63–74.

Prado, Benjamín. "¿Por qué viva Franco?" *El País* Nov. 15, 2007. http://www .elpais.com/.

Prado Moura, Ángel de. *El movimiento obrero en Valladolid durante la Segunda República.* Valladolid: Junta de Castilla y León, 1985.

Preston, Paul. *The Coming of the Spanish Civil War: Reform, Reaction and Revolution in the Second Republic.* 2nd rev. ed. New York: Routledge, 1994.

———. *Doves of War: Four Women of Spain.* London: HarperCollins, 2002.

———. *Franco.* New York: Basic Books, 1994.

———. *Las tres Españas del 36.* Barcelona: Plaza & Janés, 1998.

Price, Richard. *First-Time: The Historical Vision of an African American People.* 2nd ed. Chicago: University of Chicago Press, 2002.

Protocolos de los Sabios de Sión. Valladolid: Libertad/Afrodisio Aguado, 1934.

Radosh, Ronald, et al., eds. *Spain Betrayed: The Soviet Union in the Spanish Civil War.* New Haven: Yale University Press, 2001.

Raguer Suñer, Hilari. "L'altre fill del general Moscardó." *L'Avenç: Revista de Història i Cultura* 249 (2000): 14–19.

———. "El bisbe Guitart i les autoritats franquistes." *Anuari 1990–1991 de la Societat d'Estudis d'Història Eclesiàstica Moderna i Contemporània de Catalunya*. Tarragona: Diputació Provincial de Tarragona, Inst. Estudis Tarraconenses Ramón Berenguer IV, 1992. 249–65.

———. *Divendres de Passió: Vida i mort de Manuel Carrasco i Formiguera*. Barcelona: Publicacions de l'Abadia de Montserrat, 1984.

———. *Gunpowder and Incense: The Catholic Church and the Spanish Civil War*. London: Routledge, 2007.

———. *La pólvora y el incienso: La Iglesia y la guerra civil española (1936–1939)*. Barcelona: Península, 2001.

———. Review of *Historia de la persecución religiosa en España 1936–1939*, by Antonio Montero Moreno. *Revue d Histoire Ecclésiastique* 57 (1962): 618–30.

———. *Salvador Rial, Vicari del Cardenal de la pau*. Barcelona: Publicacions de l'Abadia de Montserrat, 1993.

———. "La Santa Sede y los bombardeos de Barcelona." *Historia y Vida* 145 (1980): 22–35.

———. *La Unió Democràtica de Catalunya i el seu temps (1931–1939)*. Barcelona: Publicaciones de l'Abadia de Montserrat, 1976.

Ranzato, Gabriele. *El pasado de bronce: La herencia de la guerra civil en la España democrática*. Barcelona: Destino, 2006.

Rappaport, Joanne. *The Politics of Memory*. Cambridge: Cambridge University Press, 1990.

Redondo, Onésimo. "El autor y el precursor de los 'Protocolos.'" *Obras completas. Edición cronológica II*. Madrid: Publicaciones Españolas, 1955.

———. *El Estado Nacional*. Barcelona: Ediciones FE, 1939.

———. "El regreso de la barbarie." *JONS Antología*. Ed. Juan Aparicio Barcelona: Editora Nacional, 1933.

Reig Tapia, Alberto. *Memoria de la Guerra Civil: Los mitos de la tribu*. Madrid: Alianza Editorial, 1999.

Renov, Michael. "Toward a Poetics of Documentary." *Theorizing Documentary*. New York: Routledge, 1993. 12–36.

Resina, Joan Ramon, ed. *Disremembering the Dictatorship: The Politics of Memory in the Spanish Transition to Democracy*. Amsterdam: Rodopi, 2000.

———. "Window of Opportunity: The Television Documentary as 'After-Image' of the War." *Teaching Representations of the Spanish Civil War*. Ed. Noël Valis. New York: Modern Language Association, 2007. 406–24.

Richard, Nelly. *Cultural Residues: Chile in Transition*. Minneapolis: University of Minnesota Press, 2004.

Richards, Michael. "From War Culture to Civil Society." *History and Memory* 14.1–2 (2002): 93–120.

————. "Morality and Biology in the Spanish Civil War: Psychiatrists, Revolution and Women Prisoners in Málaga." *Contemporary European History* 10 (2001): 395–421.

————. "'Presenting Arms to the Blessed Sacrament': Civil War and Semana Santa in the City of Málaga, 1936–1939." Ealham and Richards 196–222.

————. *Un tiempo de silencio: La guerra civil y la cultura de la represión en la España de Franco, 1936–1945.* Barcelona: Crítica, 1999.

Ricoeur, Paul. *Critique and Conviction: Conversations with François Azouvi and Marc de Launay.* Trans. Kathleen Blamey. New York: Columbia University Press, 1998.

Riera, Ignasi. *Los catalanes de Franco.* Barcelona: Plaza y Janés, 1998.

Robben, Antonius C. G. M. "The Assault on Basic Trust: Disappearance, Protest, and Reburial in Argentina." *Cultures under Siege: Collective Violence and Trauma.* Ed. Antonius C. G. M. Robben and Marcelo M. Suárez-Orozco. Cambridge: Cambridge University Press, 2000. 70–101.

————, ed. *Death, Mourning, and Burial: A Cross-Cultural Reader.* Malden, MA: Blackwell, 2004.

————. "How Traumatized Societies Remember: The Aftermath of Argentina's Dirty War." *Cultural Critique* 59 (2005): 120–64.

————. *Political Violence and Trauma in Argentina.* Philadelphia: University of Pennsylvania Press, 2005.

————. "State Terror in the Netherworld: Disappearance and Reburial in Argentina." Robben, *Death* 134–48.

Robinson, Paul. *The White Russian Army in Exile, 1920–1941.* Oxford: Clarendon Press, 2002.

Rodríguez Puértolas, Julio. *Literatura fascista española.* 2 vols. Madrid: Ediciones Akal, 1986–1987.

Rojas Marcos, Luis. "Por favor, hablad." *El País* Mar. 15, 2004. http://www.elpais.com/.

Romano, Sergio. *Due fronti: La grande polemica sulla guerra di Spagna.* Florence: Liberal Libri, 1998.

Roniger, Luis, and Mario Sznajder. "The Politics of Memory and Oblivion in Redemocratized Argentina and Uruguay." *History & Memory* 10 (1998): 133–69.

Rosaldo, R. *Ilongot Headhunting, 1883–1974: A Study in Society and History.* Stanford: Stanford University Press, 1980.

Rubia Barcia, José. *Prosas de razón y hiel: Desde el exilio, desmitificando al Franquismo y ensoñando una España mejor.* Caracas, Venezuela: Casuz Editores, 1976.

Ruiz Portella, Javier, ed. *La guerra civil: ¿Dos o tres Españas?* Barcelona: Ediciones Altera, 1999.

Ruiz Rico, Juan José. *El papel político de la Iglesia católica en la España de Franco (1936–1971)*. Madrid: Tecnos, 1977.

Ruiz Villaplana, Antonio. *Doy fe . . . un año de actuación en la España nacionalista*. Paris: Editions Imprimerie cooperative Etoile, 1937.

S., Benilde (pseudonym). Personal interview conducted by Ignacio Fernández de Mata. Apr. 16, 2003.

Sáinz Rodríguez, Pedro. *Testimonio y recuerdos*. Barcelona: Planeta, 1978.

Salas Larrázabal, Ramón. *Los datos exactos de la guerra civil española*. Madrid: Drácena, 1980.

———. *Pérdidas de la Guerra*. Barcelona: Editorial Planeta, 1977.

Sánchez, Isidro, Manuel Ortiz, and David Ruiz, eds. *España franquista: Causa general y actitudes sociales ante la dictadura*. Albacete: Ediciones de la Universidad de Castilla La-Mancha, Servicio de Publicaciones, 1993.

Sánchez, Manuel. "Emotivo homenaje a las víctimas de Franco en el Congreso." *El Mundo* Dec. 2, 2003. http://www.elmundo.es.

Sánchez, Sarah. *Fact and Fiction: Representations of the Asturian Revolution (1934–1938)*. Leeds: Maney Publishing for the Modern Humanities Research Association, 2003.

Sánchez Diana, José María. *Ramiro Ledesma Ramos: Biografía política*. Madrid: Editora Nacional, 1975.

Sánchez Recio, Glicerio. *De las dos ciudades a la resurrección de España: Magisterio pastoral y pensamiento político de Enrique Pla y Deniel*. Valladolid: Juan Gi-Albert y Ambito Ediciones, 1994.

Sanz de Diego, Rafael Ma. "Actitud del P. Huidobro ante la ejecución de prisioneros en la guerra civil: Nuevos datos." *Estudios Eclesiásticos* 60 (1985): 443–84.

Satorras Pons, Alícia. "*Soldados de Salamina* de Javier Cercas, reflexiones sobre los héroes." *Revista Hispánica Moderna* 56 (2003): 227–45.

Scarry, Elaine. *The Body in Pain: The Making and Unmaking of the World*. New York: Oxford University Press, 1985.

———. "Injury and the Structure of War." *Representations* 10 (1985): 1–51.

———. *Resisting Representation*. New York: Oxford University Press, 1994.

Sciolino, Elaine, and Emma Daly. "Spaniards at Last Confront the Ghost of Franco." *New York Times* Nov. 11, 2002: A3.

Seidman, Michael. *Republic of Egos: A Social History of the Spanish Civil War*. Madison: University of Wisconsin Press, 2002.

Semelin, Jacques. "Violencias extremas: ¿Es posible comprender?" *Revista Internacional de Ciencias Sociales* 174 (Dec. 2002). http://www.unesco.org/issj/rics174/Fulltext174spa.pdf.

Semprún, Jorge. *La escritura o la vida*. Barcelona: Círculo de Lectores, 1995.

———. *El largo viaje*. Barcelona: Seix Barral, 1994.

———. *Viviré con su nombre, morirá con el mío*. Barcelona: Tusquets, 2001.

Sennott, Charles. "Via a Grave Site, Spain Relives Harsh Divisions." *Boston Globe* Aug. 22, 2004: A6.

Serrano Suñer, Ramón. *Entre el silencio y la propaganda, la historia como fue. Memorias.* Barcelona: Planeta, 1977.

———. "Prólogo." *Masonería y pacifistas.* By Juan Tusquets. Burgos: Ediciones Antisectarias, 1939.

Sharpe, Jim. "History from Below." *New Perspectives on Historical Writing.* Ed. Peter Burke. Oxford: Blackwell, 1994. 25–42.

Silva Barrera, Emilio, and Santiago Macías. *Las fosas de Franco: Los republicanos que el dictador dejó en las cunetas.* Madrid: Temas de hoy, 2003.

Sivan, Emmanuel. "Private Pain and Public Remembrance in Israel." Winter and Sivan, *War* 177–204.

Skoutelsky, Rémi. *Novedad en el frente: Las Brigadas Internacionales en la guerra civil.* Madrid: Temas de Hoy, 2005.

Solé i Sabaté, Joseph M., and José María Villaroya. "Mayo de 1937–Abril de 1939." Juliá *Víctimas* 187–273.

Song, H. Rosi. "El patriotismo constitucional o la dimensión mnemotécnica de una nación." *Casa encantada: Lugares de memoria en la España constitucional (1978–2004).* Ed. Joan Ramon Resina and Ulrich Winter. Frankfurt am Main: Vervuert, 2005. 223–39.

Sontag, Susan. *Regarding the Pain of Others.* New York: Farrar, Straus and Giroux, 2003.

Sophocles. *Antigone.* Trans. Robert Whitelaw. *Fifteen Greek Plays.* New York: Oxford University Press, 1943. 211–48.

Southworth, Herbert. *Conspiracy and the Spanish Civil War: The Brainwashing of Francisco Franco.* London: Routledge, 2002.

———. *El mito de la cruzada de Franco.* Paris: Ruedo Ibérico, 1964.

Souto Blanco, Maria Jesus. *La represión franquista en la provincia de Lugo (1936–1940).* Sada, A Coruña: Edicios do Castro, 1998.

Spanish Episcopate. *Constructores de paz.* Feb. 20, 1986.

Steedly, Mary. *Hanging Without a Rope: Narrative Experience in Colonial and Postcolonial Karoland.* Princeton: Princeton University Press, 1993.

Stepan, John J. *The Russian Fascists: Tragedy and Farce in Exile 1925–1945.* London: Hamish Hamilton, 1978.

Stewart, Susan. "What Praise Poems Are For." *PMLA* 120.1 (2005): 235–45.

Stover, Eric, and Harvey Weinstein, eds. *My Neighbor, My Enemy: Justice and Community in the Aftermath of Mass Atrocity.* Cambridge: Cambridge University Press, 2004.

Suárez Fernández, Luis. *Francisco Franco y su tiempo.* 8 vols. Madrid: Fundación Nacional Francisco Franco, 1984.

Subirà, Joan. *Capellans en temps de Franco.* Barcelona: Editorial Mediterrània, 1996.

"Los sucesos de Badajoz." *El Imparcial,* Jan. 2, 1932.

Sueiro, Daniel. *El Valle de los Caídos: Los secretos de la cripta franquista.* 1976. Madrid: La Esfera de los Libros, 2006.

Suleiman, Susan Rubin. *Crises of Memory and the Second World War.* Cambridge: Harvard University Press, 2006.

Sztompka, Piotr. "Cultural Trauma: The Other Side of Social Change." *European Journal of Social Theory* 3 (2000): 449–66.

Taussig, Michael. "Culture of Terror, Space of Death: Roger's Casement's Putumayo Report and the Explanation of Torture." *Violence in War and Peace: An Anthology.* Ed. Nancy Scheper-Hughes and Philippe Bourgois. Malden, MA: Blackwell, 2004. 39–53.

———. *Shamanism, Colonialism and the Wild Man: A Study in Terror and Healing.* Chicago: University of Chicago Press, 1987.

Tello Lázaro, José Angel. *Ideología y política: La Iglesia católica española, 1936–1959.* Zaragoza: Pórtico, 1984.

Tesón Martín, N. "AI reclama justica para los represaliados de la Guerra Civil." *El País* July 19, 2005. http://www.elpais.com/.

Thomas, Hugh. *La guerra civil española, 1936–1939.* Barcelona: Ediciones Éxito, 1978.

Toro Muñoz, Francisco Miguel de. "Policía, denuncia y control social: Alemania y Austria durante el Tercer Reich." *Historia Social* 34 (1999): 117–34.

Torrent, Martín. *¿Qué me dice Usted de los presos?* Alcalá de Henares: Imprenta Talleres Penitenciarios, 1942.

Torres, Francesc. "The Images of Memory: A Civil Narration of History: A Photo Essay." *Journal of Spanish Cultural Studies* 9.2 (2008): 157–75.

"La tragedia de Castilblanco." *El Faro de Extremadura* (Plasencia), Jan. 9, 1932.

"La tragedia de Castilblanco." *La Opinión* (Trujilo), Jan. 7, 1932.

Tremlett, Giles. *Ghosts of Spain: Travels Through Spain and Its Silent Past.* London: Faber and Faber, 2006.

Tusell, Javier. *Franco y los católicos: La política interior española entre 1945 y 1957.* Madrid: Alianza Editorial, 1984.

———. "La Iglesia y la guerra civil." *La guerra civil Española.* Vol. 16. Ed. Manuel Tuñón de Lara. Madrid: Historia 16, 1986.

———. "El revisionismo histórico español." *El País* July 8, 2004. http://www.elpais.com/.

Tusquets, Juan. *Masones y pacifistas.* Burgos: Ediciones Antisectarias, 1939.

———. *Orígenes de la revolución española.* Barcelona: Editorial Vilamala, 1932.

———. *Los poderes ocultos en España: Los Protocolos y su aplicación a España—Infiltraciones masónicas en el catalanismo—¿El señor Macià es masón?* Barcelona: Editorial Vilamala, Biblioteca Las Sectas, 1932.

Upton, Anthony F. *The Finnish Revolution 1917–1918.* The Nordic Series 3. Minneapolis: University of Minnesota Press, 1980.

Valdés, Francisco. "Márgenes: El Afincado." *La Voz Extremeña* (Badajoz), Jan. 10, 1932.

Valdes, Rafael. *Fernando Huidobro: Intelectual y héroe.* Madrid: Editorial Apostolado de la Prensa, 1966.

El Valle de los Caídos: Lugar de reconciliación y de paz. Generalísimo Francisco Franco. 2005. http://www.generalisimofranco.com/valle_caidos/02_decreto.htm.

Vallejo Nágera, Antonio. *Eugenesia de la hispanidad y regeneración de la raza.* Burgos: Editorial Española, 1936.

———. "Psiquismo del fanatismo marxista." *Revista Semana Médica Española* 1.6 (Oct. 8, 1938).

Varela, Fernando. "Los Populares rechazan indeminzar a las víctimas gallegas del franquismo." *El País* Apr. 28, 2006: 25.

Vega, Pedro. *Historia de la Liga de Mutilados: Liga de mutilados e invalidos de la guerra de espana 1936–1939.* Madrid: Imprime M. C. Martinez, 1981.

Vegas Latapie, Eugenio. *Escritos políticos.* Madrid: Cultura Española, 1941.

———. "Maeztu y Acción Española." *ABC* 2. 1952.

———. *El Pensamiento político de Calvo Sotelo.* Madrid: Cultura Española, 1941.

Verdery, Katherine. *The Political Lives of Dead Bodies: Reburial and Postsocialist Change.* New York: Columbia University Press, 1999.

Vidal Castaño, José Antonio. *La memoria reprimida: Historias orales del maquis.* Valencia: Universitat de València, 2004.

Vidal i Barraquer, Francesc. *Arxiu. Esglesia i Estat durant la Segona República espanyola 1931/1936.* 4 vols. Monestir de Montserrat: Publicacions de l'Abadia de Montserrat, 1971–1990.

Vidarte, Juan Simeón. *El bienio negro y la insurrección de Asturias: Testimonio.* Barcelona: Grijalbo, 1978.

———. *Las Cortes Constituyentes de 1931–1933.* Barcelona: Grijalbo, 1976.

Vigón, Jorge. *General Mola (el conspirador).* Barcelona: Editorial AHR, 1957.

Vilanova, Mercedes. "Anarchism, Political Participation, and Illiteracy in Barcelona between 1934 and 1936." *American Historical Review* 97 (1992): 96–120.

Vilanova i Vila-Abadal, Francesc. *Les majories invisibles: Explotació fabril, revolució i repressió: 26 entrevistes.* Barcelona: Icaria, 1995.

———. *Repressió política i coacció econòmica: Les responsabilitats polítiques de republicans i conservadors catalans a la posguerra (1939–1942).* Barcelona: Publicacions de l'Abadia de Montserrat, 1999.

Vilar, Pierre. "Los franceses y la guerra de España." Colloquium, Perpignan, France. September 1989

Villacañas Berlanga, José Luis. *Ramiro de Maeztu y el ideal de la burguesía en España.* Madrid: Espasa Calpe, 2000.

Villarroya i Font, Joan. *Els bombardeigs de Barccelona Durant la Guerra civil (1936–1939).* Barcelona: Publicacions de l' Abadia de Montserrat, 1999.

Villena, Miguel Ángel. "Entre el miedo y la impunidad." *El País* Oct. 14, 2006: 4.

Vincent, Mary. *Catholicism in the Second Spanish Republic. Religion and Politics in Salamanca 1930–1936.* Oxford: Clarendon Press, 1996.

Vinyes, Ricard. "El estado y la restitución, hoy." *El País* Nov. 10, 2004. http://www.elpais.com/.

———. *Irredentas: Las presas políticas y sus hijos en las cárceles de Franco.* Madrid: Temas de Hoy, 2002.

———. "'Nada os pertenece . . .' Las presas de Barcelona, 1939–1945." *Historia Social* 39 (2001): 49–66.

———. "Territoris de cástig (les presons franquistas, 1939–1959)." *Notícia de la negra nit: Vides i veus a les presons franquistes, 1939–1959.* Barcelona: Diputacio de Barcelona, Xarxa de Municipis, 2001.

———, Montse Armengou, and Ricard Belis. *Los niños perdidos del franquismo* [*Franco's Forgotten Children*]. Barcelona: Plaza & Janes, 2003.

Wachtel, Nathan. *The Vision of the Vanquished: The Spanish Conquest of Peru through Indian Eyes, 1530–1570.* New York: Barnes and Noble Books, 1977.

Weinrich, Harald. *Lethe: The Art and Critique of Forgetting.* Trans. Steven Rendall. Ithaca: Cornell University Press, 2004.

White, Hayden. "Bodies and Their Plots." *Choreographing History.* Ed. S. L. Foster. Bloomington: Indiana University Press, 1995.

Wilkinson, Tracy. "Even in Death, Franco Has the Power to Divide Spaniards." *Los Angeles Times* Oct. 29, 2006.

Williams, Linda. "Mirrors without Memories: Truth, History, and the New Documentary." *Film Quarterly: Forty Years, A Selection.* Ed. Bill Henderson and Ann Martin. Berkeley: University of California Press, 1999. 308–27.

Winter, Jay, and Emmanuel Sivan, eds. *War and Remembrance in the Twentieth Century.* Cambridge: Cambridge University Press, 1999.

———. Introduction. Winter and Sivan, *War* 1–5.

Young, James. *The Texture of Memory: Holocaust Memorials and Meaning.* New Haven: Yale University Press, 1993.

Yushimoto del Valle, Carlos. "*Soldados de Salamina*: Indagaciones sobre un héroe moderno." *Espéculo: Revista de Estudios Literarios* 23 (2003). http://www.ucm.es/info/especulo/.

Zavala, José María. *Los gángsters de la guerra civil.* Barcelona: Plaza & Janés, 2006.

———. *Los horrores de la guerra civil.* Barcelona: Random House Mondadori, 2003.

About the Contributors

SAMUEL AMAGO is the author of *True Lies: Narrative Self-Consciousness in the Contemporary Spanish Novel* (Bucknell University Press, 2006). He teaches courses on modern Spanish fiction and film at the University of Notre Dame, where he is an associate professor in the Department of Romance Languages and Literatures.

MONTSE ARMENGOU MARTÍN is a television journalist for TV de Catalunya, Spain. She has directed documentaries and written accompanying books on the Spanish Civil War, such as *Los niños perdidos del franquismo* (with Ricard Vinyes and Ricard Belis, Debolsillo, 2003), *Las fosas del silencio* (with Ricard Belis, Plaza & Janés, 2004), and *El convoy de los 927* (with Ricard Belis, Plaza & Janés, 2005).

JULIÁN CASANOVA is professor of contemporary history at the University of Zaragoza (Spain). He is the author of *La Iglesia de Franco* (Crítica, 2005) and *De las calles al frente: El anarco-sindicalismo en España* (Crítica, 2007). He coauthored *Víctimas de la Guerra civil* (1999) and is a frequent contributor to Spain's *El País*.

IGNACIO FERNÁNDEZ DE MATA is associate professor of social anthropology at the University of Burgos (Spain). Relating to the subject of this volume, he has published "From Invisibility to Power: Spanish Victims and the Manipulation of their Symbolic Capital" in *Totalitarian Movements and Political Religions* (2008) and "Exorcizando la mala suerte: Esquelas y duelos inconclusos de 1936," in *La cultura tradicional en la sociedad del siglo XXI. IV Jornadas Nacionales Folclore y Sociedad* (Instituto Municipal de Cultura, 2009).

FRANCISCO FERRÁNDIZ holds the title of *científico titular* at the Instituto de Lengua, Literatura y Antropología (ILLA) at the Centro de Ciencias Humanas y Sociales (CCHS), and the Consejo Superior de Investigaciones Científicas (CSIC). He is the author of "Cries and Whispers: Exhuming and Narrating Defeat in Spain Today," *Journal of Spanish Cultural Studies* (2008), and "The Return of Civil War Ghosts: The Ethnography of Exhumations in Contemporary Spain," *Anthropology Today* (2006).

SOLEDAD FOX is associate professor of Romance languages at Williams College. She is the author of *Constancia de la Mora in War and Exile: International Voice for the Spanish Republic,* (Sussex, 2006) and "Análisis de *Para una crítica de la violencia* de Walter Benjamin," published in *Cultura Moderna* (Sevilla, 2006).

ANTONIO GÓMEZ LÓPEZ-QUIÑONES is assistant professor at Dartmouth College. He is the author of *Borges y el Nazismo: Sur (1937–1946)* (Universidad de Granada, 2004) and *La guerra persistente: Memoria violencia y utopía: Representaciones contemporáneas de la guerra civil española* (Vervuert/Iberoamericana, 2006).

ANNE E. HARDCASTLE is associate professor of Spanish and a member of the executive committee for the Film Studies program at Wake Forest University. Her most recent publications on contemporary Spanish fiction and film have appeared in *Film Criticism* and the *Vanderbilt e-Journal of Luso-Hispanic Studies.*

GINA HERRMANN is associate professor of Spanish literature at the University of Oregon. She is the author of *Written in Red: The Communist Memoir in Spain* (University of Illinois Press, 2010).

CARLOS JEREZ-FARRÁN is professor of Spanish at the University of Notre Dame. He is the author of *Un Lorca desconocido: Análisis de un teatro 'irrepresentable'* (Biblioteca Nueva, 2004) and, more recently, *La pasión de San Lorca y el placer de morir* (Visor, 2006).

JO LABANYI is professor of Spanish and director of the King Juan Carlos I of Spain Center, New York University. She is the editor of the volume *Constructing Identity in Contemporary Spain* (Oxford University Press, 2002) and *The Politics of Memory in Contemporary Spain,* a special issue of *Journal of Spanish Cultural Studies* (2008).

PAUL PRESTON is the Príncipe de Asturias Professor of Contemporary Spanish Studies, London School of Economics. He has authored *The Politics of Revenge: Fascism and the Military in Twentieth-Century Spain* (Routledge, 1990), *Franco: A Biography* (Grijalbo, 2002), *The Spanish Civil War: Reaction, Revolution and Revenge* (Harper Perennial, 2006), and, most recently, *We Saw Spain Die: Foreign Correspondents in the Spanish Civil War* (Constable and Robinson, 2008).

HILARI RAGUER SUÑER resides at Montserrat Abbey in Barcelona, Spain. He is professor in law (Barcelona) and D. E. S. in political sciences (Paris). He is the author of *Gunpowder and Incense: The Catholic Church and the Spanish Civil War* (Routledge, 2007) and of *Requiem por la Cristiandad: El Concilio Vaticano II y su impacto en España* (Península, 2006).

JOAN RAMON RESINA is professor and chair of the Department of Iberian and Latin American Cultures at Stanford University. He is author of *Hispanismo y Estado: La cultura al servicio de una idea imperial* (Biblioteca Nueva, 2009) and *Barcelona's Vocation of Modernity: Rise and Decline of an Urban Image* (Stanford University Press, 2008).

MICHAEL RICHARDS is reader in Spanish history at the University of the West of England, Bristol, and is coeditor of *The Splintering of Spain: Cultural History and the Spanish Civil War, 1936–39* (Cambridge University Press, 2005). He is currently completing an extensive study of the relationship between war and postwar in Spain, 1936–2006.

ANTONIUS C. G. M. ROBBEN is professor of anthropology at Utrecht University, the Netherlands. Two of his recent books are *Death, Mourning, and Burial: A Cross-Cultural Reader* (Blackwell, 2004) and the award-winning ethnography *Political Violence and Trauma in Argentina* (University of Pennsylvania Press, 2005).

GILES TREMLETT is Spain correspondent for the *Guardian* and the *Economist*. He is the author of *Ghosts of Spain: Travels Through Spain and Its Silent Past* (Faber and Faber, 2007).

Index